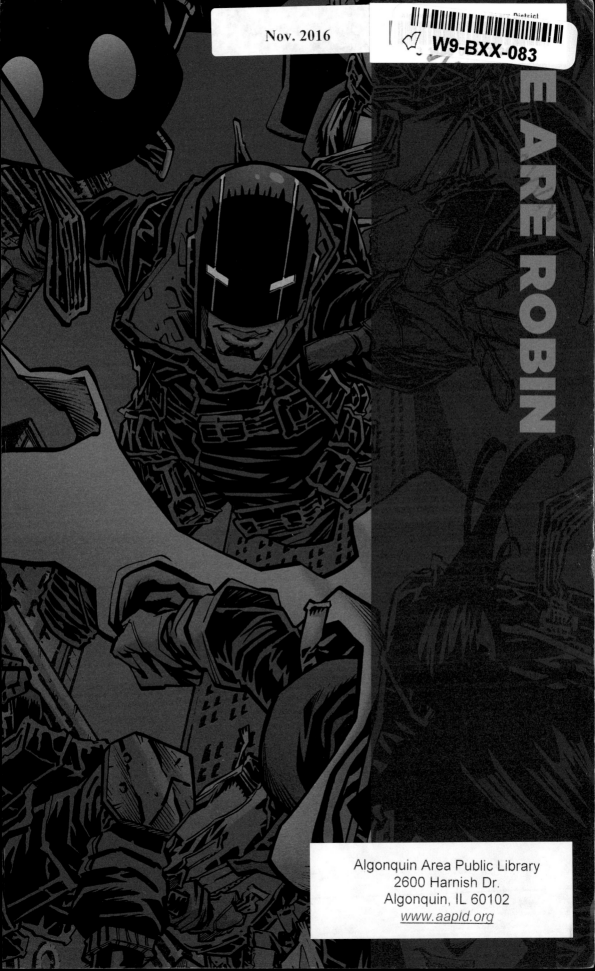

WE ARE ROBIN

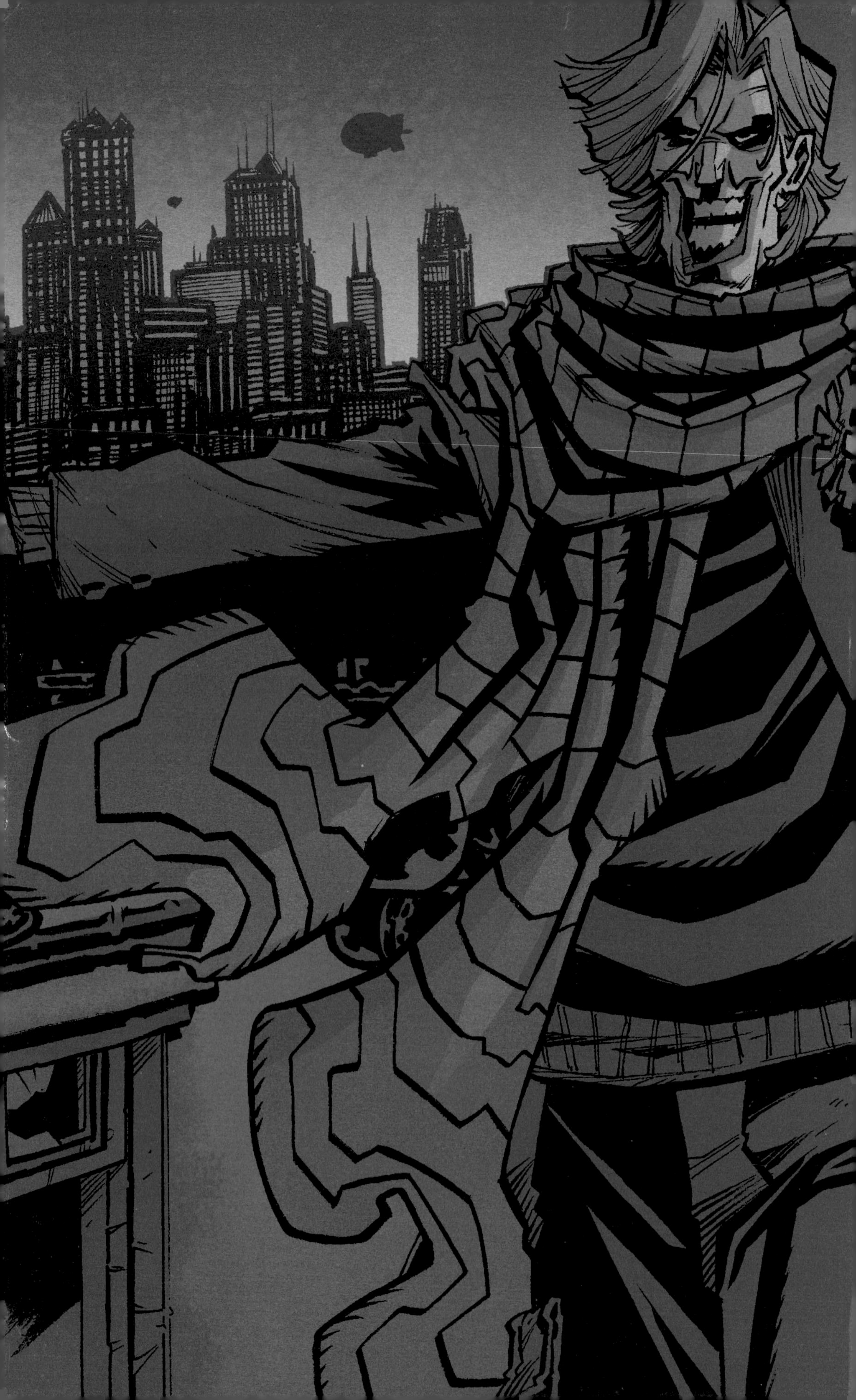

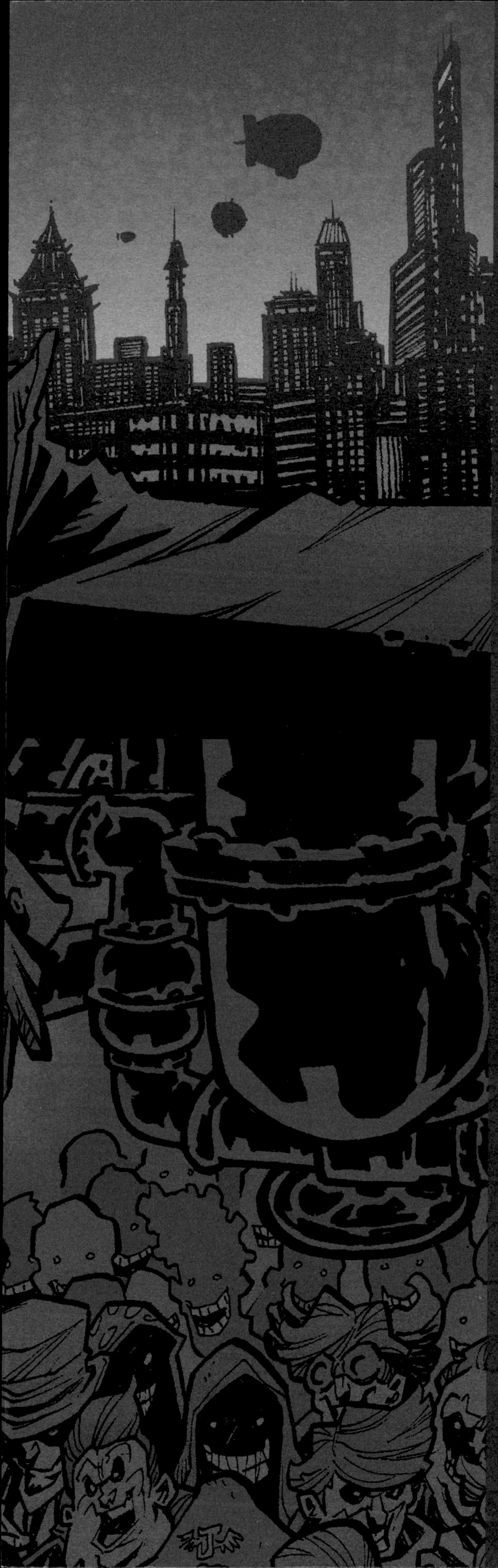

WE ARE ROBIN

VOLUME 2
JOKERS

WRITTEN BY
LEE BERMEJO

ART BY
JORGE CORONA
ROB HAYNES
CARMINE DI GIANDOMENICO

COLORS BY
TRISH MULVIHILL
MAT LOPES
CRIS PETER

LETTERS BY
JARED K. FLETCHER

COLLECTION COVER BY
LEE BERMEJO

MARK DOYLE Editor – Original Series
REBECCA TAYLOR Associate Editor – Original Series
JEB WOODARD Group Editor – Collected Editions
ROBIN WILDMAN Editor – Collected Edition
STEVE COOK Design Director – Books
DAMIAN RYLAND Publication Design

BOB HARRAS Senior VP – Editor-in-Chief, DC Comics

DIANE NELSON President
DAN DIDIO and JIM LEE Co-Publishers
GEOFF JOHNS Chief Creative Officer
AMIT DESAI Senior VP – Marketing & Global Franchise Management
NAIRI GARDINER Senior VP – Finance
SAM ADES VP – Digital Marketing
BOBBIE CHASE VP – Talent Development
MARK CHIARELLO Senior VP – Art, Design & Collected Editions
JOHN CUNNINGHAM VP – Content Strategy
ANNE DEPIES VP – Strategy Planning & Reporting
DON FALLETTI VP – Manufacturing Operations
LAWRENCE GANEM VP – Editorial Administration & Talent Relations
ALISON GILL Senior VP – Manufacturing & Operations
HANK KANALZ Senior VP – Editorial Strategy & Administration
JAY KOGAN VP – Legal Affairs
DEREK MADDALENA Senior VP – Sales & Business Development
JACK MAHAN VP – Business Affairs
DAN MIRON VP – Sales Planning & Trade Development
NICK NAPOLITANO VP – Manufacturing Administration
CAROL ROEDER VP – Marketing
EDDIE SCANNELL VP – Mass Account & Digital Sales
COURTNEY SIMMONS Senior VP – Publicity & Communications
JIM (SKI) SOKOLOWSKI VP – Comic Book Specialty & Newsstand Sales
SANDY YI Senior VP – Global Franchise Management

WE ARE ROBIN VOLUME 2: JOKERS

DC Comics, 2900 West Alameda Ave., Burbank, CA 91505
Printed by RR Donnelley, Salem, VA, USA. 9/9/16. First Printing.
ISBN: 978-1-4012-6490-1

Library of Congress Cataloging-in-Publication Data is available.

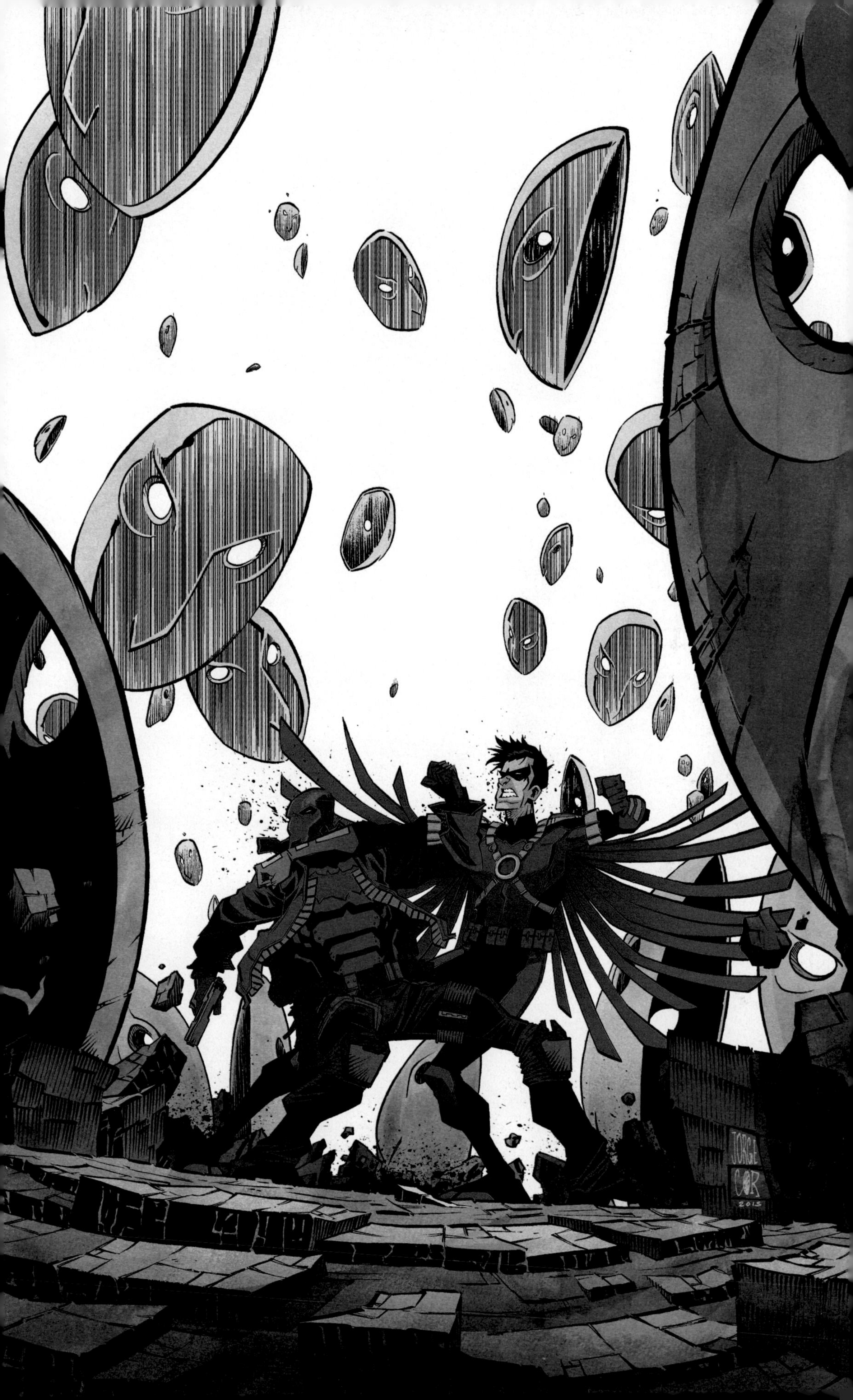
JORGE
COR
2015

PREVIOUSLY IN ROBIN WAR...

In an effort to stop the city's new gang of amateur Robins, Gotham Councilwoman Athene Noctua has made wearing or possessing Robin emblems illegal. The young vigilantes were driven underground, where they were found by the real Robin, Damian Wayne, and the three former Robins—Dick Grayson, Jason Todd and Tim Drake. To protect the untrained teens, Dick tipped off the Gotham police to their location, leading to the arrest of the entire group. Dick intended to keep the children safe, but now they are facing destruction at the hands of the Court of Owls and its elite killers, the Talons. Meanwhile, Dick is off on his own mysterious mission...

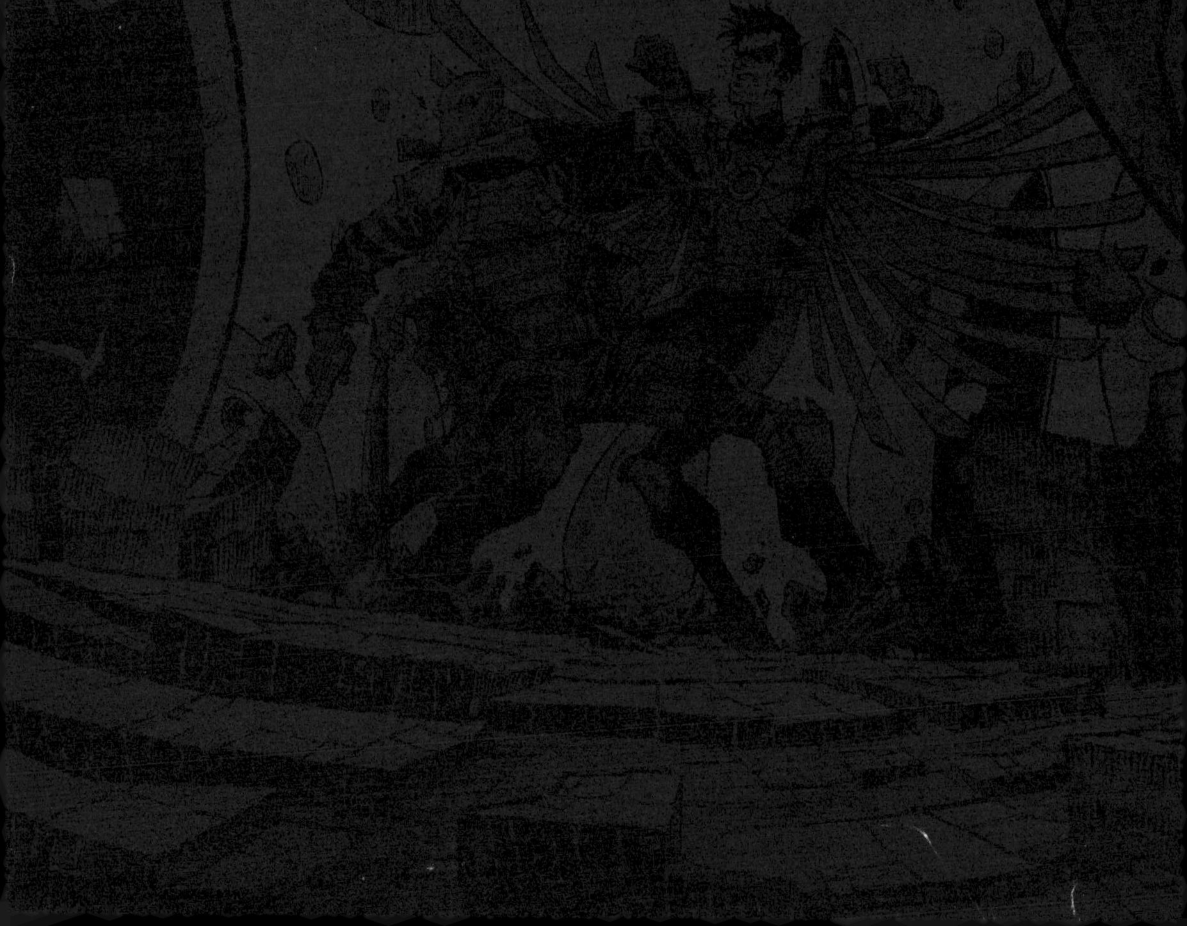

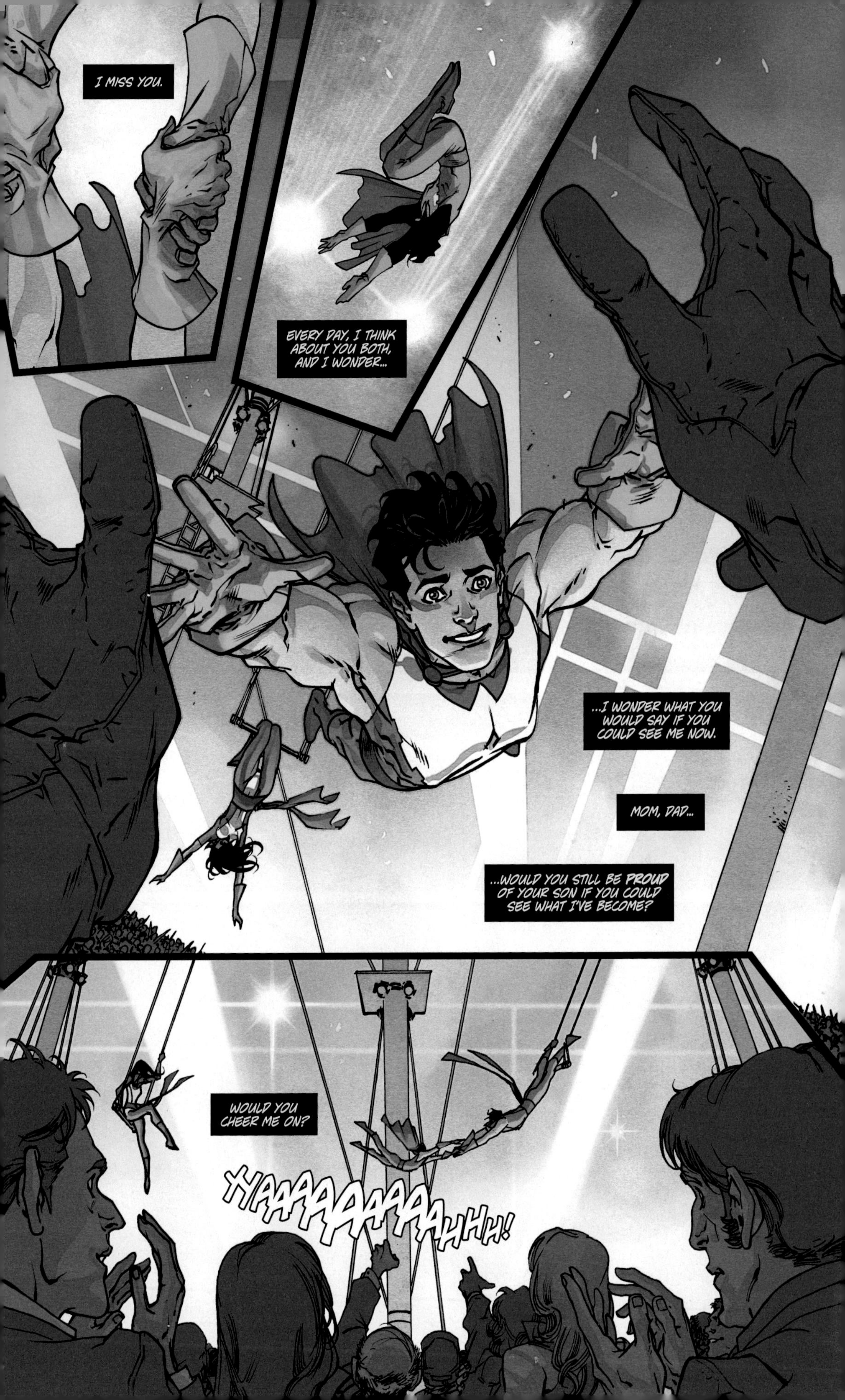
I MISS YOU.
EVERY DAY, I THINK ABOUT YOU BOTH, AND I WONDER...
...I WONDER WHAT YOU WOULD SAY IF YOU COULD SEE ME NOW.
MOM, DAD...
...WOULD YOU STILL BE PROUD OF YOUR SON IF YOU COULD SEE WHAT I'VE BECOME?
WOULD YOU CHEER ME ON?
YAAAAAAAAAAHHH!

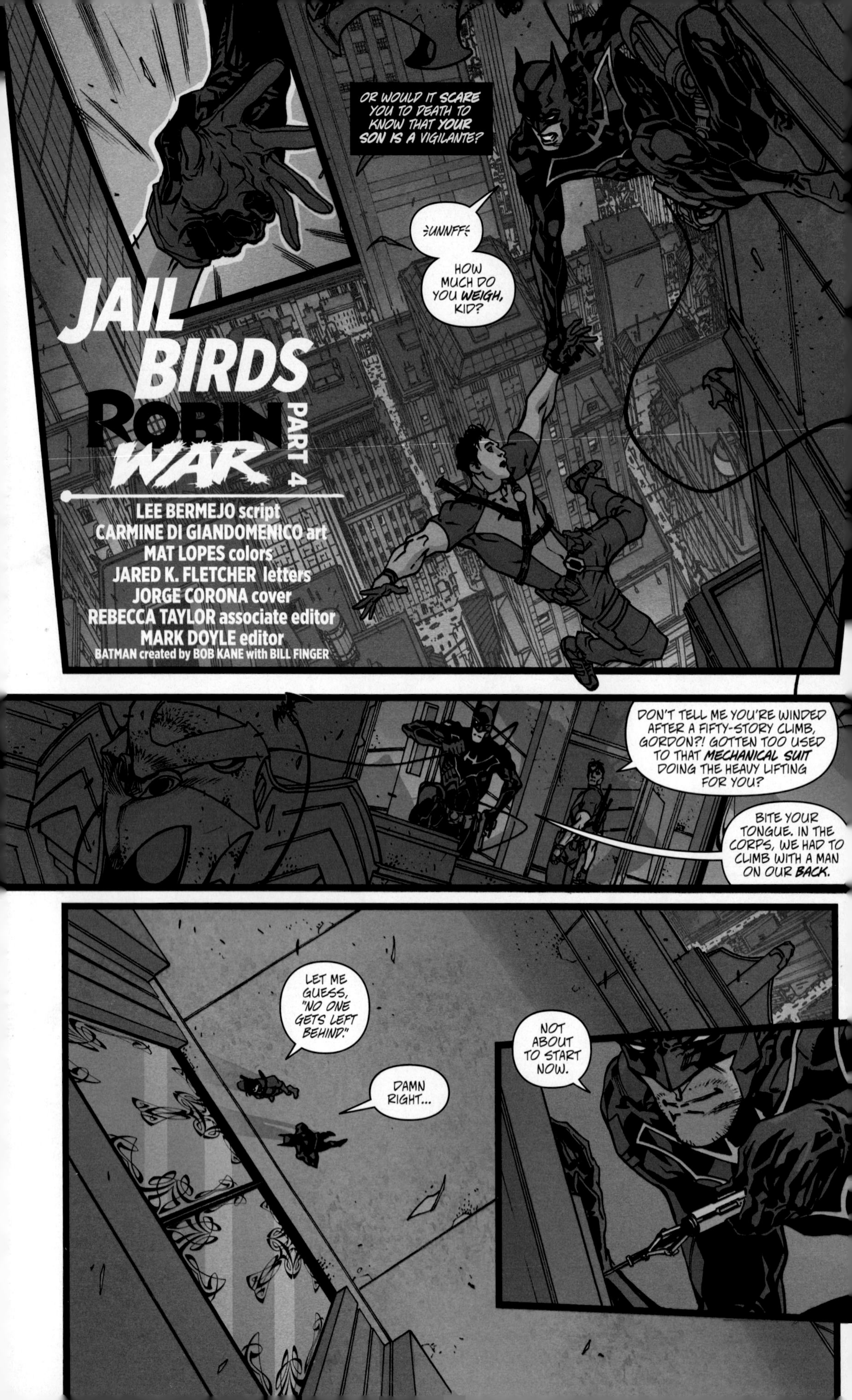

OR WOULD IT SCARE YOU TO DEATH TO KNOW THAT YOUR SON IS A VIGILANTE?
UNNFF
HOW MUCH DO YOU WEIGH, KID?
JAIL BIRDS
ROBIN WAR PART 4
LEE BERMEJO script
CARMINE DI GIANDOMENICO art
MAT LOPES colors
JARED K. FLETCHER letters
JORGE CORONA cover
REBECCA TAYLOR associate editor
MARK DOYLE editor
BATMAN created by BOB KANE with BILL FINGER
DON'T TELL ME YOU'RE WINDED AFTER A FIFTY-STORY CLIMB, GORDON?! GOTTEN TOO USED TO THAT MECHANICAL SUIT DOING THE HEAVY LIFTING FOR YOU?
BITE YOUR TONGUE. IN THE CORPS, WE HAD TO CLIMB WITH A MAN ON OUR BACK.
LET ME GUESS, "NO ONE GETS LEFT BEHIND."
DAMN RIGHT...
NOT ABOUT TO START NOW.

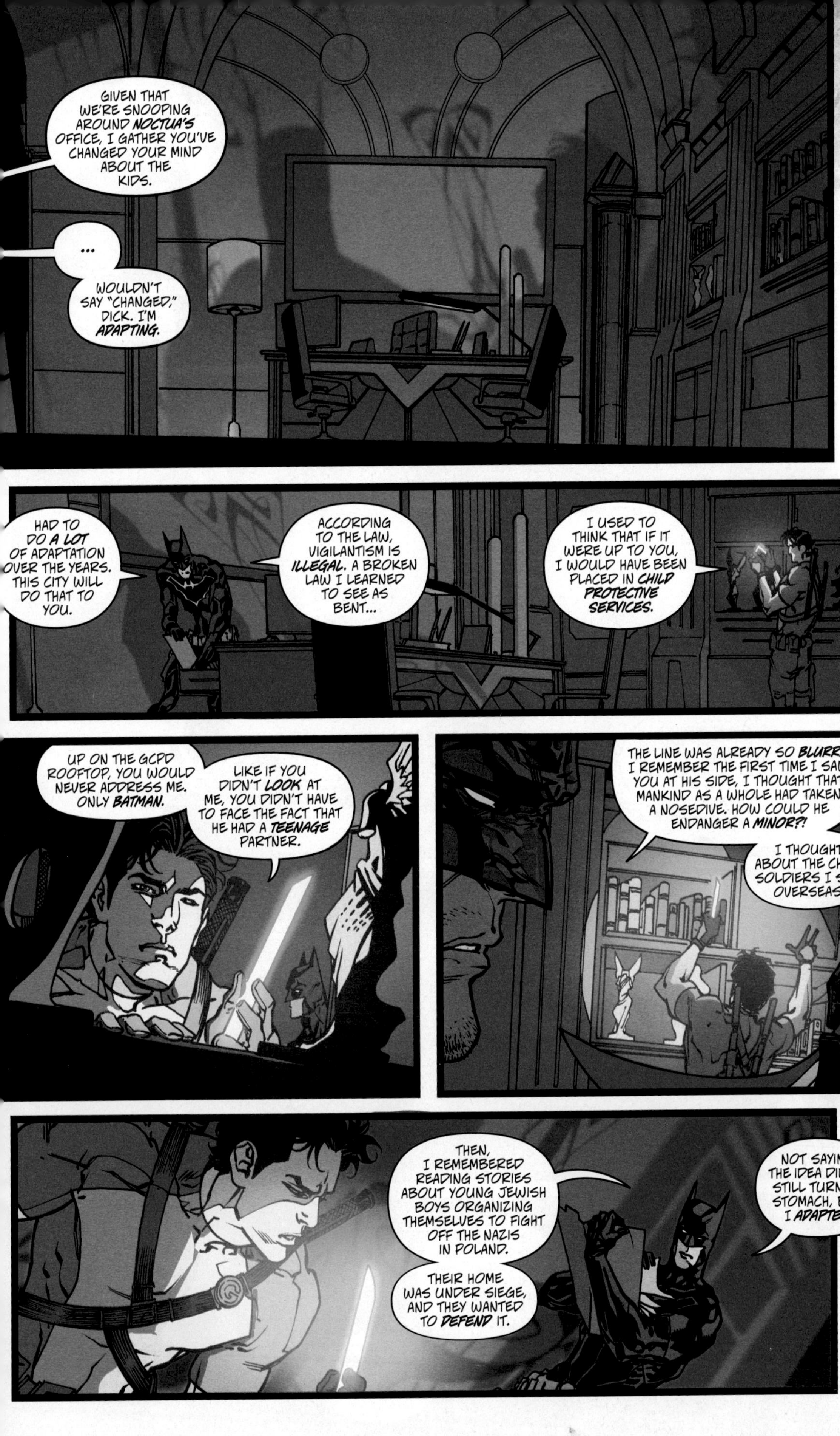
GIVEN THAT WE'RE SNOOPING AROUND NOCTUA'S OFFICE, I GATHER YOU'VE CHANGED YOUR MIND ABOUT THE KIDS.
...
WOULDN'T SAY "CHANGED," DICK. I'M ADAPTING.
HAD TO DO A LOT OF ADAPTATION OVER THE YEARS. THIS CITY WILL DO THAT TO YOU.
ACCORDING TO THE LAW, VIGILANTISM IS ILLEGAL. A BROKEN LAW I LEARNED TO SEE AS BENT...
I USED TO THINK THAT IF IT WERE UP TO YOU, I WOULD HAVE BEEN PLACED IN CHILD PROTECTIVE SERVICES.
UP ON THE GCPD ROOFTOP, YOU WOULD NEVER ADDRESS ME. ONLY BATMAN.
LIKE IF YOU DIDN'T LOOK AT ME, YOU DIDN'T HAVE TO FACE THE FACT THAT HE HAD A TEENAGE PARTNER.
THE LINE WAS ALREADY SO BLURRY. I REMEMBER THE FIRST TIME I SAW YOU AT HIS SIDE, I THOUGHT THAT MANKIND AS A WHOLE HAD TAKEN A NOSEDIVE. HOW COULD HE ENDANGER A MINOR?!
I THOUGHT ABOUT THE CHILD SOLDIERS I SAW OVERSEAS.
THEN, I REMEMBERED READING STORIES ABOUT YOUNG JEWISH BOYS ORGANIZING THEMSELVES TO FIGHT OFF THE NAZIS IN POLAND.
THEIR HOME WAS UNDER SIEGE, AND THEY WANTED TO DEFEND IT.
NOT SAYING THE IDEA DIDN'T STILL TURN MY STOMACH, BUT I ADAPTED.

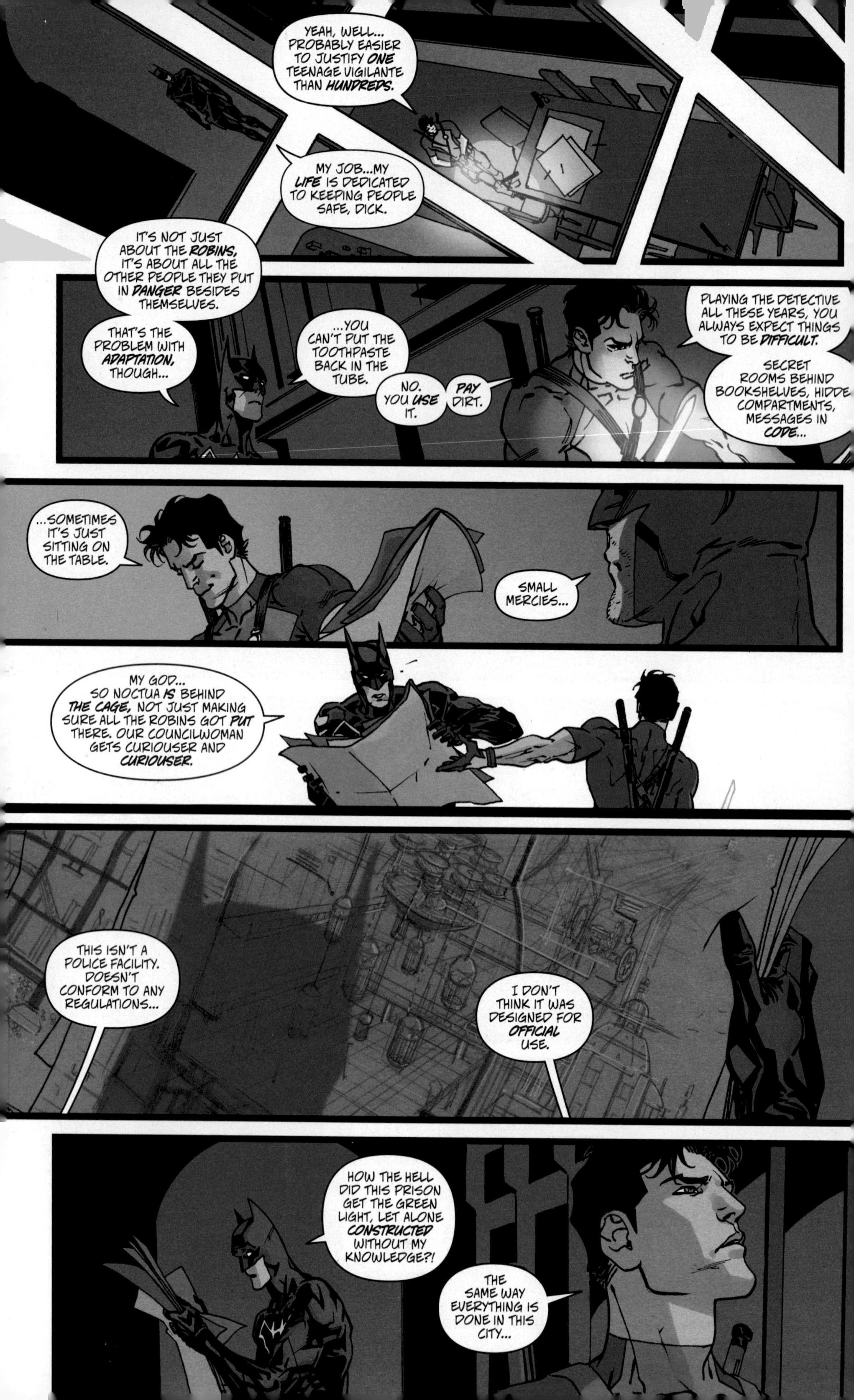
YEAH, WELL... PROBABLY EASIER TO JUSTIFY ONE TEENAGE VIGILANTE THAN HUNDREDS.
MY JOB...MY LIFE IS DEDICATED TO KEEPING PEOPLE SAFE, DICK.
IT'S NOT JUST ABOUT THE ROBINS, IT'S ABOUT ALL THE OTHER PEOPLE THEY PUT IN DANGER BESIDES THEMSELVES.
THAT'S THE PROBLEM WITH ADAPTATION, THOUGH...
...YOU CAN'T PUT THE TOOTHPASTE BACK IN THE TUBE.
NO. YOU USE IT.
PAY DIRT.
PLAYING THE DETECTIVE ALL THESE YEARS, YOU ALWAYS EXPECT THINGS TO BE DIFFICULT.
SECRET ROOMS BEHIND BOOKSHELVES, HIDDE COMPARTMENTS, MESSAGES IN CODE...
...SOMETIMES IT'S JUST SITTING ON THE TABLE.
SMALL MERCIES...
MY GOD... SO NOCTUA IS BEHIND THE CAGE, NOT JUST MAKING SURE ALL THE ROBINS GOT PUT THERE. OUR COUNCILWOMAN GETS CURIOUSER AND CURIOUSER.
THIS ISN'T A POLICE FACILITY. DOESN'T CONFORM TO ANY REGULATIONS...
I DON'T THINK IT WAS DESIGNED FOR OFFICIAL USE.
HOW THE HELL DID THIS PRISON GET THE GREEN LIGHT, LET ALONE CONSTRUCTED WITHOUT MY KNOWLEDGE?!
THE SAME WAY EVERYTHING IS DONE IN THIS CITY...

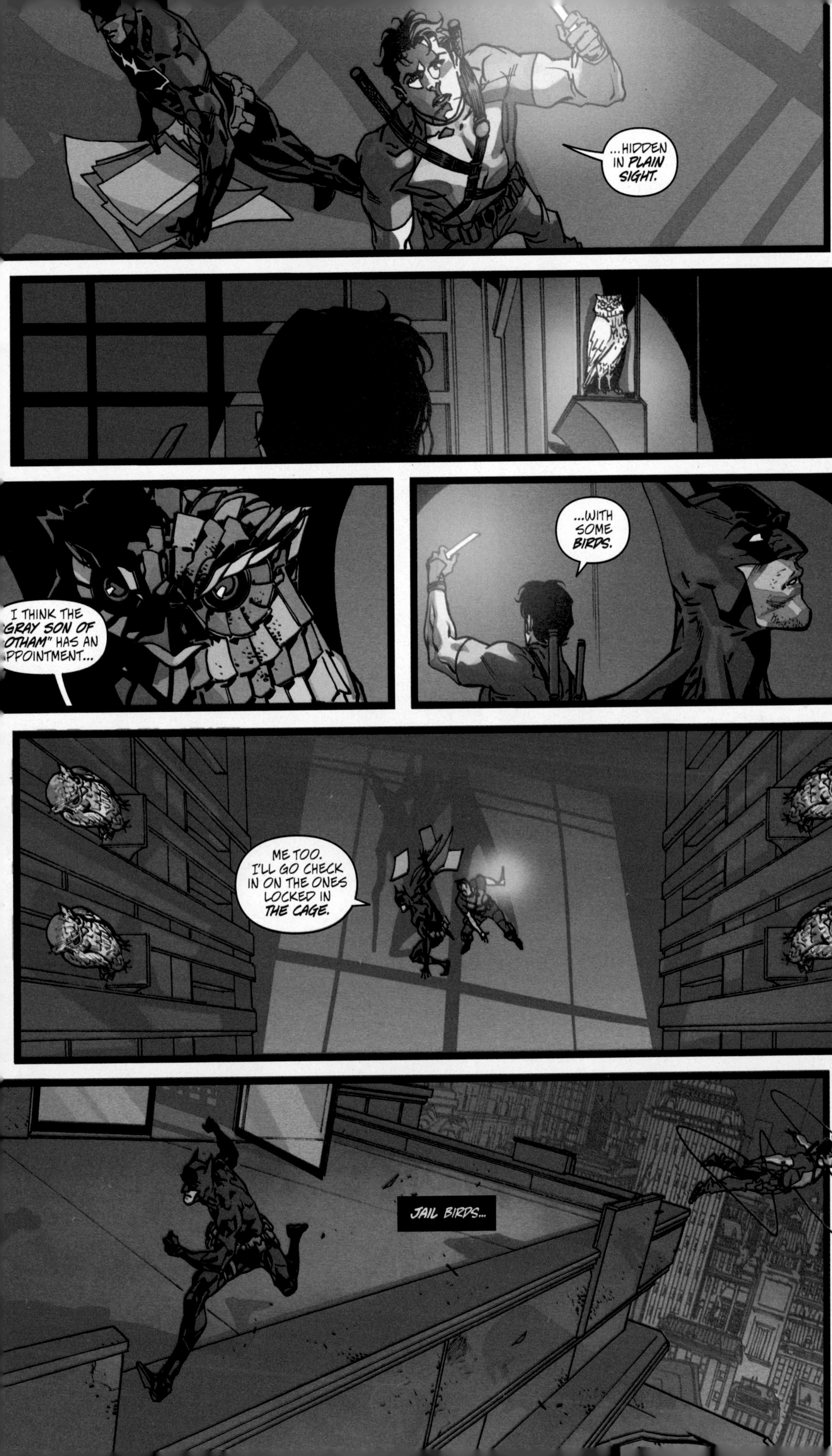

...HIDDEN IN PLAIN SIGHT.
I THINK THE "GRAY SON OF GOTHAM" HAS AN APPOINTMENT...
...WITH SOME BIRDS.
ME TOO. I'LL GO CHECK IN ON THE ONES LOCKED IN THE CAGE.
JAIL BIRDS...

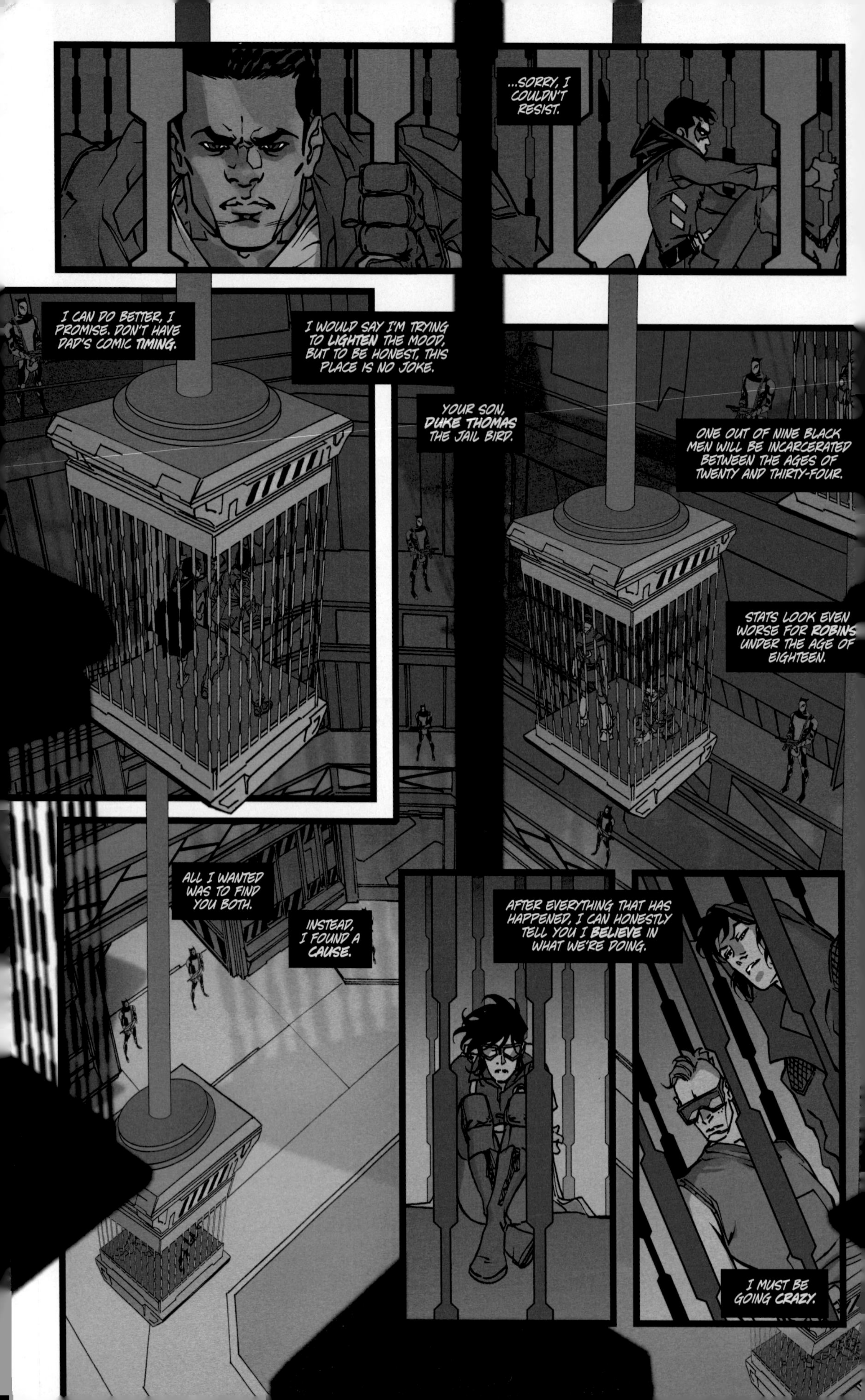
...SORRY, I COULDN'T RESIST.
I CAN DO BETTER, I PROMISE. DON'T HAVE DAD'S COMIC TIMING.
I WOULD SAY I'M TRYING TO LIGHTEN THE MOOD, BUT TO BE HONEST, THIS PLACE IS NO JOKE.
YOUR SON, DUKE THOMAS THE JAIL BIRD.
ONE OUT OF NINE BLACK MEN WILL BE INCARCERATED BETWEEN THE AGES OF TWENTY AND THIRTY-FOUR.
STATS LOOK EVEN WORSE FOR ROBINS UNDER THE AGE OF EIGHTEEN.
ALL I WANTED WAS TO FIND YOU BOTH.
INSTEAD, I FOUND A CAUSE.
AFTER EVERYTHING THAT HAS HAPPENED, I CAN HONESTLY TELL YOU I BELIEVE IN WHAT WE'RE DOING.
I MUST BE GOING CRAZY.

NOT AS CRAZY AS **THIS** GUY, THOUGH. CLAIMS TO BE THE REAL ROBIN. WHATEVER. REAL PAIN IN MY **ASS**.

URRRGHHHH...

AMATEURS... UURGHH.

YOU'RE GOING TO GIVE YOURSELF A HERNIA.

HERNIAS ARE FOR **AMATEURS**.

EVERY STRUCTURE HAS A WEAKNESS WAITING TO BE **EXPLOITED**.

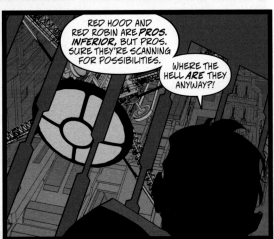

RED HOOD AND RED ROBIN ARE **PROS**. **INFERIOR,** BUT PROS. SURE THEY'RE SCANNING FOR POSSIBILITIES.

WHERE THE HELL **ARE** THEY ANYWAY?!

THINK SOMETHING UP ABOVE US IS CONTROLLING THESE CELLS.

CAN'T BE SURE UNLESS I GET A CLOSER LOOK. CAN'T GET A CLOSER LOOK UNLESS I GET **OUT**.

CAN'T GET **OUT** WITHOUT A DISTRACTION...**OR** SOME GEAR IN MY UTILITY BELT.

WOULD **KILL** FOR MY UTILITY BELT RIGHT ABOUT NOW.

ALWAYS WANTED ONE OF THOSE.

CAN'T SEE IZZY OR RIKO. THINK I SEE DRE AND DAX. THEY LOOK LIKE THEY'RE OKAY...

INSTEAD OF WORRYING ABOUT THE OTHER **AMATEURS**, WHY NOT PUT YOURSELF TO GOOD USE AND HELP ME GET THE GUARDS IN HERE...

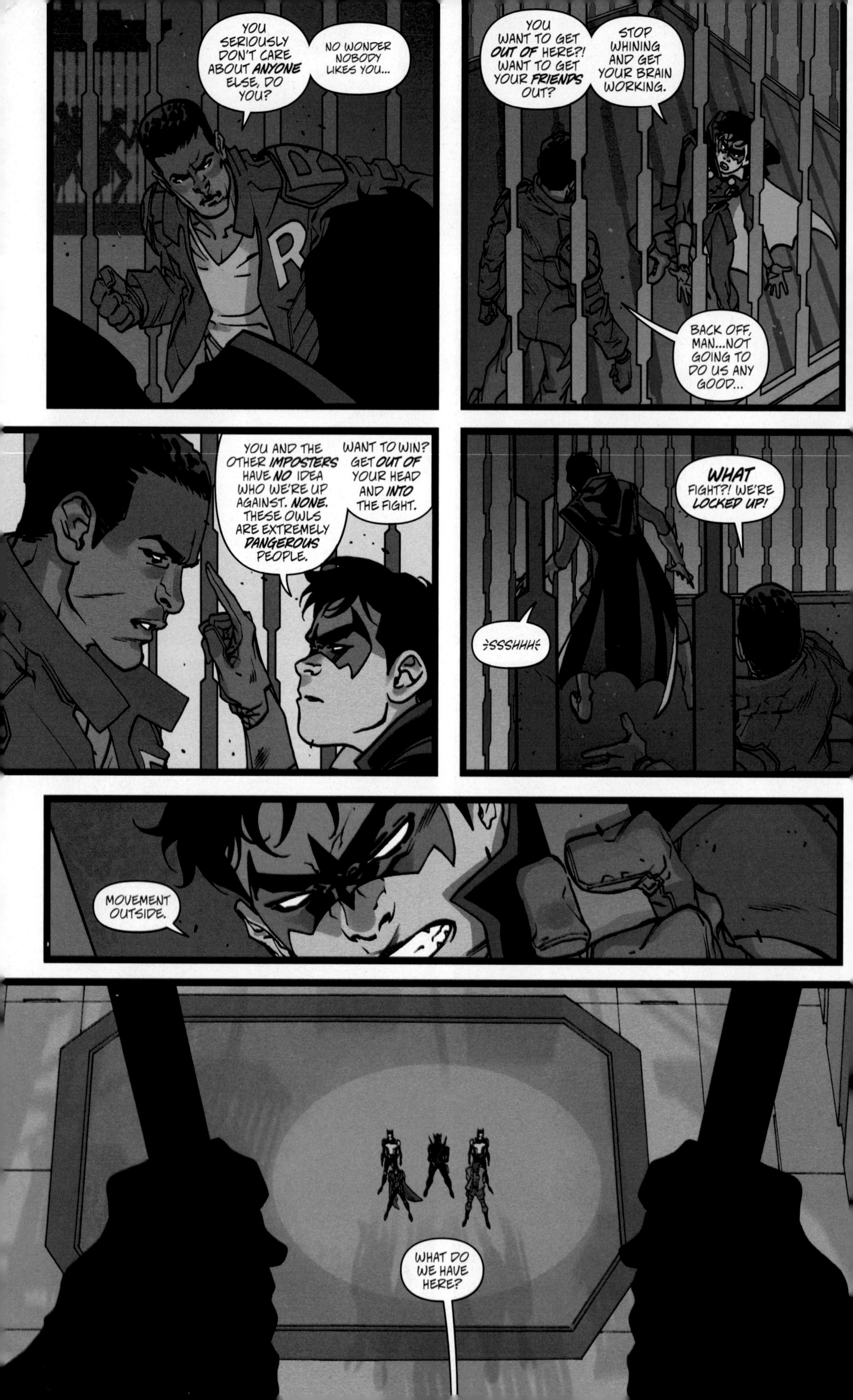
YOU SERIOUSLY DON'T CARE ABOUT ANYONE ELSE, DO YOU?
NO WONDER NOBODY LIKES YOU...
YOU WANT TO GET OUT OF HERE?! WANT TO GET YOUR FRIENDS OUT?
STOP WHINING AND GET YOUR BRAIN WORKING.
BACK OFF, MAN...NOT GOING TO DO US ANY GOOD...
YOU AND THE OTHER IMPOSTERS HAVE NO IDEA WHO WE'RE UP AGAINST. NONE. THESE OWLS ARE EXTREMELY DANGEROUS PEOPLE.
WANT TO WIN? GET OUT OF YOUR HEAD AND INTO THE FIGHT.
WHAT FIGHT?! WE'RE LOCKED UP!
SSSHHH
MOVEMENT OUTSIDE.
WHAT DO WE HAVE HERE?

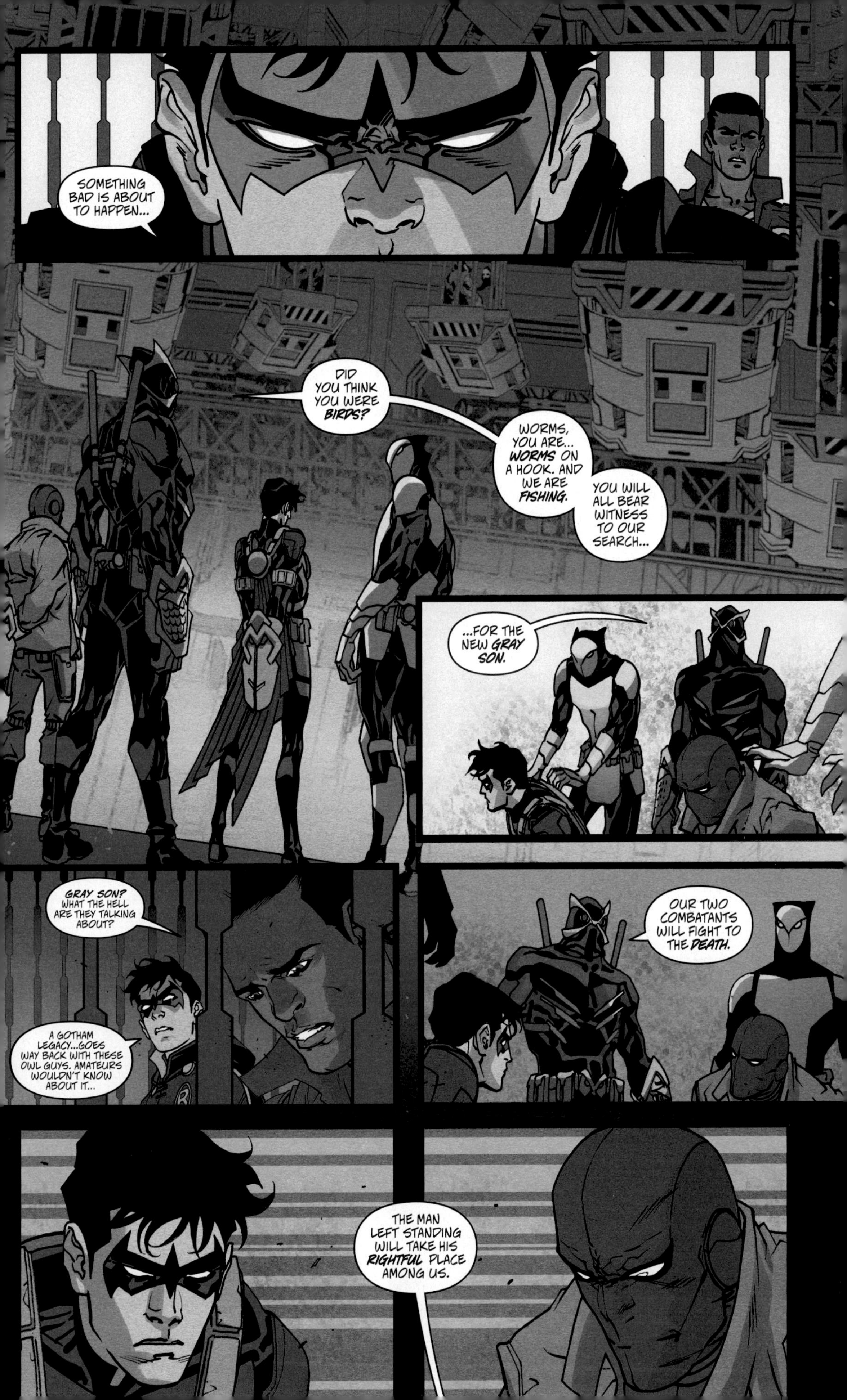
SOMETHING BAD IS ABOUT TO HAPPEN...
DID YOU THINK YOU WERE BIRDS?
WORMS, YOU ARE... WORMS ON A HOOK. AND WE ARE FISHING.
YOU WILL ALL BEAR WITNESS TO OUR SEARCH...
...FOR THE NEW GRAY SON.
GRAY SON? WHAT THE HELL ARE THEY TALKING ABOUT?
A GOTHAM LEGACY...GOES WAY BACK WITH THESE OWL GUYS. AMATEURS WOULDN'T KNOW ABOUT IT...
OUR TWO COMBATANTS WILL FIGHT TO THE DEATH.
THE MAN LEFT STANDING WILL TAKE HIS RIGHTFUL PLACE AMONG US.

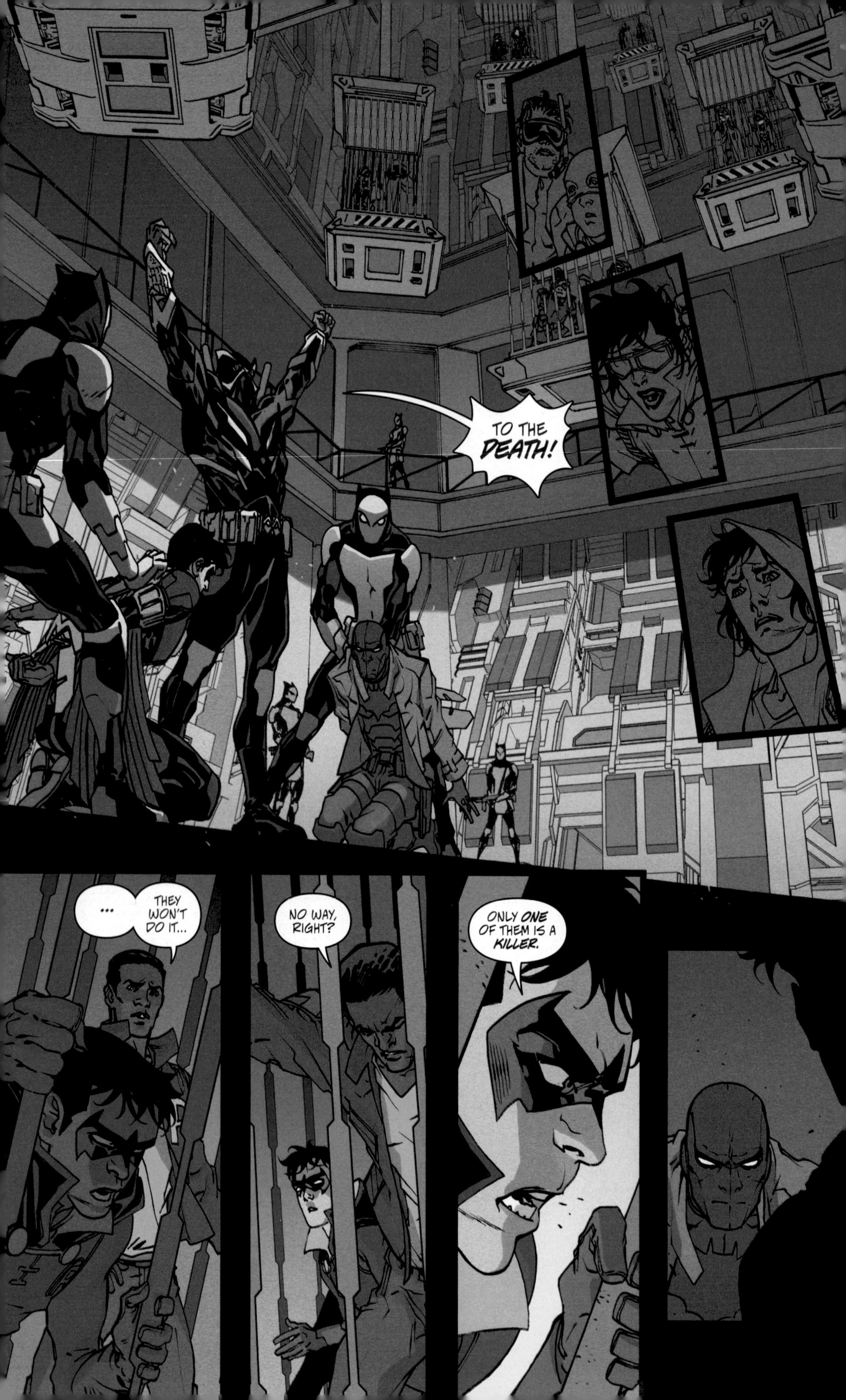

TO THE DEATH!
...
THEY WON'T DO IT...
NO WAY, RIGHT?
ONLY ONE OF THEM IS A KILLER.

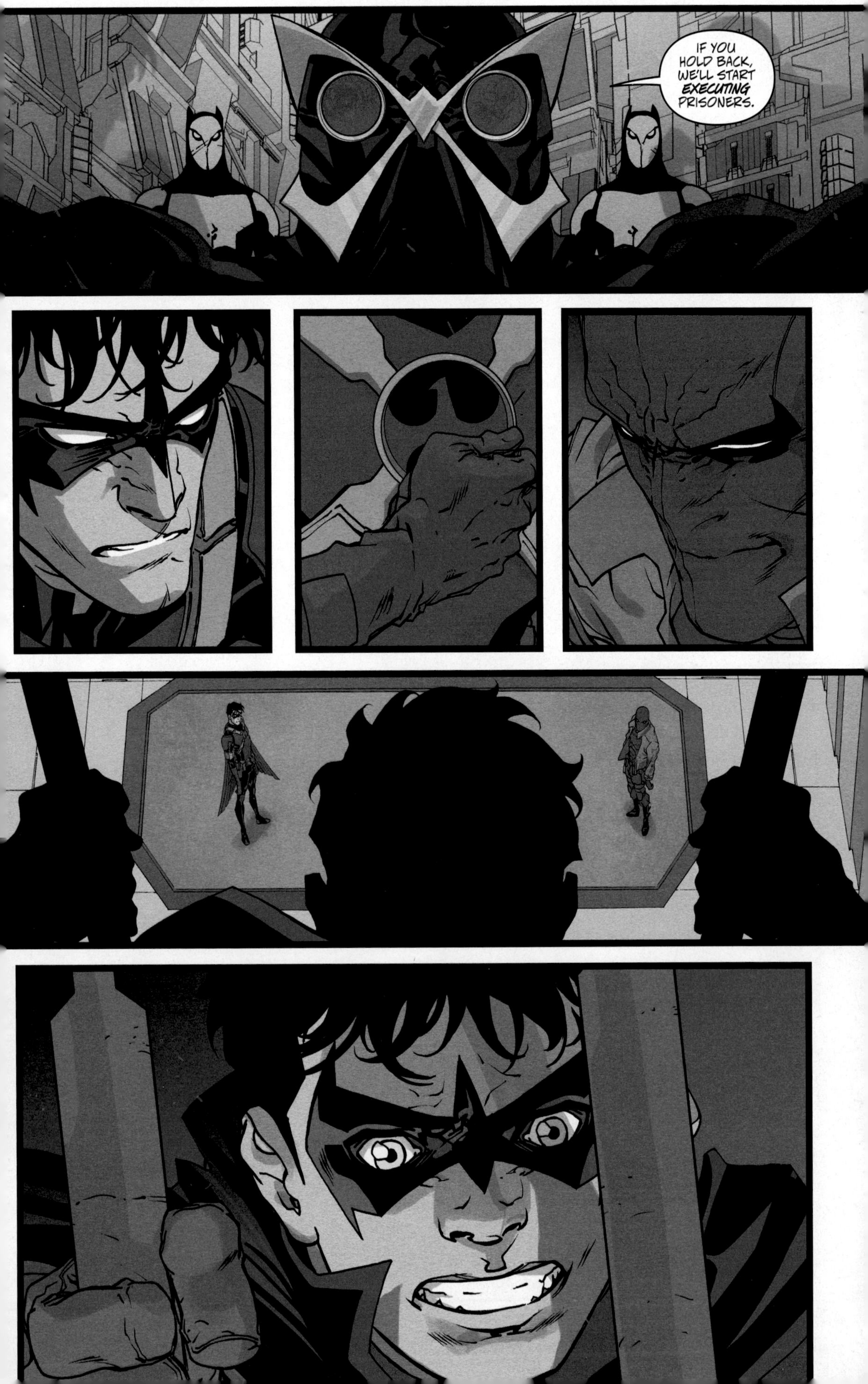
IF YOU HOLD BACK, WE'LL START EXECUTING PRISONERS.

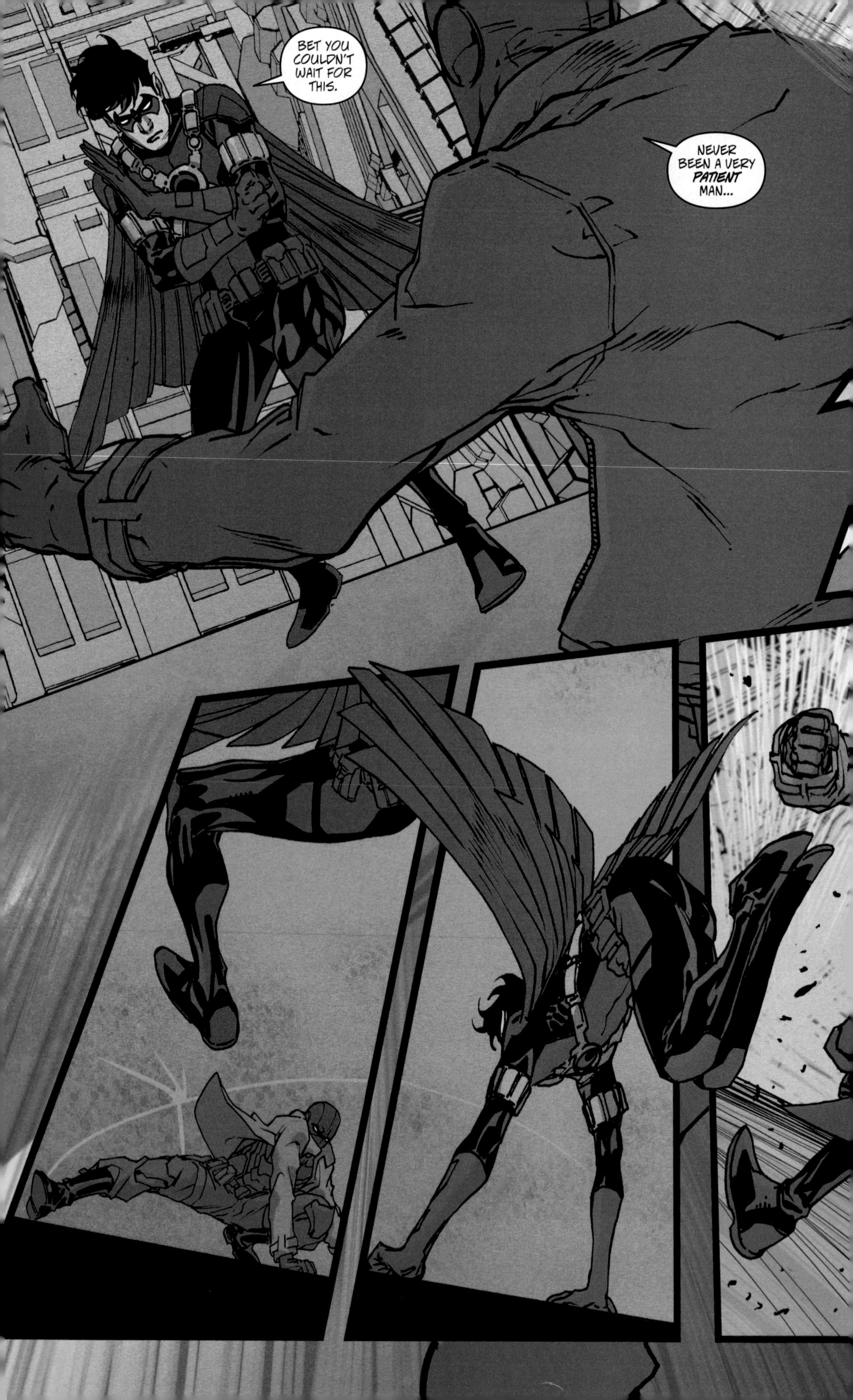
BET YOU COULDN'T WAIT FOR THIS.
NEVER BEEN A VERY PATIENT MAN...

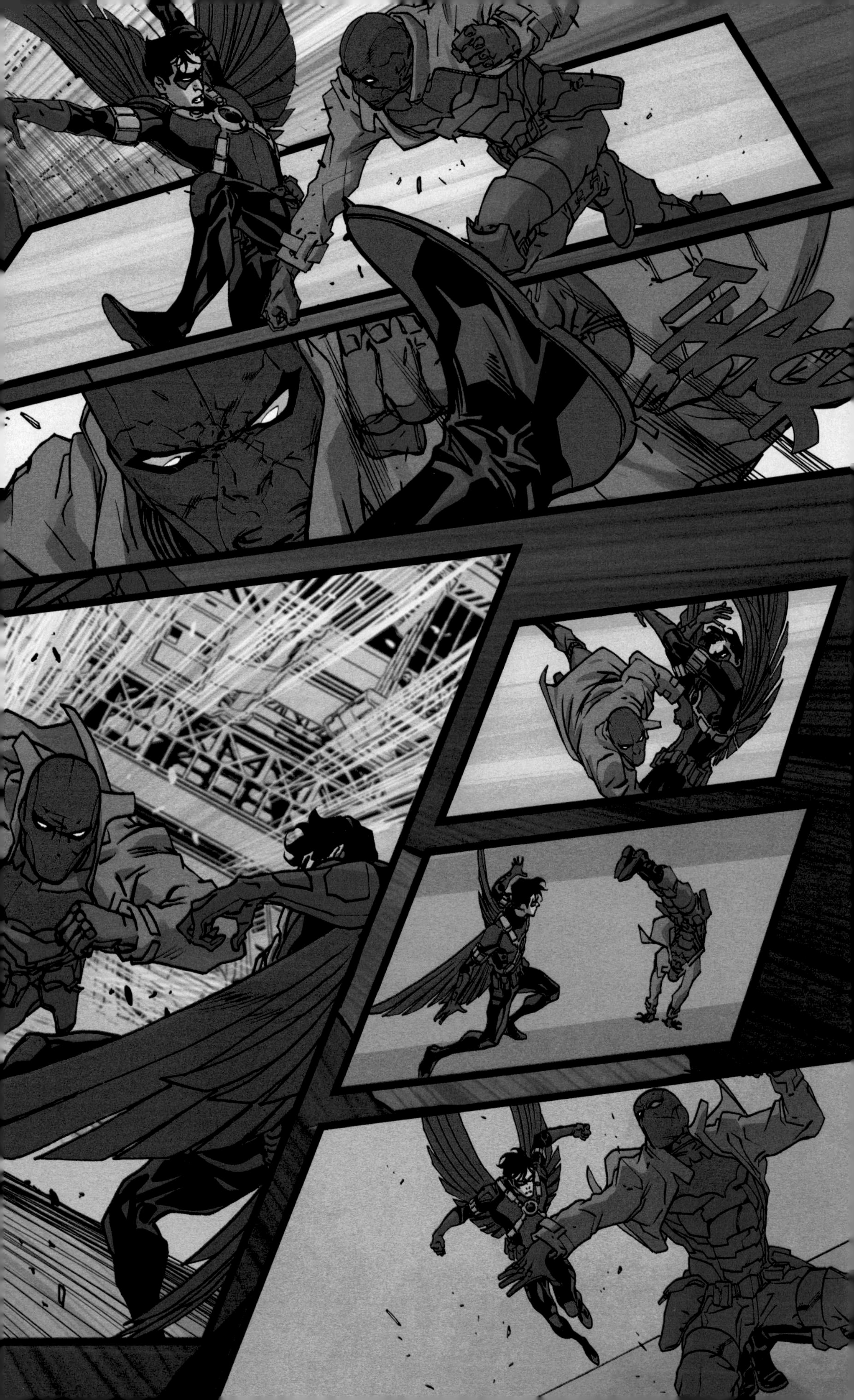
THACK

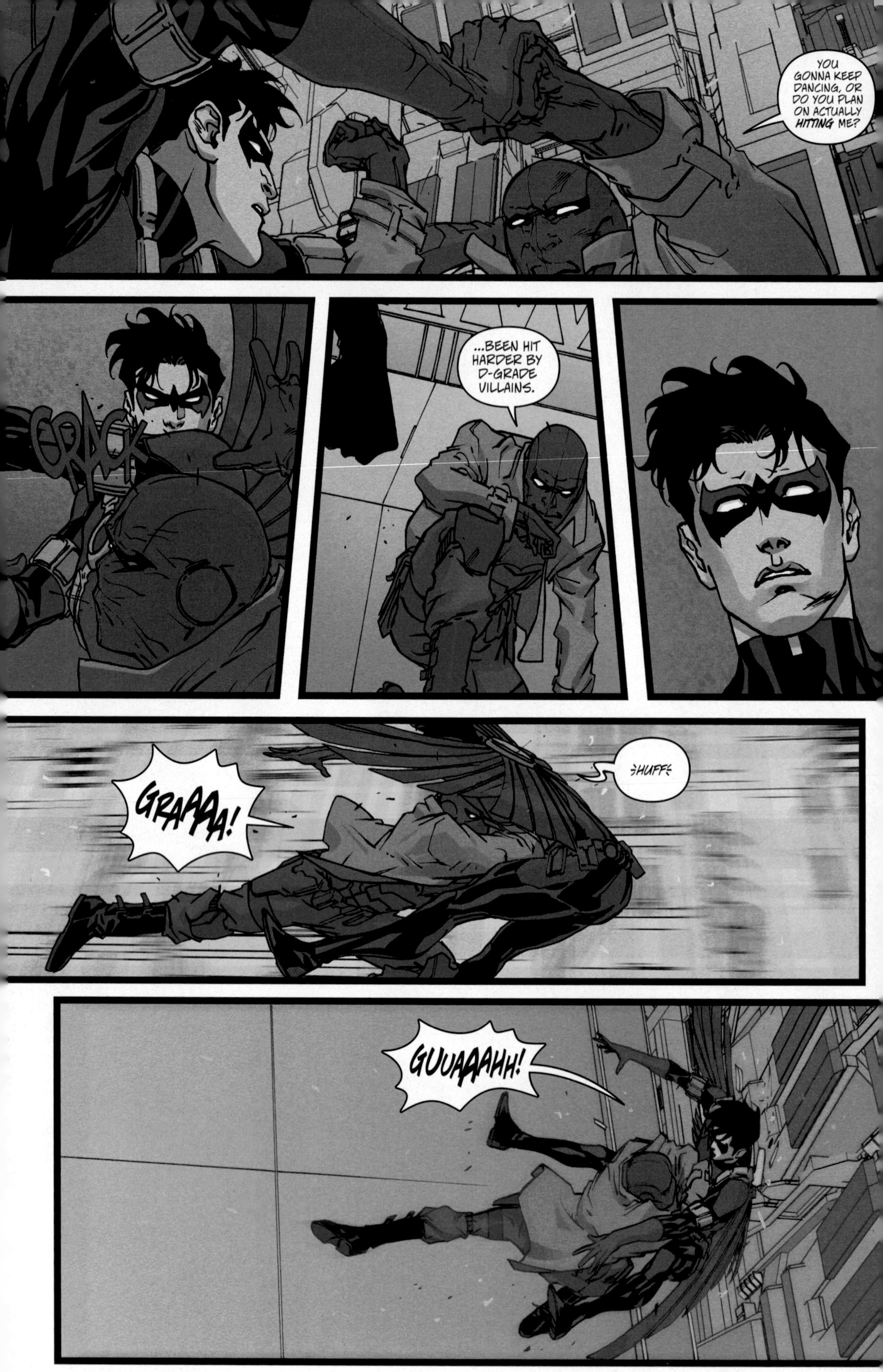
YOU GONNA KEEP DANCING, OR DO YOU PLAN ON ACTUALLY HITTING ME?
CRACK
...BEEN HIT HARDER BY D-GRADE VILLAINS.
GRAAAA!
HUFF
GUUAAAHH!

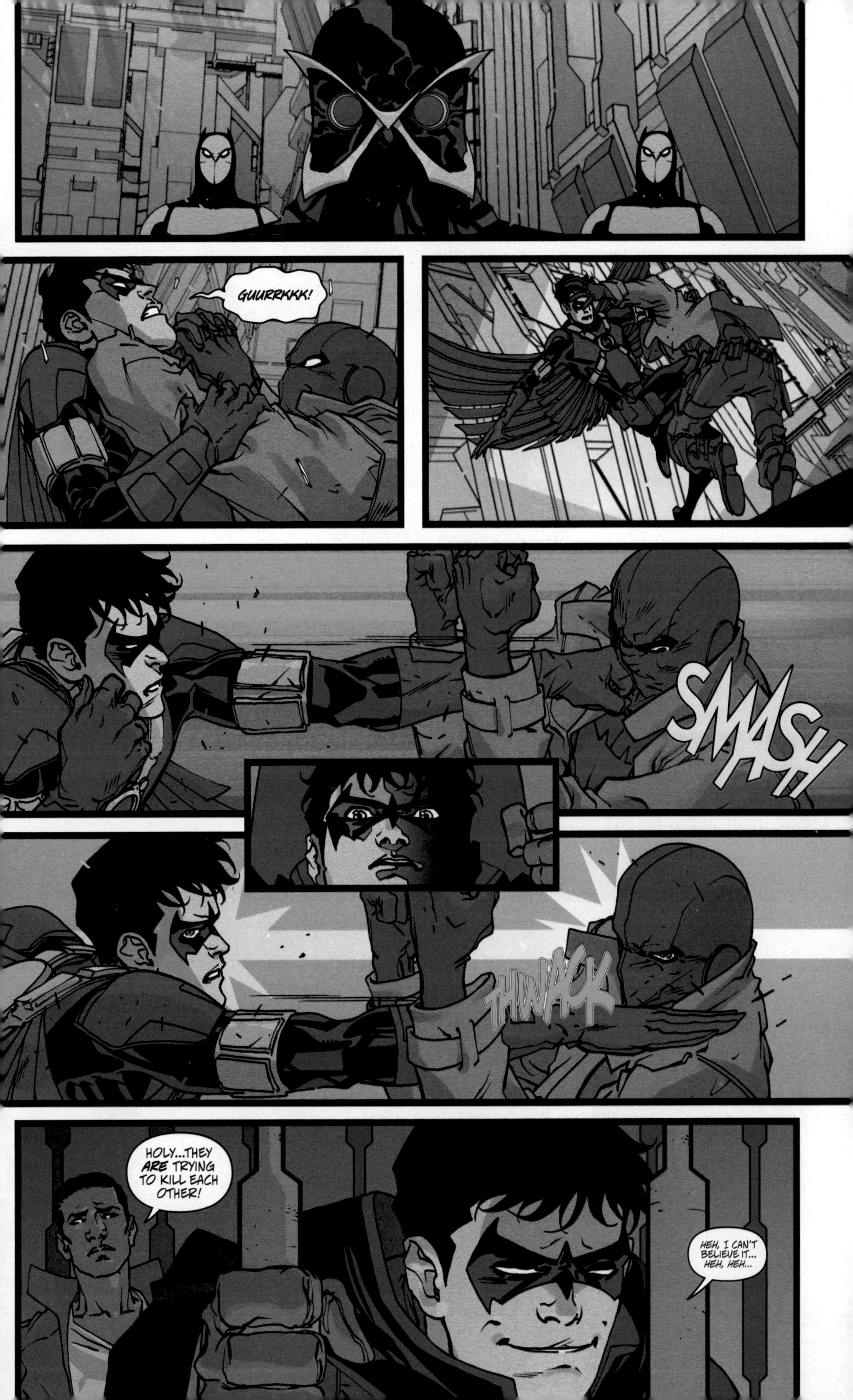
GUURRKKK!
SMASH
THWACK
HOLY...THEY ARE TRYING TO KILL EACH OTHER!
HEH, I CAN'T BELIEVE IT... HEH, HEH...

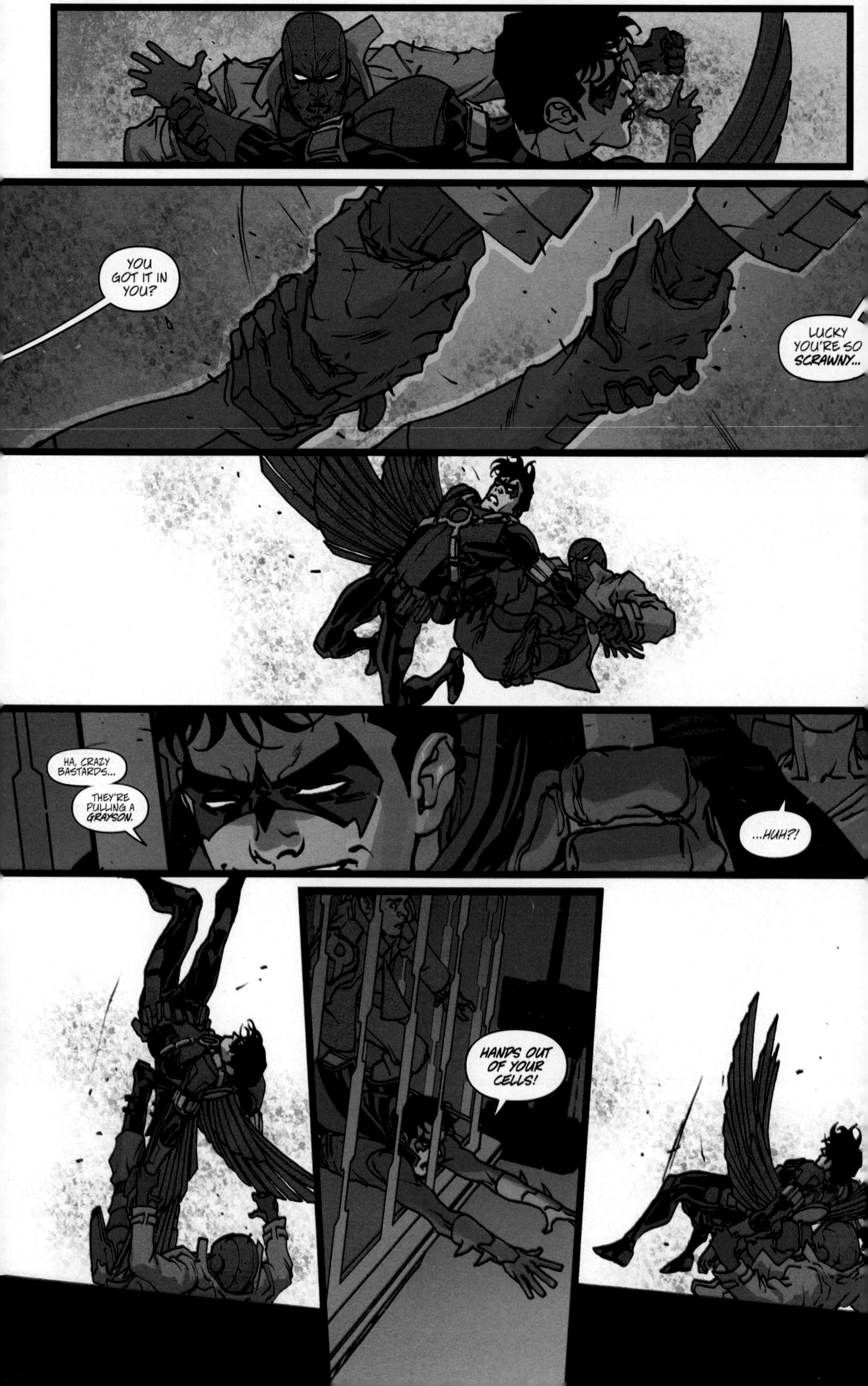
YOU GOT IT IN YOU?
LUCKY YOU'RE SO SCRAWNY...
HA, CRAZY BASTARDS...
THEY'RE PULLING A GRAYSON.
...HUH?!
HANDS OUT OF YOUR CELLS!

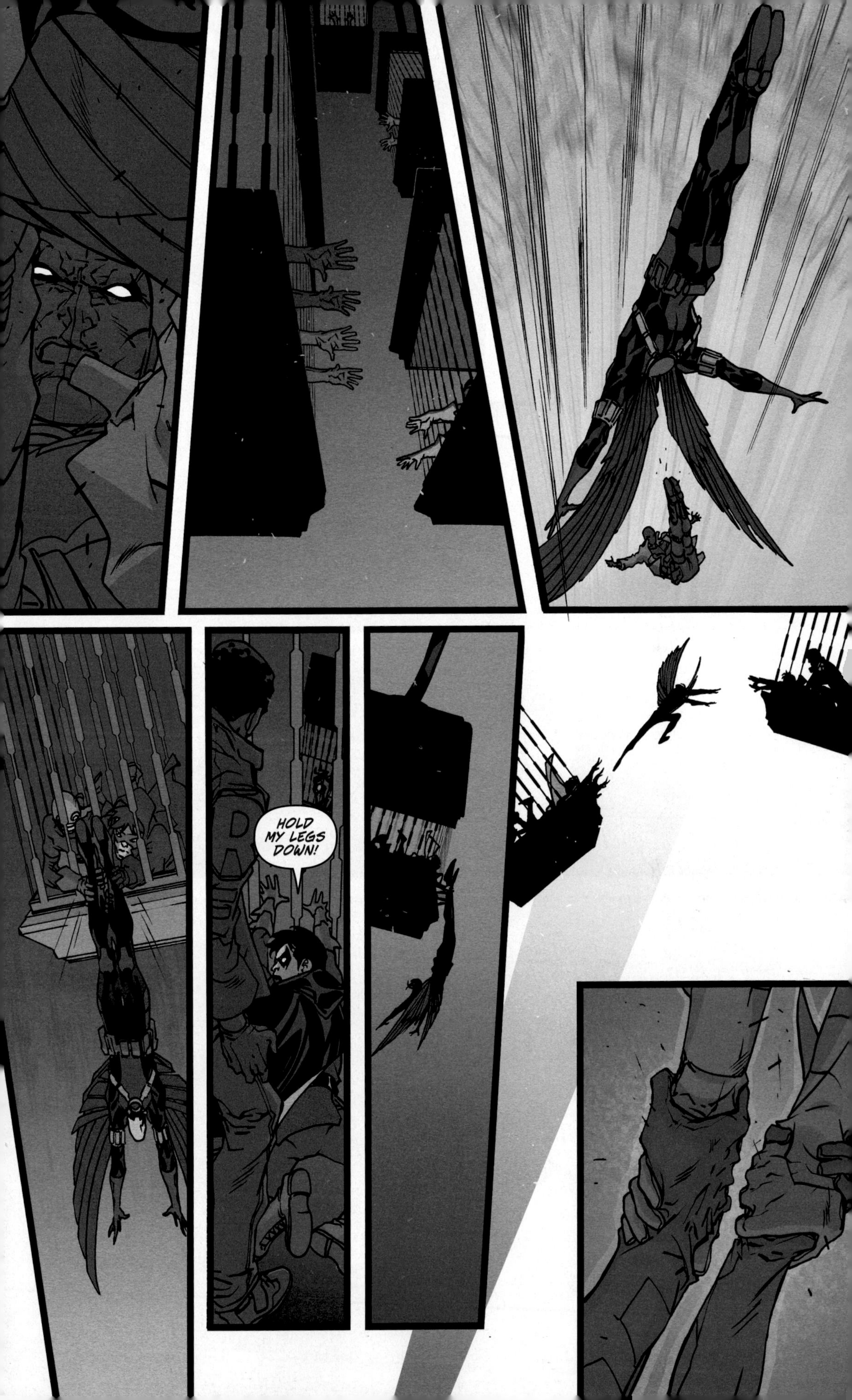
HOLD MY LEGS DOWN!

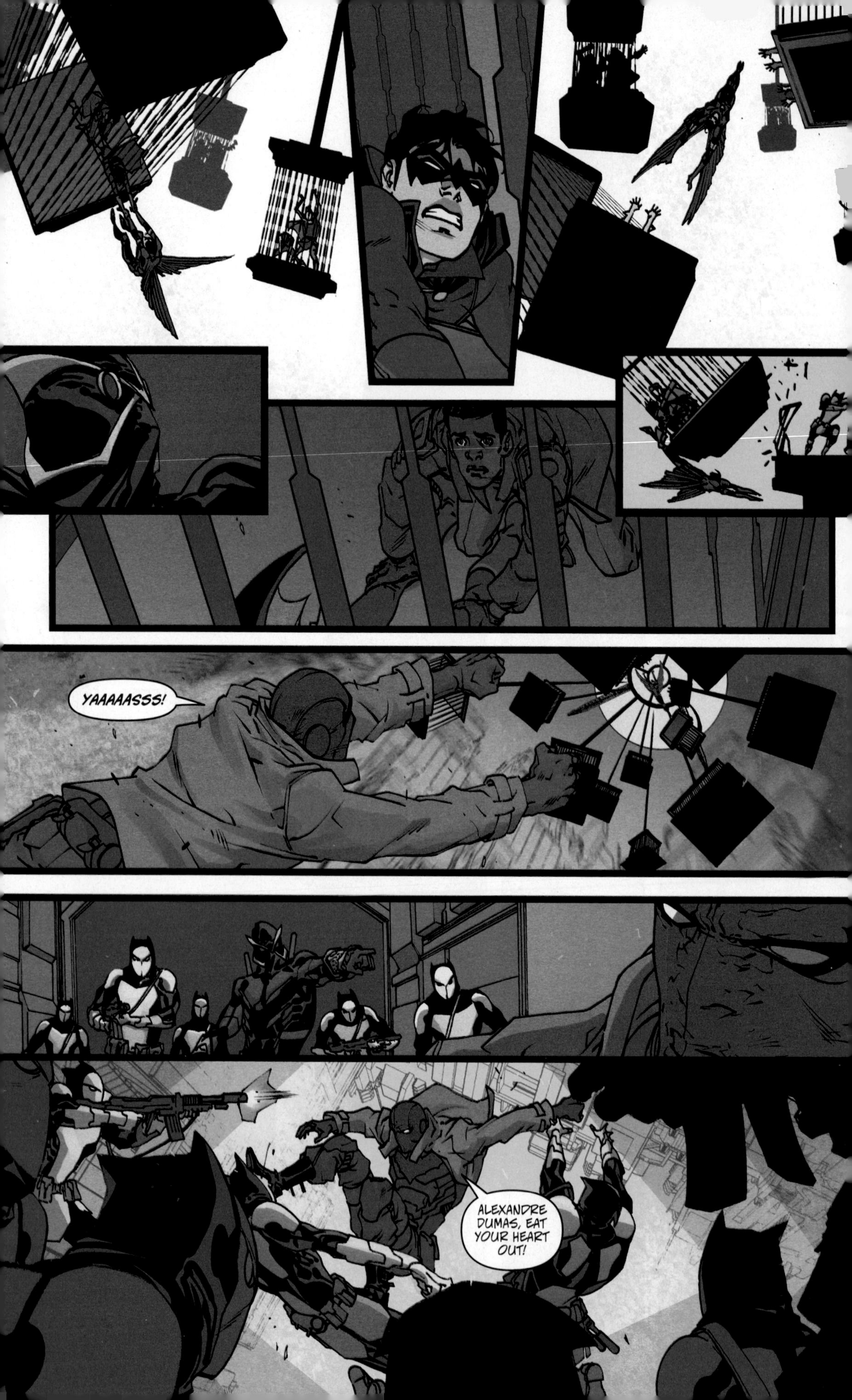
YAAAAASSS!
ALEXANDRE DUMAS, EAT YOUR HEART OUT!

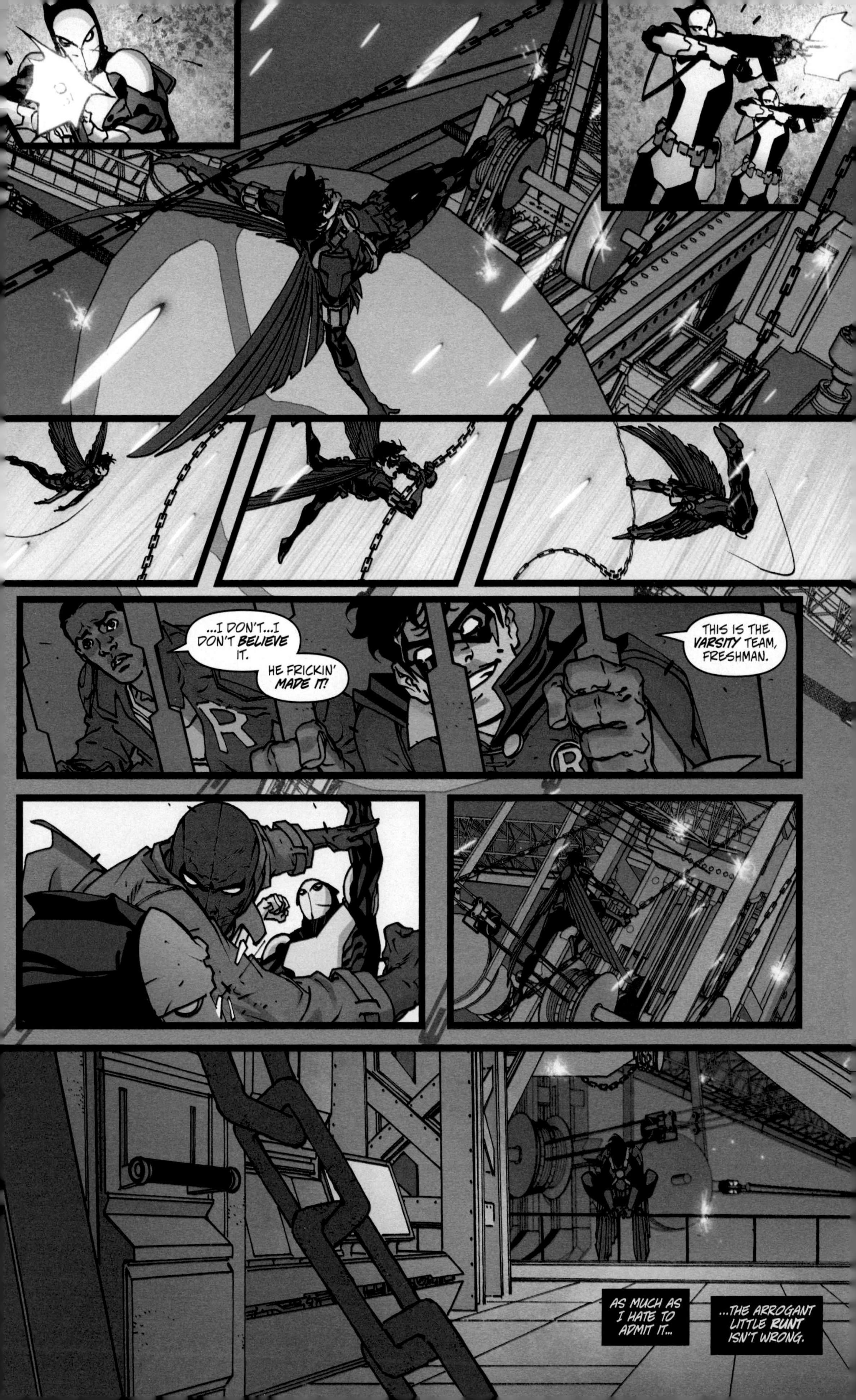
...I DON'T...I DON'T BELIEVE IT.
HE FRICKIN' MADE IT!
THIS IS THE VARSITY TEAM, FRESHMAN.
AS MUCH AS I HATE TO ADMIT IT...
...THE ARROGANT LITTLE RUNT ISN'T WRONG.

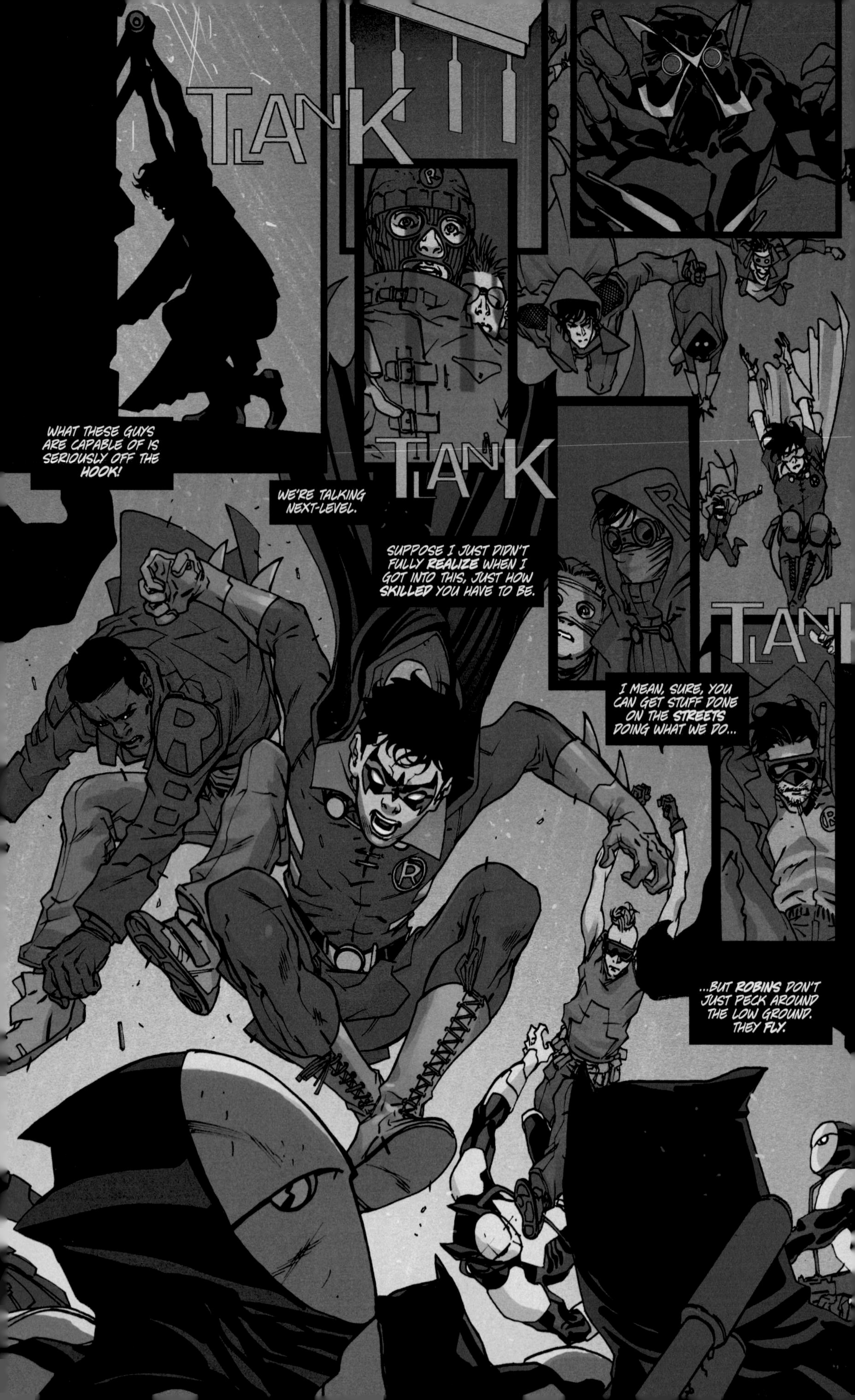
TLANK
WHAT THESE GUYS ARE CAPABLE OF IS SERIOUSLY OFF THE HOOK!
WE'RE TALKING NEXT-LEVEL.
TLANK
SUPPOSE I JUST DIDN'T FULLY REALIZE WHEN I GOT INTO THIS, JUST HOW SKILLED YOU HAVE TO BE.
TLANK
I MEAN, SURE, YOU CAN GET STUFF DONE ON THE STREETS DOING WHAT WE DO...
...BUT ROBINS DON'T JUST PECK AROUND THE LOW GROUND. THEY FLY.

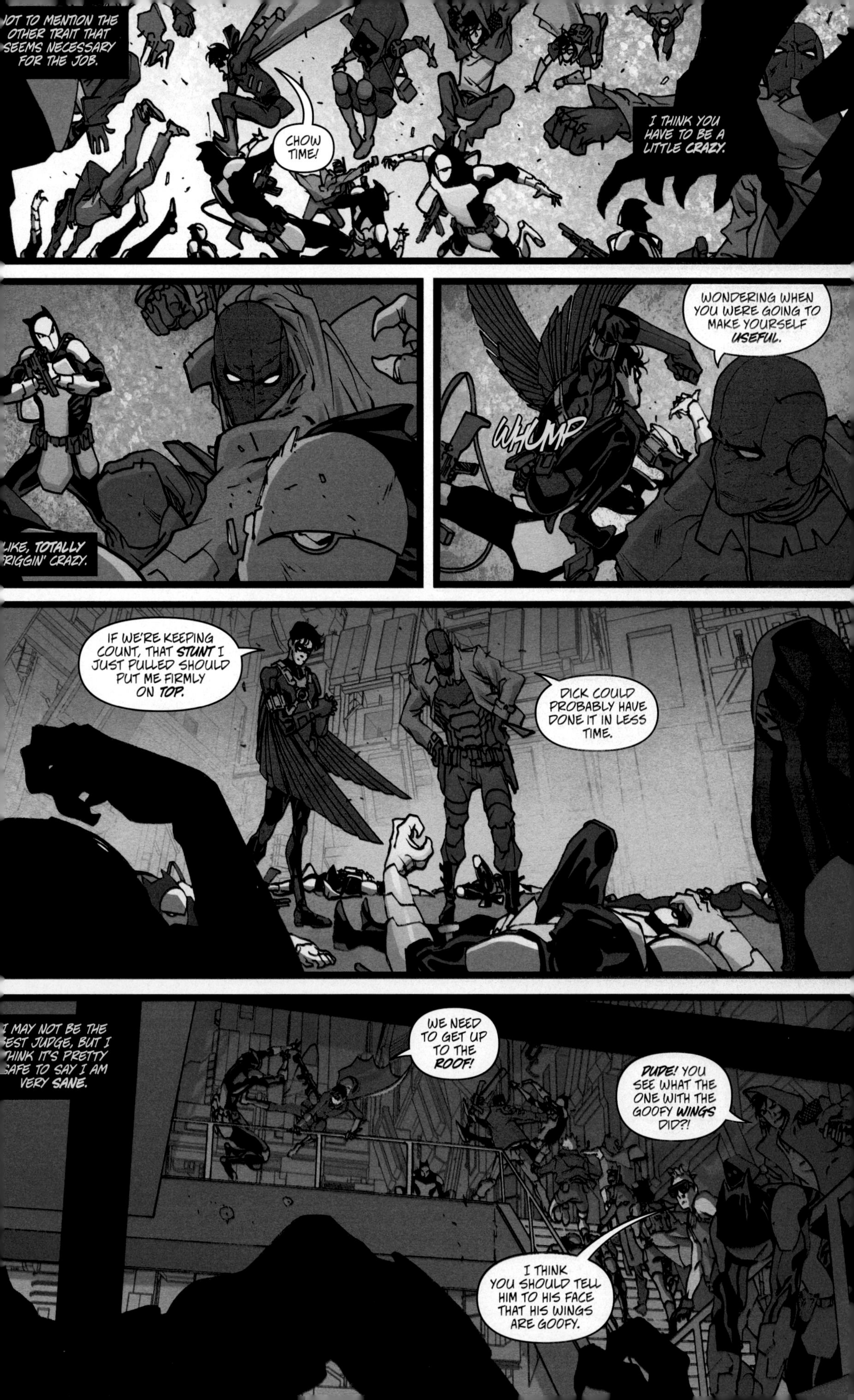

NOT TO MENTION THE OTHER TRAIT THAT SEEMS NECESSARY FOR THE JOB.
CHOW TIME!
I THINK YOU HAVE TO BE A LITTLE CRAZY.
LIKE, TOTALLY FRIGGIN' CRAZY.
WONDERING WHEN YOU WERE GOING TO MAKE YOURSELF USEFUL.
WHUMP
IF WE'RE KEEPING COUNT, THAT STUNT I JUST PULLED SHOULD PUT ME FIRMLY ON TOP.
DICK COULD PROBABLY HAVE DONE IT IN LESS TIME.
I MAY NOT BE THE BEST JUDGE, BUT I THINK IT'S PRETTY SAFE TO SAY I AM VERY SANE.
WE NEED TO GET UP TO THE ROOF!
DUDE! YOU SEE WHAT THE ONE WITH THE GOOFY WINGS DID?!
I THINK YOU SHOULD TELL HIM TO HIS FACE THAT HIS WINGS ARE GOOFY.

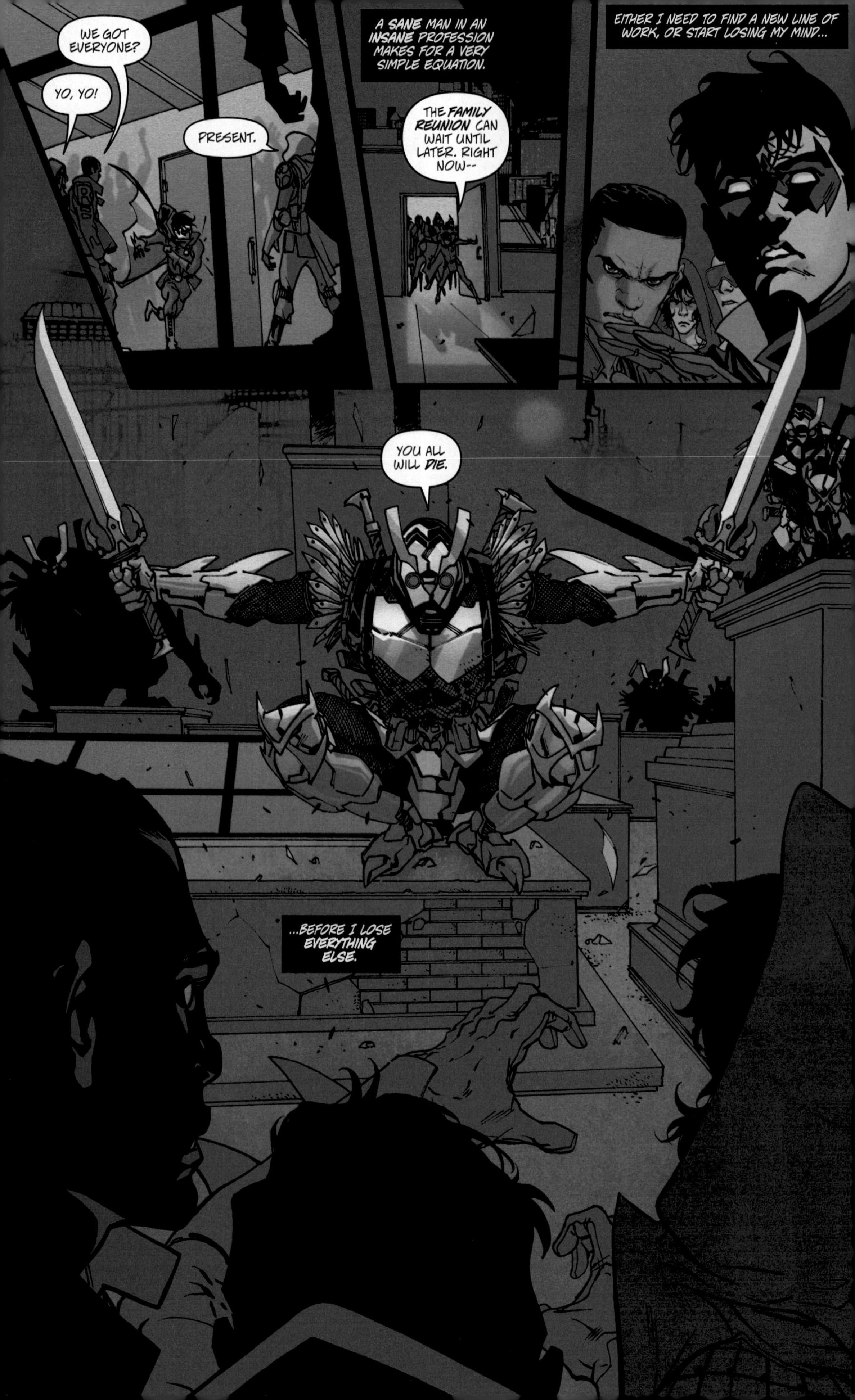
WE GOT EVERYONE?
YO, YO!
PRESENT.
A SANE MAN IN AN INSANE PROFESSION MAKES FOR A VERY SIMPLE EQUATION.
THE FAMILY REUNION CAN WAIT UNTIL LATER. RIGHT NOW--
EITHER I NEED TO FIND A NEW LINE OF WORK, OR START LOSING MY MIND...
YOU ALL WILL DIE.
...BEFORE I LOSE EVERYTHING ELSE.

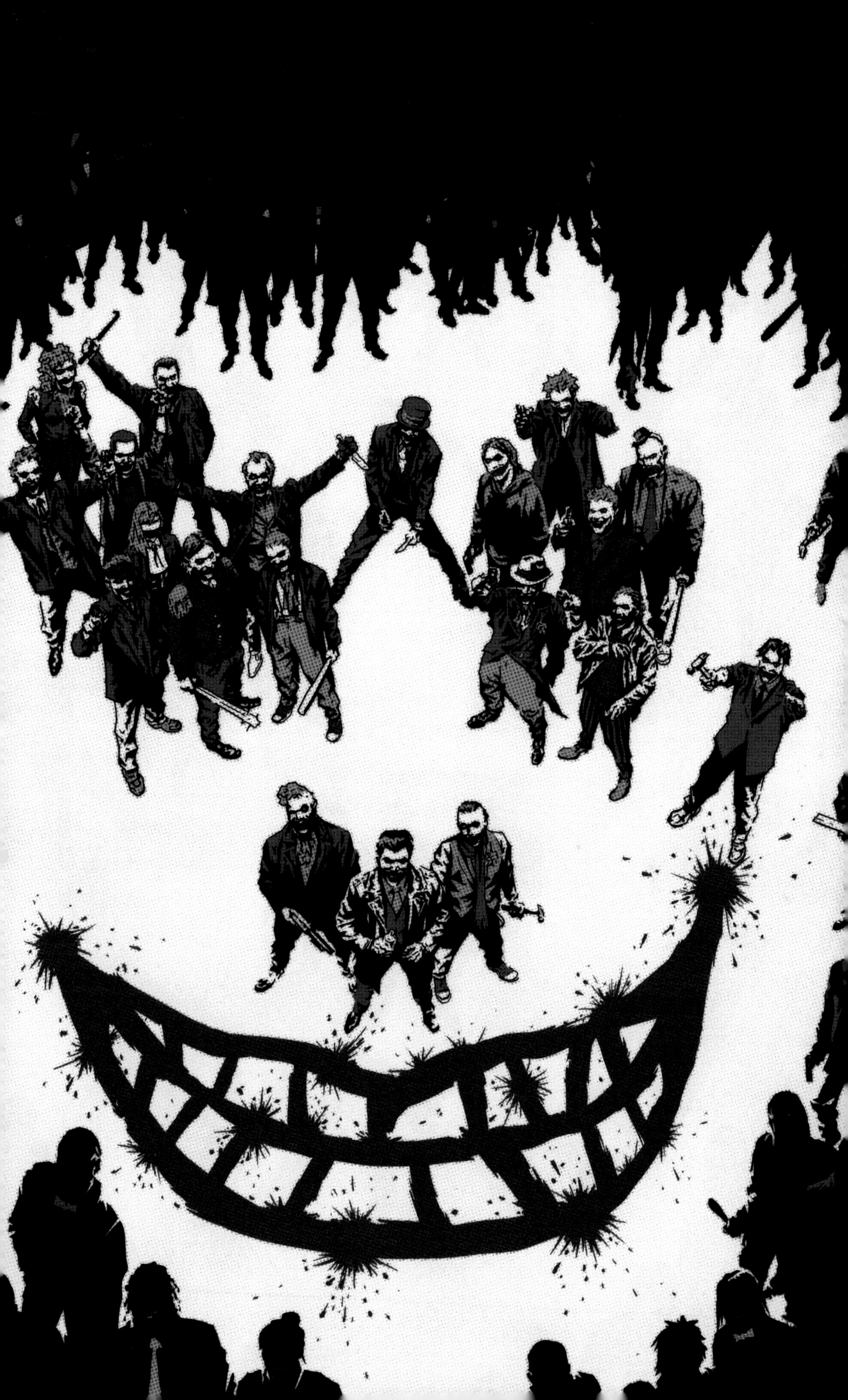

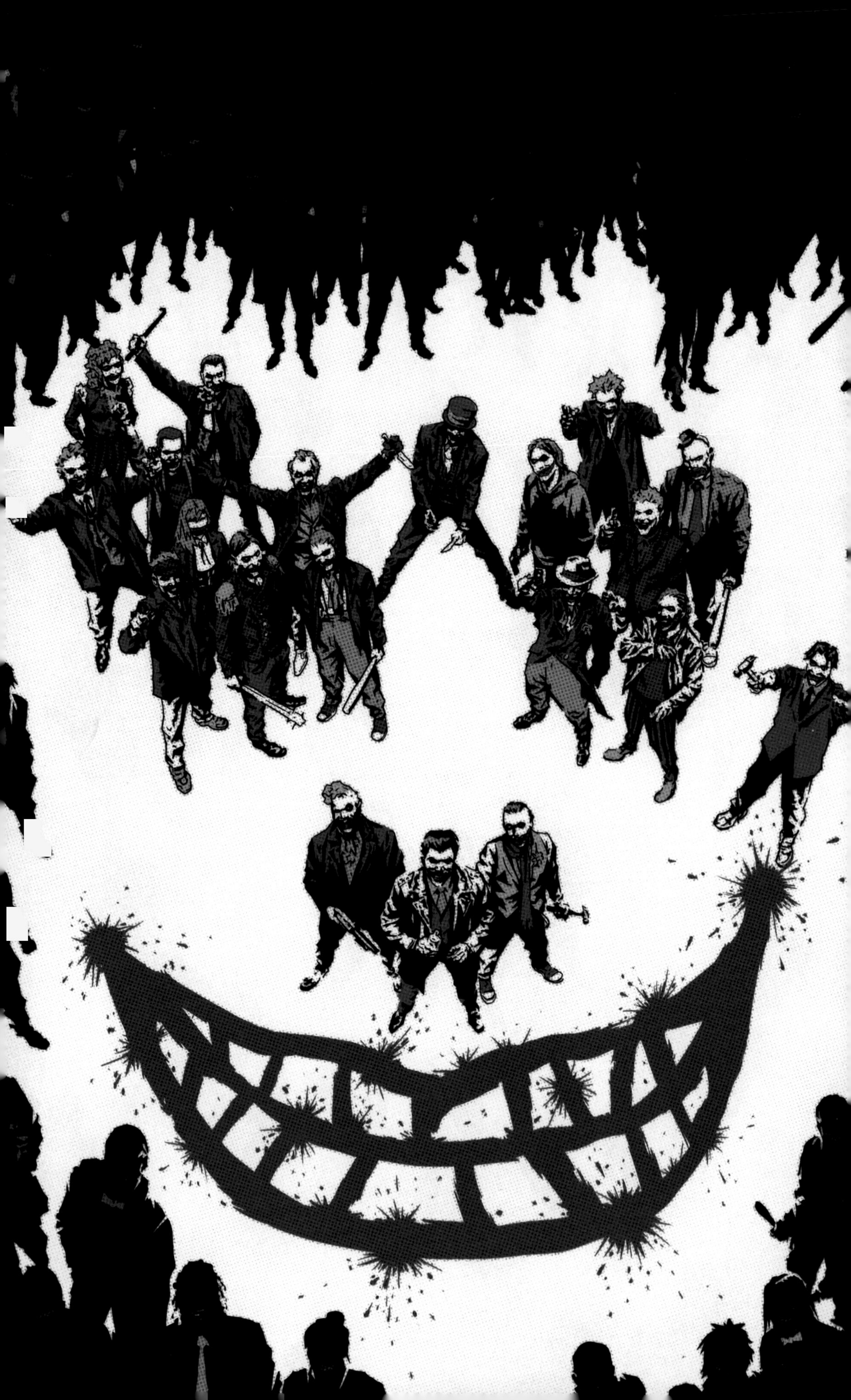

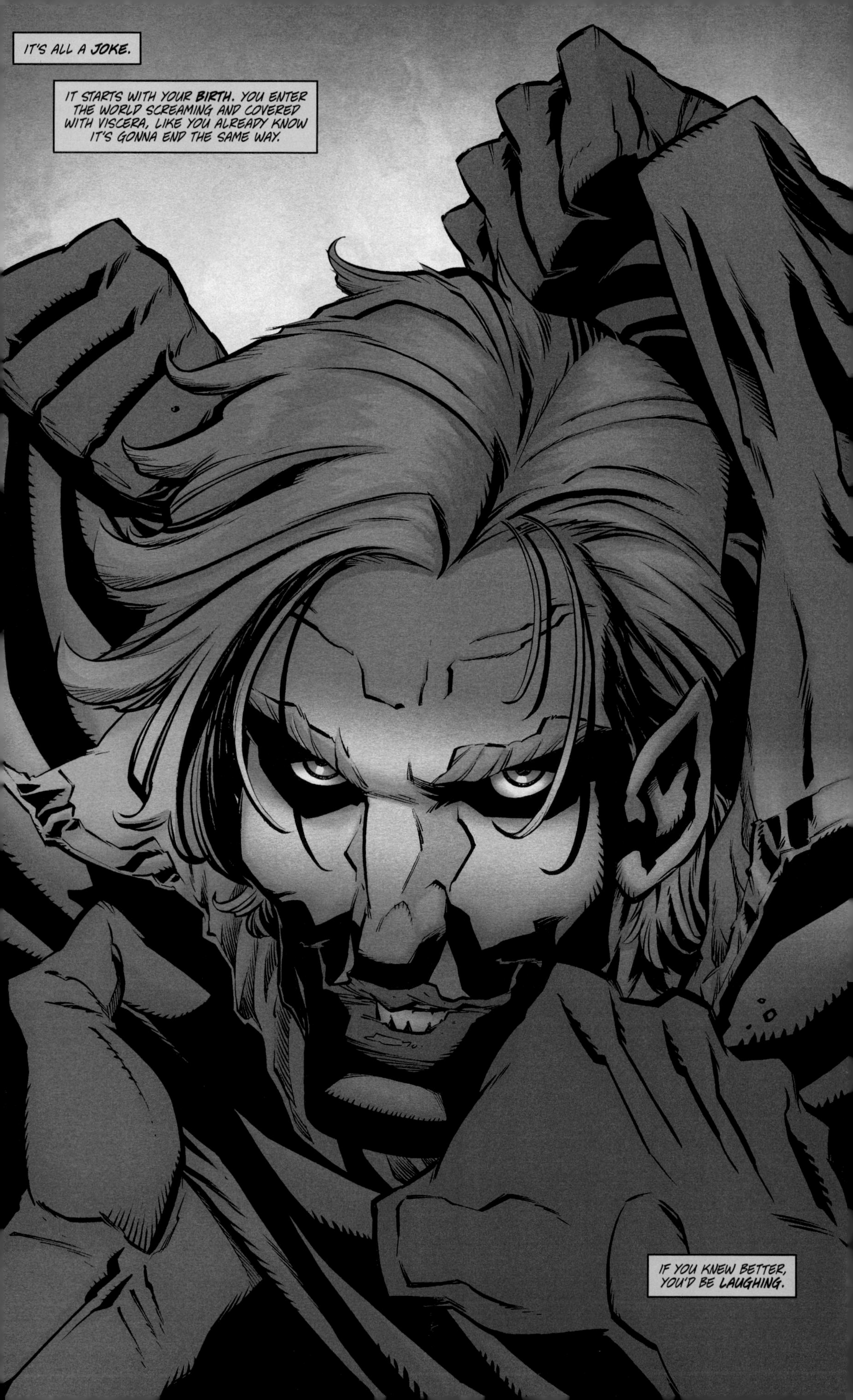
IT'S ALL A JOKE.
IT STARTS WITH YOUR BIRTH. YOU ENTER THE WORLD SCREAMING AND COVERED WITH VISCERA, LIKE YOU ALREADY KNOW IT'S GONNA END THE SAME WAY.
IF YOU KNEW BETTER, YOU'D BE LAUGHING.

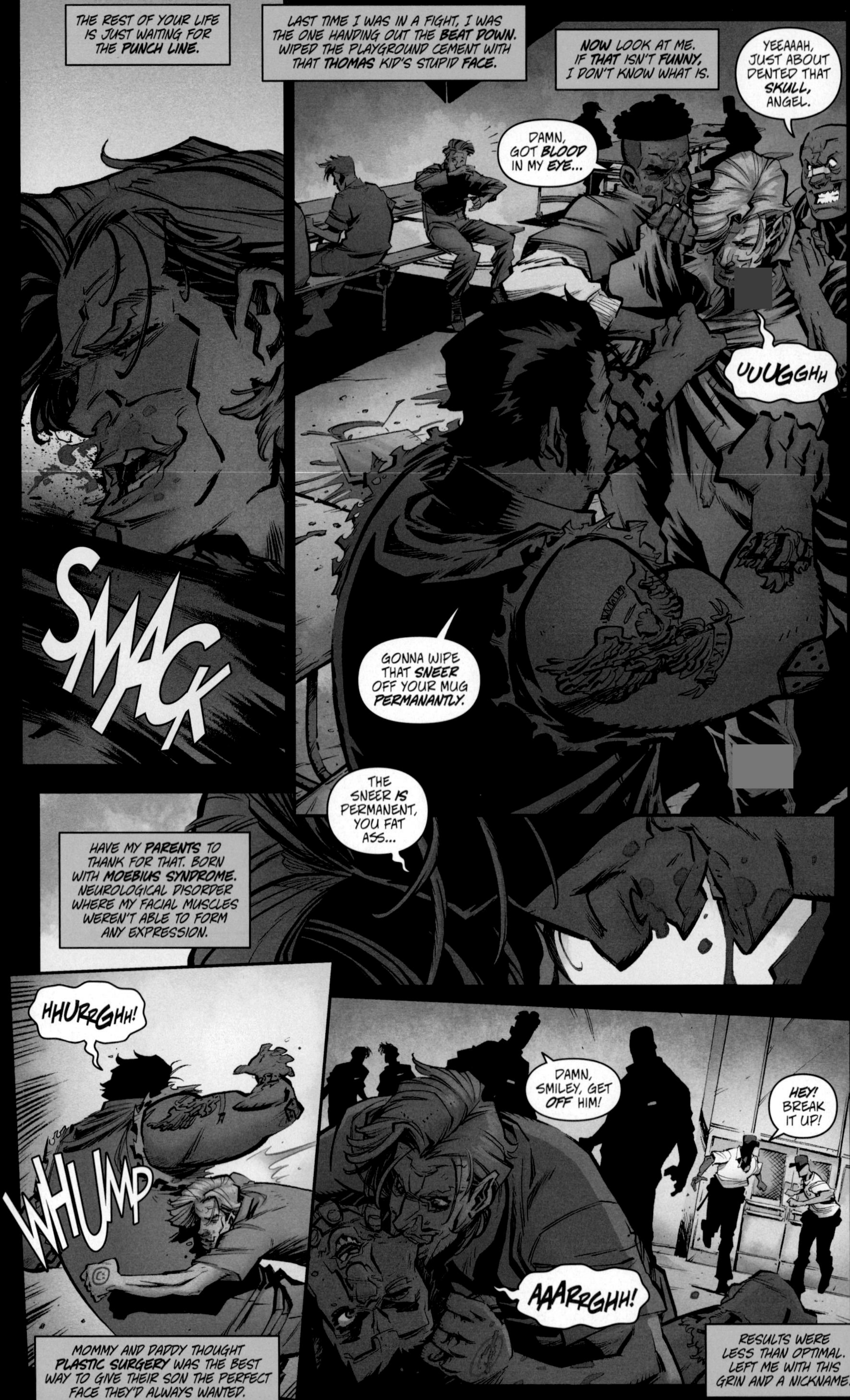
THE REST OF YOUR LIFE IS JUST WAITING FOR THE PUNCH LINE.
SMACK
LAST TIME I WAS IN A FIGHT, I WAS THE ONE HANDING OUT THE BEAT DOWN. WIPED THE PLAYGROUND CEMENT WITH THAT THOMAS KID'S STUPID FACE.
NOW LOOK AT ME. IF THAT ISN'T FUNNY, I DON'T KNOW WHAT IS.
YEEAAAH, JUST ABOUT DENTED THAT SKULL, ANGEL.
DAMN, GOT BLOOD IN MY EYE...
UUUGGHH
GONNA WIPE THAT SNEER OFF YOUR MUG PERMANANTLY.
THE SNEER IS PERMANENT, YOU FAT ASS...
HAVE MY PARENTS TO THANK FOR THAT. BORN WITH MOEBIUS SYNDROME. NEUROLOGICAL DISORDER WHERE MY FACIAL MUSCLES WEREN'T ABLE TO FORM ANY EXPRESSION.
HHURRGHH!
WHUMP
MOMMY AND DADDY THOUGHT PLASTIC SURGERY WAS THE BEST WAY TO GIVE THEIR SON THE PERFECT FACE THEY'D ALWAYS WANTED.
DAMN, SMILEY, GET OFF HIM!
HEY! BREAK IT UP!
AAARRGHH!
RESULTS WERE LESS THAN OPTIMAL. LEFT ME WITH THIS GRIN AND A NICKNAME.

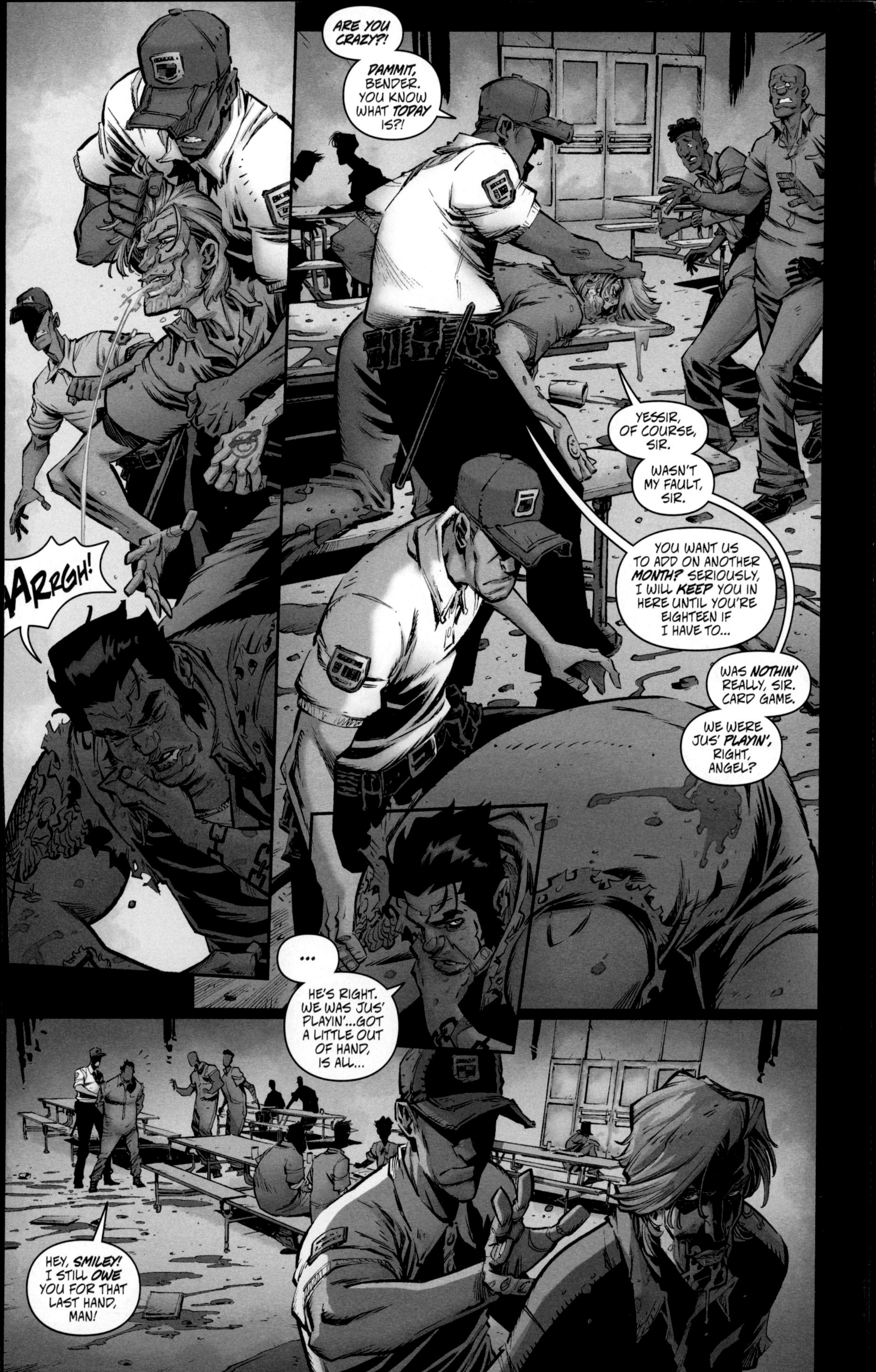
AARRGH!
ARE YOU CRAZY?!
DAMMIT, BENDER. YOU KNOW WHAT TODAY IS?!
YESSIR, OF COURSE, SIR.
WASN'T MY FAULT, SIR.
YOU WANT US TO ADD ON ANOTHER MONTH? SERIOUSLY, I WILL KEEP YOU IN HERE UNTIL YOU'RE EIGHTEEN IF I HAVE TO...
WAS NOTHIN' REALLY, SIR. CARD GAME.
WE WERE JUS' PLAYIN', RIGHT, ANGEL?
...
HE'S RIGHT. WE WAS JUS' PLAYIN'...GOT A LITTLE OUT OF HAND, IS ALL...
HEY, SMILEY! I STILL OWE YOU FOR THAT LAST HAND, MAN!

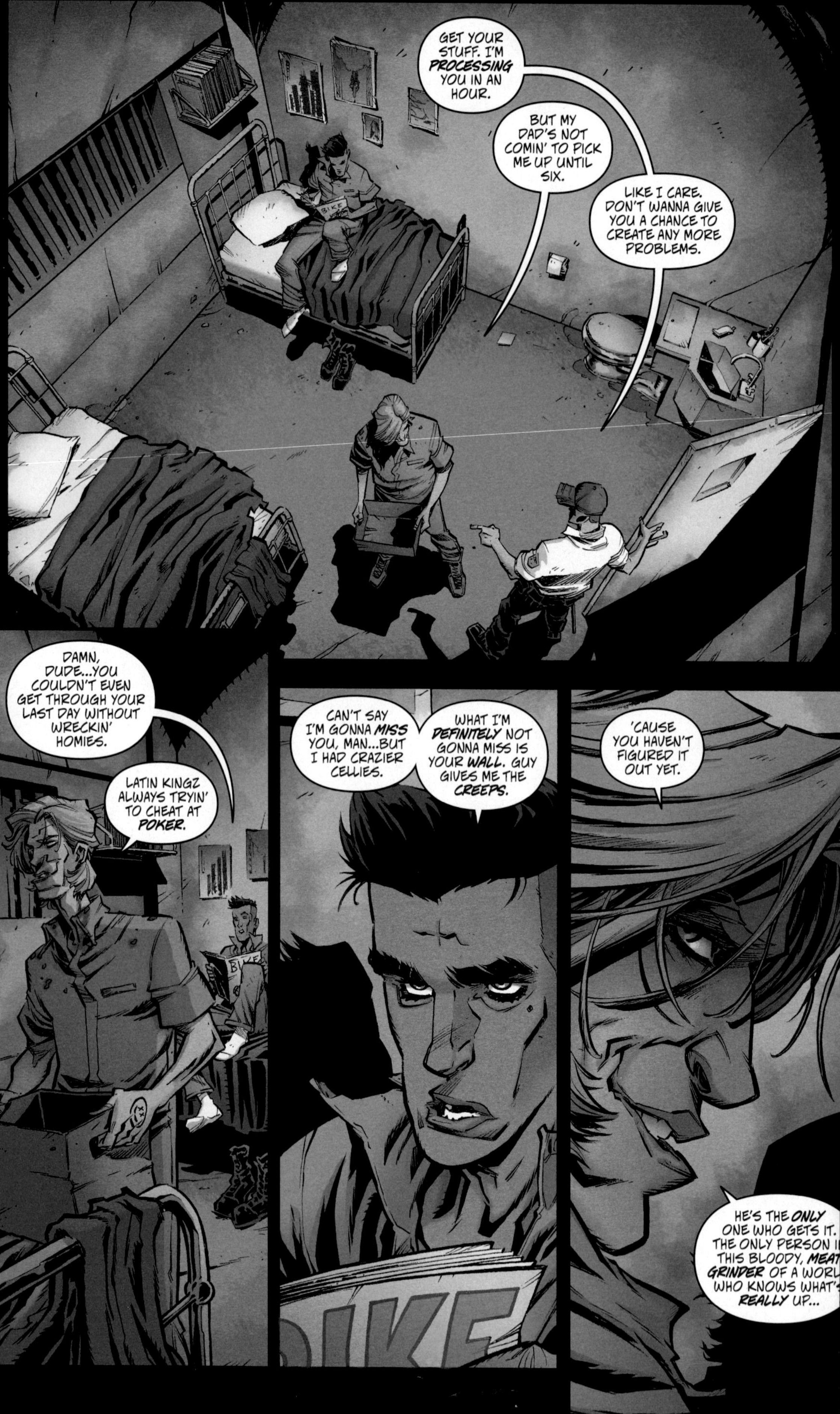
GET YOUR STUFF. I'M PROCESSING YOU IN AN HOUR.
BUT MY DAD'S NOT COMIN' TO PICK ME UP UNTIL SIX.
LIKE I CARE. DON'T WANNA GIVE YOU A CHANCE TO CREATE ANY MORE PROBLEMS.
BIKE
DAMN, DUDE...YOU COULDN'T EVEN GET THROUGH YOUR LAST DAY WITHOUT WRECKIN' HOMIES.
LATIN KINGZ ALWAYS TRYIN' TO CHEAT AT POKER.
CAN'T SAY I'M GONNA MISS YOU, MAN...BUT I HAD CRAZIER CELLIES.
WHAT I'M DEFINITELY NOT GONNA MISS IS YOUR WALL. GUY GIVES ME THE CREEPS.
'CAUSE YOU HAVEN'T FIGURED IT OUT YET.
HE'S THE ONLY ONE WHO GETS IT. THE ONLY PERSON I THIS BLOODY, MEAT GRINDER OF A WORL WHO KNOWS WHAT'S REALLY UP...

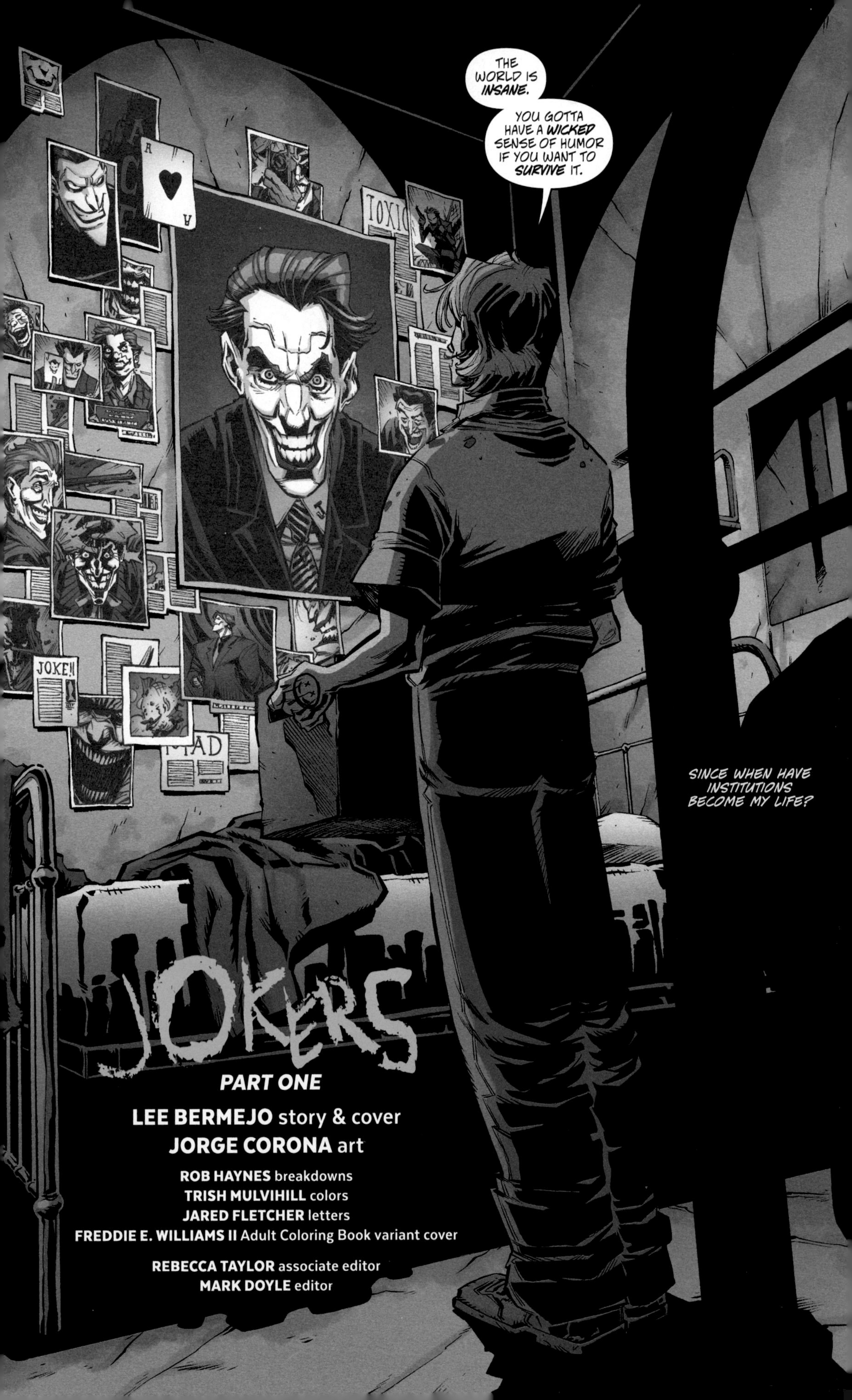
THE WORLD IS INSANE.
YOU GOTTA HAVE A WICKED SENSE OF HUMOR IF YOU WANT TO SURVIVE IT.
SINCE WHEN HAVE INSTITUTIONS BECOME MY LIFE?
JOKERS
PART ONE
LEE BERMEJO story & cover
JORGE CORONA art
ROB HAYNES breakdowns
TRISH MULVIHILL colors
JARED FLETCHER letters
FREDDIE E. WILLIAMS II Adult Coloring Book variant cover
REBECCA TAYLOR associate editor
MARK DOYLE editor

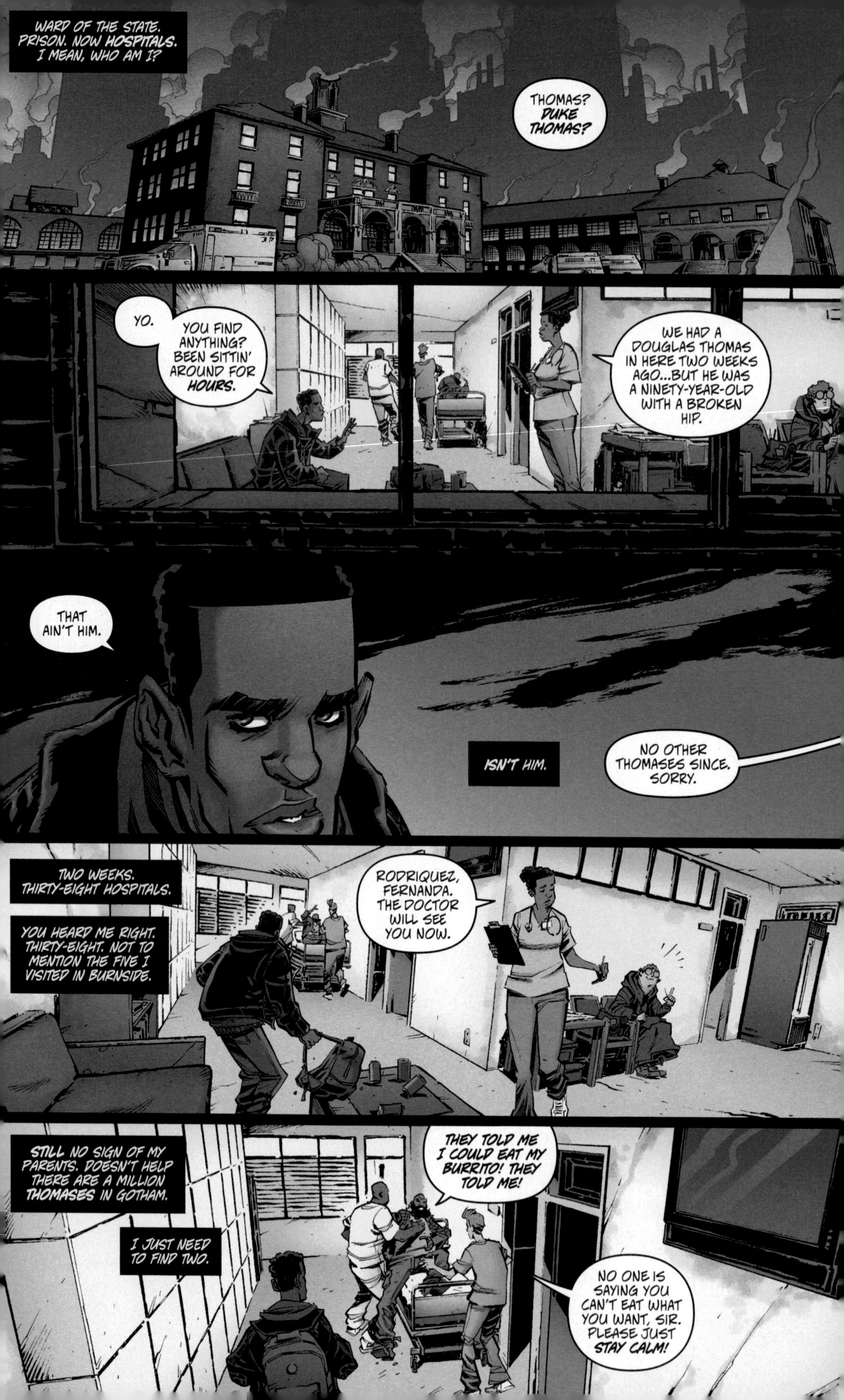
WARD OF THE STATE. PRISON. NOW HOSPITALS. I MEAN, WHO AM I?
THOMAS? DUKE THOMAS?
YO.
YOU FIND ANYTHING? BEEN SITTIN' AROUND FOR HOURS.
WE HAD A DOUGLAS THOMAS IN HERE TWO WEEKS AGO...BUT HE WAS A NINETY-YEAR-OLD WITH A BROKEN HIP.
THAT AIN'T HIM.
ISN'T HIM.
NO OTHER THOMASES SINCE. SORRY.
TWO WEEKS. THIRTY-EIGHT HOSPITALS.
YOU HEARD ME RIGHT. THIRTY-EIGHT. NOT TO MENTION THE FIVE I VISITED IN BURNSIDE.
RODRIQUEZ, FERNANDA. THE DOCTOR WILL SEE YOU NOW.
STILL NO SIGN OF MY PARENTS. DOESN'T HELP THERE ARE A MILLION THOMASES IN GOTHAM.
I JUST NEED TO FIND TWO.
THEY TOLD ME I COULD EAT MY BURRITO! THEY TOLD ME!
NO ONE IS SAYING YOU CAN'T EAT WHAT YOU WANT, SIR. PLEASE JUST STAY CALM!

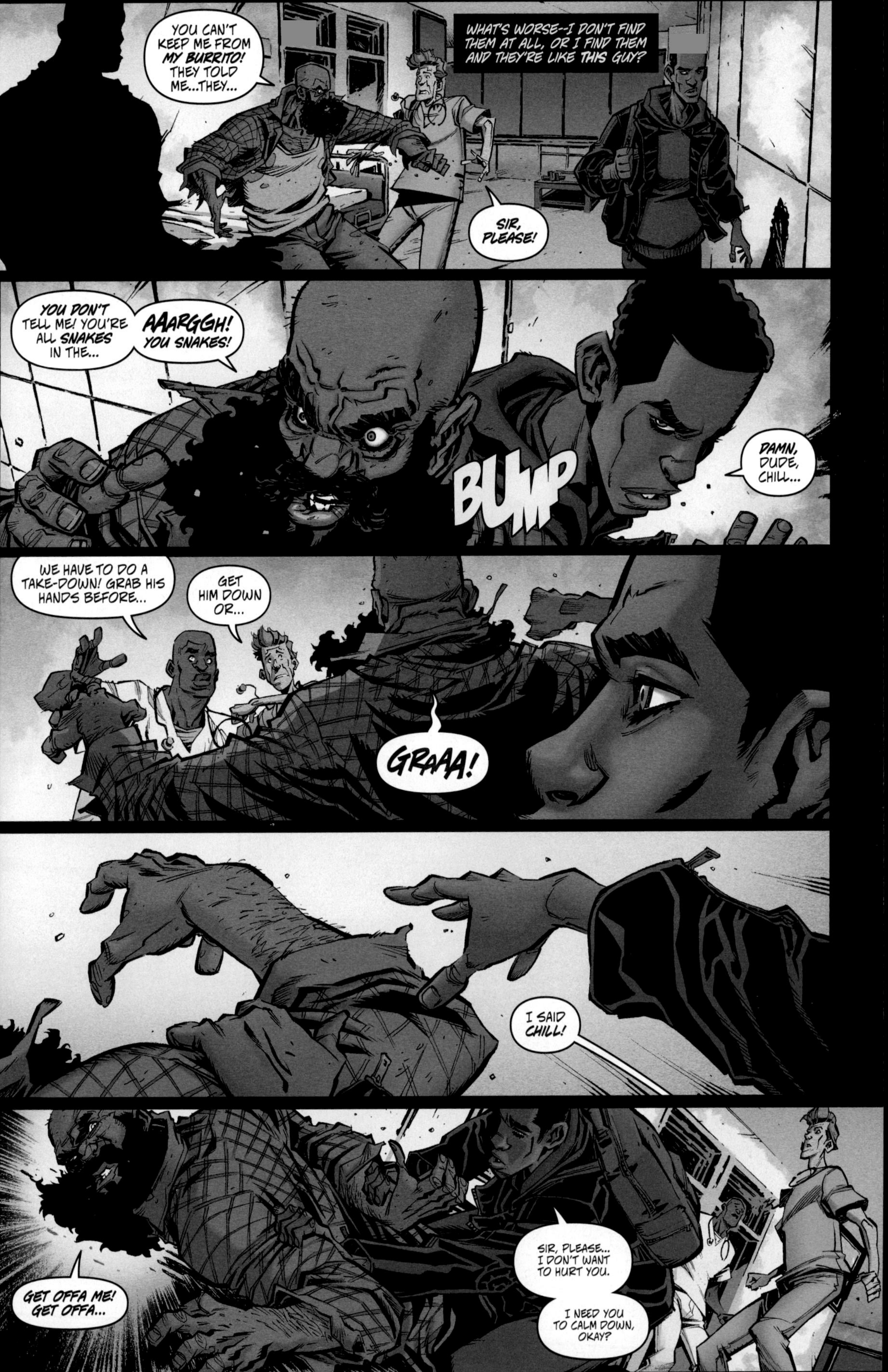
YOU CAN'T KEEP ME FROM MY BURRITO! THEY TOLD ME...THEY...
WHAT'S WORSE--I DON'T FIND THEM AT ALL, OR I FIND THEM AND THEY'RE LIKE THIS GUY?
SIR, PLEASE!
YOU DON'T TELL ME! YOU'RE ALL SNAKES IN THE...
AAARGGH! YOU SNAKES!
BUMP
DAMN, DUDE, CHILL...
WE HAVE TO DO A TAKE-DOWN! GRAB HIS HANDS BEFORE...
GET HIM DOWN OR...
GRAAA!
I SAID CHILL!
GET OFFA ME! GET OFFA...
SIR, PLEASE... I DON'T WANT TO HURT YOU.
I NEED YOU TO CALM DOWN, OKAY?

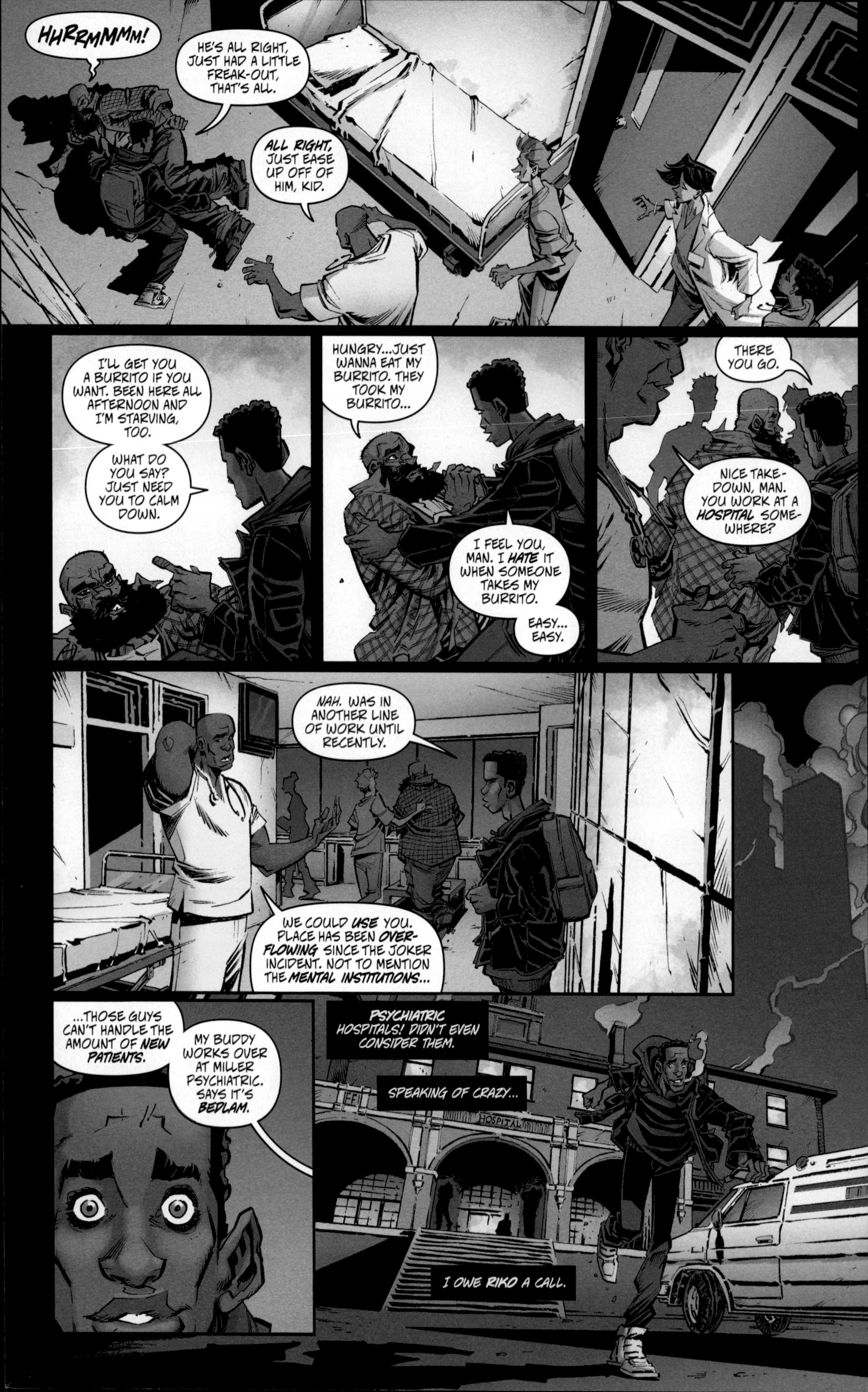
HHRRMMMM!
HE'S ALL RIGHT, JUST HAD A LITTLE FREAK-OUT, THAT'S ALL.
ALL RIGHT, JUST EASE UP OFF OF HIM, KID.
I'LL GET YOU A BURRITO IF YOU WANT. BEEN HERE ALL AFTERNOON AND I'M STARVING, TOO.
WHAT DO YOU SAY? JUST NEED YOU TO CALM DOWN.
HUNGRY...JUST WANNA EAT MY BURRITO. THEY TOOK MY BURRITO...
I FEEL YOU, MAN. I HATE IT WHEN SOMEONE TAKES MY BURRITO.
EASY... EASY.
THERE YOU GO.
NICE TAKE-DOWN, MAN. YOU WORK AT A HOSPITAL SOMEWHERE?
NAH. WAS IN ANOTHER LINE OF WORK UNTIL RECENTLY.
WE COULD USE YOU. PLACE HAS BEEN OVERFLOWING SINCE THE JOKER INCIDENT. NOT TO MENTION THE MENTAL INSTITUTIONS...
...THOSE GUYS CAN'T HANDLE THE AMOUNT OF NEW PATIENTS.
MY BUDDY WORKS OVER AT MILLER PSYCHIATRIC. SAYS IT'S BEDLAM.
PSYCHIATRIC HOSPITALS! DIDN'T EVEN CONSIDER THEM.
SPEAKING OF CRAZY...
HOSPITAL
I OWE RIKO A CALL.

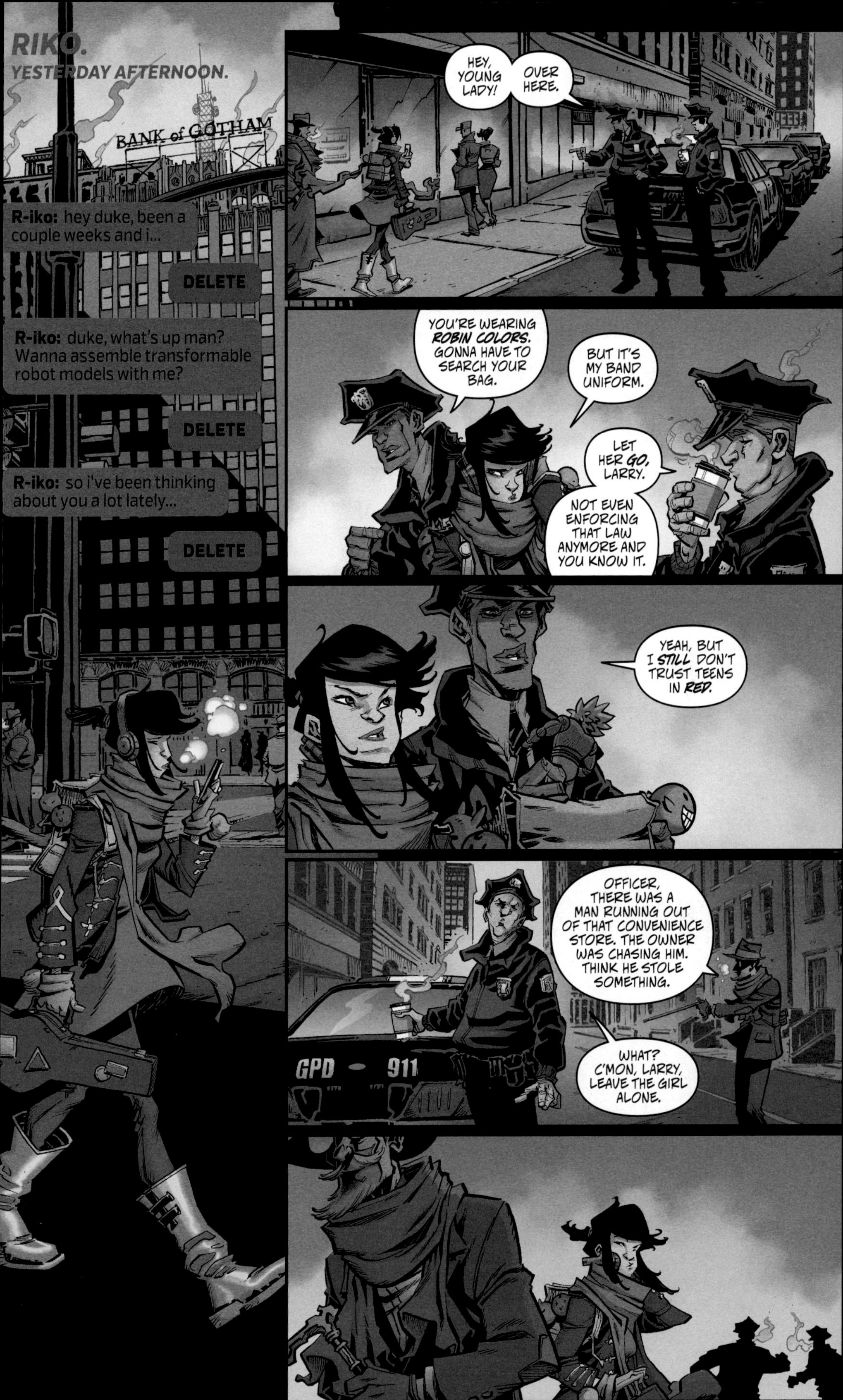

RIKO.
YESTERDAY AFTERNOON.
BANK of GOTHAM
R-iko: hey duke, been a couple weeks and i...
DELETE
R-iko: duke, what's up man? Wanna assemble transformable robot models with me?
DELETE
R-iko: so i've been thinking about you a lot lately...
DELETE
HEY, YOUNG LADY!
OVER HERE.
YOU'RE WEARING ROBIN COLORS. GONNA HAVE TO SEARCH YOUR BAG.
BUT IT'S MY BAND UNIFORM.
LET HER GO, LARRY.
NOT EVEN ENFORCING THAT LAW ANYMORE AND YOU KNOW IT.
YEAH, BUT I STILL DON'T TRUST TEENS IN RED.
OFFICER, THERE WAS A MAN RUNNING OUT OF THAT CONVENIENCE STORE. THE OWNER WAS CHASING HIM. THINK HE STOLE SOMETHING.
GPD - 911
WHAT? C'MON, LARRY, LEAVE THE GIRL ALONE.

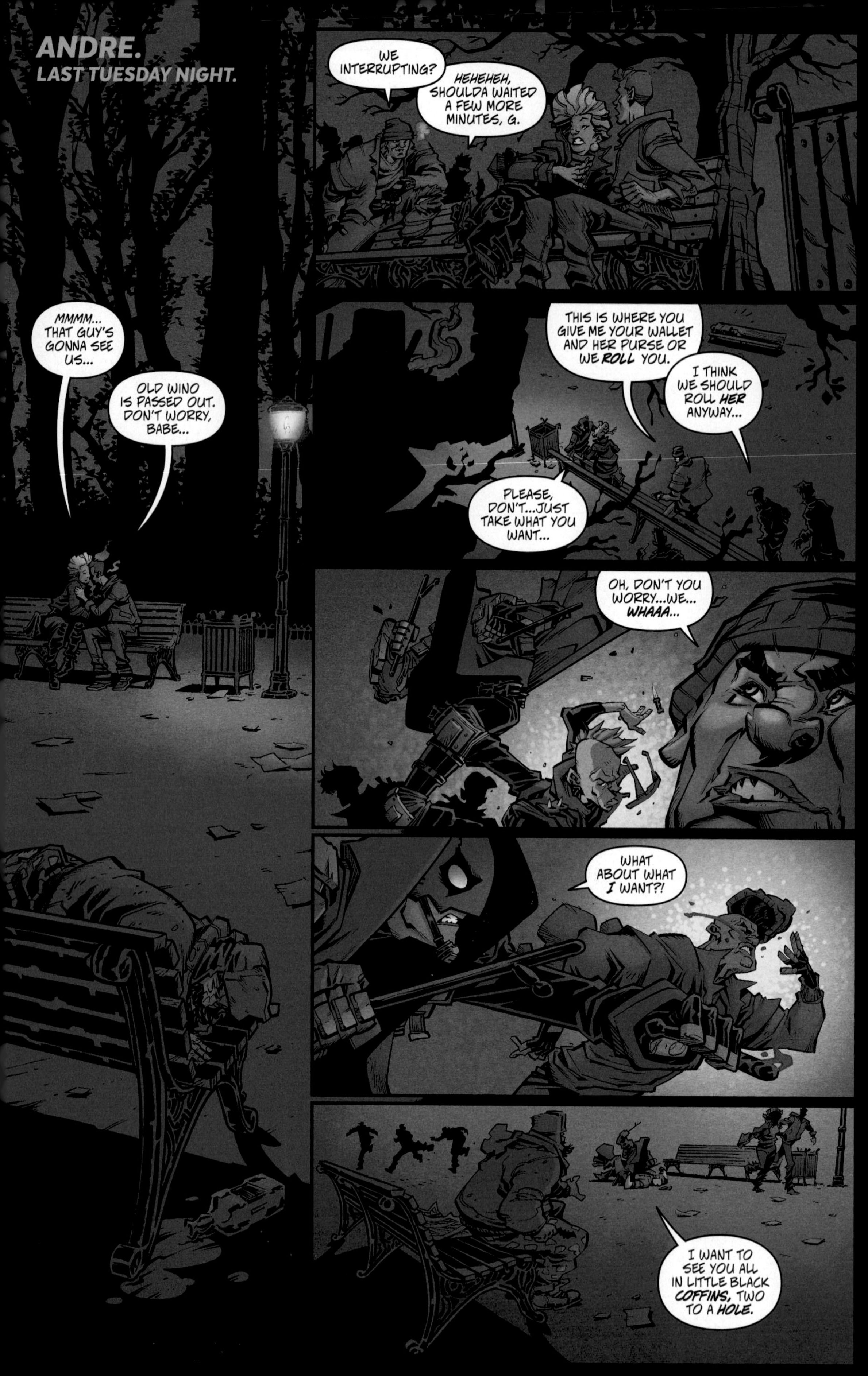
ANDRE.
LAST TUESDAY NIGHT.
MMMM... THAT GUY'S GONNA SEE US...
OLD WINO IS PASSED OUT. DON'T WORRY, BABE...
WE INTERRUPTING?
HEHEHEH, SHOULDA WAITED A FEW MORE MINUTES, G.
THIS IS WHERE YOU GIVE ME YOUR WALLET AND HER PURSE OR WE ROLL YOU.
I THINK WE SHOULD ROLL HER ANYWAY...
PLEASE, DON'T...JUST TAKE WHAT YOU WANT...
OH, DON'T YOU WORRY...WE... WHAAA...
WHAT ABOUT WHAT I WANT?!
I WANT TO SEE YOU ALL IN LITTLE BLACK COFFINS, TWO TO A HOLE.

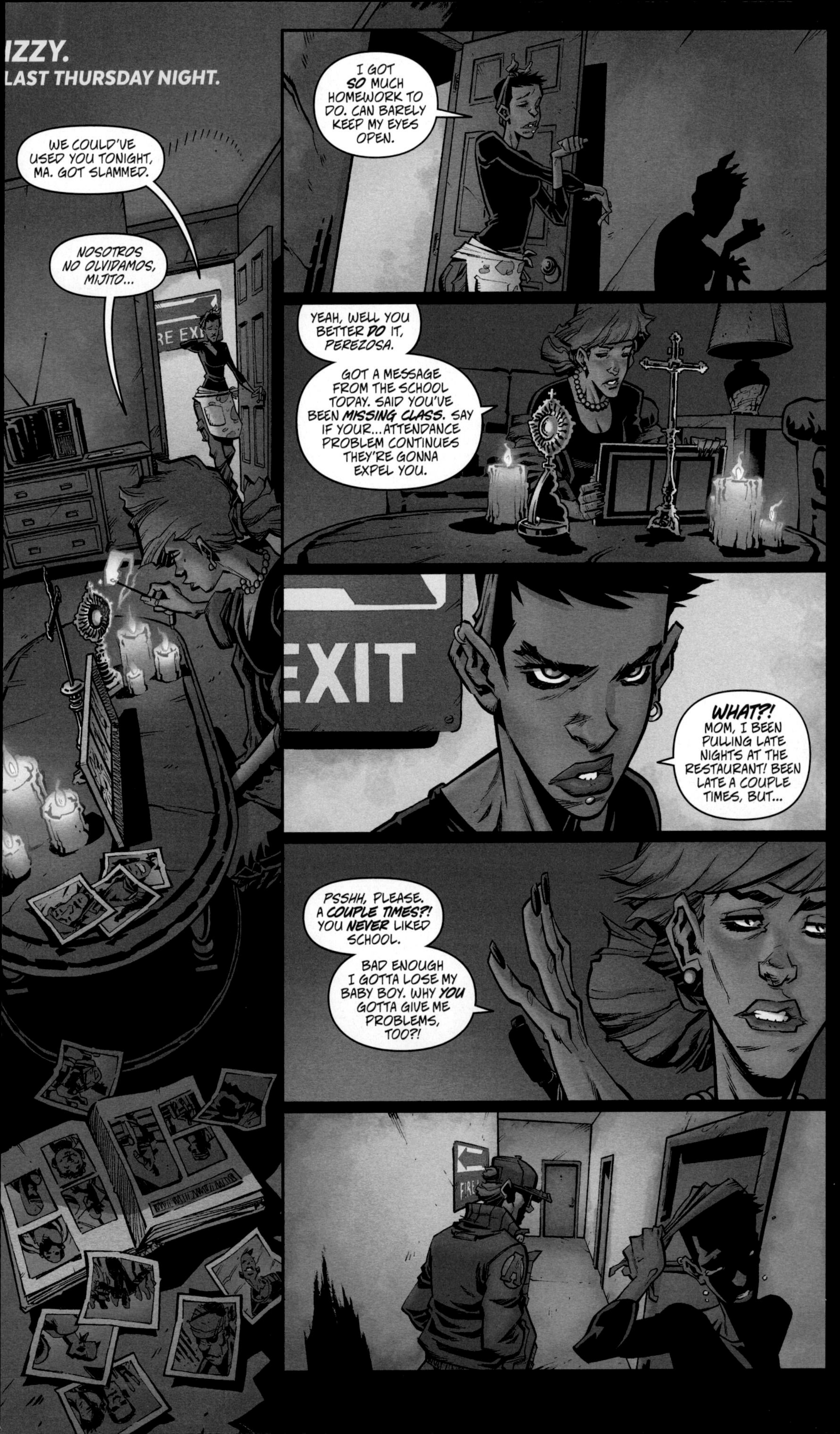
IZZY.
LAST THURSDAY NIGHT.
WE COULD'VE USED YOU TONIGHT, MA. GOT SLAMMED.
NOSOTROS NO OLVIDAMOS, MIJITO...
I GOT SO MUCH HOMEWORK TO DO. CAN BARELY KEEP MY EYES OPEN.
YEAH, WELL YOU BETTER DO IT, PEREZOSA.
GOT A MESSAGE FROM THE SCHOOL TODAY. SAID YOU'VE BEEN MISSING CLASS. SAY IF YOUR...ATTENDANCE PROBLEM CONTINUES THEY'RE GONNA EXPEL YOU.
EXIT
WHAT?! MOM, I BEEN PULLING LATE NIGHTS AT THE RESTAURANT! BEEN LATE A COUPLE TIMES, BUT...
PSSHH, PLEASE. A COUPLE TIMES?! YOU NEVER LIKED SCHOOL.
BAD ENOUGH I GOTTA LOSE MY BABY BOY. WHY YOU GOTTA GIVE ME PROBLEMS, TOO?!

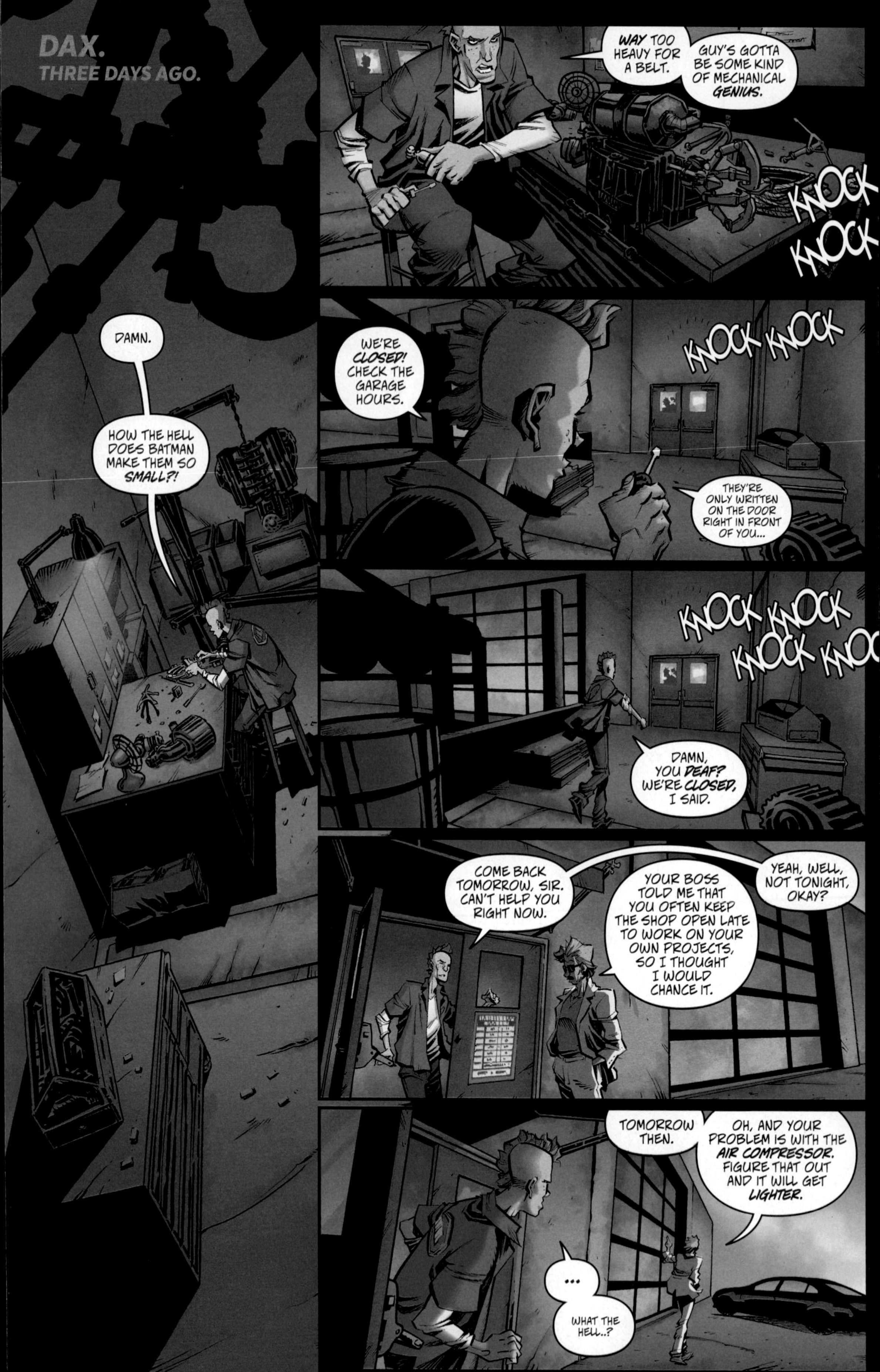
DAX.
THREE DAYS AGO.
WAY TOO HEAVY FOR A BELT.
GUY'S GOTTA BE SOME KIND OF MECHANICAL GENIUS.
KNOCK KNOCK
DAMN.
HOW THE HELL DOES BATMAN MAKE THEM SO SMALL?!
KNOCK KNOCK
WE'RE CLOSED! CHECK THE GARAGE HOURS.
THEY'RE ONLY WRITTEN ON THE DOOR RIGHT IN FRONT OF YOU...
KNOCK KNOCK KNOCK KNOC
DAMN, YOU DEAF? WE'RE CLOSED, I SAID.
COME BACK TOMORROW, SIR. CAN'T HELP YOU RIGHT NOW.
YOUR BOSS TOLD ME THAT YOU OFTEN KEEP THE SHOP OPEN LATE TO WORK ON YOUR OWN PROJECTS, SO I THOUGHT I WOULD CHANCE IT.
YEAH, WELL, NOT TONIGHT, OKAY?
TOMORROW THEN.
OH, AND YOUR PROBLEM IS WITH THE AIR COMPRESSOR. FIGURE THAT OUT AND IT WILL GET LIGHTER.
...
WHAT THE HELL..?

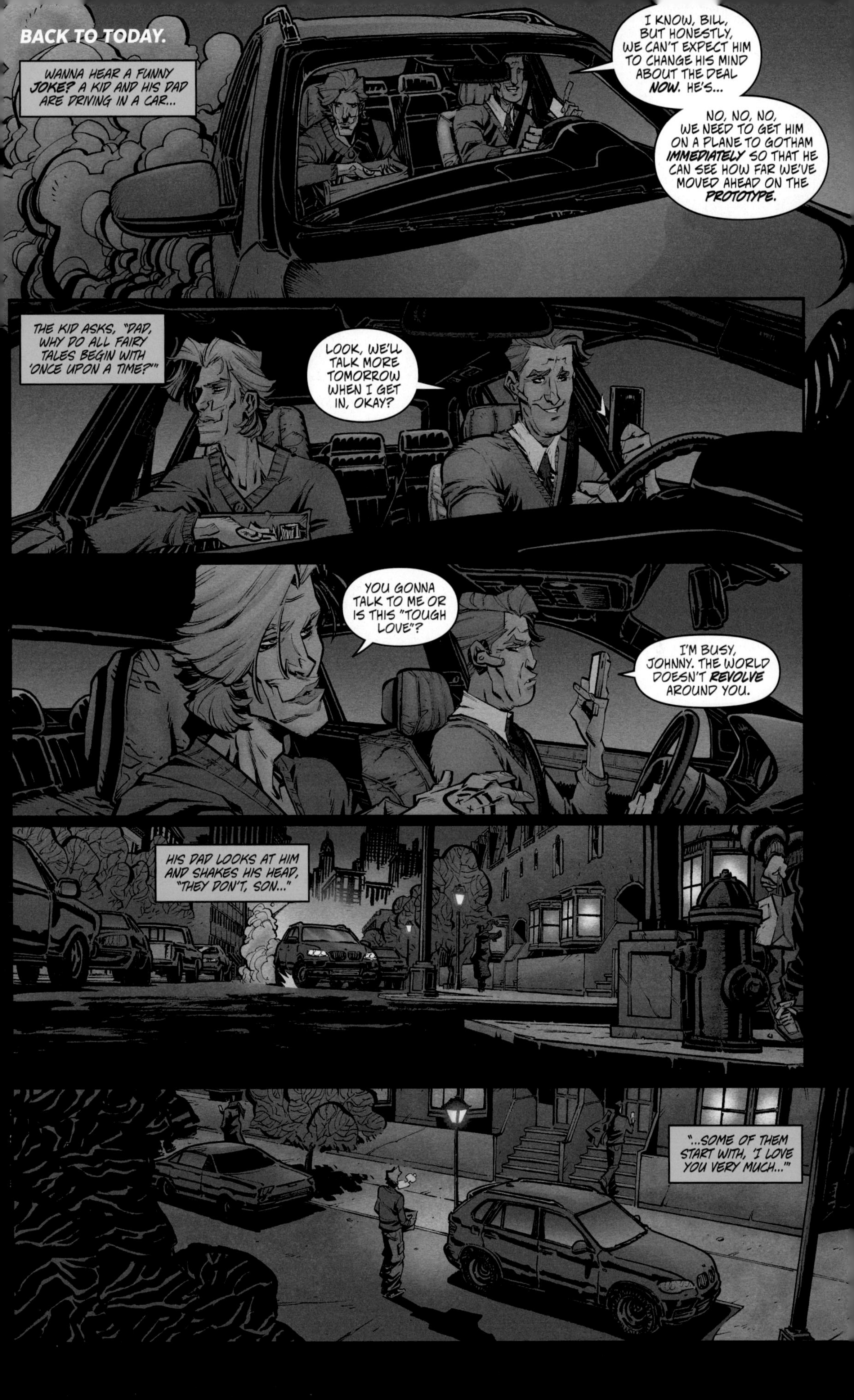
BACK TO TODAY.
WANNA HEAR A FUNNY JOKE? A KID AND HIS DAD ARE DRIVING IN A CAR...
I KNOW, BILL, BUT HONESTLY, WE CAN'T EXPECT HIM TO CHANGE HIS MIND ABOUT THE DEAL NOW. HE'S...
NO, NO, NO, WE NEED TO GET HIM ON A PLANE TO GOTHAM IMMEDIATELY SO THAT HE CAN SEE HOW FAR WE'VE MOVED AHEAD ON THE PROTOTYPE.
THE KID ASKS, "DAD, WHY DO ALL FAIRY TALES BEGIN WITH 'ONCE UPON A TIME?'"
LOOK, WE'LL TALK MORE TOMORROW WHEN I GET IN, OKAY?
YOU GONNA TALK TO ME OR IS THIS "TOUGH LOVE"?
I'M BUSY, JOHNNY. THE WORLD DOESN'T REVOLVE AROUND YOU.
HIS DAD LOOKS AT HIM AND SHAKES HIS HEAD, "THEY DON'T, SON..."
"...SOME OF THEM START WITH, 'I LOVE YOU VERY MUCH...'"

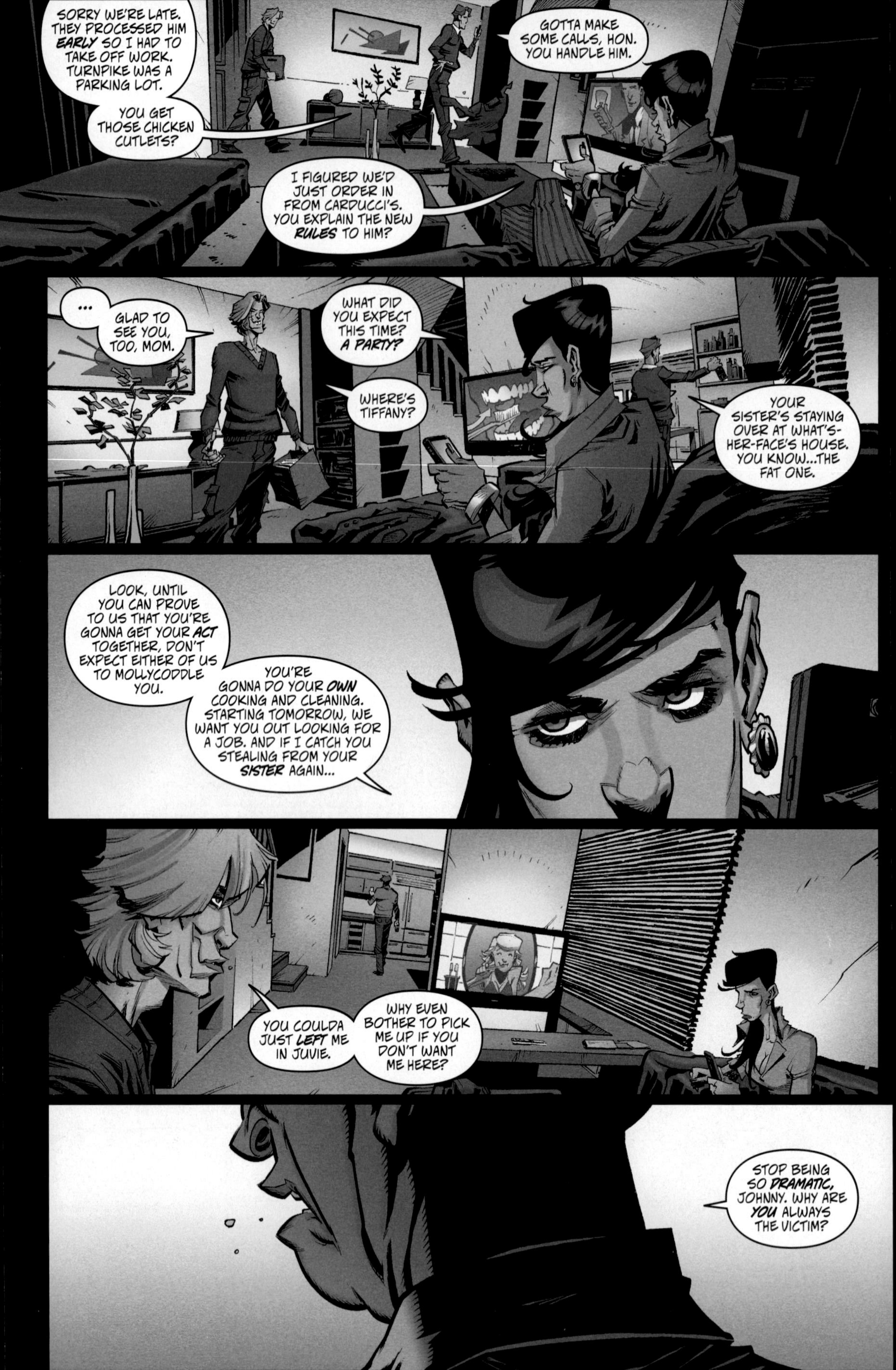
SORRY WE'RE LATE. THEY PROCESSED HIM EARLY SO I HAD TO TAKE OFF WORK. TURNPIKE WAS A PARKING LOT.
GOTTA MAKE SOME CALLS, HON. YOU HANDLE HIM.
YOU GET THOSE CHICKEN CUTLETS?
I FIGURED WE'D JUST ORDER IN FROM CARDUCCI'S. YOU EXPLAIN THE NEW RULES TO HIM?
...
GLAD TO SEE YOU, TOO, MOM.
WHAT DID YOU EXPECT THIS TIME? A PARTY?
WHERE'S TIFFANY?
YOUR SISTER'S STAYING OVER AT WHAT'S-HER-FACE'S HOUSE. YOU KNOW...THE FAT ONE.
LOOK, UNTIL YOU CAN PROVE TO US THAT YOU'RE GONNA GET YOUR ACT TOGETHER, DON'T EXPECT EITHER OF US TO MOLLYCODDLE YOU.
YOU'RE GONNA DO YOUR OWN COOKING AND CLEANING. STARTING TOMORROW, WE WANT YOU OUT LOOKING FOR A JOB. AND IF I CATCH YOU STEALING FROM YOUR SISTER AGAIN...
YOU COULDA JUST LEFT ME IN JUVIE.
WHY EVEN BOTHER TO PICK ME UP IF YOU DON'T WANT ME HERE?
STOP BEING SO DRAMATIC, JOHNNY. WHY ARE YOU ALWAYS THE VICTIM?

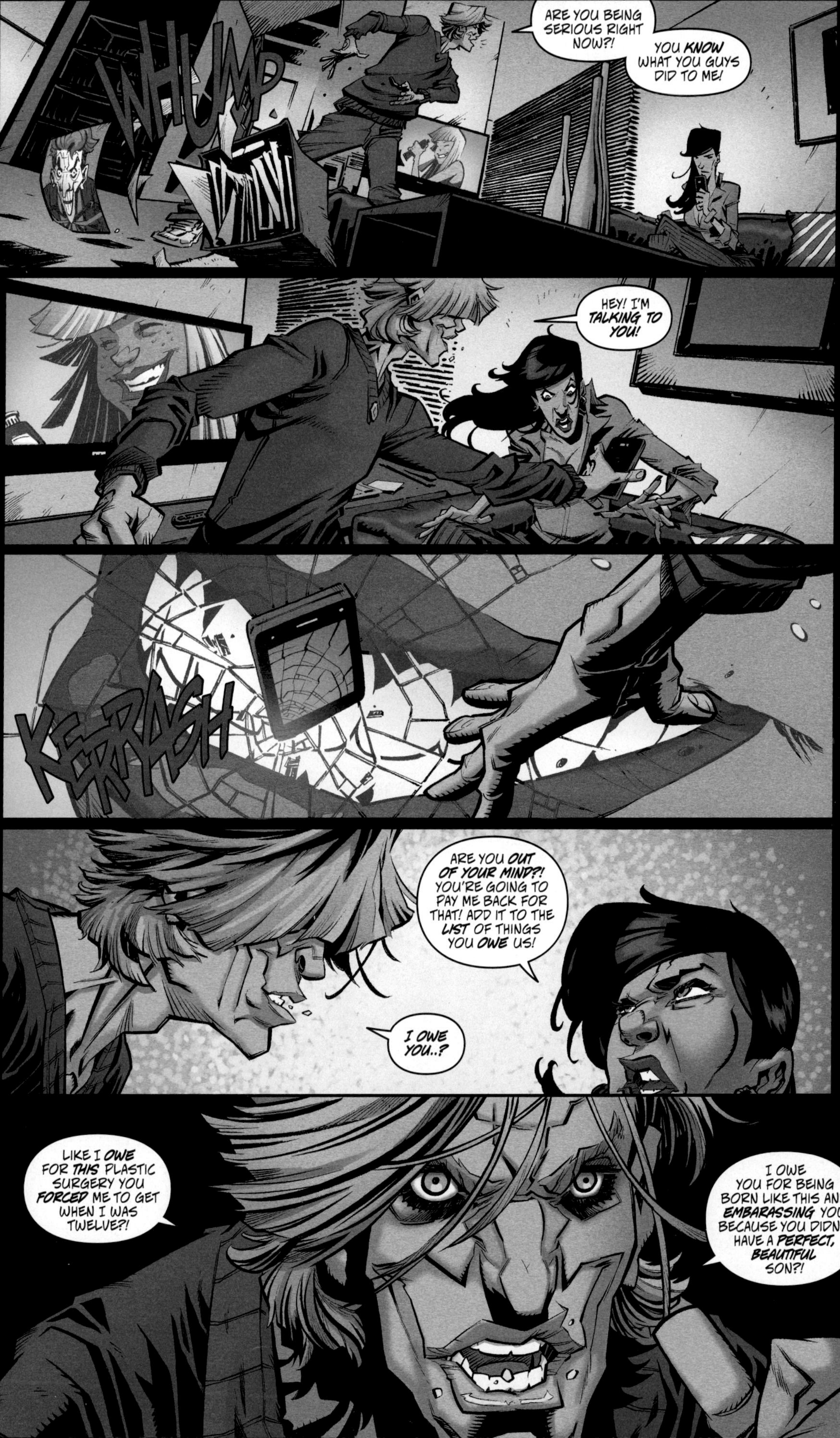

WHUMP
ARE YOU BEING SERIOUS RIGHT NOW?!
YOU **KNOW** WHAT YOU GUYS DID TO ME!
HEY! I'M **TALKING TO YOU!**
KERRASH
ARE YOU **OUT OF YOUR MIND?!** YOU'RE GOING TO PAY ME BACK FOR THAT! ADD IT TO THE **LIST** OF THINGS YOU **OWE** US!
I OWE YOU..?
LIKE I **OWE** FOR **THIS** PLASTIC SURGERY YOU **FORCED** ME TO GET WHEN I WAS TWELVE?!
I OWE YOU FOR BEING BORN LIKE THIS AND **EMBARASSING** YOU BECAUSE YOU DIDN'T HAVE A **PERFECT, BEAUTIFUL** SON?!

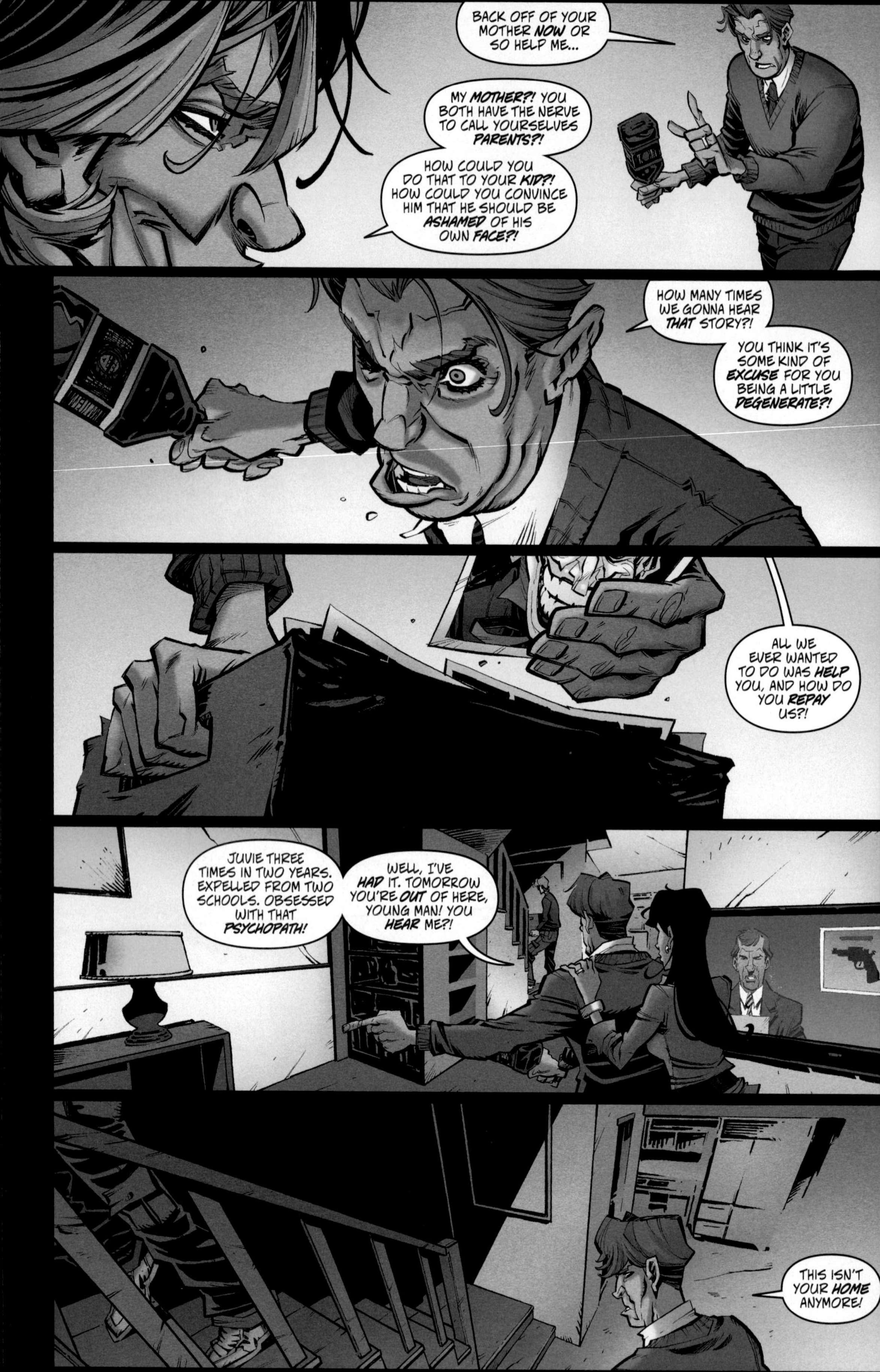
BACK OFF OF YOUR MOTHER NOW OR SO HELP ME...
MY MOTHER?! YOU BOTH HAVE THE NERVE TO CALL YOURSELVES PARENTS?!
HOW COULD YOU DO THAT TO YOUR KID?! HOW COULD YOU CONVINCE HIM THAT HE SHOULD BE ASHAMED OF HIS OWN FACE?!
HOW MANY TIMES WE GONNA HEAR THAT STORY?!
YOU THINK IT'S SOME KIND OF EXCUSE FOR YOU BEING A LITTLE DEGENERATE?!
ALL WE EVER WANTED TO DO WAS HELP YOU, AND HOW DO YOU REPAY US?!
JUVIE THREE TIMES IN TWO YEARS. EXPELLED FROM TWO SCHOOLS. OBSESSED WITH THAT PSYCHOPATH!
WELL, I'VE HAD IT. TOMORROW YOU'RE OUT OF HERE, YOUNG MAN! YOU HEAR ME?!
THIS ISN'T YOUR HOME ANYMORE!

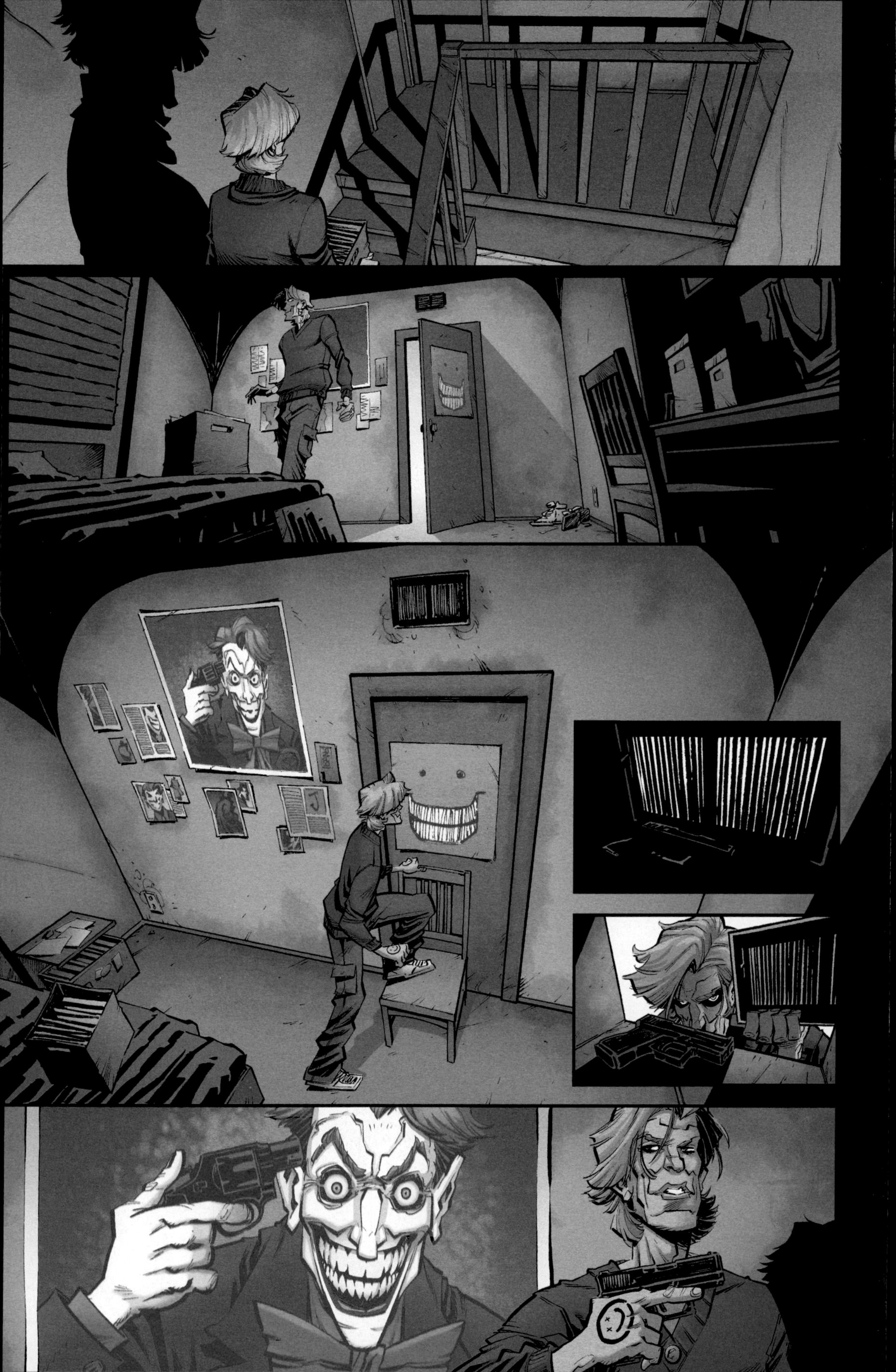

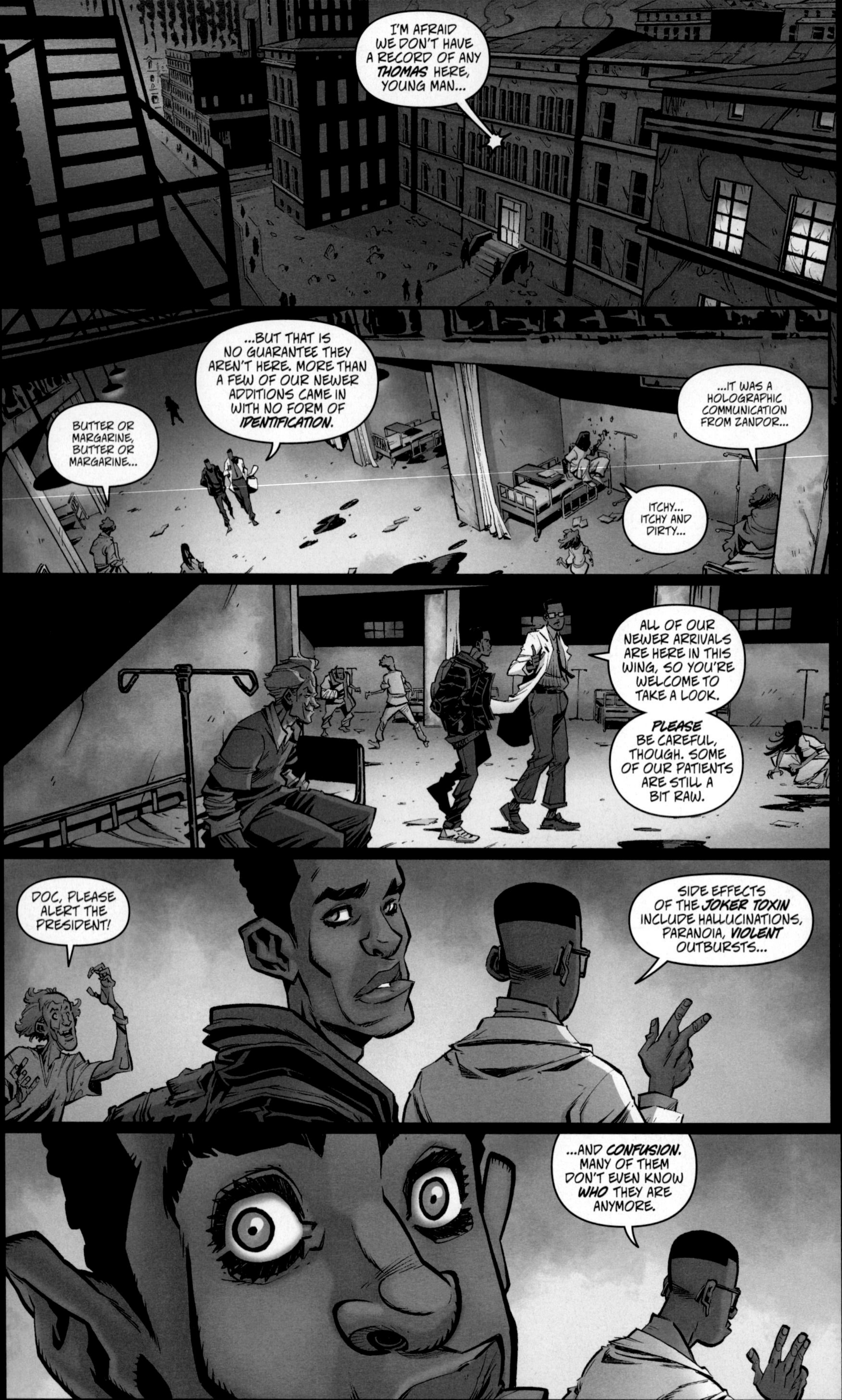
I'M AFRAID WE DON'T HAVE A RECORD OF ANY THOMAS HERE, YOUNG MAN...
...BUT THAT IS NO GUARANTEE THEY AREN'T HERE. MORE THAN A FEW OF OUR NEWER ADDITIONS CAME IN WITH NO FORM OF IDENTIFICATION.
BUTTER OR MARGARINE, BUTTER OR MARGARINE...
...IT WAS A HOLOGRAPHIC COMMUNICATION FROM ZANDOR...
ITCHY... ITCHY AND DIRTY...
ALL OF OUR NEWER ARRIVALS ARE HERE IN THIS WING, SO YOU'RE WELCOME TO TAKE A LOOK.
PLEASE BE CAREFUL, THOUGH. SOME OF OUR PATIENTS ARE STILL A BIT RAW.
DOC, PLEASE ALERT THE PRESIDENT!
SIDE EFFECTS OF THE JOKER TOXIN INCLUDE HALLUCINATIONS, PARANOIA, VIOLENT OUTBURSTS...
...AND CONFUSION. MANY OF THEM DON'T EVEN KNOW WHO THEY ARE ANYMORE.

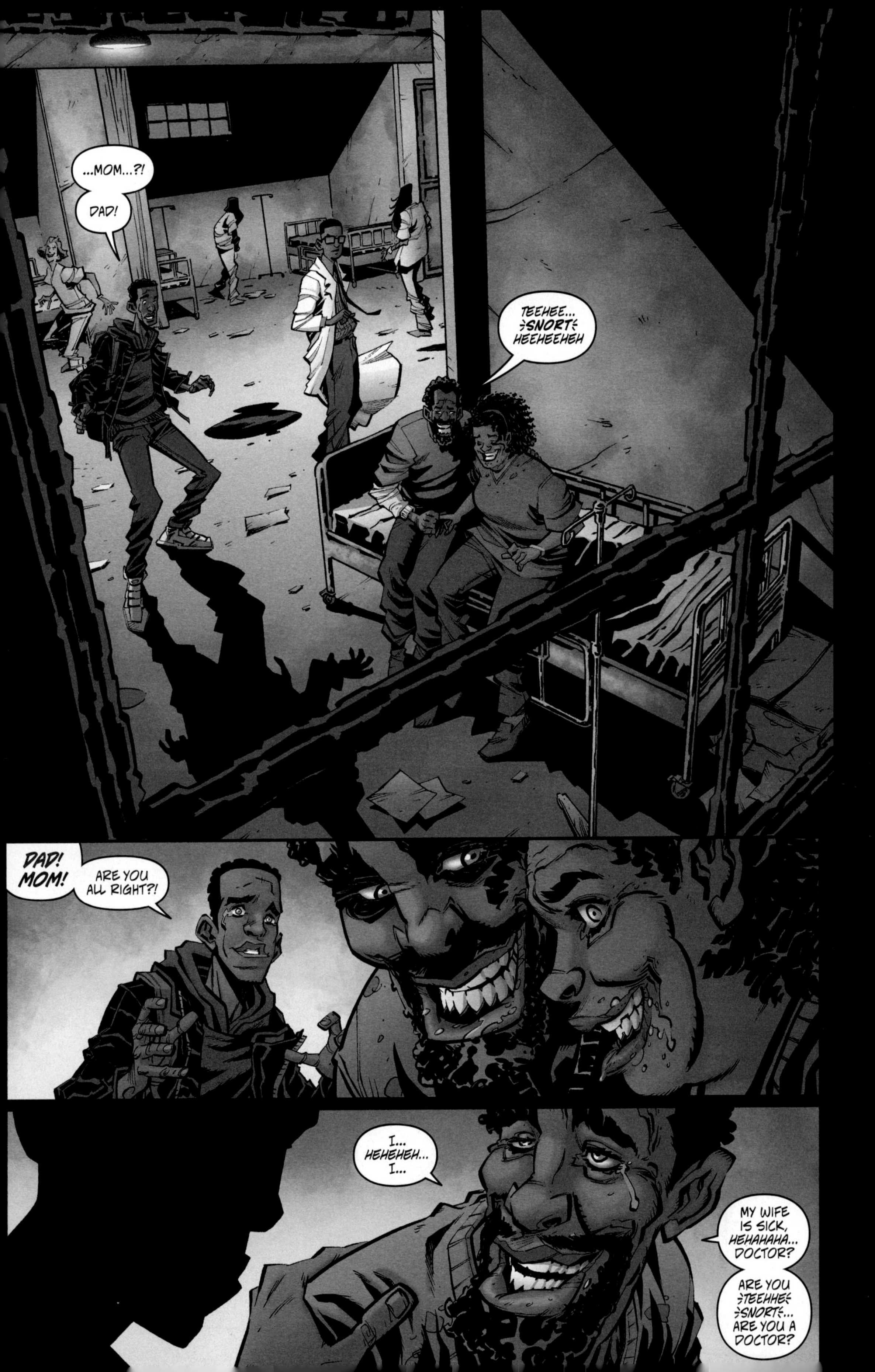
...MOM...?!
DAD!
TEEHEE... SNORT HEEHEEHEH
DAD! MOM!
ARE YOU ALL RIGHT?!
I... HEHEHEH... I...
MY WIFE IS SICK, HEHAHAHA... DOCTOR?
ARE YOU TEEHHE SNORT... ARE YOU A DOCTOR?

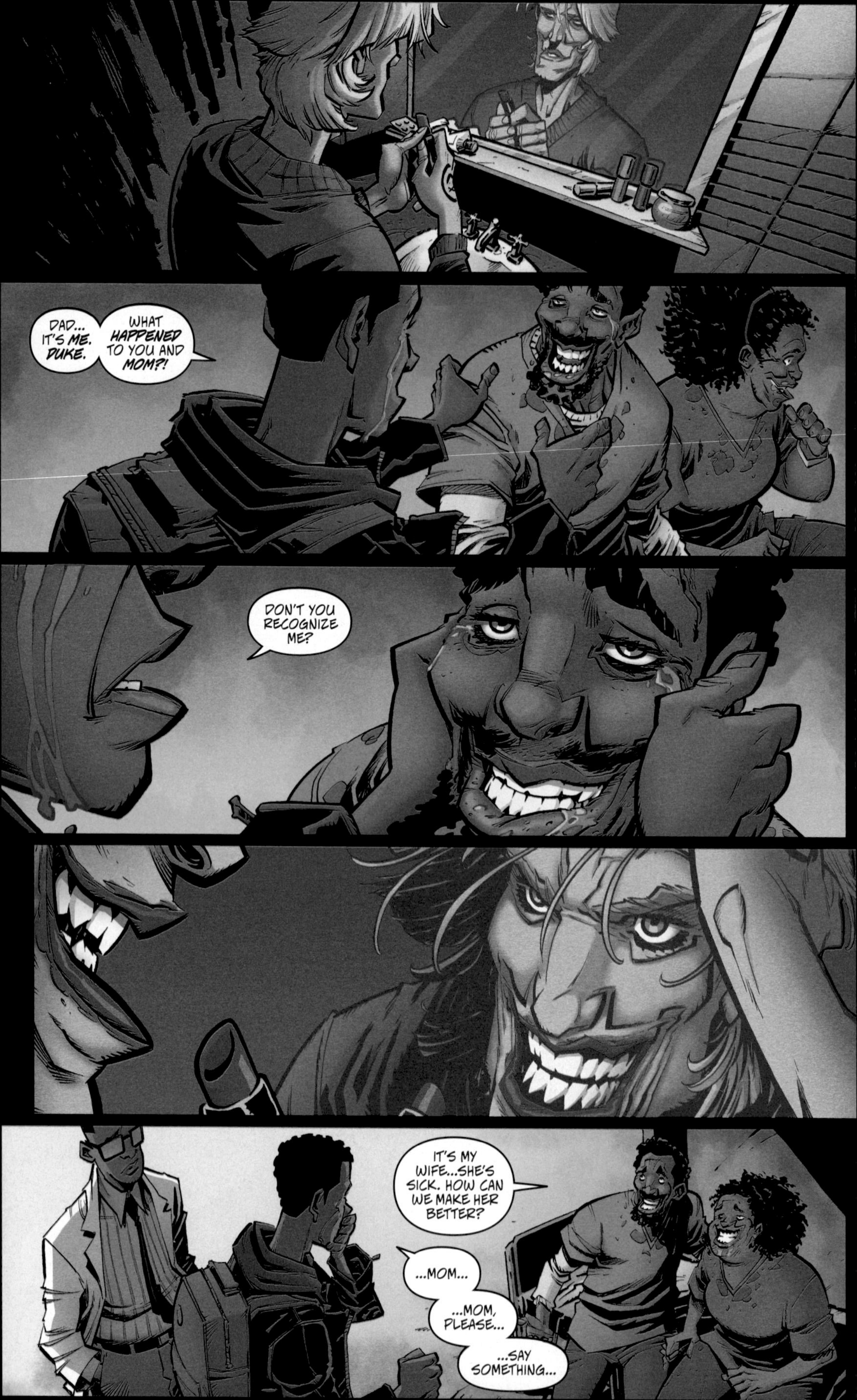
DAD... IT'S ME. DUKE.
WHAT HAPPENED TO YOU AND MOM?!
DON'T YOU RECOGNIZE ME?
IT'S MY WIFE...SHE'S SICK. HOW CAN WE MAKE HER BETTER?
...MOM...
...MOM, PLEASE...
...SAY SOMETHING...

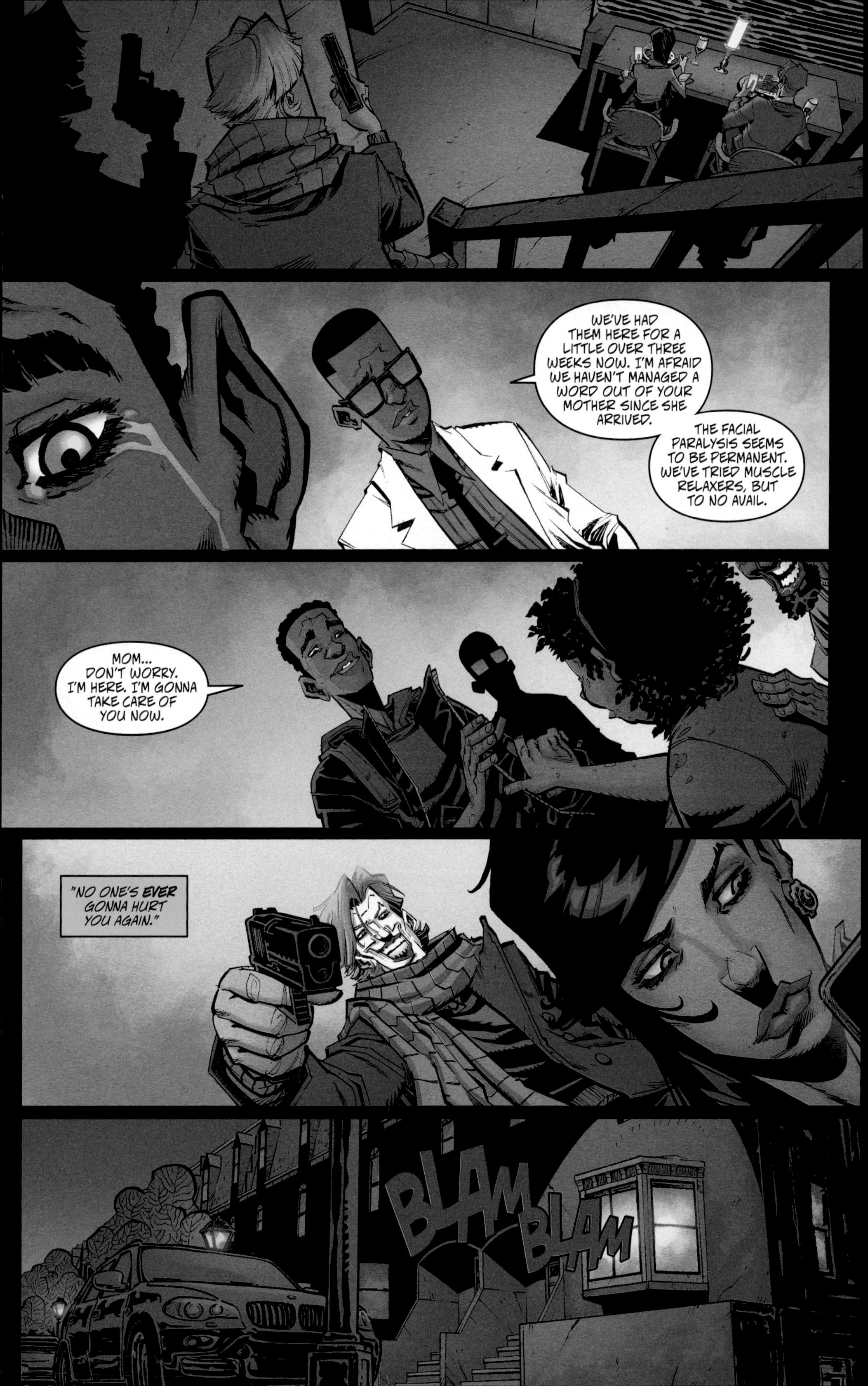
WE'VE HAD THEM HERE FOR A LITTLE OVER THREE WEEKS NOW. I'M AFRAID WE HAVEN'T MANAGED A WORD OUT OF YOUR MOTHER SINCE SHE ARRIVED.
THE FACIAL PARALYSIS SEEMS TO BE PERMANENT. WE'VE TRIED MUSCLE RELAXERS, BUT TO NO AVAIL.
MOM... DON'T WORRY. I'M HERE. I'M GONNA TAKE CARE OF YOU NOW.
"NO ONE'S **EVER** GONNA HURT YOU AGAIN."
BLAM
BLAM

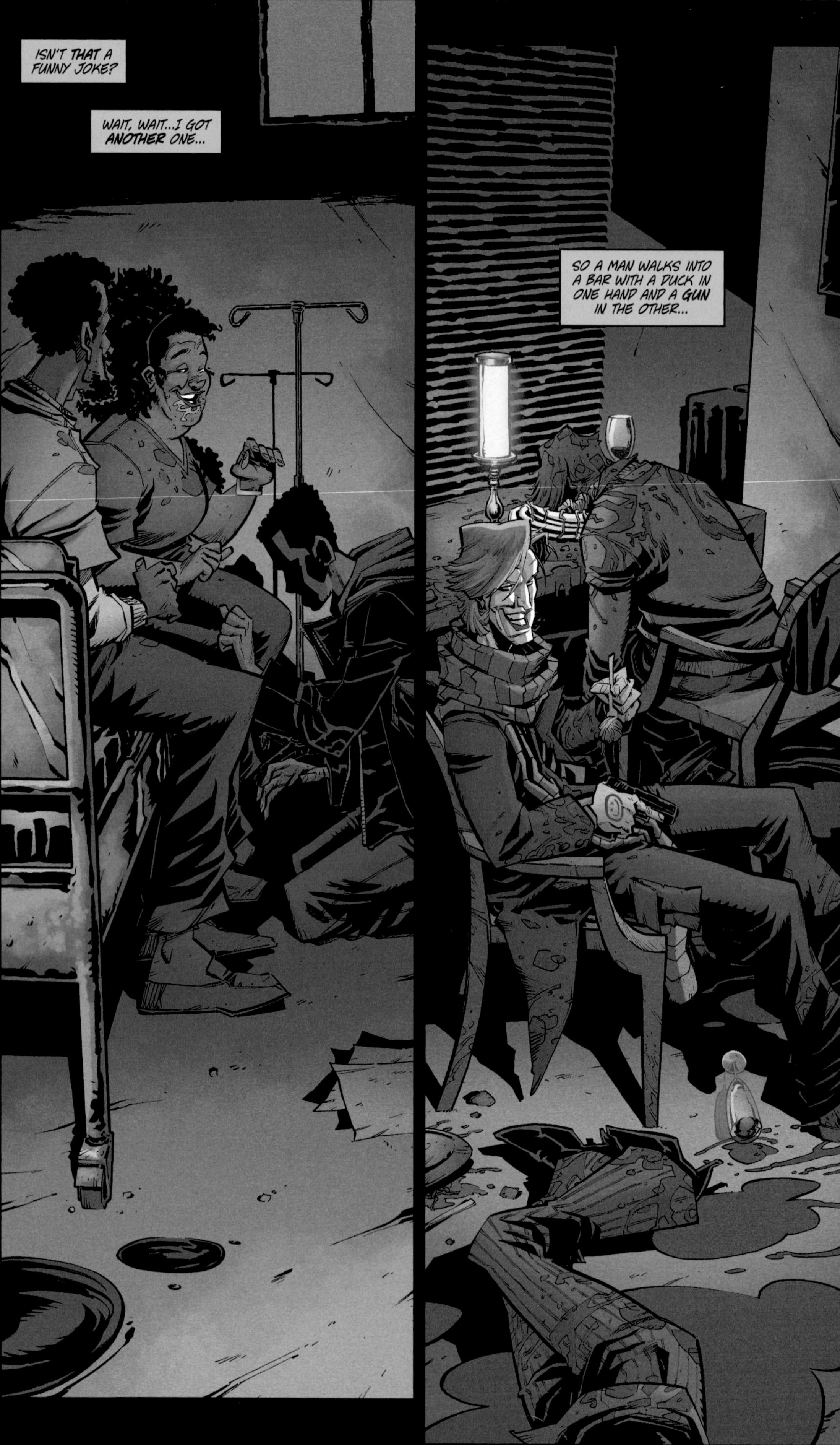
ISN'T THAT A FUNNY JOKE?
WAIT, WAIT...I GOT ANOTHER ONE...
SO A MAN WALKS INTO A BAR WITH A DUCK IN ONE HAND AND A GUN IN THE OTHER...

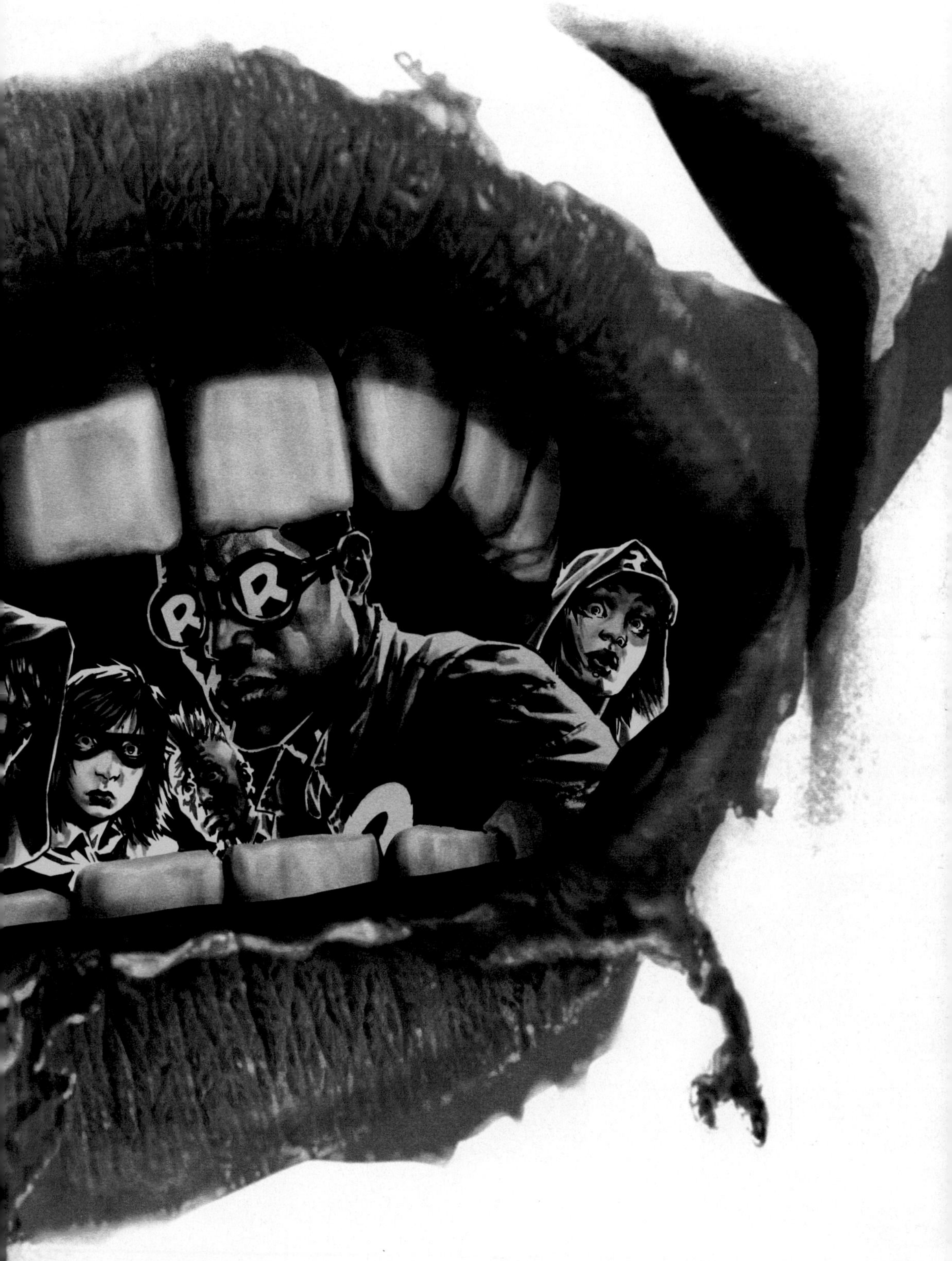

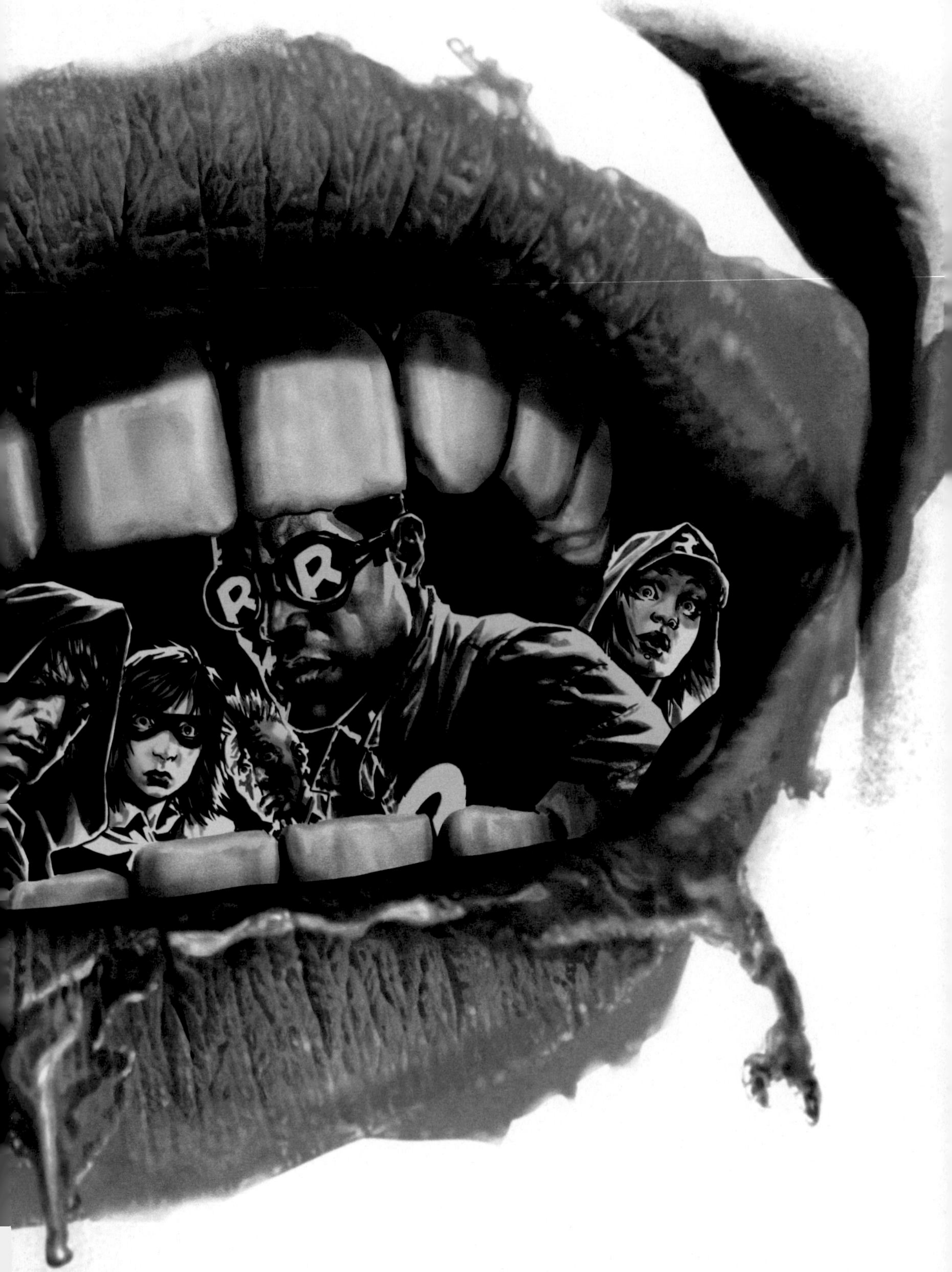

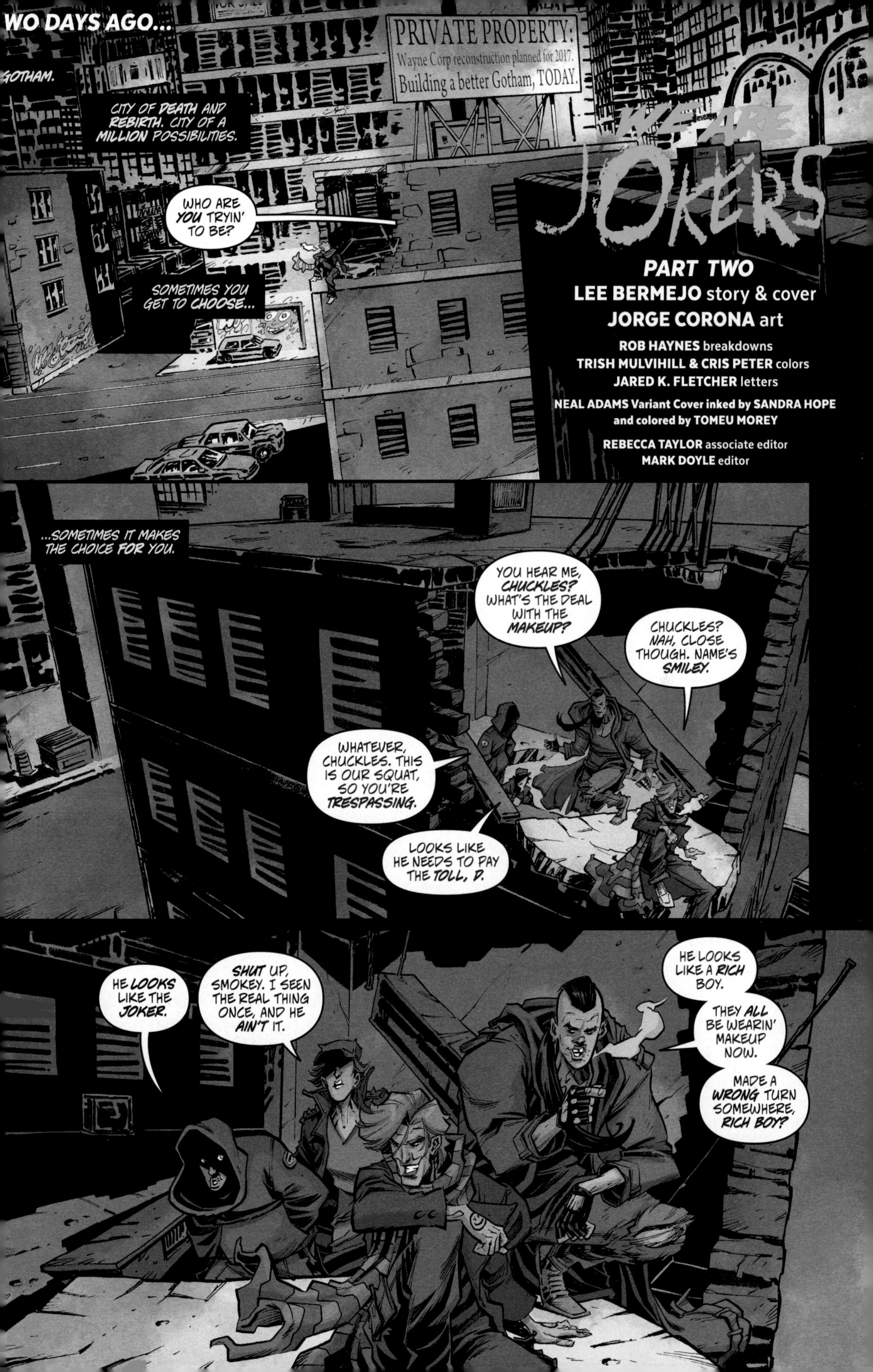
WO DAYS AGO...
PRIVATE PROPERTY: Wayne Corp reconstruction planned for 2017. Building a better Gotham, TODAY.
GOTHAM.
CITY OF DEATH AND REBIRTH. CITY OF A MILLION POSSIBILITIES.
WHO ARE YOU TRYIN' TO BE?
SOMETIMES YOU GET TO CHOOSE...
WE ARE JOKERS
PART TWO
LEE BERMEJO story & cover
JORGE CORONA art
ROB HAYNES breakdowns
TRISH MULVIHILL & CRIS PETER colors
JARED K. FLETCHER letters
NEAL ADAMS Variant Cover inked by SANDRA HOPE and colored by TOMEU MOREY
REBECCA TAYLOR associate editor
MARK DOYLE editor
...SOMETIMES IT MAKES THE CHOICE FOR YOU.
YOU HEAR ME, CHUCKLES? WHAT'S THE DEAL WITH THE MAKEUP?
CHUCKLES? NAH, CLOSE THOUGH. NAME'S SMILEY.
WHATEVER, CHUCKLES. THIS IS OUR SQUAT, SO YOU'RE TRESPASSING.
LOOKS LIKE HE NEEDS TO PAY THE TOLL, D.
HE LOOKS LIKE THE JOKER.
SHUT UP, SMOKEY. I SEEN THE REAL THING ONCE, AND HE AIN'T IT.
HE LOOKS LIKE A RICH BOY.
THEY ALL BE WEARIN' MAKEUP NOW.
MADE A WRONG TURN SOMEWHERE, RICH BOY?

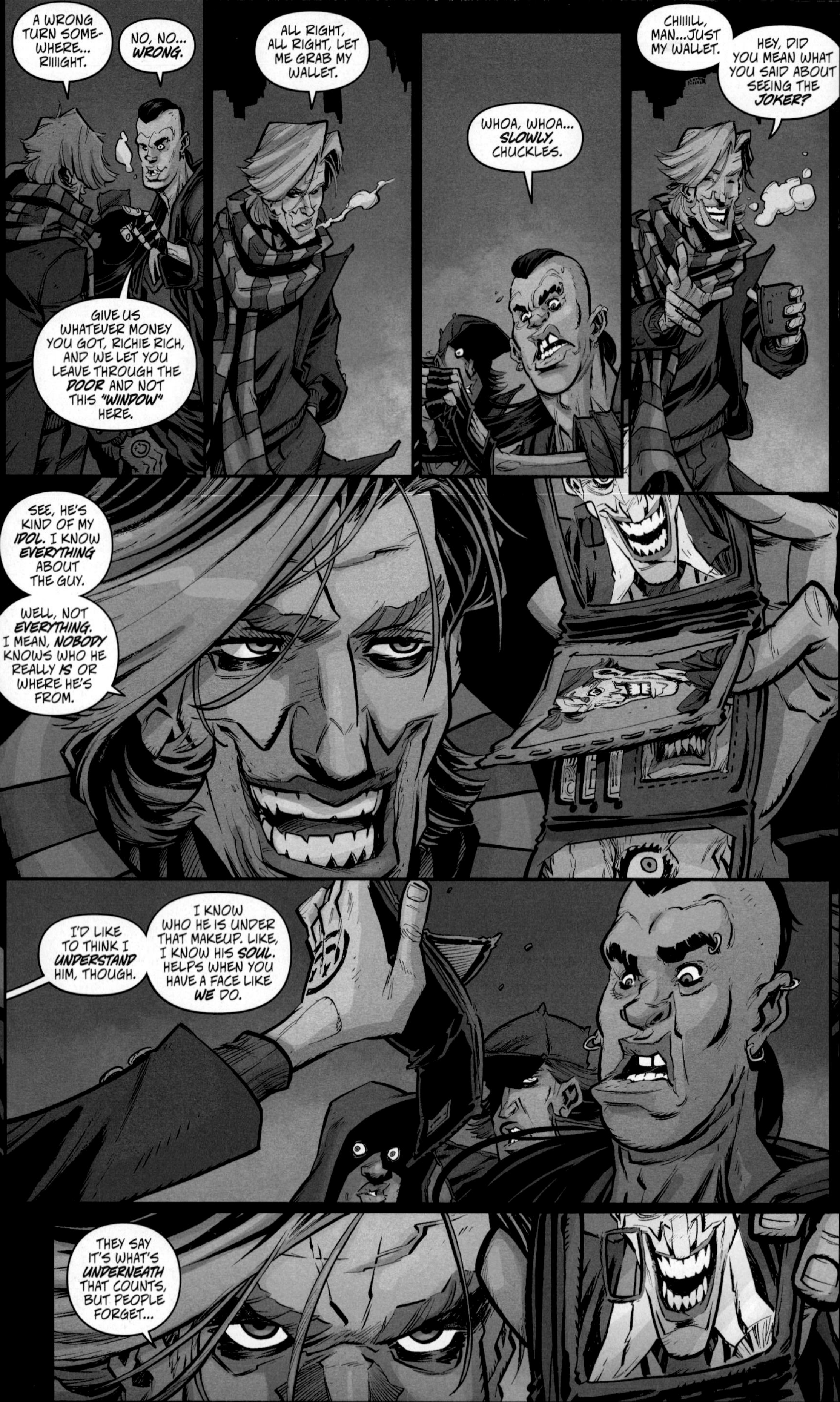

A WRONG TURN SOME-WHERE... RIIIIGHT.
NO, NO... WRONG.
GIVE US WHATEVER MONEY YOU GOT, RICHIE RICH, AND WE LET YOU LEAVE THROUGH THE DOOR AND NOT THIS "WINDOW" HERE.
ALL RIGHT, ALL RIGHT, LET ME GRAB MY WALLET.
WHOA, WHOA... SLOWLY, CHUCKLES.
CHIIIILL, MAN...JUST MY WALLET.
HEY, DID YOU MEAN WHAT YOU SAID ABOUT SEEING THE JOKER?
SEE, HE'S KIND OF MY IDOL. I KNOW EVERYTHING ABOUT THE GUY.
WELL, NOT EVERYTHING. I MEAN, NOBODY KNOWS WHO HE REALLY IS OR WHERE HE'S FROM.
I'D LIKE TO THINK I UNDERSTAND HIM, THOUGH.
I KNOW WHO HE IS UNDER THAT MAKEUP. LIKE, I KNOW HIS SOUL. HELPS WHEN YOU HAVE A FACE LIKE WE DO.
THEY SAY IT'S WHAT'S UNDERNEATH THAT COUNTS, BUT PEOPLE FORGET...

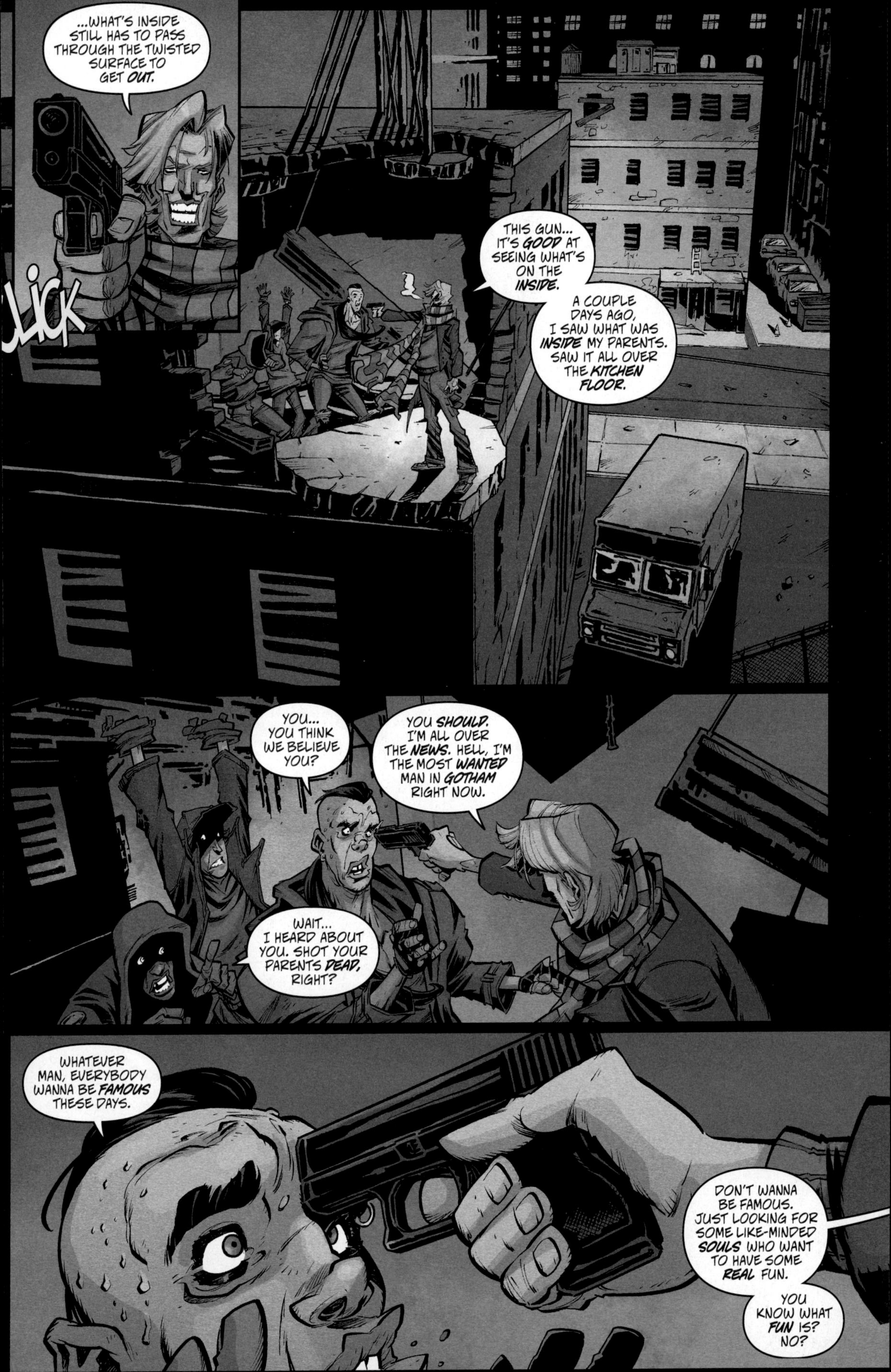
...WHAT'S INSIDE STILL HAS TO PASS THROUGH THE TWISTED SURFACE TO GET OUT.
CLICK
THIS GUN... IT'S GOOD AT SEEING WHAT'S ON THE INSIDE.
A COUPLE DAYS AGO, I SAW WHAT WAS INSIDE MY PARENTS. SAW IT ALL OVER THE KITCHEN FLOOR.
YOU... YOU THINK WE BELIEVE YOU?
YOU SHOULD. I'M ALL OVER THE NEWS. HELL, I'M THE MOST WANTED MAN IN GOTHAM RIGHT NOW.
WAIT... I HEARD ABOUT YOU. SHOT YOUR PARENTS DEAD, RIGHT?
WHATEVER MAN, EVERYBODY WANNA BE FAMOUS THESE DAYS.
DON'T WANNA BE FAMOUS. JUST LOOKING FOR SOME LIKE-MINDED SOULS WHO WANT TO HAVE SOME REAL FUN.
YOU KNOW WHAT FUN IS? NO?

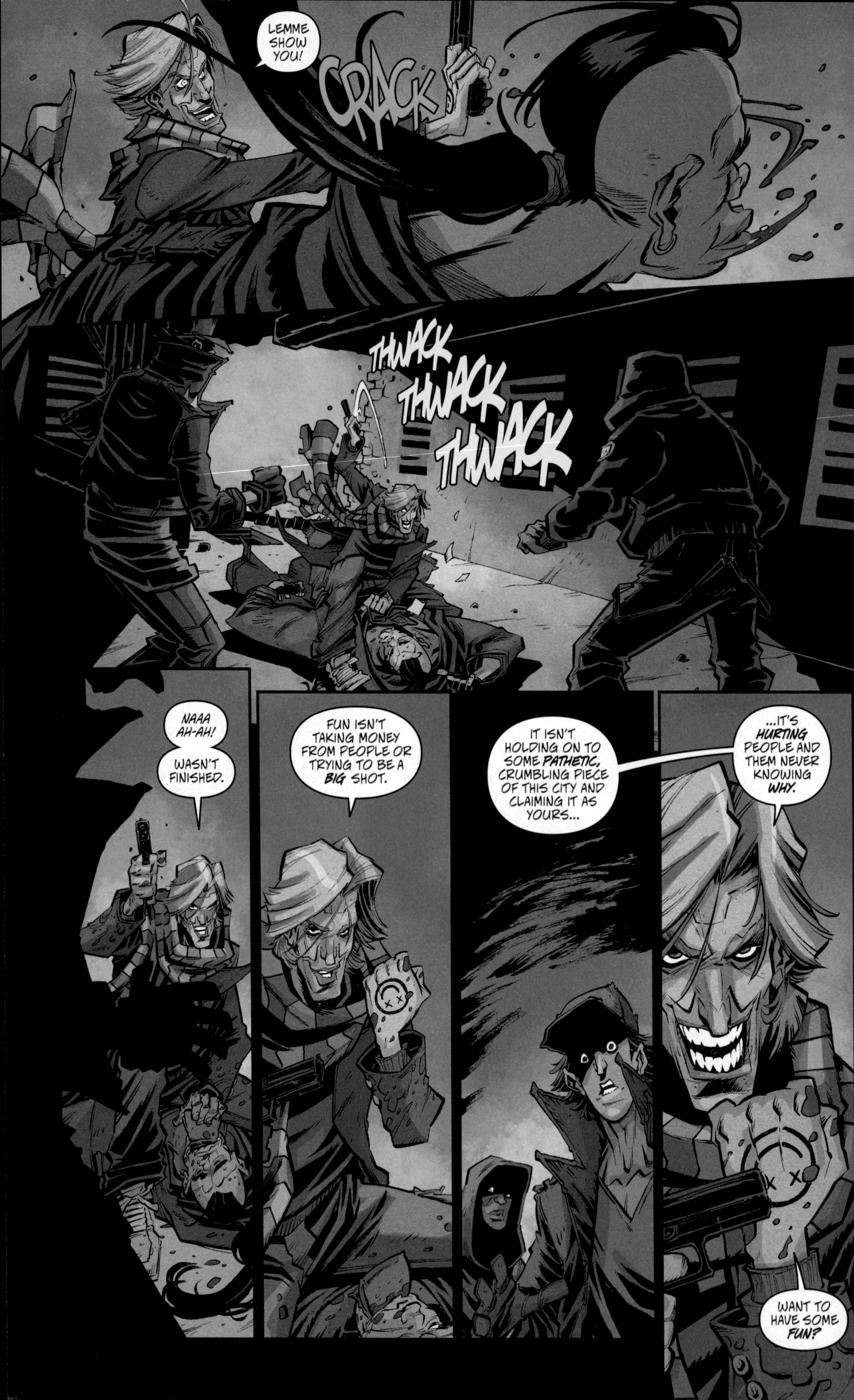
LEMME SHOW YOU!
CRACK
THWACK
THWACK
THWACK
NAAA AH-AH!
WASN'T FINISHED.
FUN ISN'T TAKING MONEY FROM PEOPLE OR TRYING TO BE A BIG SHOT.
IT ISN'T HOLDING ON TO SOME PATHETIC, CRUMBLING PIECE OF THIS CITY AND CLAIMING IT AS YOURS...
...IT'S HURTING PEOPLE AND THEM NEVER KNOWING WHY.
WANT TO HAVE SOME FUN?

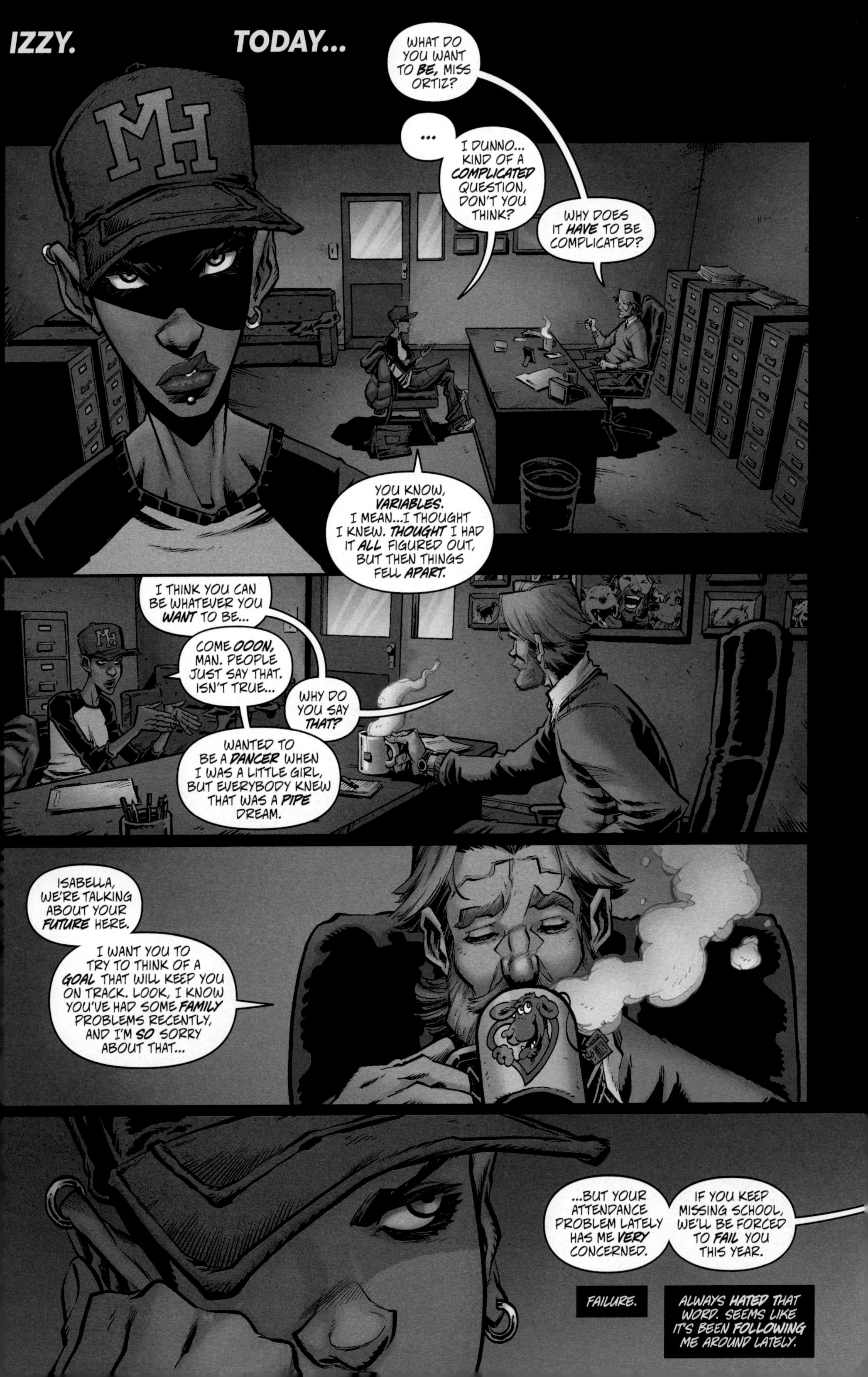
IZZY.
TODAY...
WHAT DO YOU WANT TO BE, MISS ORTIZ?
...
I DUNNO... KIND OF A COMPLICATED QUESTION, DON'T YOU THINK?
WHY DOES IT HAVE TO BE COMPLICATED?
YOU KNOW, VARIABLES. I MEAN...I THOUGHT I KNEW. THOUGHT I HAD IT ALL FIGURED OUT, BUT THEN THINGS FELL APART.
I THINK YOU CAN BE WHATEVER YOU WANT TO BE...
COME OOON, MAN. PEOPLE JUST SAY THAT. ISN'T TRUE...
WHY DO YOU SAY THAT?
WANTED TO BE A DANCER WHEN I WAS A LITTLE GIRL, BUT EVERYBODY KNEW THAT WAS A PIPE DREAM.
ISABELLA, WE'RE TALKING ABOUT YOUR FUTURE HERE.
I WANT YOU TO TRY TO THINK OF A GOAL THAT WILL KEEP YOU ON TRACK. LOOK, I KNOW YOU'VE HAD SOME FAMILY PROBLEMS RECENTLY, AND I'M SO SORRY ABOUT THAT...
...BUT YOUR ATTENDANCE PROBLEM LATELY HAS ME VERY CONCERNED.
IF YOU KEEP MISSING SCHOOL, WE'LL BE FORCED TO FAIL YOU THIS YEAR.
FAILURE.
ALWAYS HATED THAT WORD. SEEMS LIKE IT'S BEEN FOLLOWING ME AROUND LATELY.

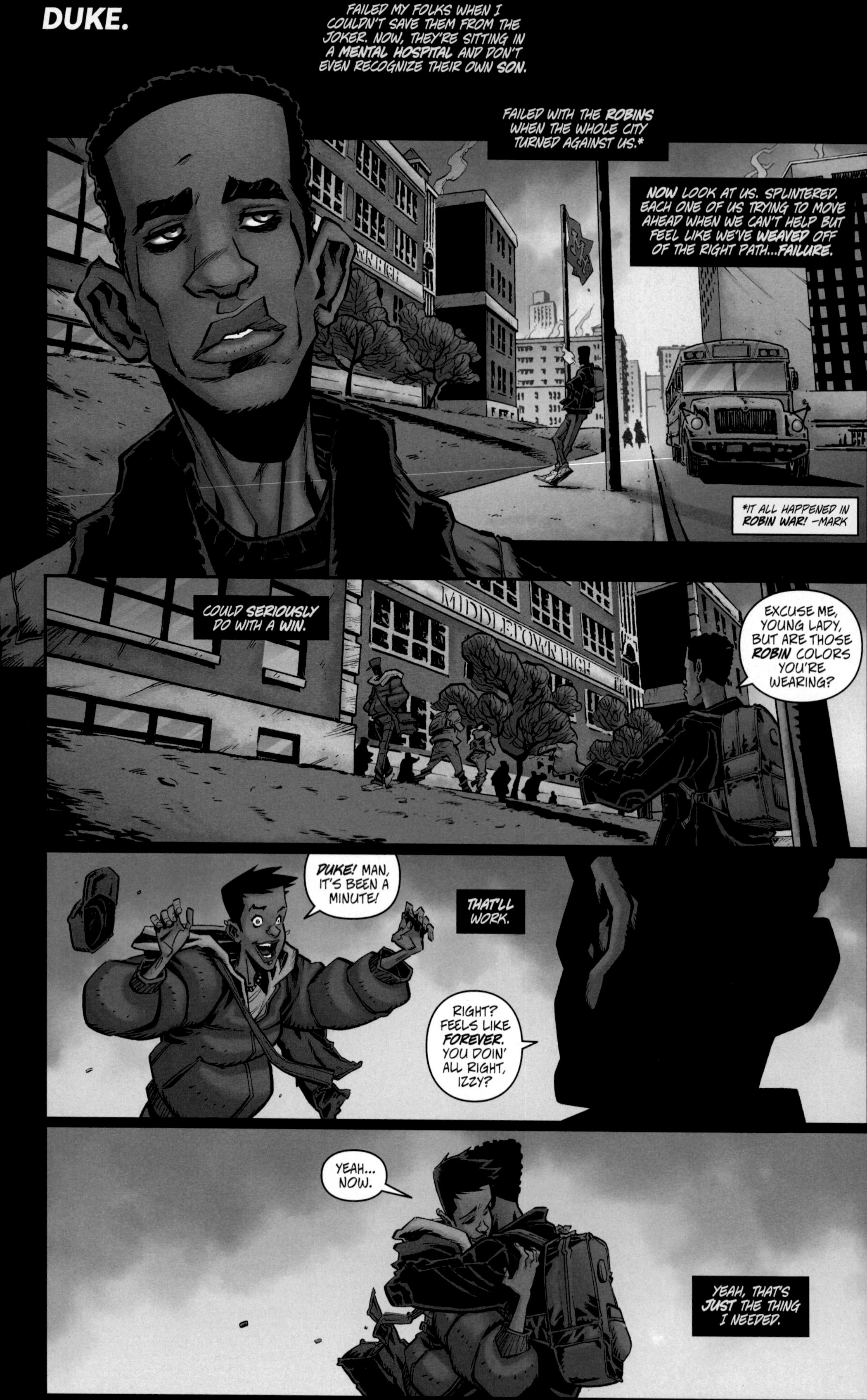
DUKE.
FAILED MY FOLKS WHEN I COULDN'T SAVE THEM FROM THE JOKER. NOW, THEY'RE SITTING IN A MENTAL HOSPITAL AND DON'T EVEN RECOGNIZE THEIR OWN SON.
FAILED WITH THE ROBINS WHEN THE WHOLE CITY TURNED AGAINST US.*
NOW LOOK AT US. SPLINTERED. EACH ONE OF US TRYING TO MOVE AHEAD WHEN WE CAN'T HELP BUT FEEL LIKE WE'VE WEAVED OFF OF THE RIGHT PATH...FAILURE.
*IT ALL HAPPENED IN ROBIN WAR! –MARK
COULD SERIOUSLY DO WITH A WIN.
MIDDLETOWN HIGH
EXCUSE ME, YOUNG LADY, BUT ARE THOSE ROBIN COLORS YOU'RE WEARING?
DUKE! MAN, IT'S BEEN A MINUTE!
THAT'LL WORK.
RIGHT? FEELS LIKE FOREVER. YOU DOIN' ALL RIGHT, IZZY?
YEAH... NOW.
YEAH, THAT'S JUST THE THING I NEEDED.

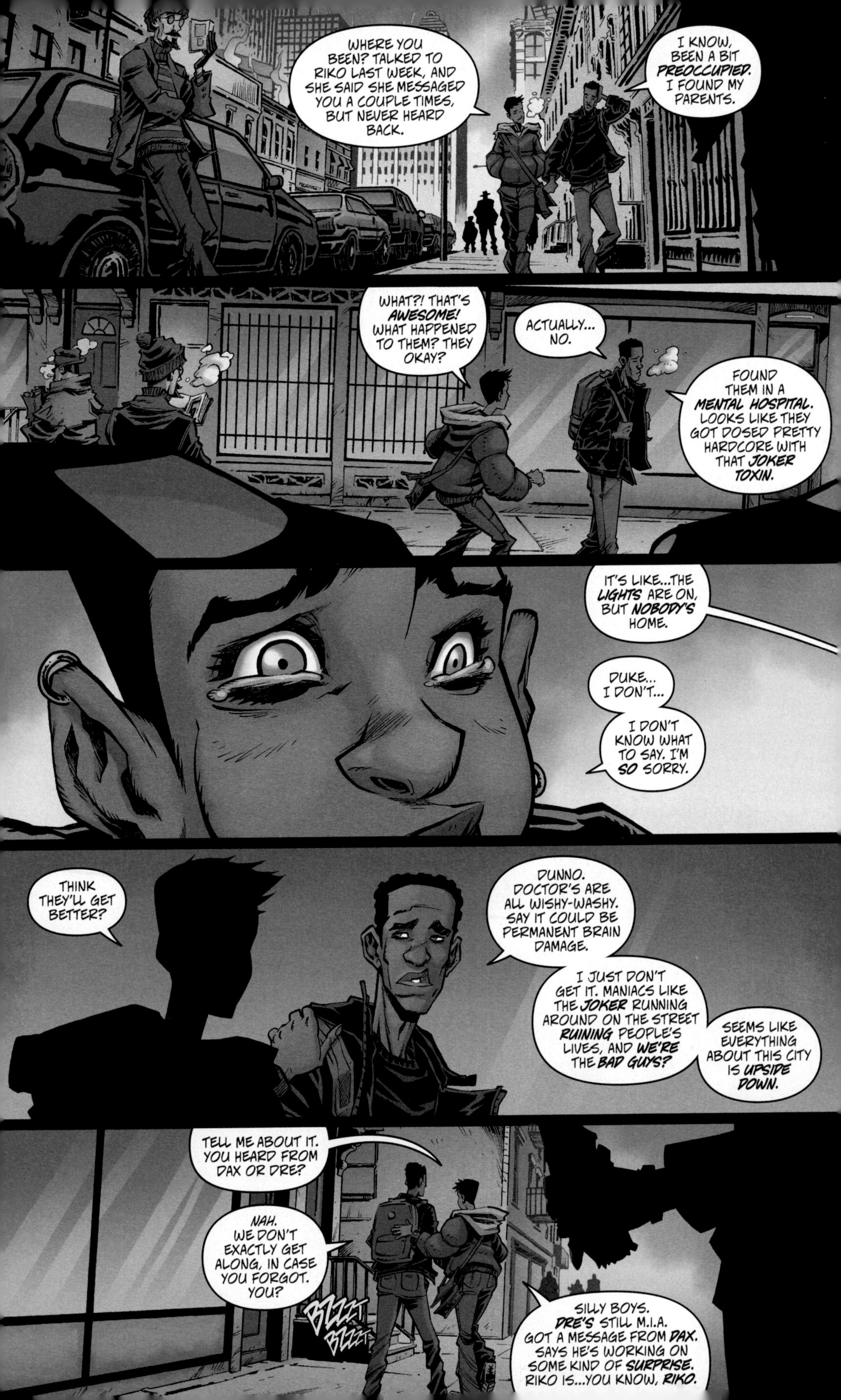

WHERE YOU BEEN? TALKED TO RIKO LAST WEEK, AND SHE SAID SHE MESSAGED YOU A COUPLE TIMES, BUT NEVER HEARD BACK.
I KNOW, BEEN A BIT PREOCCUPIED. I FOUND MY PARENTS.
WHAT?! THAT'S AWESOME! WHAT HAPPENED TO THEM? THEY OKAY?
ACTUALLY... NO.
FOUND THEM IN A MENTAL HOSPITAL. LOOKS LIKE THEY GOT DOSED PRETTY HARDCORE WITH THAT JOKER TOXIN.
IT'S LIKE...THE LIGHTS ARE ON, BUT NOBODY'S HOME.
DUKE... I DON'T...
I DON'T KNOW WHAT TO SAY. I'M SO SORRY.
THINK THEY'LL GET BETTER?
DUNNO. DOCTOR'S ARE ALL WISHY-WASHY. SAY IT COULD BE PERMANENT BRAIN DAMAGE.
I JUST DON'T GET IT. MANIACS LIKE THE JOKER RUNNING AROUND ON THE STREET RUINING PEOPLE'S LIVES, AND WE'RE THE BAD GUYS?
SEEMS LIKE EVERYTHING ABOUT THIS CITY IS UPSIDE DOWN.
TELL ME ABOUT IT. YOU HEARD FROM DAX OR DRE?
NAH. WE DON'T EXACTLY GET ALONG, IN CASE YOU FORGOT. YOU?
BZZZT BZZZT
SILLY BOYS. DRE'S STILL M.I.A. GOT A MESSAGE FROM DAX. SAYS HE'S WORKING ON SOME KIND OF SURPRISE. RIKO IS...YOU KNOW, RIKO.

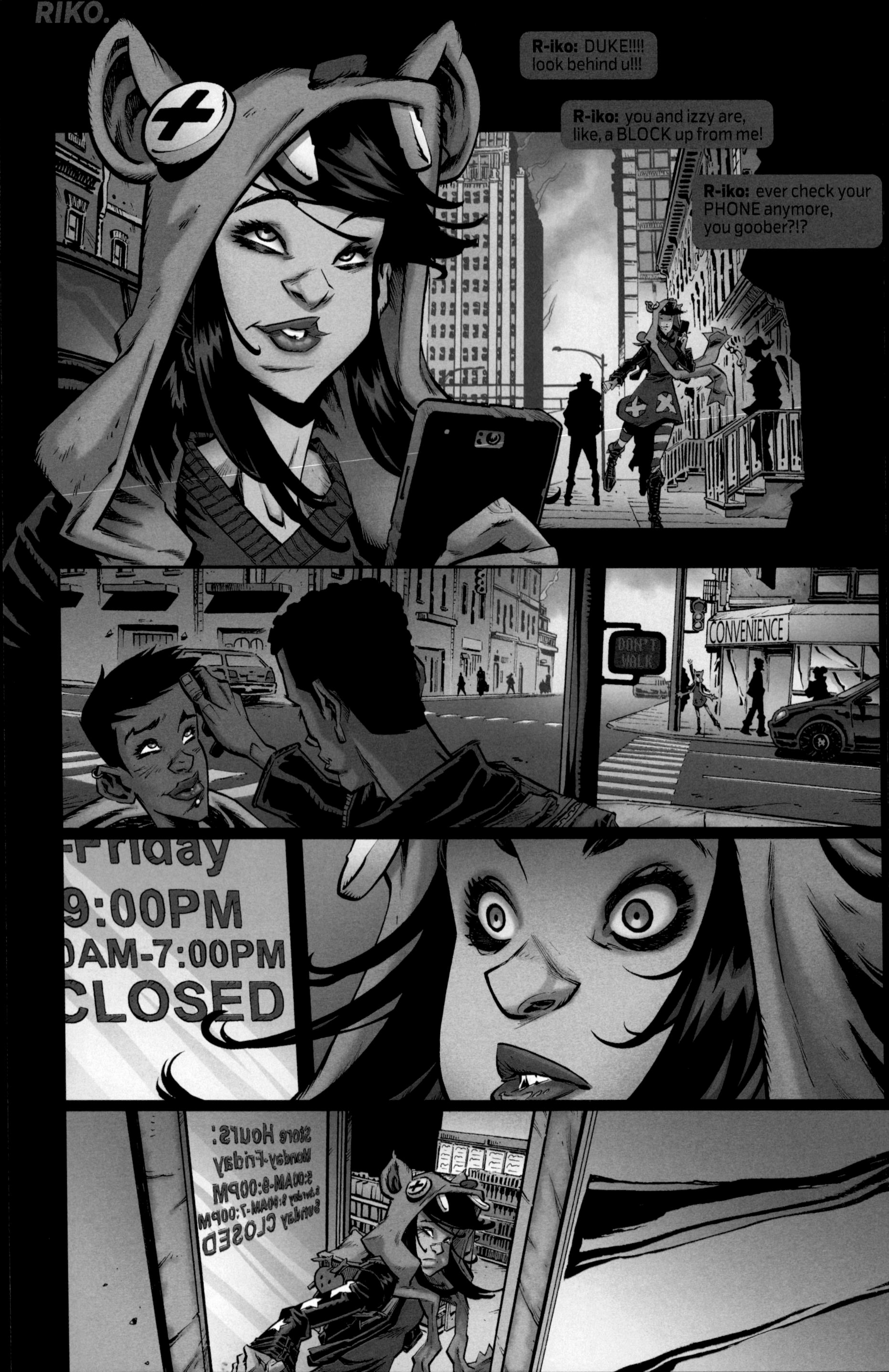
RIKO.
R-iko: DUKE!!!! look behind u!!!
R-iko: you and izzy are, like, a BLOCK up from me!
R-iko: ever check your PHONE anymore, you goober?!?
DON'T WALK
CONVENIENCE
Friday
9:00PM
0AM-7:00PM
CLOSED

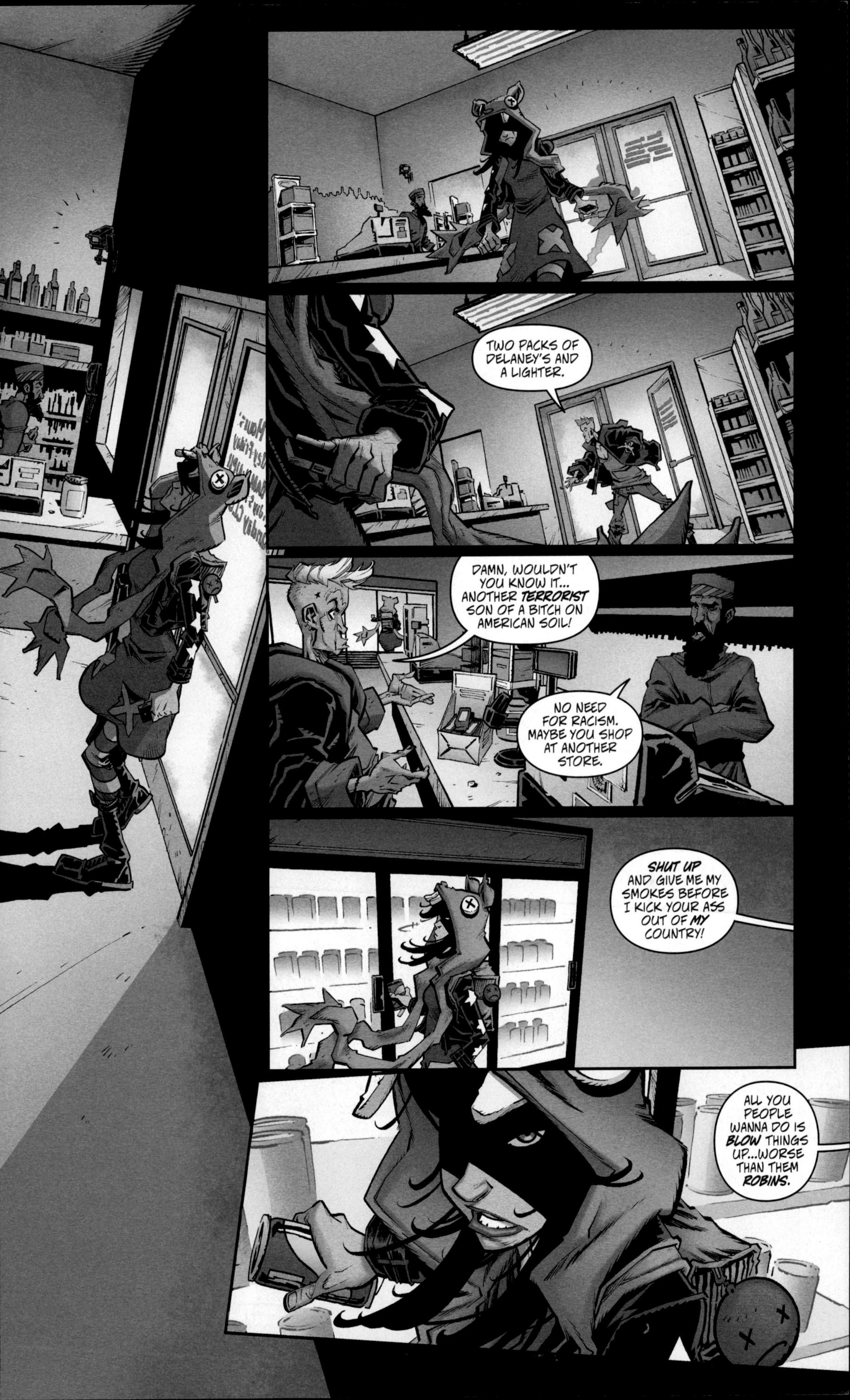
TWO PACKS OF DELANEY'S AND A LIGHTER.
DAMN, WOULDN'T YOU KNOW IT... ANOTHER TERRORIST SON OF A BITCH ON AMERICAN SOIL!
NO NEED FOR RACISM. MAYBE YOU SHOP AT ANOTHER STORE.
SHUT UP AND GIVE ME MY SMOKES BEFORE I KICK YOUR ASS OUT OF MY COUNTRY!
ALL YOU PEOPLE WANNA DO IS BLOW THINGS UP...WORSE THAN THEM ROBINS.

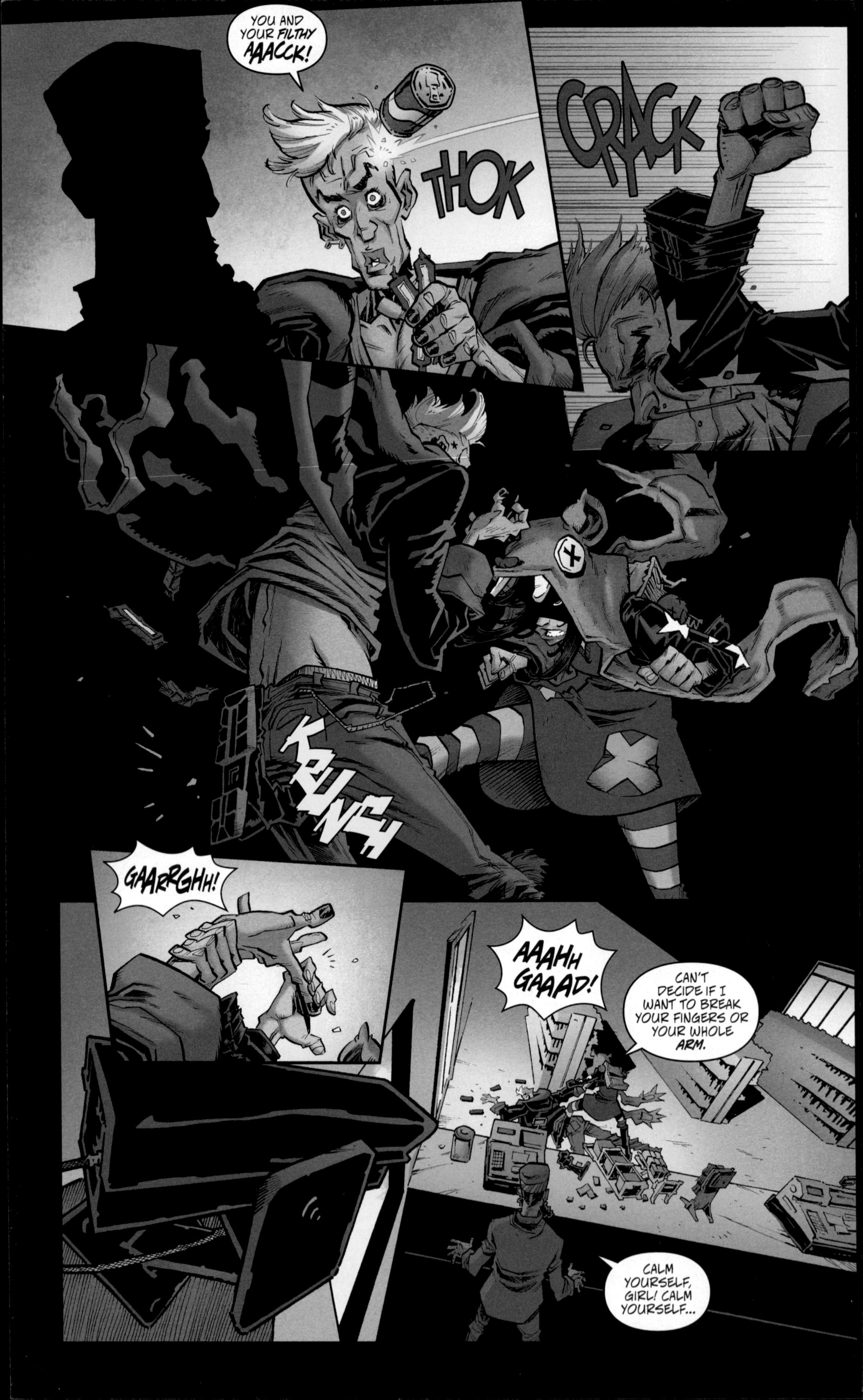
YOU AND YOUR FILTHY AAACCK!
THOK
CRACK
KRUNCH
GAARRGHH!
AAAHH GAAAD!
CAN'T DECIDE IF I WANT TO BREAK YOUR FINGERS OR YOUR WHOLE ARM.
CALM YOURSELF, GIRL! CALM YOURSELF...

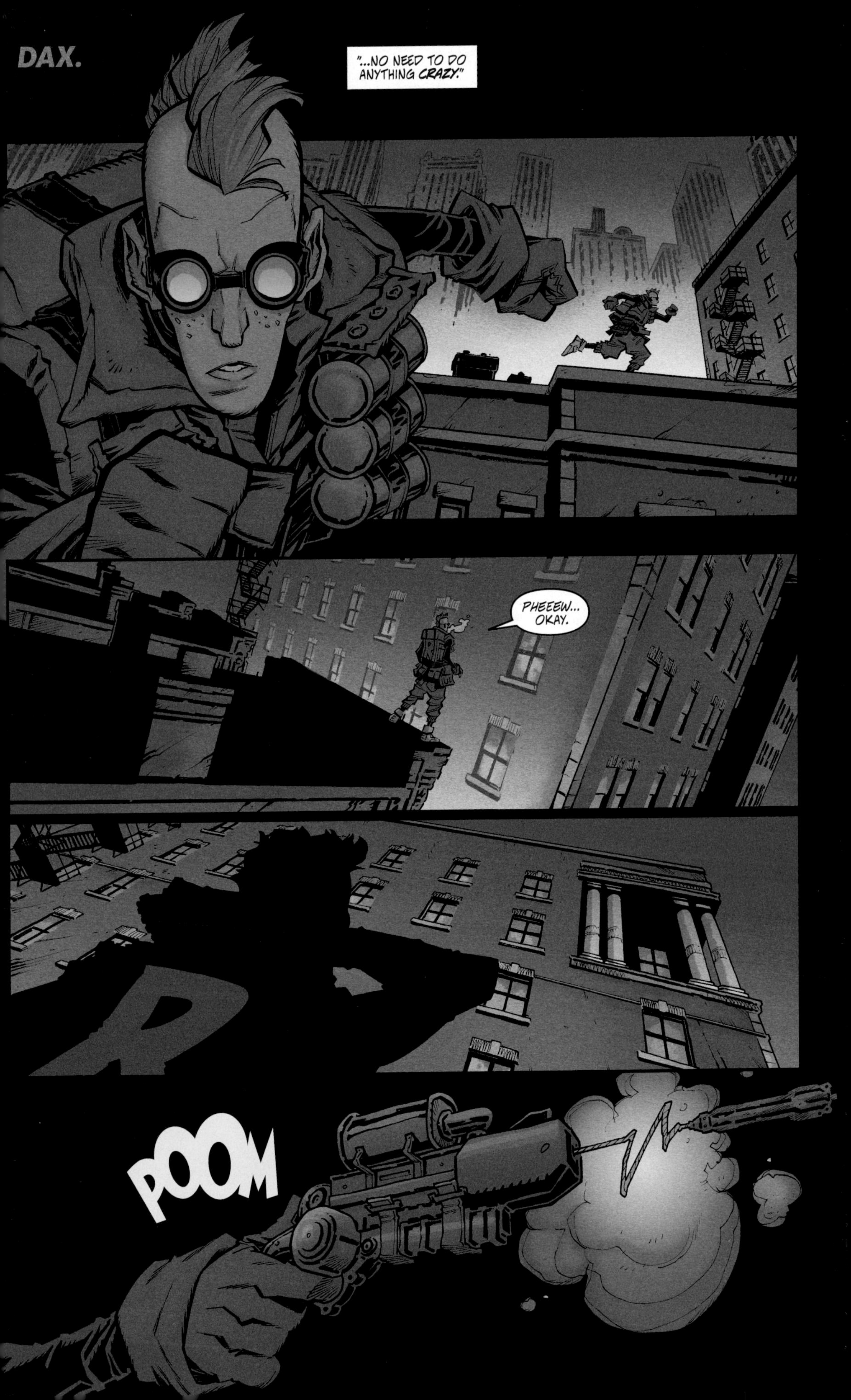
DAX.
"...NO NEED TO DO ANYTHING CRAZY."
PHEEEW... OKAY.
POOM

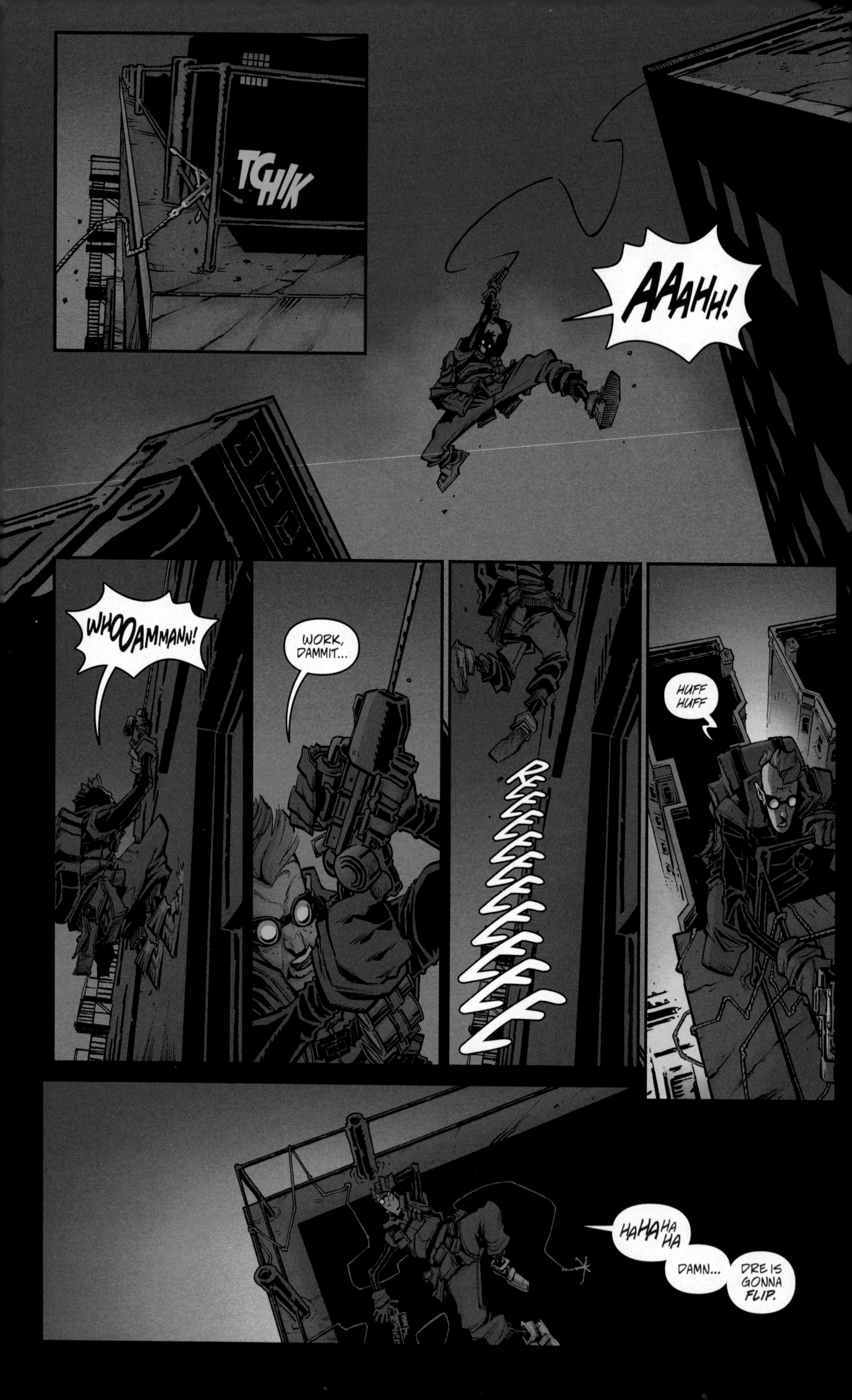
TCHIK
AAAHH!
WHOOAMMANN!
WORK, DAMMIT...
REEEEEEEEEEEEE
HUFF HUFF
HAHAHAHA
DAMN...
DRE IS GONNA FLIP.

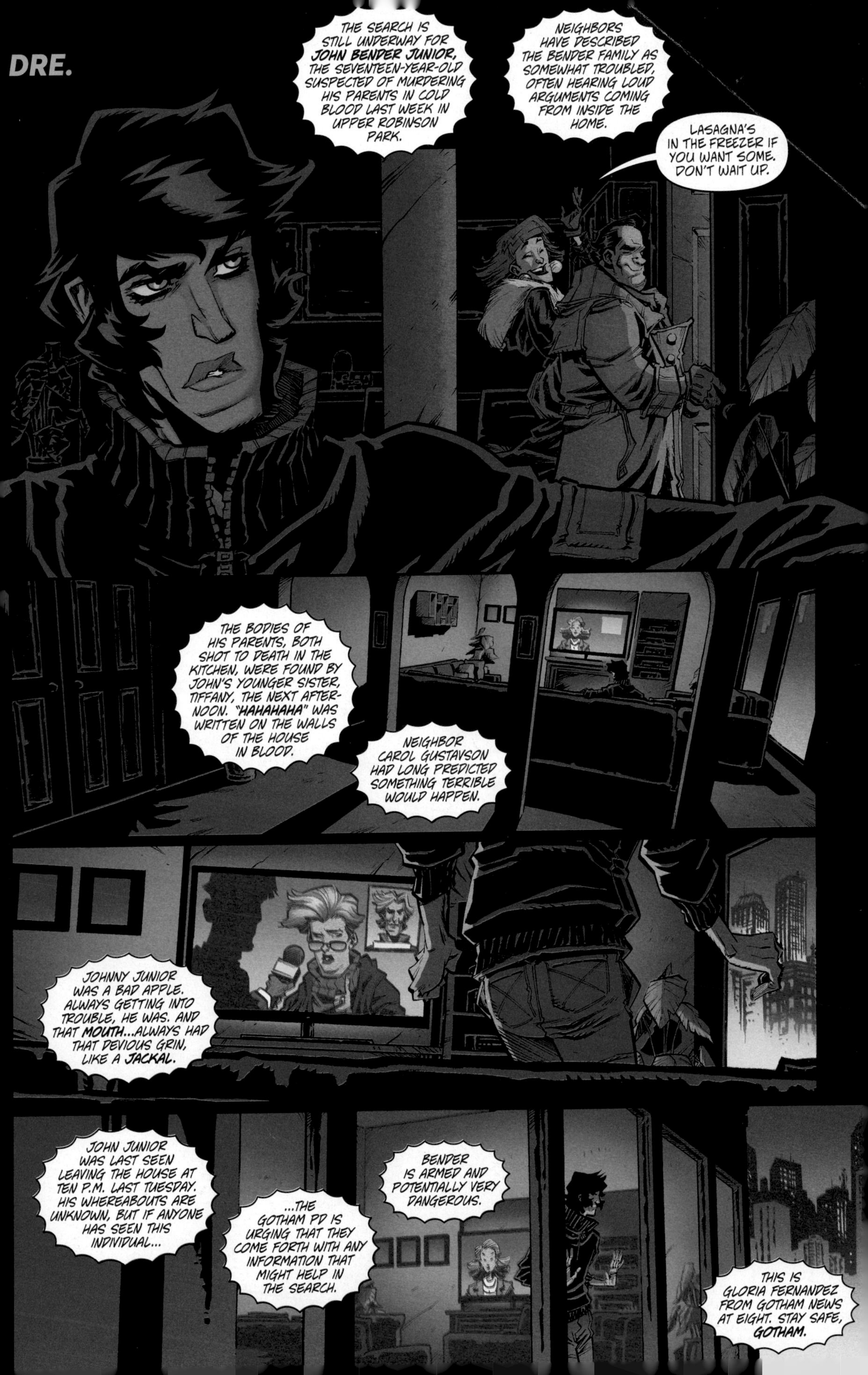
DRE.
THE SEARCH IS STILL UNDERWAY FOR JOHN BENDER JUNIOR, THE SEVENTEEN-YEAR-OLD SUSPECTED OF MURDERING HIS PARENTS IN COLD BLOOD LAST WEEK IN UPPER ROBINSON PARK.
NEIGHBORS HAVE DESCRIBED THE BENDER FAMILY AS SOMEWHAT TROUBLED, OFTEN HEARING LOUD ARGUMENTS COMING FROM INSIDE THE HOME.
LASAGNA'S IN THE FREEZER IF YOU WANT SOME. DON'T WAIT UP.
THE BODIES OF HIS PARENTS, BOTH SHOT TO DEATH IN THE KITCHEN, WERE FOUND BY JOHN'S YOUNGER SISTER, TIFFANY, THE NEXT AFTER-NOON. "HAHAHAHA" WAS WRITTEN ON THE WALLS OF THE HOUSE IN BLOOD.
NEIGHBOR CAROL GUSTAVSON HAD LONG PREDICTED SOMETHING TERRIBLE WOULD HAPPEN.
JOHNNY JUNIOR WAS A BAD APPLE. ALWAYS GETTING INTO TROUBLE, HE WAS. AND THAT MOUTH...ALWAYS HAD THAT DEVIOUS GRIN, LIKE A JACKAL.
JOHN JUNIOR WAS LAST SEEN LEAVING THE HOUSE AT TEN P.M. LAST TUESDAY. HIS WHEREABOUTS ARE UNKNOWN, BUT IF ANYONE HAS SEEN THIS INDIVIDUAL...
...THE GOTHAM PD IS URGING THAT THEY COME FORTH WITH ANY INFORMATION THAT MIGHT HELP IN THE SEARCH.
BENDER IS ARMED AND POTENTIALLY VERY DANGEROUS.
THIS IS GLORIA FERNANDEZ FROM GOTHAM NEWS AT EIGHT. STAY SAFE, GOTHAM.

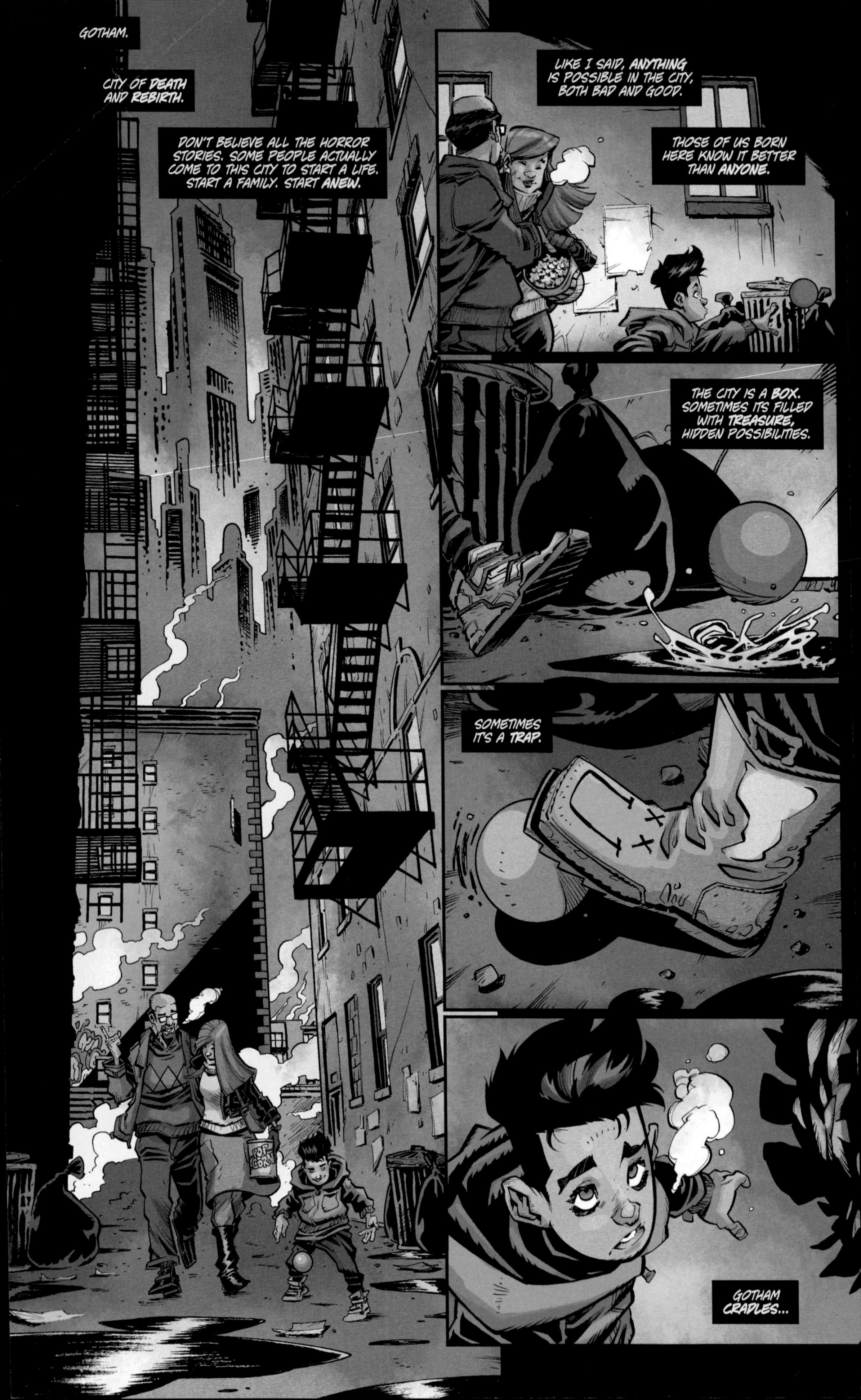
GOTHAM.
CITY OF DEATH AND REBIRTH.
DON'T BELIEVE ALL THE HORROR STORIES. SOME PEOPLE ACTUALLY COME TO THIS CITY TO START A LIFE. START A FAMILY. START ANEW.
POP CORN
LIKE I SAID, ANYTHING IS POSSIBLE IN THE CITY, BOTH BAD AND GOOD.
THOSE OF US BORN HERE KNOW IT BETTER THAN ANYONE.
THE CITY IS A BOX. SOMETIMES ITS FILLED WITH TREASURE, HIDDEN POSSIBILITIES.
SOMETIMES IT'S A TRAP.
GOTHAM CRADLES...

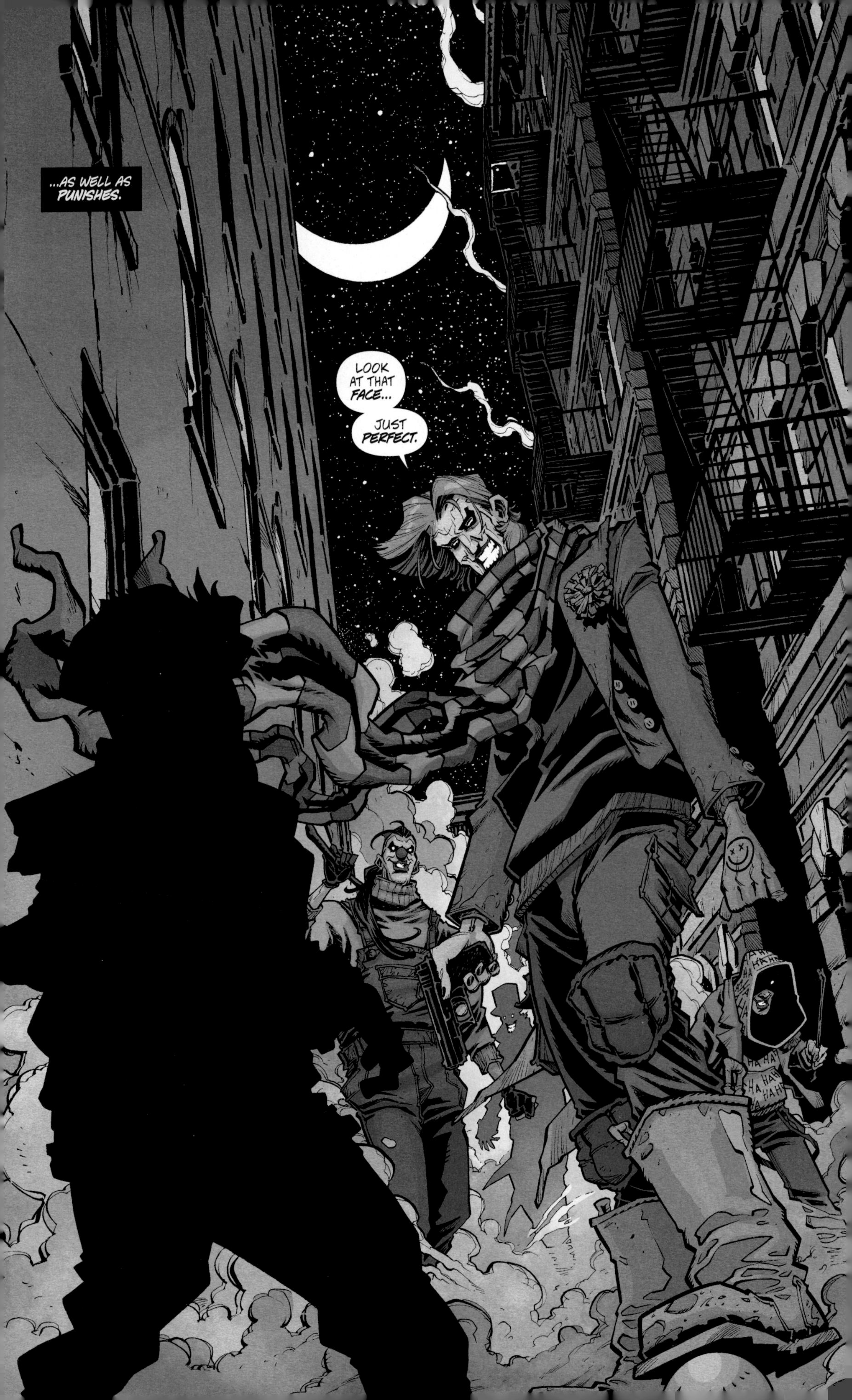
...AS WELL AS PUNISHES.
LOOK AT THAT FACE...
JUST PERFECT.

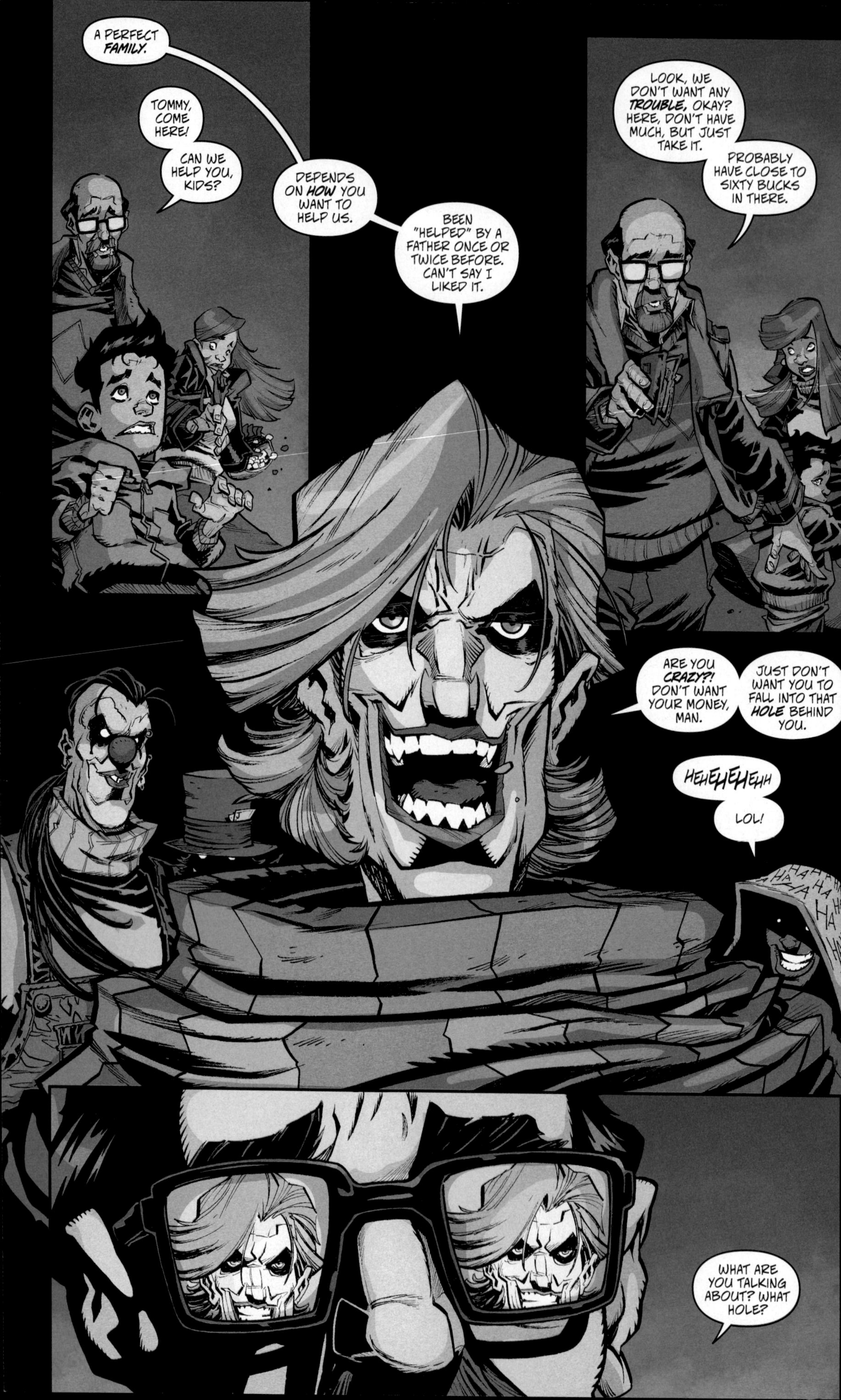

A PERFECT FAMILY.
TOMMY, COME HERE!
CAN WE HELP YOU, KIDS?
DEPENDS ON HOW YOU WANT TO HELP US.
BEEN "HELPED" BY A FATHER ONCE OR TWICE BEFORE. CAN'T SAY I LIKED IT.
LOOK, WE DON'T WANT ANY TROUBLE, OKAY? HERE, DON'T HAVE MUCH, BUT JUST TAKE IT.
PROBABLY HAVE CLOSE TO SIXTY BUCKS IN THERE.
ARE YOU CRAZY?! DON'T WANT YOUR MONEY, MAN.
JUST DON'T WANT YOU TO FALL INTO THAT HOLE BEHIND YOU.
HEHEHEHEHEHH
LOL!
WHAT ARE YOU TALKING ABOUT? WHAT HOLE?

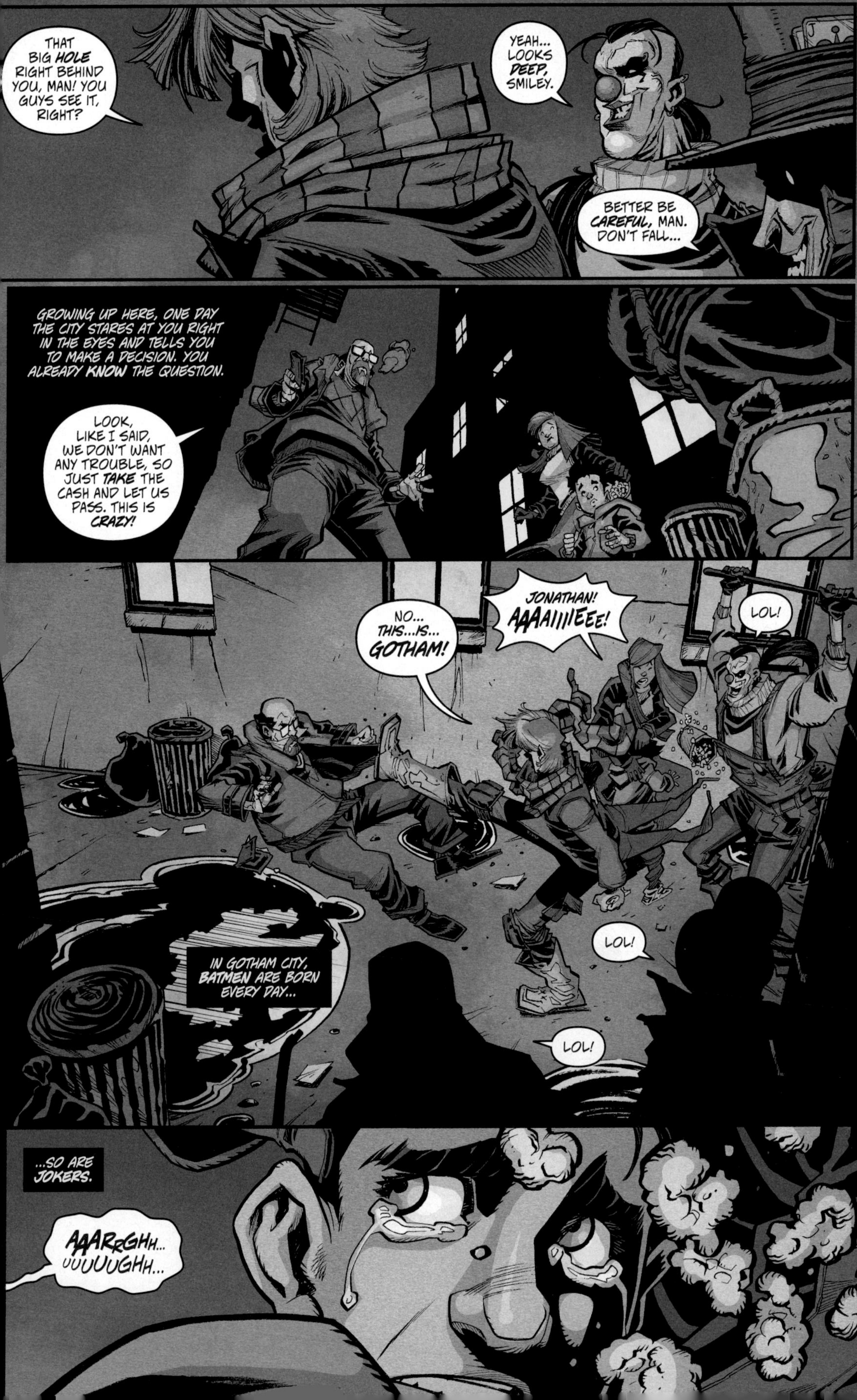
THAT BIG HOLE RIGHT BEHIND YOU, MAN! YOU GUYS SEE IT, RIGHT?
YEAH... LOOKS DEEP, SMILEY.
BETTER BE CAREFUL, MAN. DON'T FALL...
GROWING UP HERE, ONE DAY THE CITY STARES AT YOU RIGHT IN THE EYES AND TELLS YOU TO MAKE A DECISION. YOU ALREADY KNOW THE QUESTION.
LOOK, LIKE I SAID, WE DON'T WANT ANY TROUBLE, SO JUST TAKE THE CASH AND LET US PASS. THIS IS CRAZY!
NO... THIS...IS... GOTHAM!
JONATHAN! AAAAIIIIEEE!
LOL!
LOL!
IN GOTHAM CITY, BATMEN ARE BORN EVERY DAY...
LOL!
...SO ARE JOKERS.
AAARRGHH... UUUUGHH...

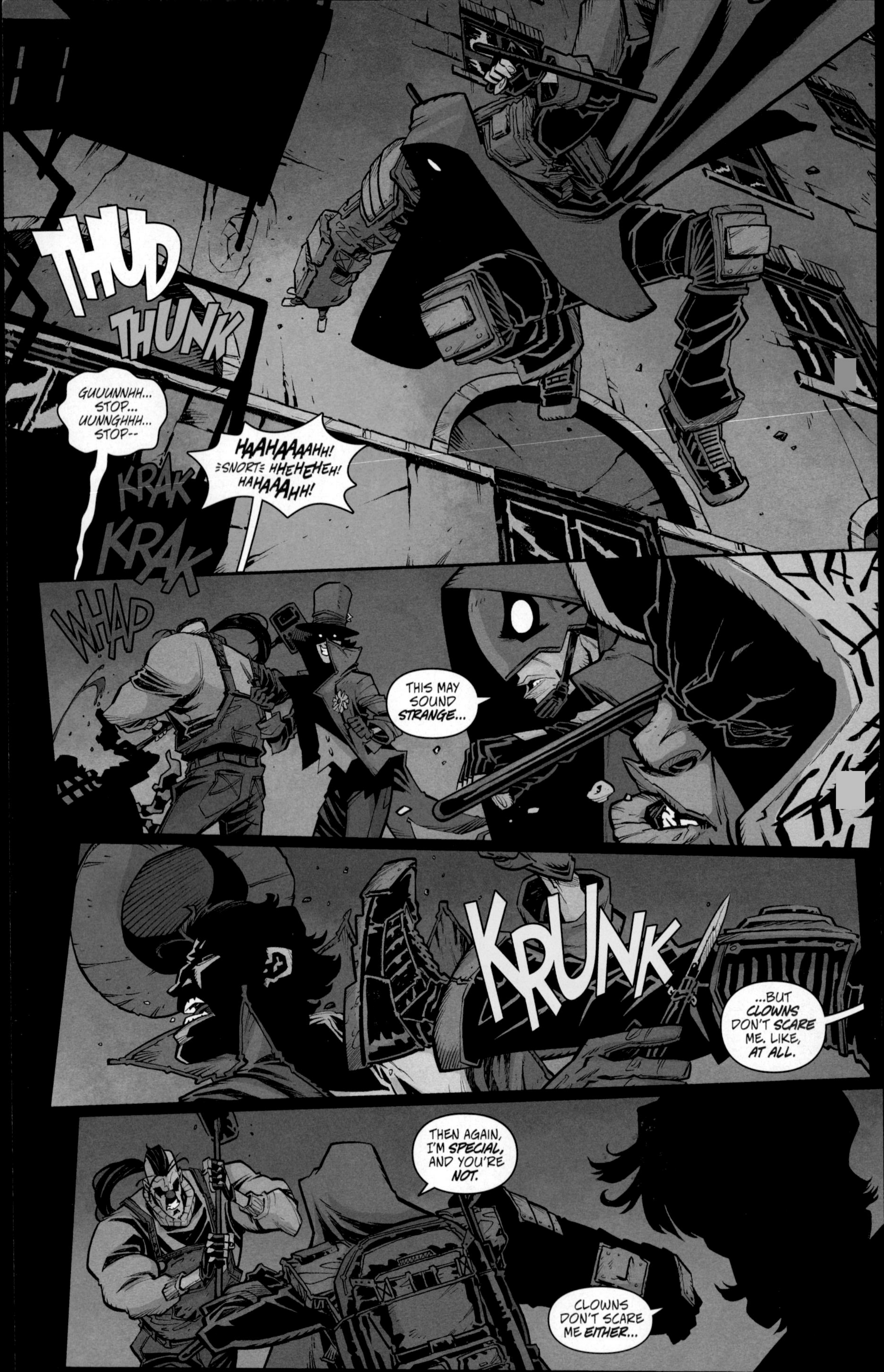
THUD
THUNK
GUUUNNHH... STOP... UUNNGHHH... STOP--
HAAHAAAAHH! SNORT HHEHEHEH! HAHAAAHH!
KRAK
KRAK
WHAP
THIS MAY SOUND STRANGE...
KRUNK
...BUT CLOWNS DON'T SCARE ME. LIKE, AT ALL.
THEN AGAIN, I'M SPECIAL, AND YOU'RE NOT.
CLOWNS DON'T SCARE ME EITHER...

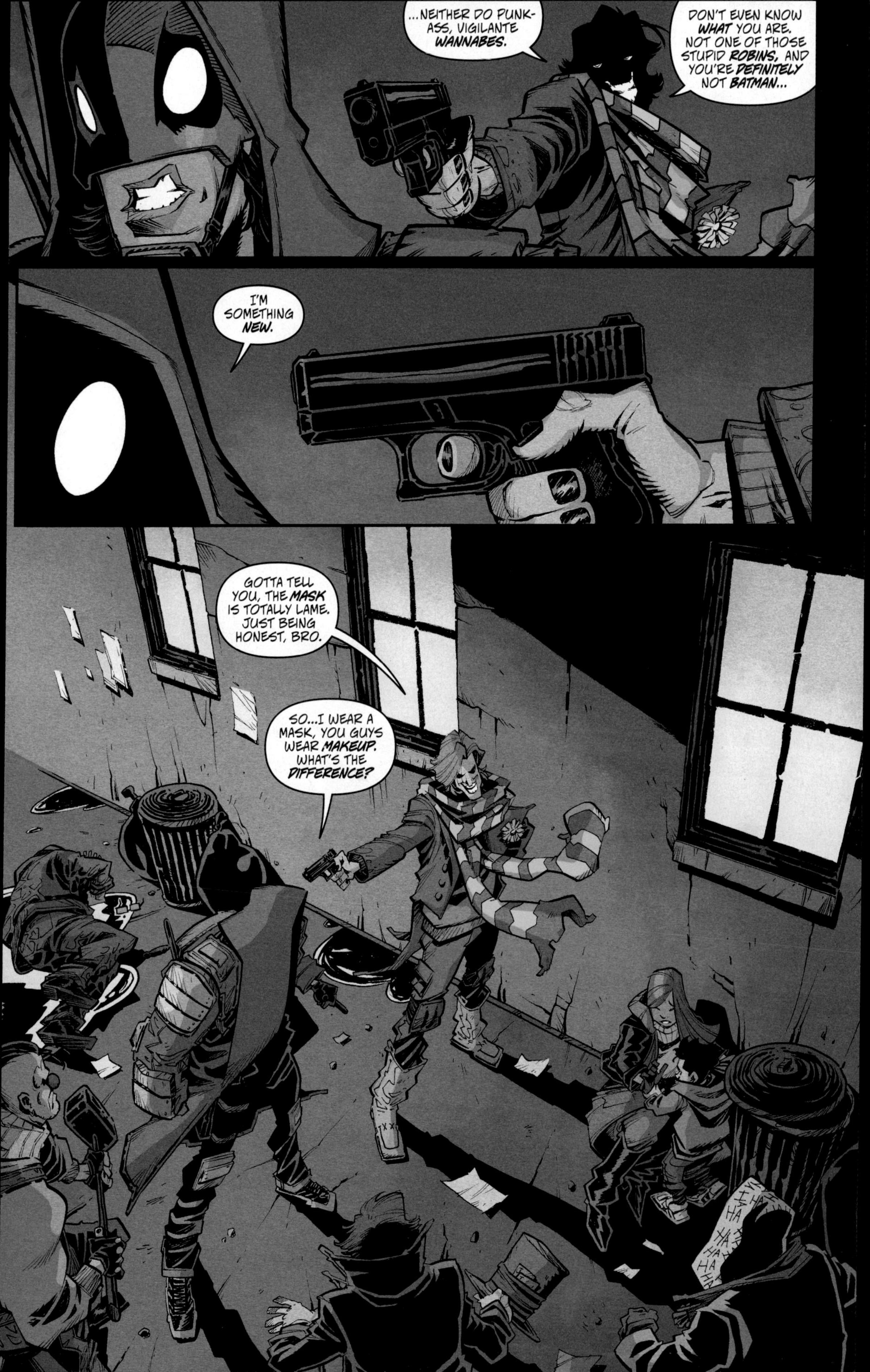
...NEITHER DO PUNK-ASS, VIGILANTE WANNABES.
DON'T EVEN KNOW WHAT YOU ARE. NOT ONE OF THOSE STUPID ROBINS, AND YOU'RE DEFINITELY NOT BATMAN...
I'M SOMETHING NEW.
GOTTA TELL YOU, THE MASK IS TOTALLY LAME. JUST BEING HONEST, BRO.
SO...I WEAR A MASK, YOU GUYS WEAR MAKEUP. WHAT'S THE DIFFERENCE?

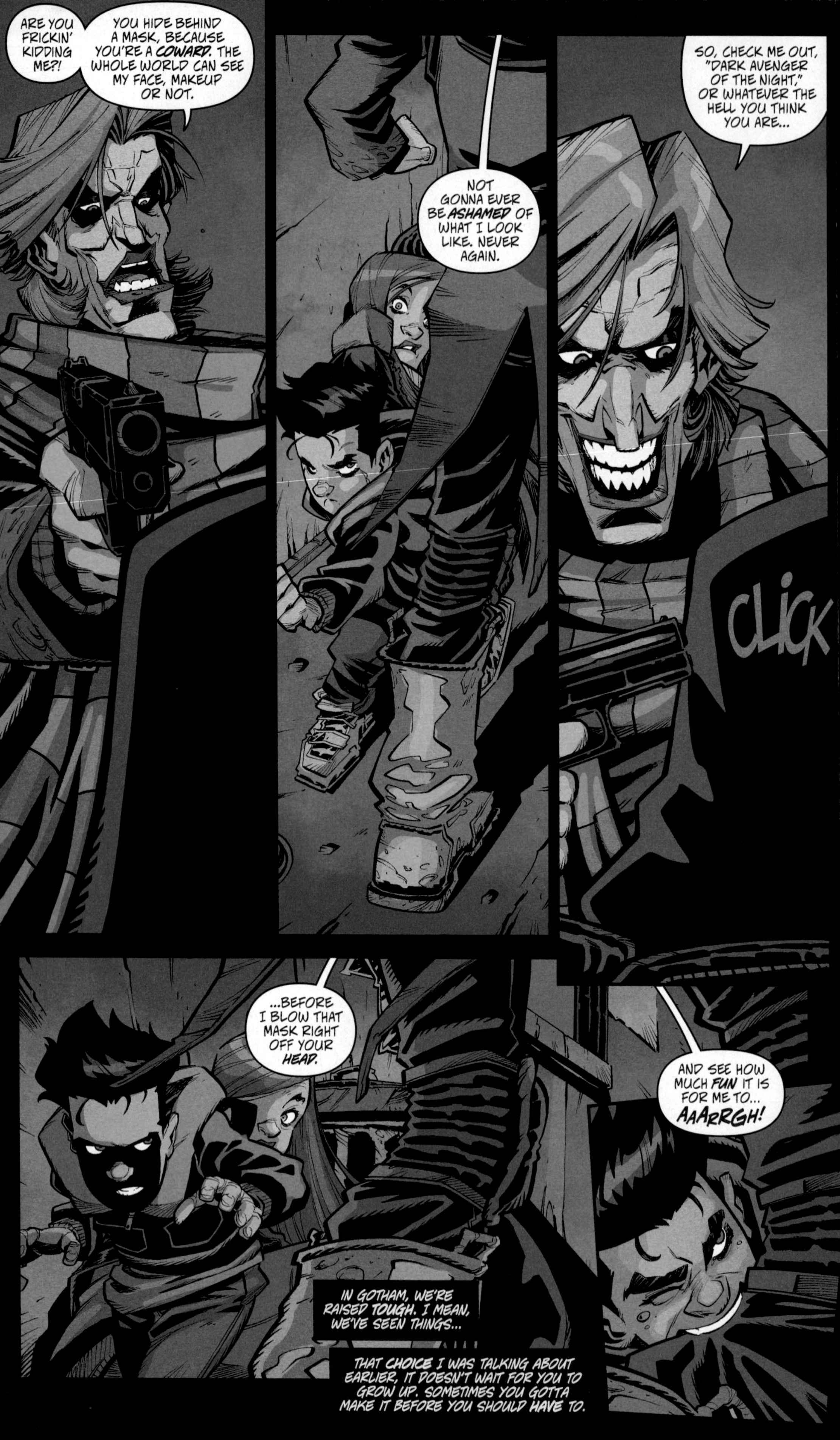
ARE YOU FRICKIN' KIDDING ME?!
YOU HIDE BEHIND A MASK, BECAUSE YOU'RE A COWARD. THE WHOLE WORLD CAN SEE MY FACE, MAKEUP OR NOT.
NOT GONNA EVER BE ASHAMED OF WHAT I LOOK LIKE. NEVER AGAIN.
SO, CHECK ME OUT, "DARK AVENGER OF THE NIGHT," OR WHATEVER THE HELL YOU THINK YOU ARE...
CLICK
...BEFORE I BLOW THAT MASK RIGHT OFF YOUR HEAD.
AND SEE HOW MUCH FUN IT IS FOR ME TO... AAARRGH!
IN GOTHAM, WE'RE RAISED TOUGH. I MEAN, WE'VE SEEN THINGS...
THAT CHOICE I WAS TALKING ABOUT EARLIER, IT DOESN'T WAIT FOR YOU TO GROW UP. SOMETIMES YOU GOTTA MAKE IT BEFORE YOU SHOULD HAVE TO.

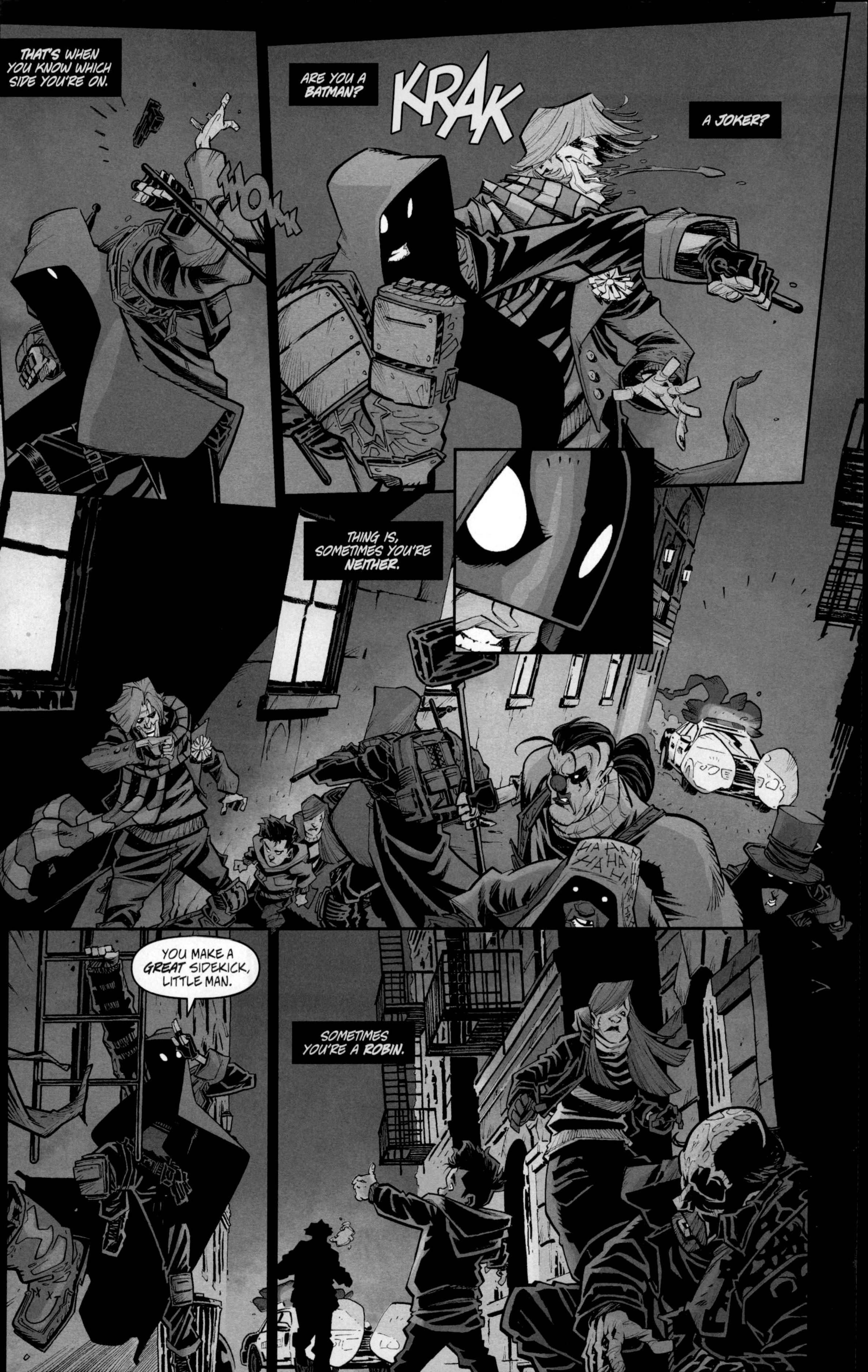
THAT'S WHEN YOU KNOW WHICH SIDE YOU'RE ON.
WHOK
ARE YOU A BATMAN?
KRAK
A JOKER?
THING IS, SOMETIMES YOU'RE NEITHER.
YOU MAKE A GREAT SIDEKICK, LITTLE MAN.
SOMETIMES YOU'RE A ROBIN.

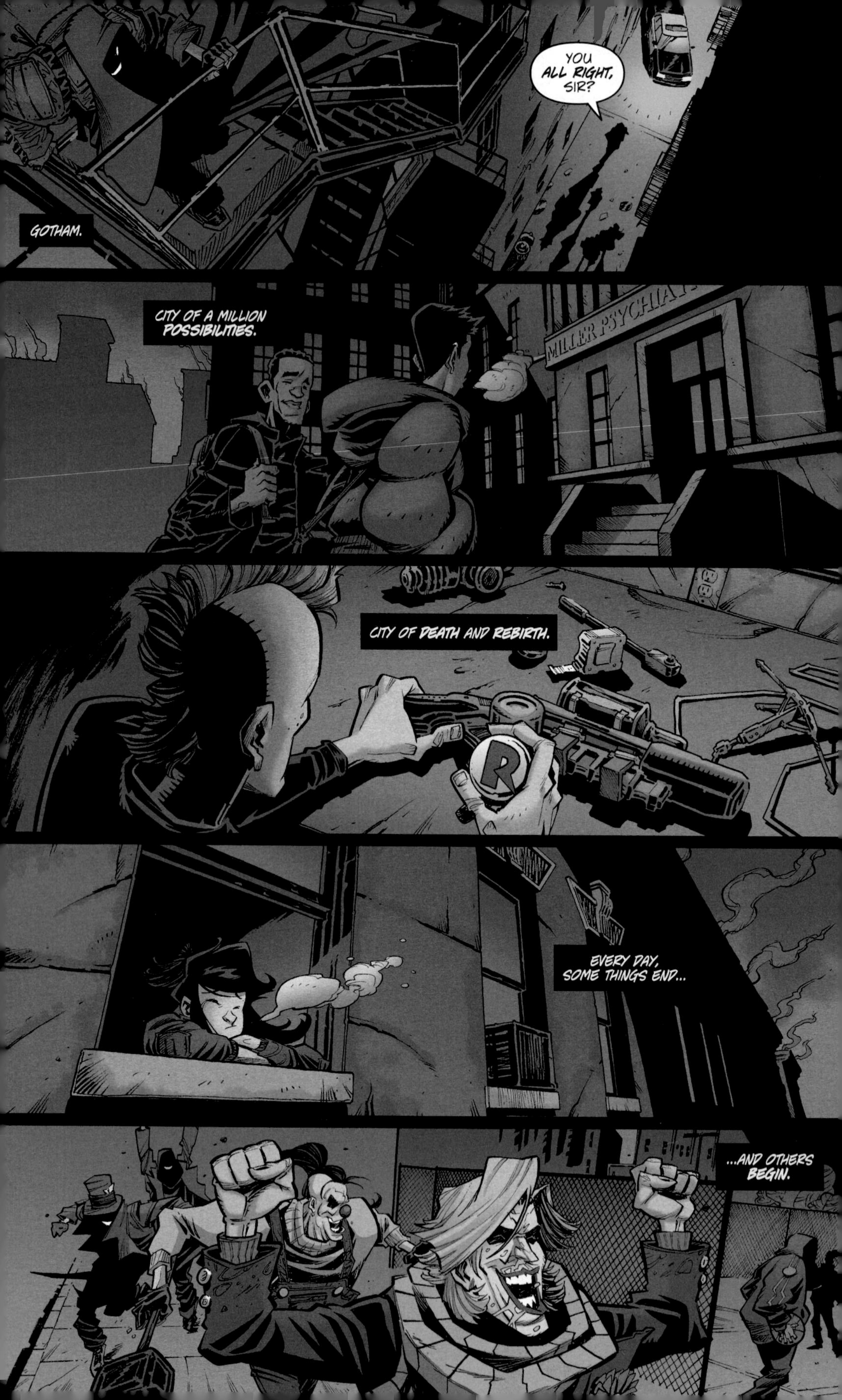
GOTHAM.
YOU ALL RIGHT, SIR?
CITY OF A MILLION POSSIBILITIES.
CITY OF DEATH AND REBIRTH.
EVERY DAY, SOME THINGS END...
...AND OTHERS BEGIN.

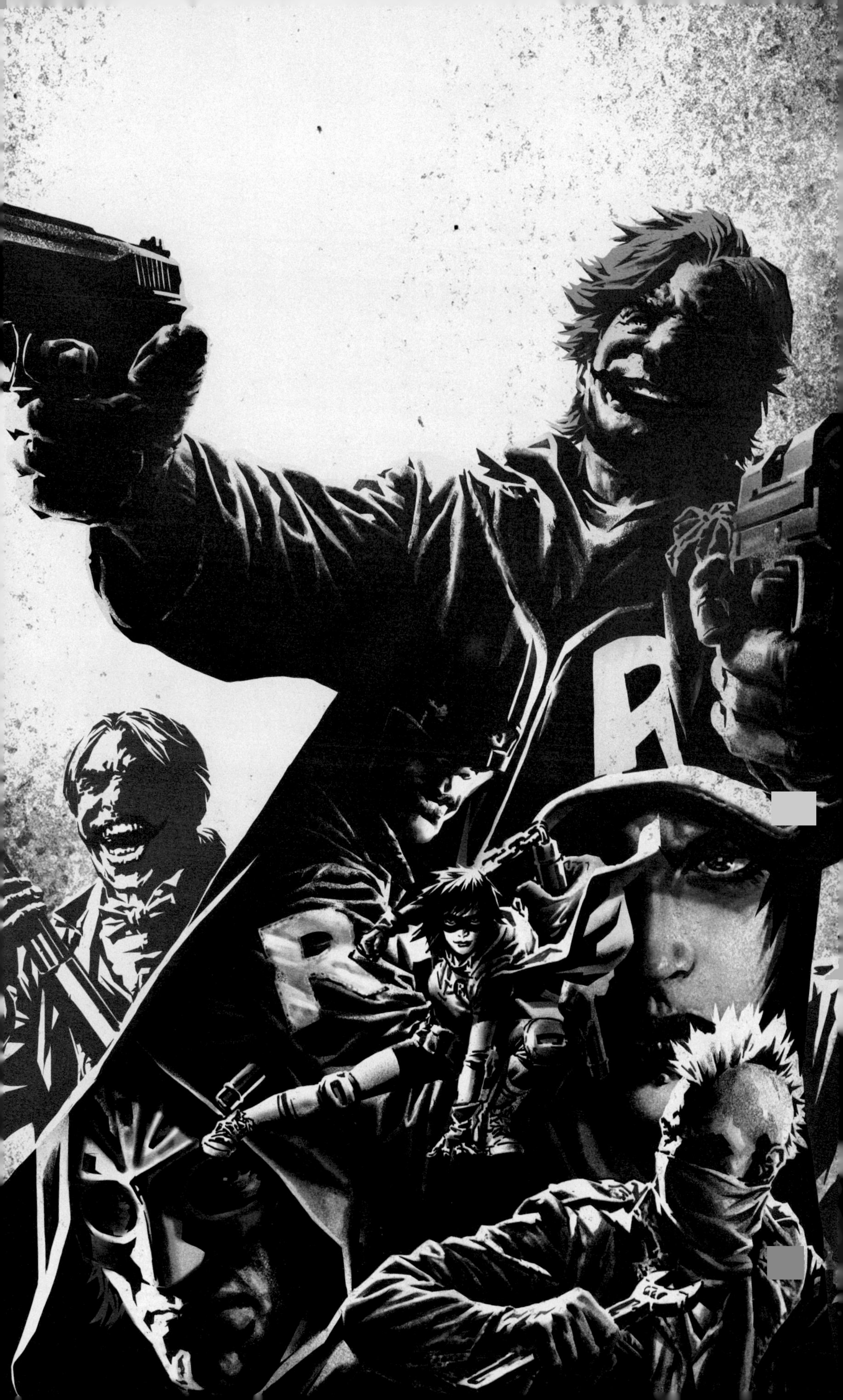

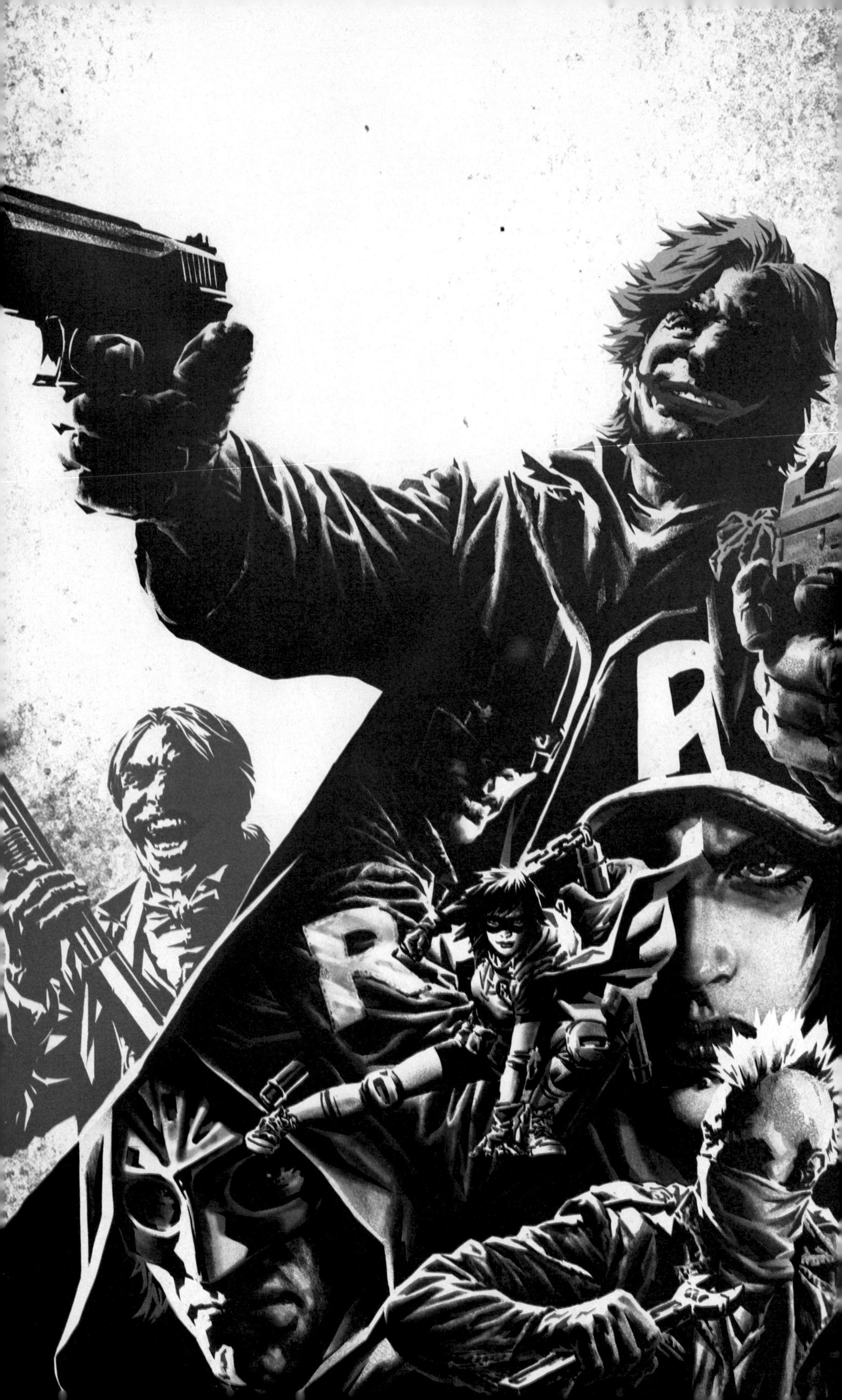

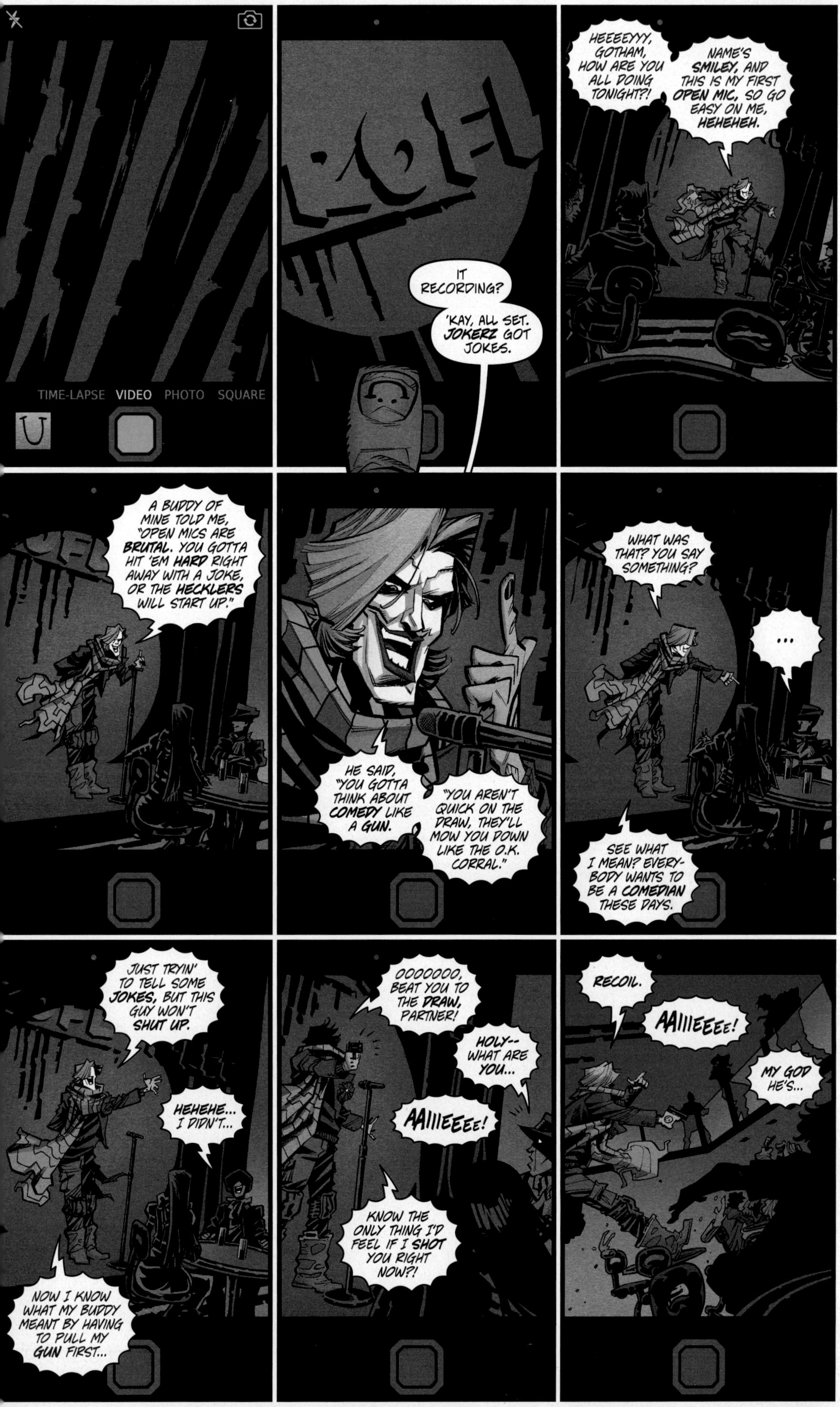
TIME-LAPSE VIDEO PHOTO SQUARE
IT RECORDING?
'KAY, ALL SET. JOKERZ GOT JOKES.
HEEEEYYY, GOTHAM, HOW ARE YOU ALL DOING TONIGHT?!
NAME'S SMILEY, AND THIS IS MY FIRST OPEN MIC, SO GO EASY ON ME, HEHEHEH.
A BUDDY OF MINE TOLD ME, "OPEN MICS ARE BRUTAL. YOU GOTTA HIT 'EM HARD RIGHT AWAY WITH A JOKE, OR THE HECKLERS WILL START UP."
HE SAID, "YOU GOTTA THINK ABOUT COMEDY LIKE A GUN.
"YOU AREN'T QUICK ON THE DRAW, THEY'LL MOW YOU DOWN LIKE THE O.K. CORRAL."
WHAT WAS THAT? YOU SAY SOMETHING?
...
SEE WHAT I MEAN? EVERY-BODY WANTS TO BE A COMEDIAN THESE DAYS.
JUST TRYIN' TO TELL SOME JOKES, BUT THIS GUY WON'T SHUT UP.
HEHEHE... I DIDN'T...
NOW I KNOW WHAT MY BUDDY MEANT BY HAVING TO PULL MY GUN FIRST...
OOOOOOO, BEAT YOU TO THE DRAW, PARTNER!
HOLY-- WHAT ARE YOU...
AAIIIEEEE!
KNOW THE ONLY THING I'D FEEL IF I SHOT YOU RIGHT NOW?!
RECOIL.
AAIIIEEEE!
MY GOD HE'S...

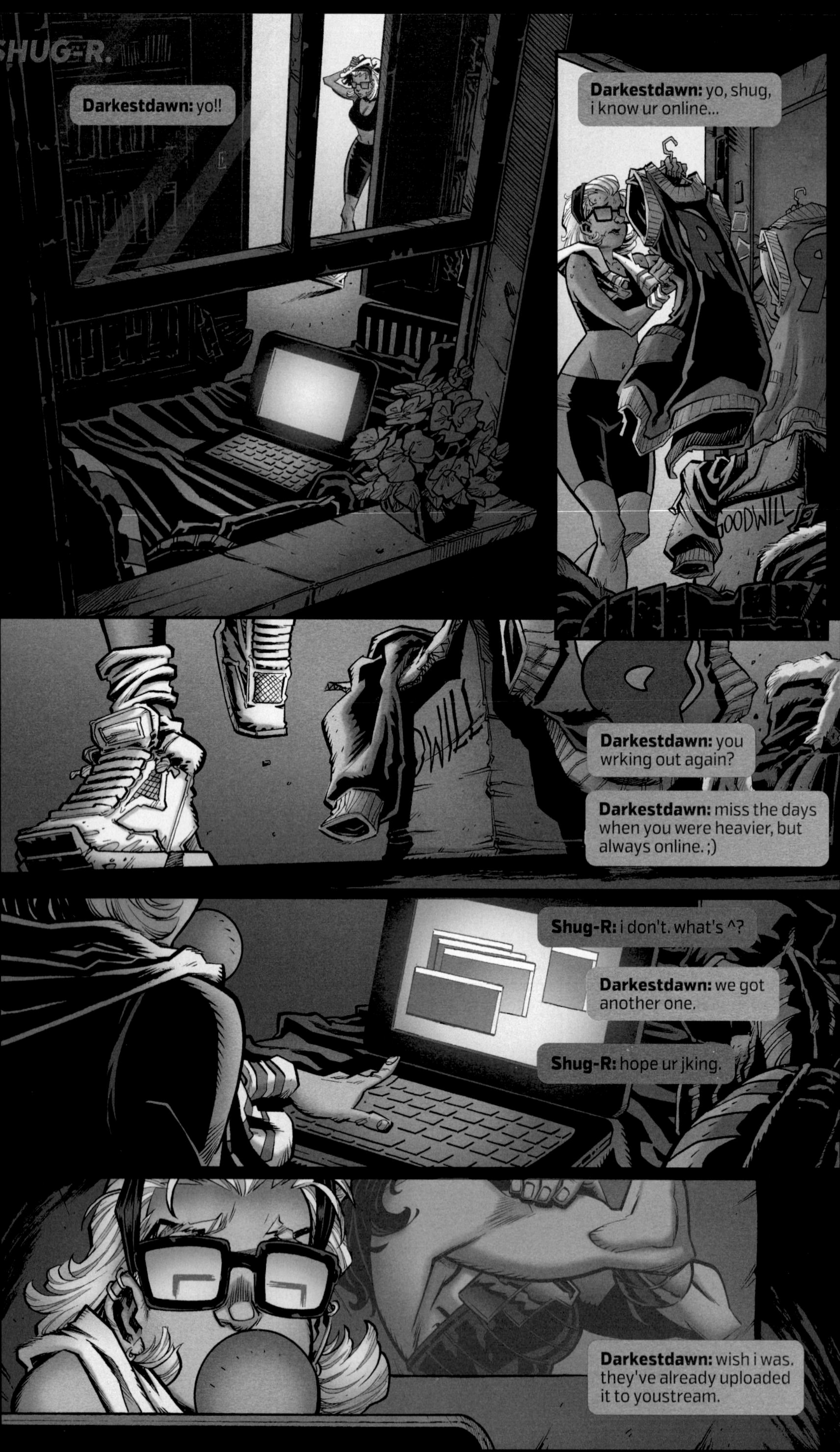
SHUG-R.
Darkestdawn: yo!!
Darkestdawn: yo, shug, i know ur online...
GOODWILL
DWILL
Darkestdawn: you wrking out again?
Darkestdawn: miss the days when you were heavier, but always online. ;)
Shug-R: i don't. what's ^?
Darkestdawn: we got another one.
Shug-R: hope ur jking.
Darkestdawn: wish i was. they've already uploaded it to youstream.

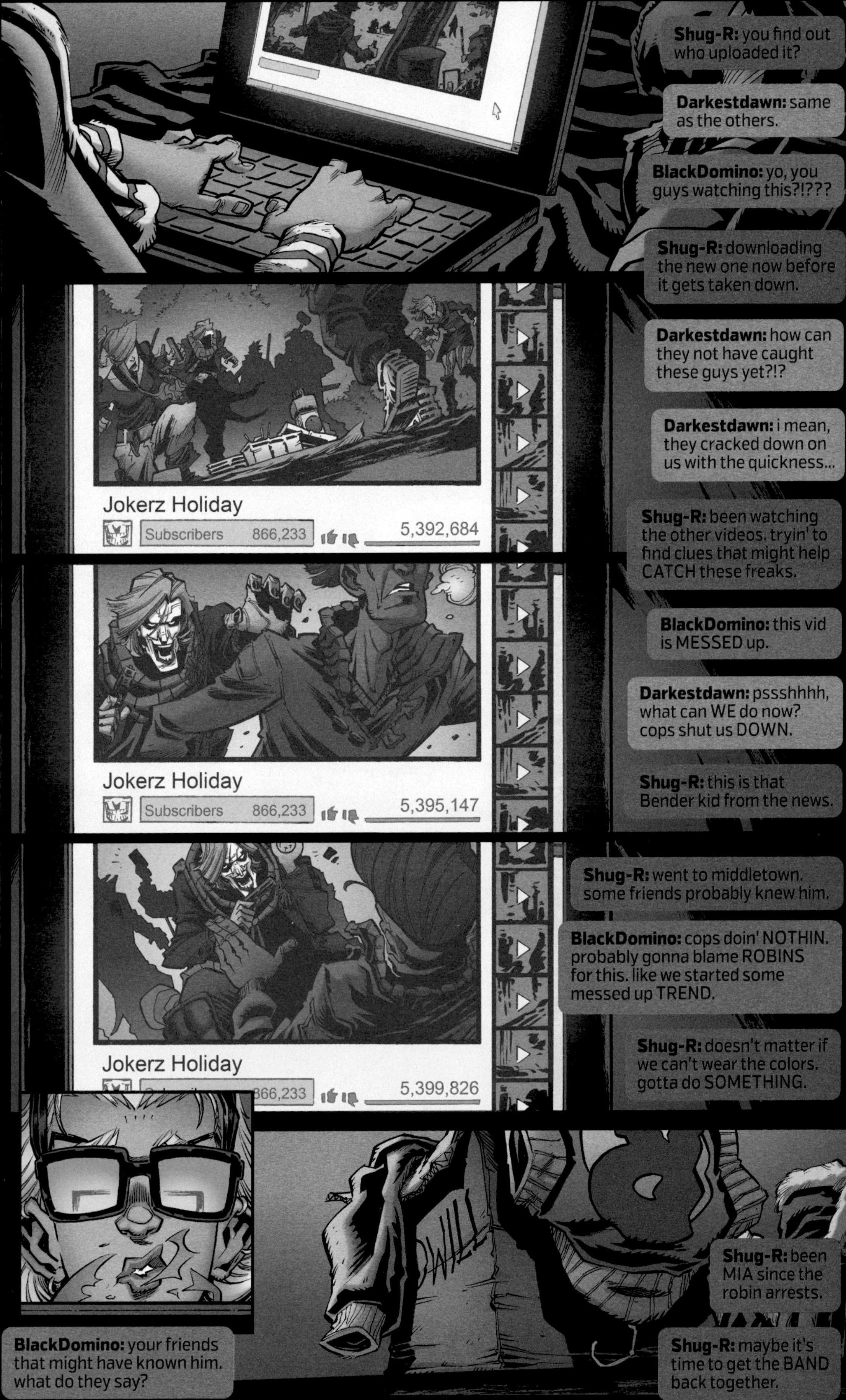
Shug-R: you find out who uploaded it?
Darkestdawn: same as the others.
BlackDomino: yo, you guys watching this?!???
Shug-R: downloading the new one now before it gets taken down.
Darkestdawn: how can they not have caught these guys yet?!?
Darkestdawn: i mean, they cracked down on us with the quickness...
Shug-R: been watching the other videos. tryin' to find clues that might help CATCH these freaks.
Jokerz Holiday
Subscribers 866,233
5,392,684
BlackDomino: this vid is MESSED up.
Darkestdawn: pssshhhh, what can WE do now? cops shut us DOWN.
Shug-R: this is that Bender kid from the news.
Jokerz Holiday
Subscribers 866,233
5,395,147
Shug-R: went to middletown. some friends probably knew him.
BlackDomino: cops doin' NOTHIN. probably gonna blame ROBINS for this. like we started some messed up TREND.
Shug-R: doesn't matter if we can't wear the colors. gotta do SOMETHING.
Jokerz Holiday
866,233
5,399,826
BlackDomino: your friends that might have known him. what do they say?
Shug-R: been MIA since the robin arrests.
Shug-R: maybe it's time to get the BAND back together.

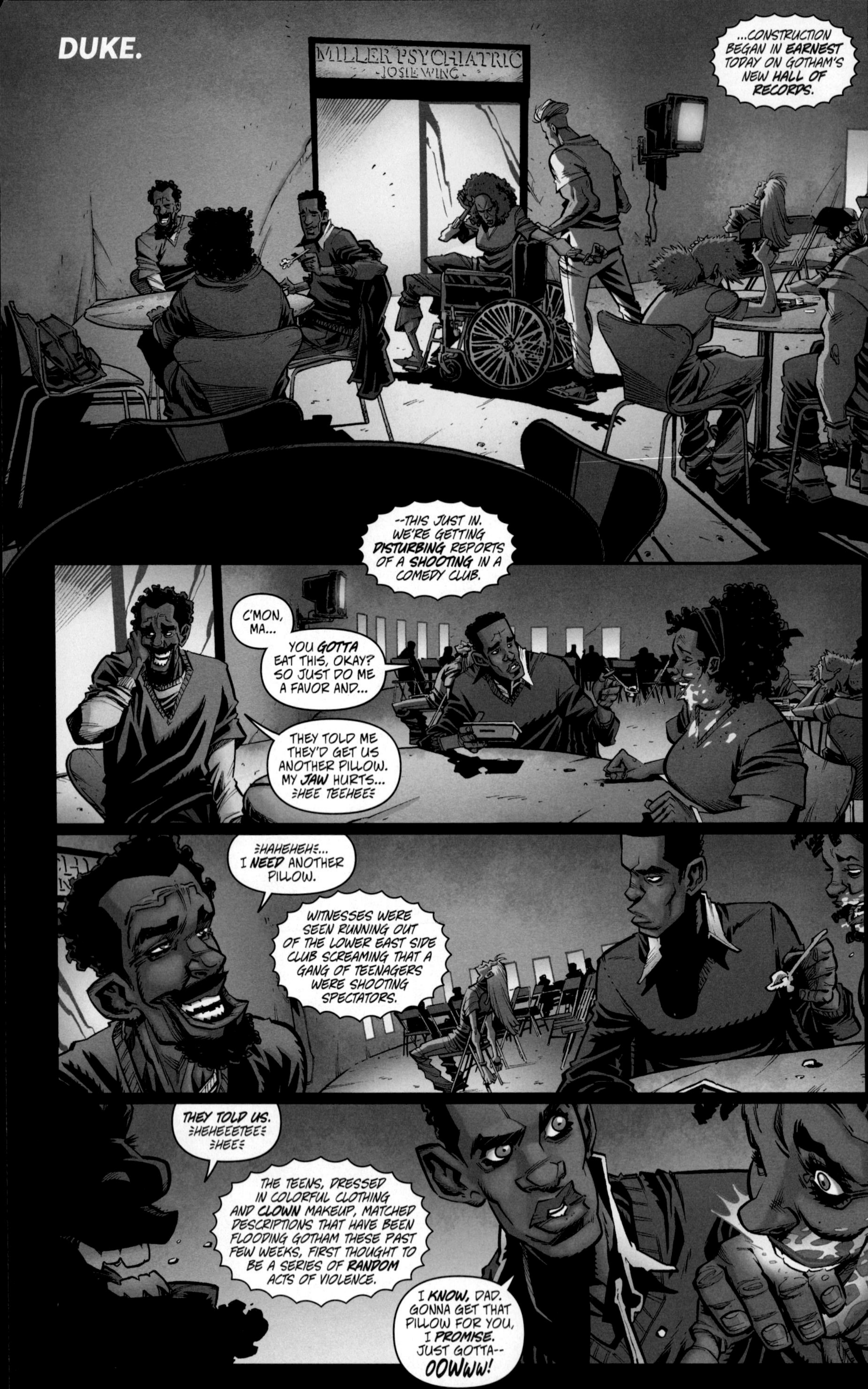
DUKE.
MILLER PSYCHIATRIC
-JOSIE WING-
...CONSTRUCTION BEGAN IN EARNEST TODAY ON GOTHAM'S NEW HALL OF RECORDS.
--THIS JUST IN. WE'RE GETTING DISTURBING REPORTS OF A SHOOTING IN A COMEDY CLUB.
C'MON, MA...
YOU GOTTA EAT THIS, OKAY? SO JUST DO ME A FAVOR AND...
THEY TOLD ME THEY'D GET US ANOTHER PILLOW. MY JAW HURTS... HEE TEEHEE
HAHEHEH... I NEED ANOTHER PILLOW.
WITNESSES WERE SEEN RUNNING OUT OF THE LOWER EAST SIDE CLUB SCREAMING THAT A GANG OF TEENAGERS WERE SHOOTING SPECTATORS.
THEY TOLD US. HEHEEETEE HEE
THE TEENS, DRESSED IN COLORFUL CLOTHING AND CLOWN MAKEUP, MATCHED DESCRIPTIONS THAT HAVE BEEN FLOODING GOTHAM THESE PAST FEW WEEKS, FIRST THOUGHT TO BE A SERIES OF RANDOM ACTS OF VIOLENCE.
I KNOW, DAD. GONNA GET THAT PILLOW FOR YOU, I PROMISE. JUST GOTTA--
OOWWW!

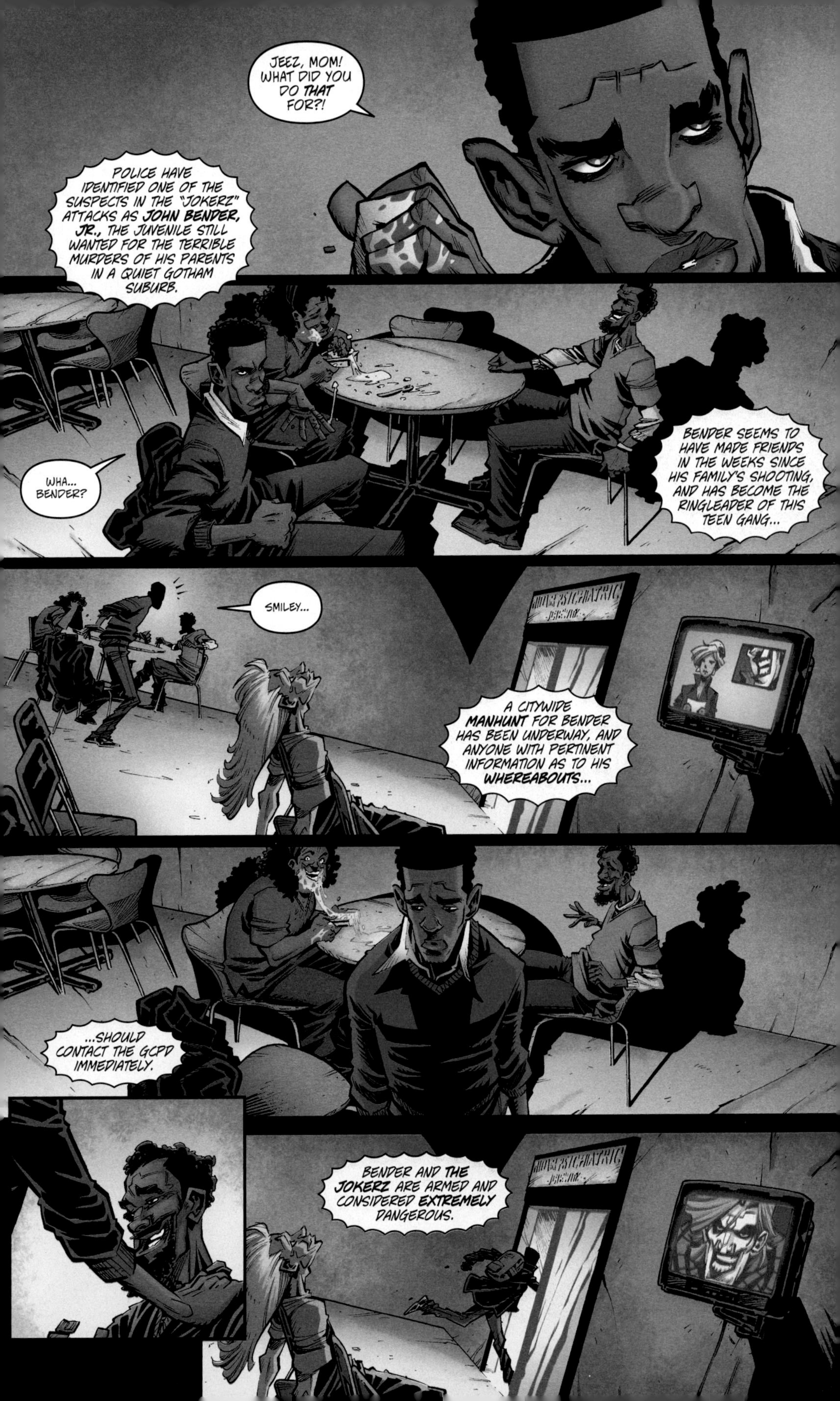

JEEZ, MOM! WHAT DID YOU DO THAT FOR?!
POLICE HAVE IDENTIFIED ONE OF THE SUSPECTS IN THE "JOKERZ" ATTACKS AS JOHN BENDER, JR., THE JUVENILE STILL WANTED FOR THE TERRIBLE MURDERS OF HIS PARENTS IN A QUIET GOTHAM SUBURB.
WHA... BENDER?
BENDER SEEMS TO HAVE MADE FRIENDS IN THE WEEKS SINCE HIS FAMILY'S SHOOTING, AND HAS BECOME THE RINGLEADER OF THIS TEEN GANG...
SMILEY...
A CITYWIDE MANHUNT FOR BENDER HAS BEEN UNDERWAY, AND ANYONE WITH PERTINENT INFORMATION AS TO HIS WHEREABOUTS...
...SHOULD CONTACT THE GCPD IMMEDIATELY.
BENDER AND THE JOKERZ ARE ARMED AND CONSIDERED EXTREMELY DANGEROUS.

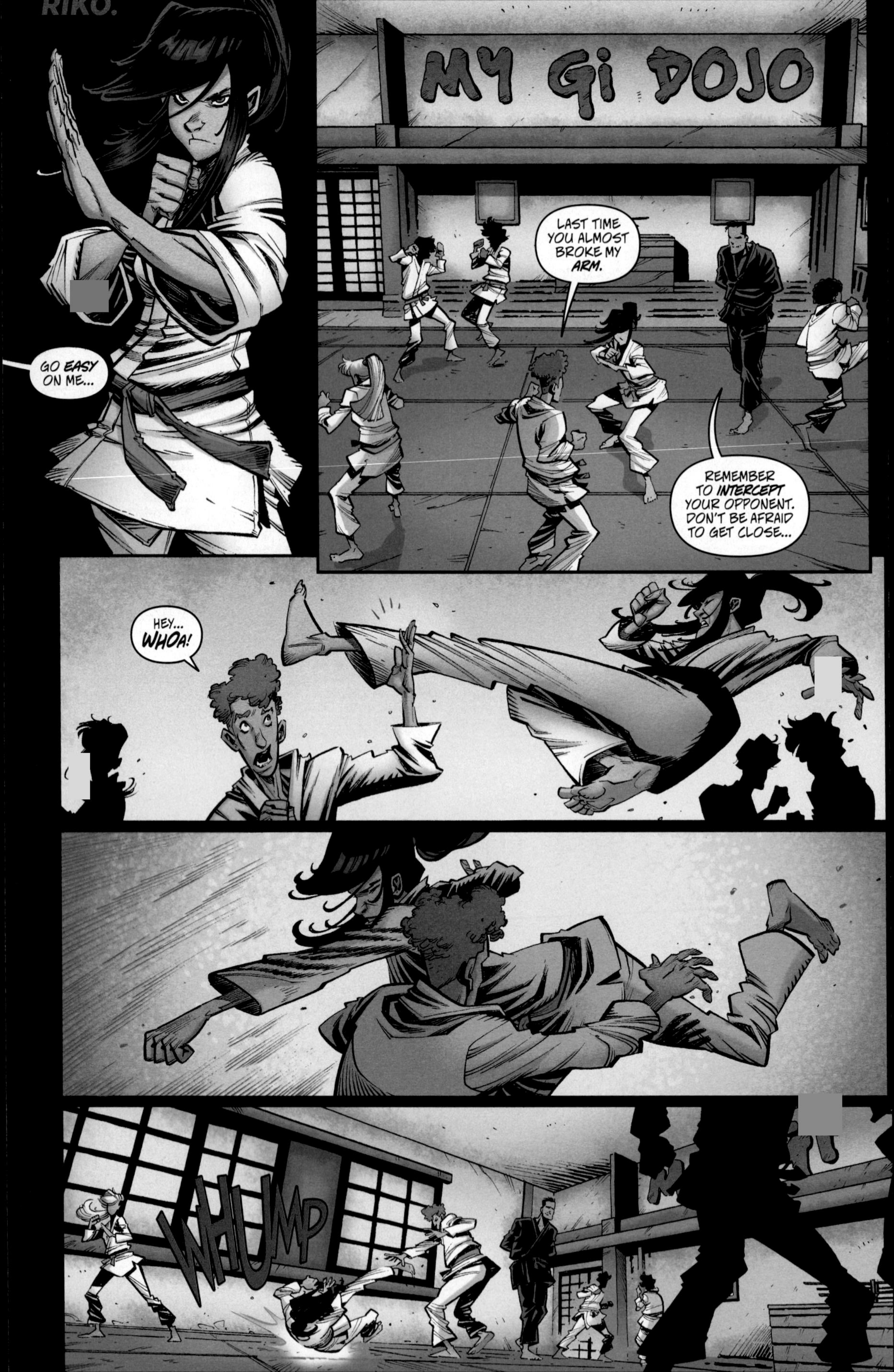
RIKO.
GO EASY ON ME...
MY Gi DOJO
LAST TIME YOU ALMOST BROKE MY ARM.
REMEMBER TO INTERCEPT YOUR OPPONENT. DON'T BE AFRAID TO GET CLOSE...
HEY... WHOA!
WHUMP

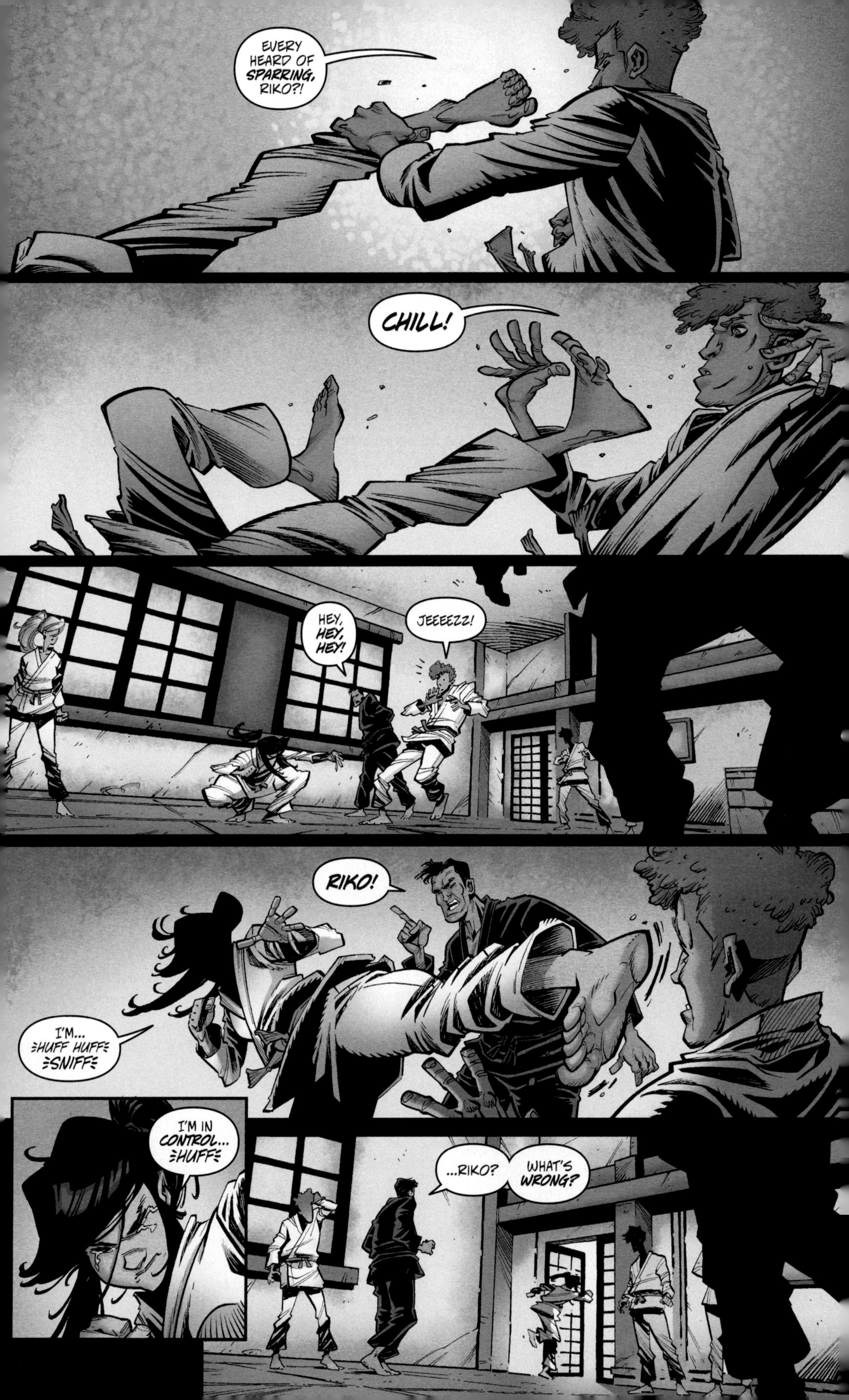

EVERY HEARD OF SPARRING, RIKO?!
CHILL!
HEY, HEY, HEY!
JEEEEZZ!
RIKO!
I'M... HUFF HUFF SNIFF
I'M IN CONTROL... HUFF
...RIKO?
WHAT'S WRONG?

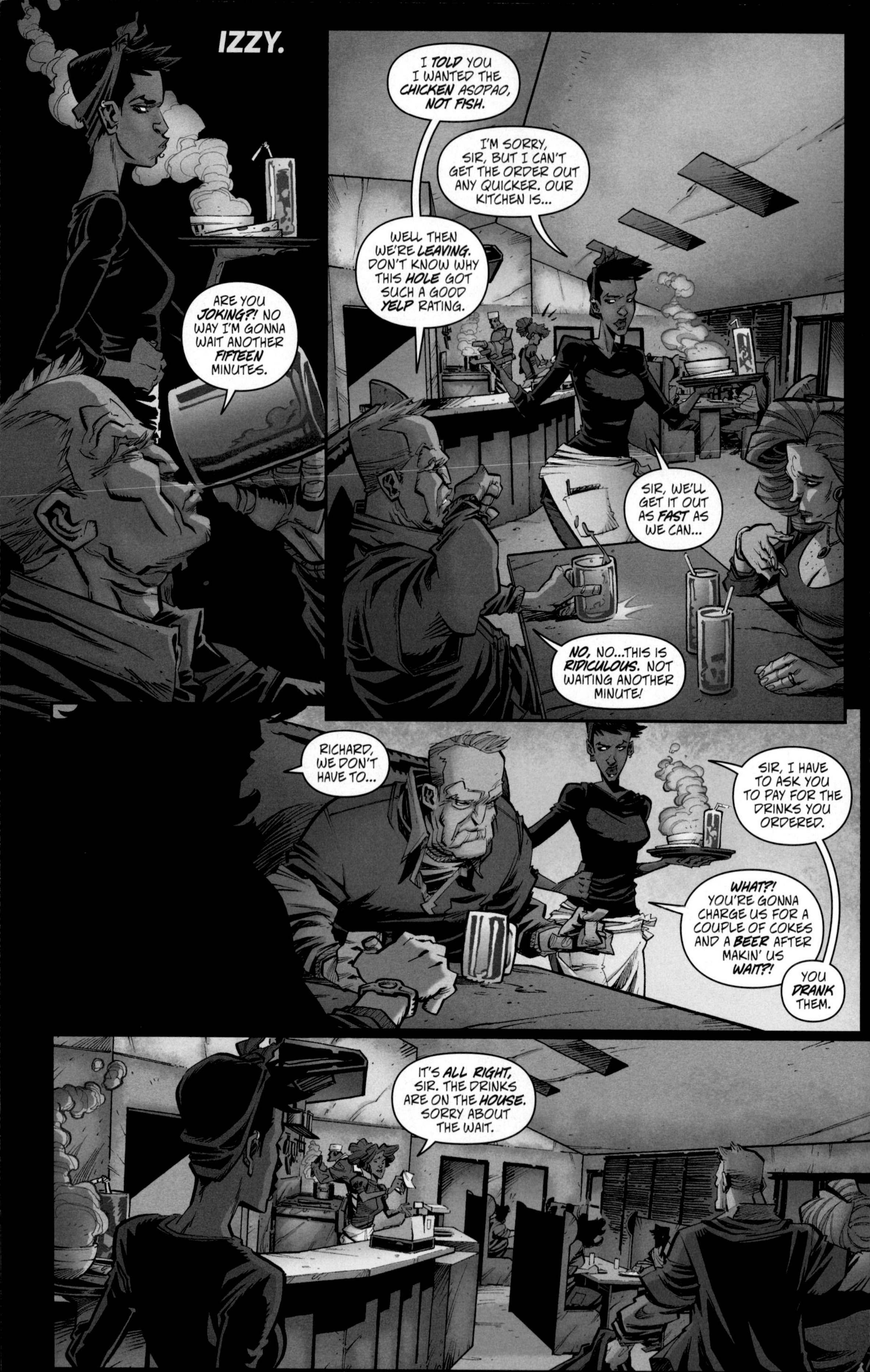
IZZY.
I TOLD YOU I WANTED THE CHICKEN ASOPAO, NOT FISH.
I'M SORRY, SIR, BUT I CAN'T GET THE ORDER OUT ANY QUICKER. OUR KITCHEN IS...
WELL THEN WE'RE LEAVING. DON'T KNOW WHY THIS HOLE GOT SUCH A GOOD YELP RATING.
ARE YOU JOKING?! NO WAY I'M GONNA WAIT ANOTHER FIFTEEN MINUTES.
SIR, WE'LL GET IT OUT AS FAST AS WE CAN...
NO, NO...THIS IS RIDICULOUS. NOT WAITING ANOTHER MINUTE!
RICHARD, WE DON'T HAVE TO...
SIR, I HAVE TO ASK YOU TO PAY FOR THE DRINKS YOU ORDERED.
WHAT?! YOU'RE GONNA CHARGE US FOR A COUPLE OF COKES AND A BEER AFTER MAKIN' US WAIT?!
YOU DRANK THEM.
IT'S ALL RIGHT, SIR. THE DRINKS ARE ON THE HOUSE. SORRY ABOUT THE WAIT.

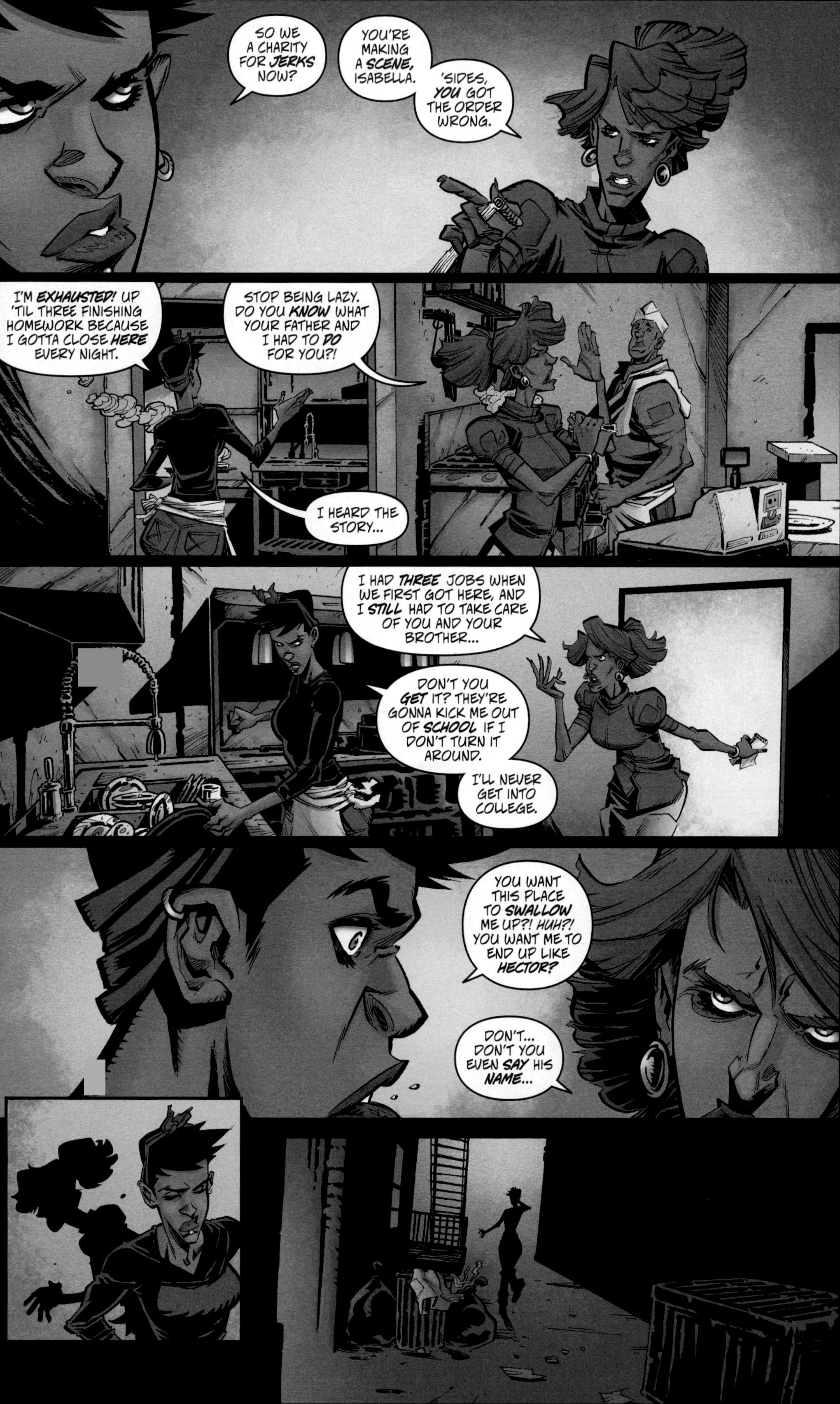

SO WE A CHARITY FOR JERKS NOW?
YOU'RE MAKING A SCENE, ISABELLA.
'SIDES, YOU GOT THE ORDER WRONG.
I'M EXHAUSTED! UP 'TIL THREE FINISHING HOMEWORK BECAUSE I GOTTA CLOSE HERE EVERY NIGHT.
STOP BEING LAZY. DO YOU KNOW WHAT YOUR FATHER AND I HAD TO DO FOR YOU?!
I HEARD THE STORY...
I HAD THREE JOBS WHEN WE FIRST GOT HERE, AND I STILL HAD TO TAKE CARE OF YOU AND YOUR BROTHER...
DON'T YOU GET IT? THEY'RE GONNA KICK ME OUT OF SCHOOL IF I DON'T TURN IT AROUND.
I'LL NEVER GET INTO COLLEGE.
YOU WANT THIS PLACE TO SWALLOW ME UP?! HUH?! YOU WANT ME TO END UP LIKE HECTOR?
DON'T... DON'T YOU EVEN SAY HIS NAME...

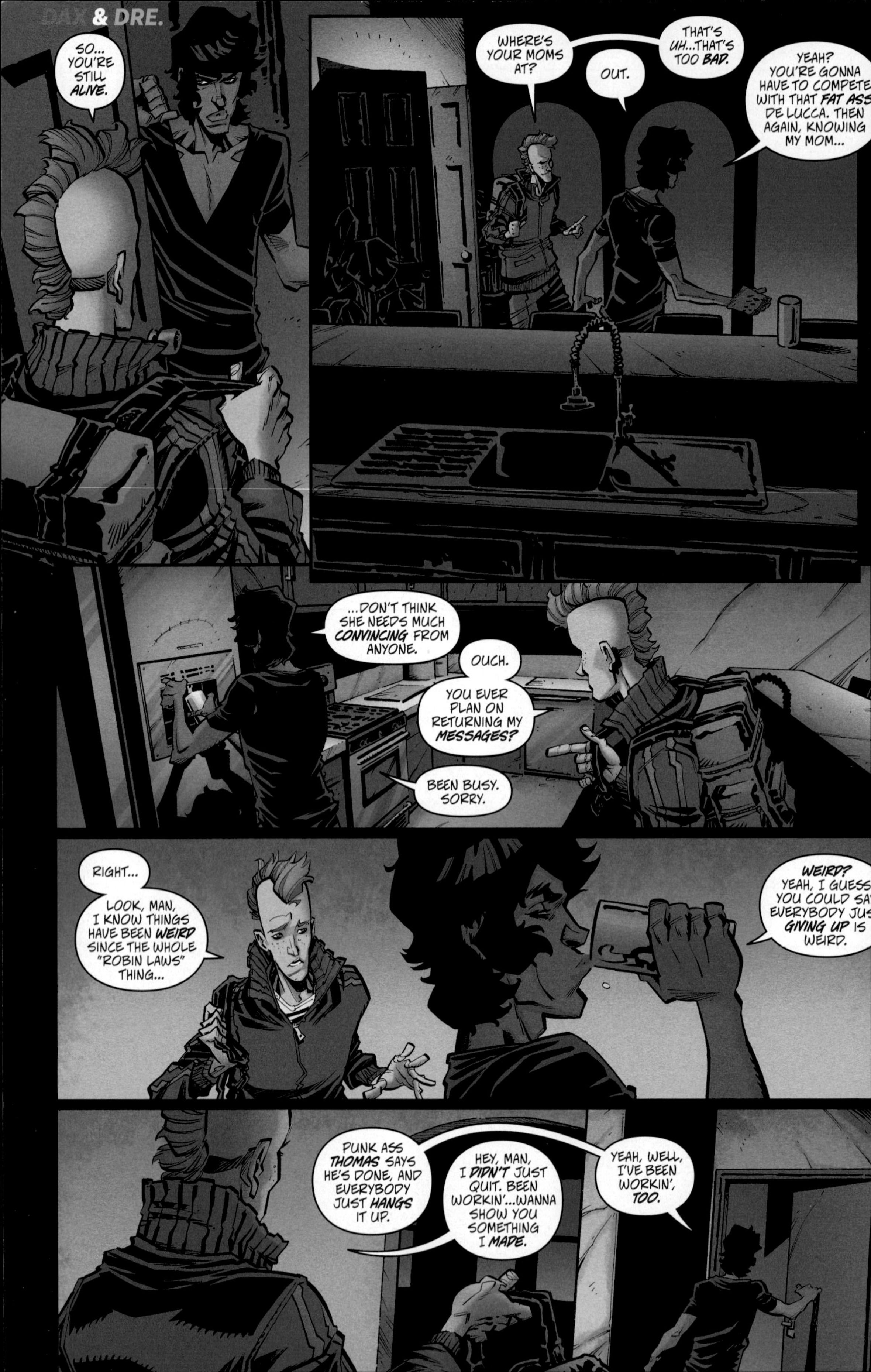
SO... YOU'RE STILL ALIVE.
WHERE'S YOUR MOMS AT?
OUT.
THAT'S UH...THAT'S TOO BAD.
YEAH? YOU'RE GONNA HAVE TO COMPETE WITH THAT FAT ASS DE LUCCA. THEN AGAIN, KNOWING MY MOM...
...DON'T THINK SHE NEEDS MUCH CONVINCING FROM ANYONE.
OUCH.
YOU EVER PLAN ON RETURNING MY MESSAGES?
BEEN BUSY. SORRY.
RIGHT...
LOOK, MAN, I KNOW THINGS HAVE BEEN WEIRD SINCE THE WHOLE "ROBIN LAWS" THING...
WEIRD? YEAH, I GUESS YOU COULD SA EVERYBODY JUS GIVING UP IS WEIRD.
PUNK ASS THOMAS SAYS HE'S DONE, AND EVERYBODY JUST HANGS IT UP.
YEAH, WELL, I'VE BEEN WORKIN', TOO.
HEY, MAN, I DIDN'T JUST QUIT. BEEN WORKIN'...WANNA SHOW YOU SOMETHING I MADE.

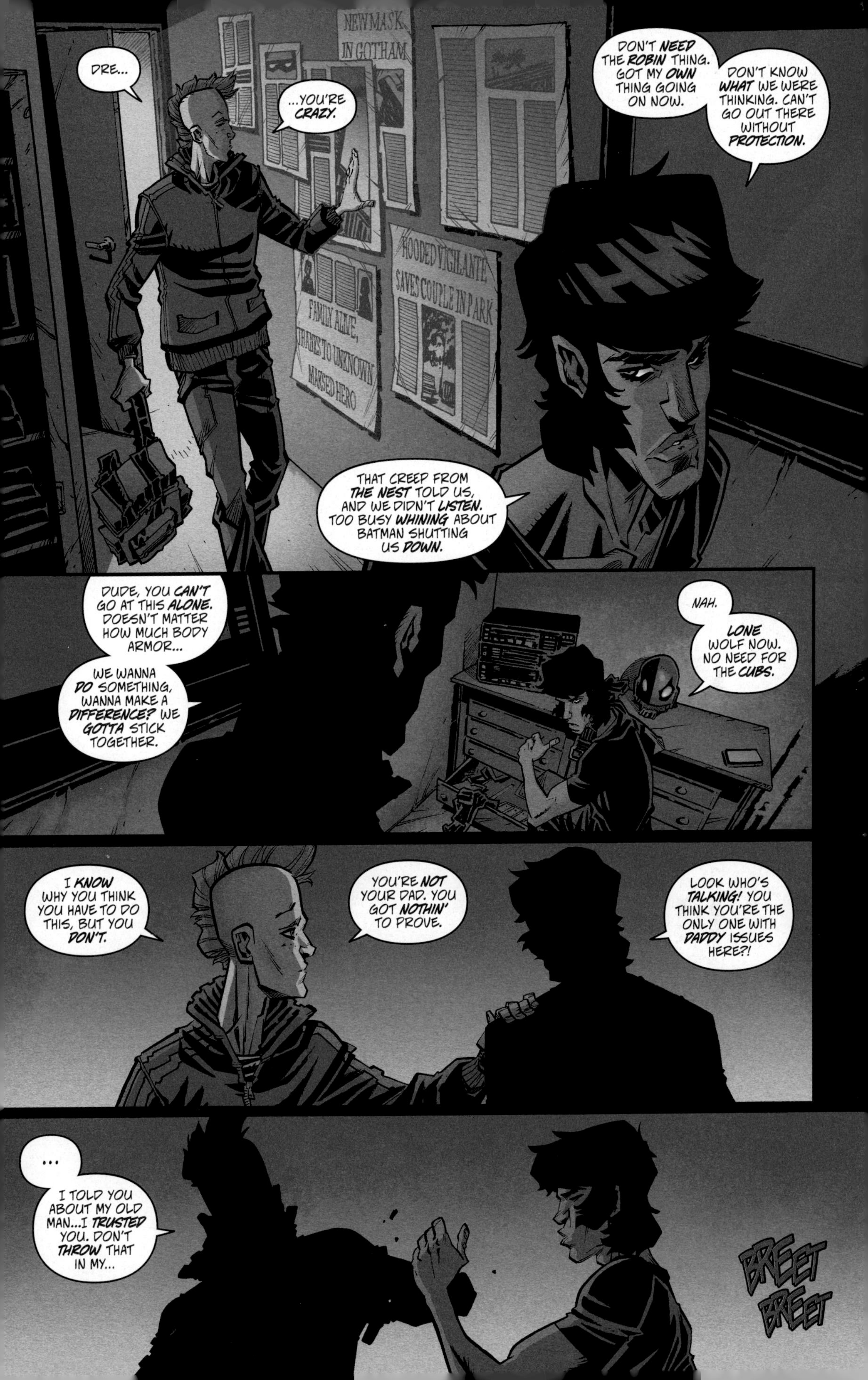
DRE...
...YOU'RE CRAZY.
NEW MASK IN GOTHAM
HOODED VIGILANTE SAVES COUPLE IN PARK
FAMILY ALIVE, THANKS TO UNKNOWN MAKSED HERO
DON'T NEED THE ROBIN THING. GOT MY OWN THING GOING ON NOW.
DON'T KNOW WHAT WE WERE THINKING. CAN'T GO OUT THERE WITHOUT PROTECTION.
THAT CREEP FROM THE NEST TOLD US, AND WE DIDN'T LISTEN. TOO BUSY WHINING ABOUT BATMAN SHUTTING US DOWN.
DUDE, YOU CAN'T GO AT THIS ALONE. DOESN'T MATTER HOW MUCH BODY ARMOR...
WE WANNA DO SOMETHING, WANNA MAKE A DIFFERENCE? WE GOTTA STICK TOGETHER.
NAH.
LONE WOLF NOW. NO NEED FOR THE CUBS.
I KNOW WHY YOU THINK YOU HAVE TO DO THIS, BUT YOU DON'T.
YOU'RE NOT YOUR DAD. YOU GOT NOTHIN' TO PROVE.
LOOK WHO'S TALKING! YOU THINK YOU'RE THE ONLY ONE WITH DADDY ISSUES HERE?!
...
I TOLD YOU ABOUT MY OLD MAN...I TRUSTED YOU. DON'T THROW THAT IN MY...
BREEET BREEET

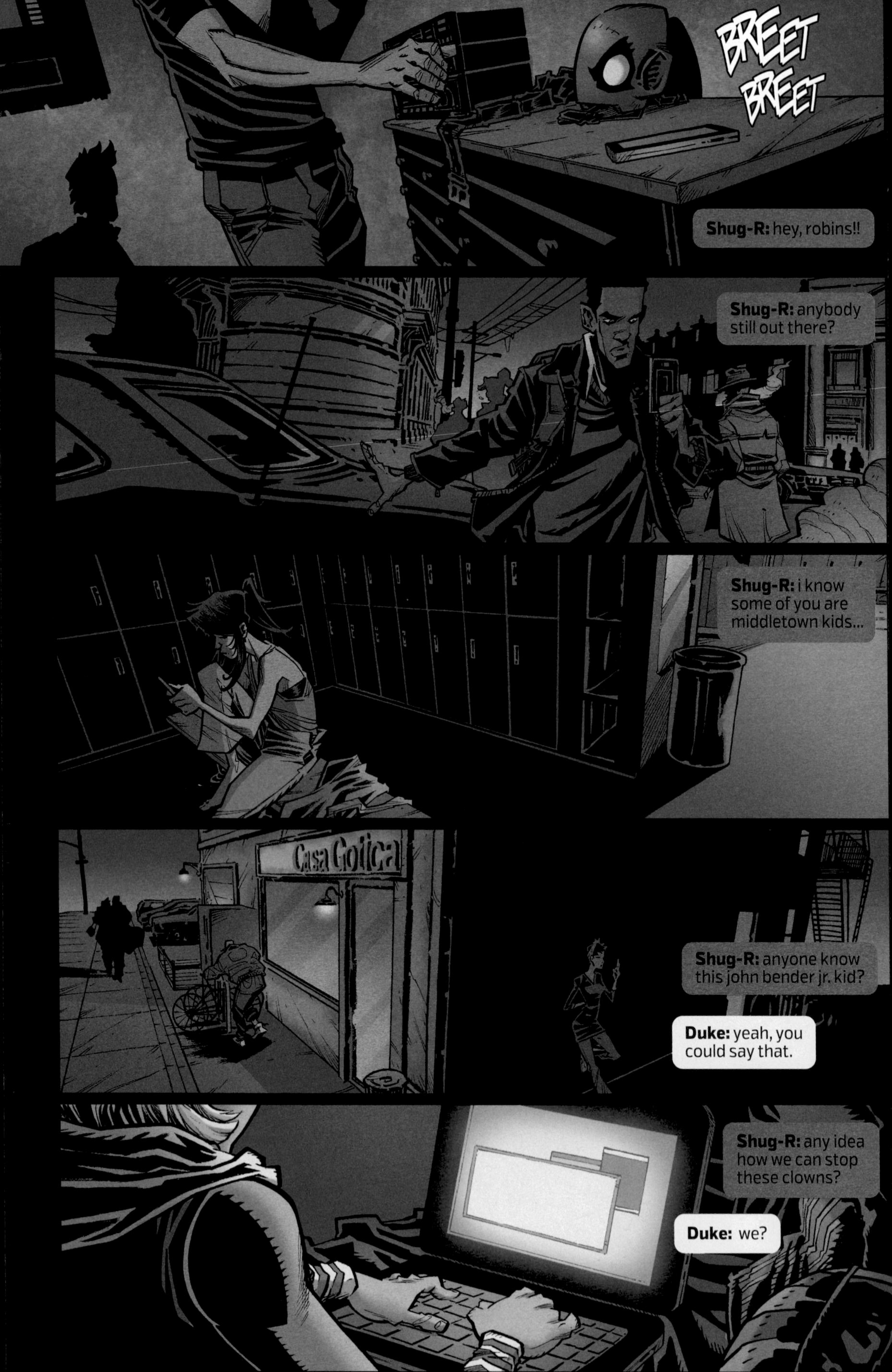

BREEET BREEET
Shug-R: hey, robins!!
Shug-R: anybody still out there?
Shug-R: i know some of you are middletown kids...
Casa Gotica
Shug-R: anyone know this john bender jr. kid?
Duke: yeah, you could say that.
Shug-R: any idea how we can stop these clowns?
Duke: we?

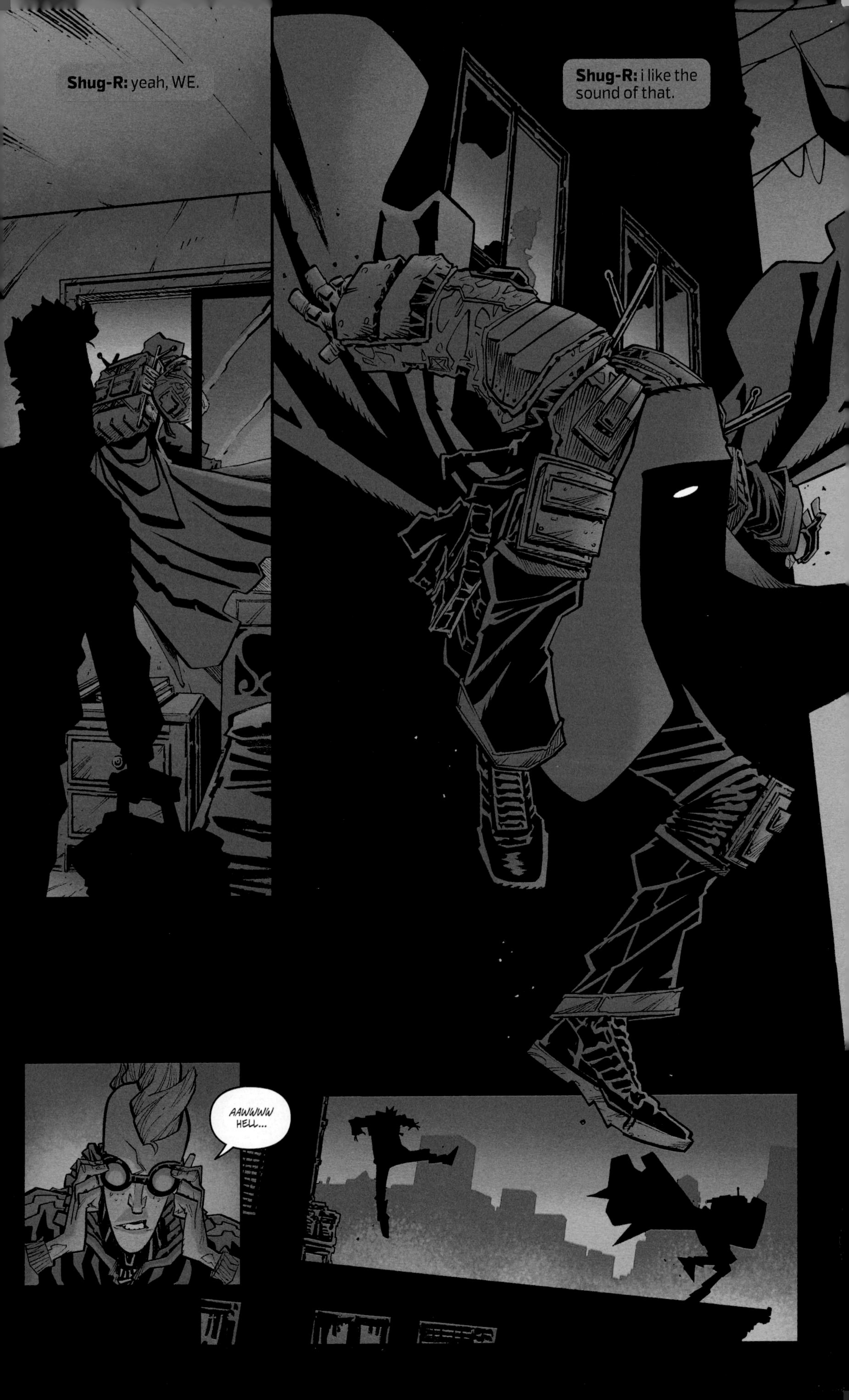
Shug-R: yeah, WE.
Shug-R: i like the sound of that.
AAWWWW HELL...

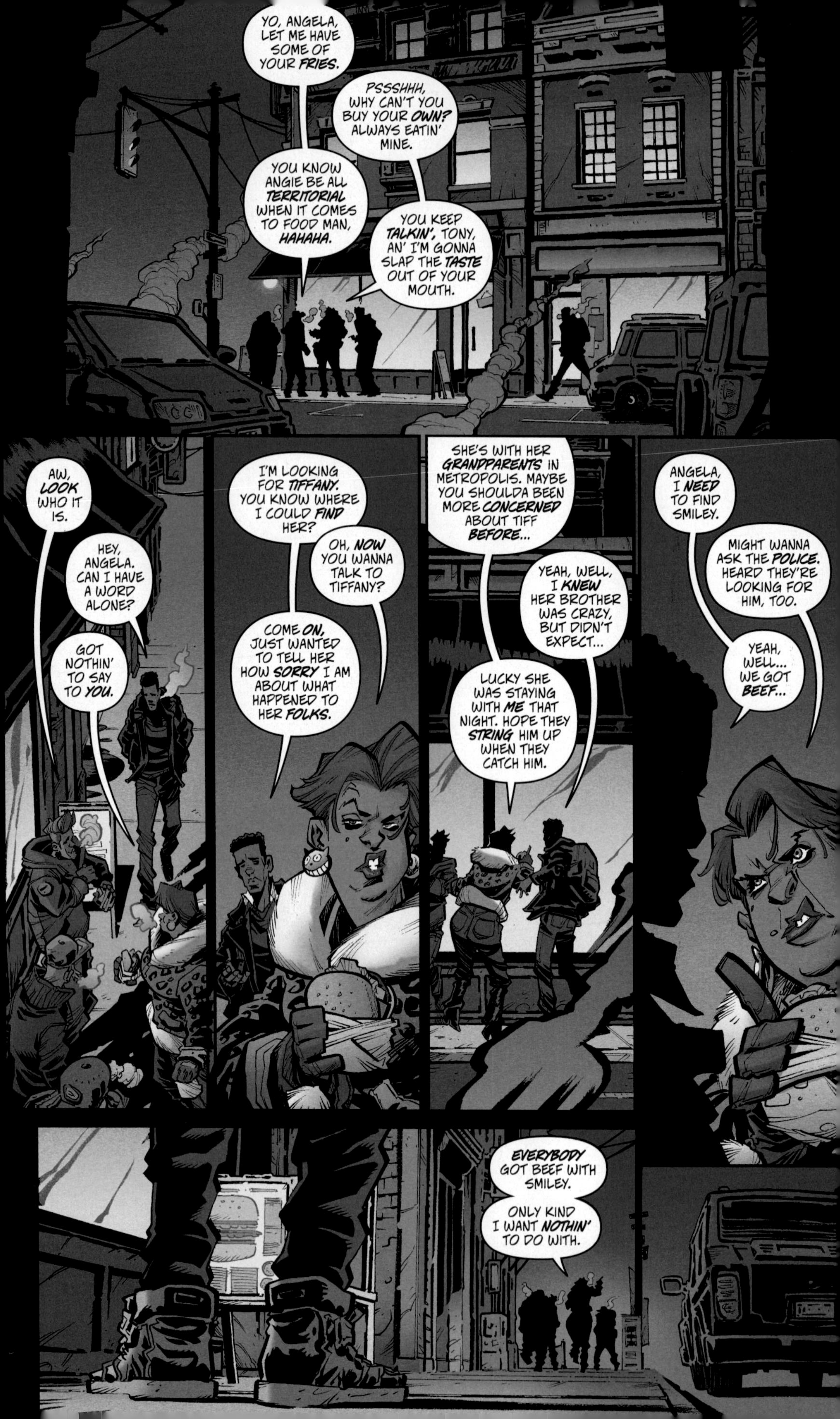
YO, ANGELA, LET ME HAVE SOME OF YOUR FRIES.
PSSSHHH, WHY CAN'T YOU BUY YOUR OWN? ALWAYS EATIN' MINE.
YOU KNOW ANGIE BE ALL TERRITORIAL WHEN IT COMES TO FOOD MAN, HAHAHA.
YOU KEEP TALKIN', TONY, AN' I'M GONNA SLAP THE TASTE OUT OF YOUR MOUTH.
AW, LOOK WHO IT IS.
HEY, ANGELA. CAN I HAVE A WORD ALONE?
GOT NOTHIN' TO SAY TO YOU.
I'M LOOKING FOR TIFFANY. YOU KNOW WHERE I COULD FIND HER?
OH, NOW YOU WANNA TALK TO TIFFANY?
COME ON, JUST WANTED TO TELL HER HOW SORRY I AM ABOUT WHAT HAPPENED TO HER FOLKS.
SHE'S WITH HER GRANDPARENTS IN METROPOLIS. MAYBE YOU SHOULDA BEEN MORE CONCERNED ABOUT TIFF BEFORE...
YEAH, WELL, I KNEW HER BROTHER WAS CRAZY, BUT DIDN'T EXPECT...
LUCKY SHE WAS STAYING WITH ME THAT NIGHT. HOPE THEY STRING HIM UP WHEN THEY CATCH HIM.
ANGELA, I NEED TO FIND SMILEY.
MIGHT WANNA ASK THE POLICE. HEARD THEY'RE LOOKING FOR HIM, TOO.
YEAH, WELL... WE GOT BEEF...
EVERYBODY GOT BEEF WITH SMILEY.
ONLY KIND I WANT NOTHIN' TO DO WITH.

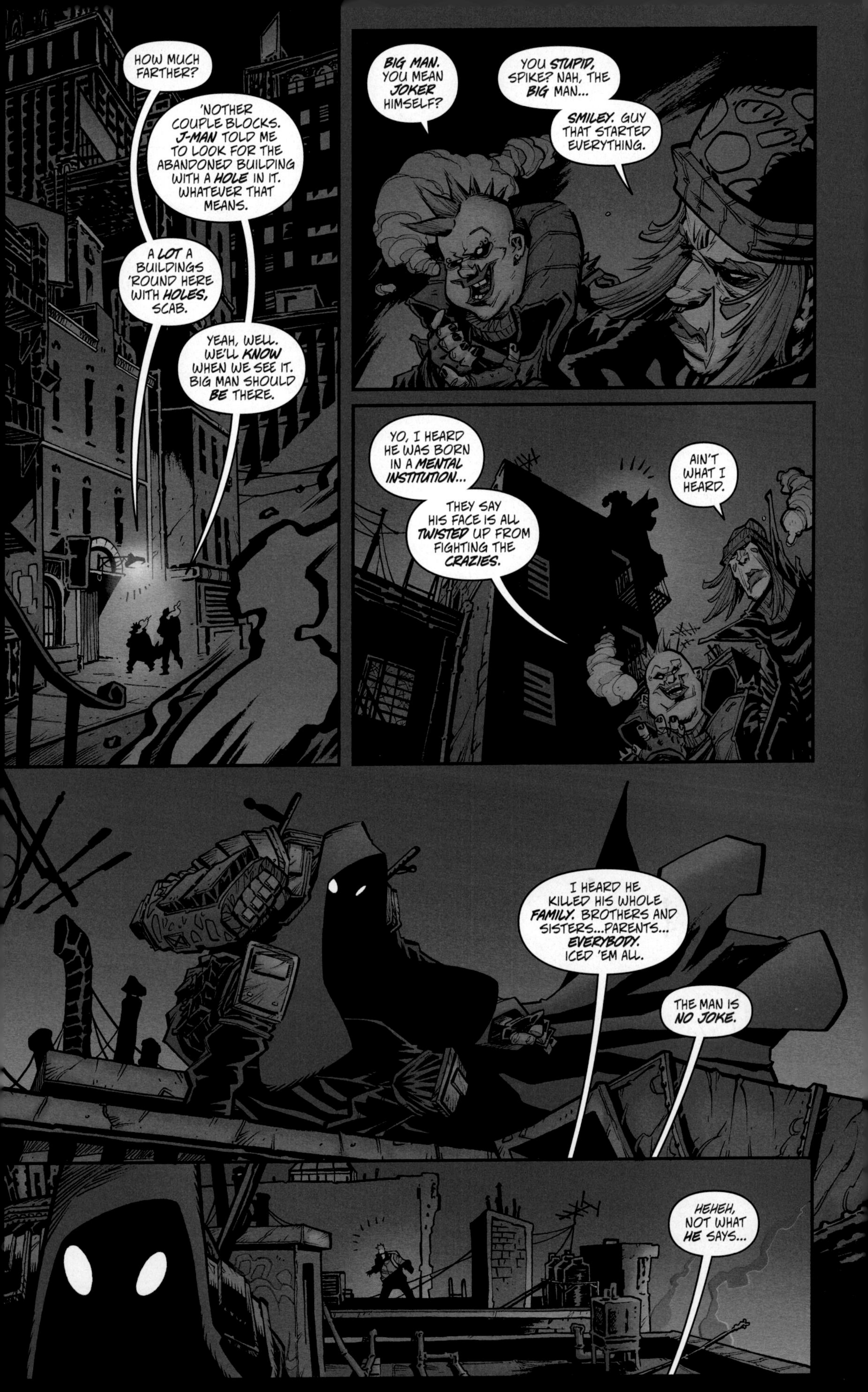
HOW MUCH FARTHER?
'NOTHER COUPLE BLOCKS. J-MAN TOLD ME TO LOOK FOR THE ABANDONED BUILDING WITH A HOLE IN IT. WHATEVER THAT MEANS.
A LOT A BUILDINGS 'ROUND HERE WITH HOLES, SCAB.
YEAH, WELL. WE'LL KNOW WHEN WE SEE IT. BIG MAN SHOULD BE THERE.
BIG MAN. YOU MEAN JOKER HIMSELF?
YOU STUPID, SPIKE? NAH, THE BIG MAN...
SMILEY. GUY THAT STARTED EVERYTHING.
YO, I HEARD HE WAS BORN IN A MENTAL INSTITUTION...
THEY SAY HIS FACE IS ALL TWISTED UP FROM FIGHTING THE CRAZIES.
AIN'T WHAT I HEARD.
I HEARD HE KILLED HIS WHOLE FAMILY. BROTHERS AND SISTERS...PARENTS... EVERYBODY. ICED 'EM ALL.
THE MAN IS NO JOKE.
HEHEH, NOT WHAT HE SAYS...

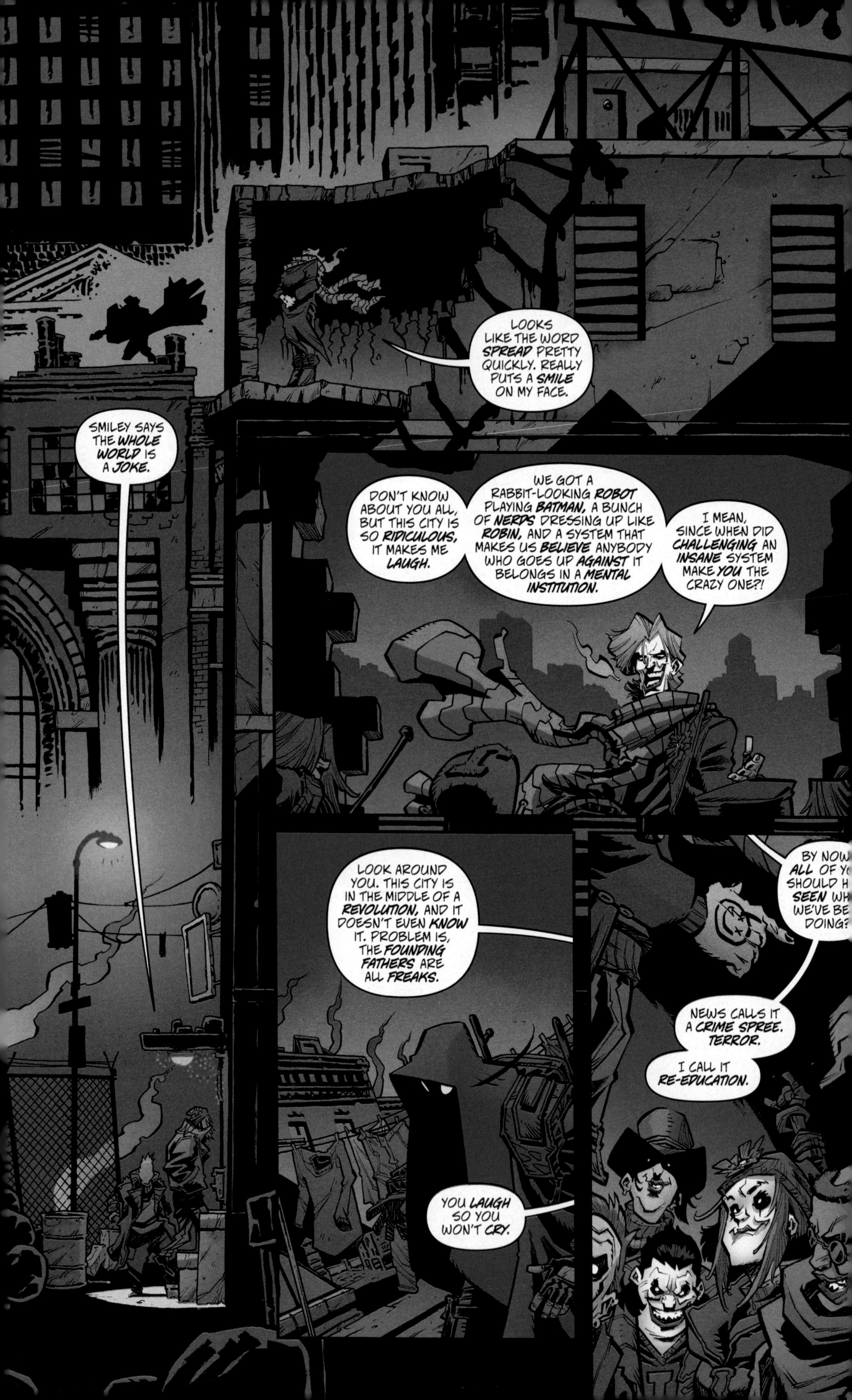
LOOKS LIKE THE WORD SPREAD PRETTY QUICKLY. REALLY PUTS A SMILE ON MY FACE.
SMILEY SAYS THE WHOLE WORLD IS A JOKE.
DON'T KNOW ABOUT YOU ALL, BUT THIS CITY IS SO RIDICULOUS, IT MAKES ME LAUGH.
WE GOT A RABBIT-LOOKING ROBOT PLAYING BATMAN, A BUNCH OF NERDS DRESSING UP LIKE ROBIN, AND A SYSTEM THAT MAKES US BELIEVE ANYBODY WHO GOES UP AGAINST IT BELONGS IN A MENTAL INSTITUTION.
I MEAN, SINCE WHEN DID CHALLENGING AN INSANE SYSTEM MAKE YOU THE CRAZY ONE?!
LOOK AROUND YOU. THIS CITY IS IN THE MIDDLE OF A REVOLUTION, AND IT DOESN'T EVEN KNOW IT. PROBLEM IS, THE FOUNDING FATHERS ARE ALL FREAKS.
BY NOW ALL OF Y SHOULD H SEEN WH WE'VE BE DOING?
NEWS CALLS IT A CRIME SPREE. TERROR.
I CALL IT RE-EDUCATION.
YOU LAUGH SO YOU WON'T CRY.

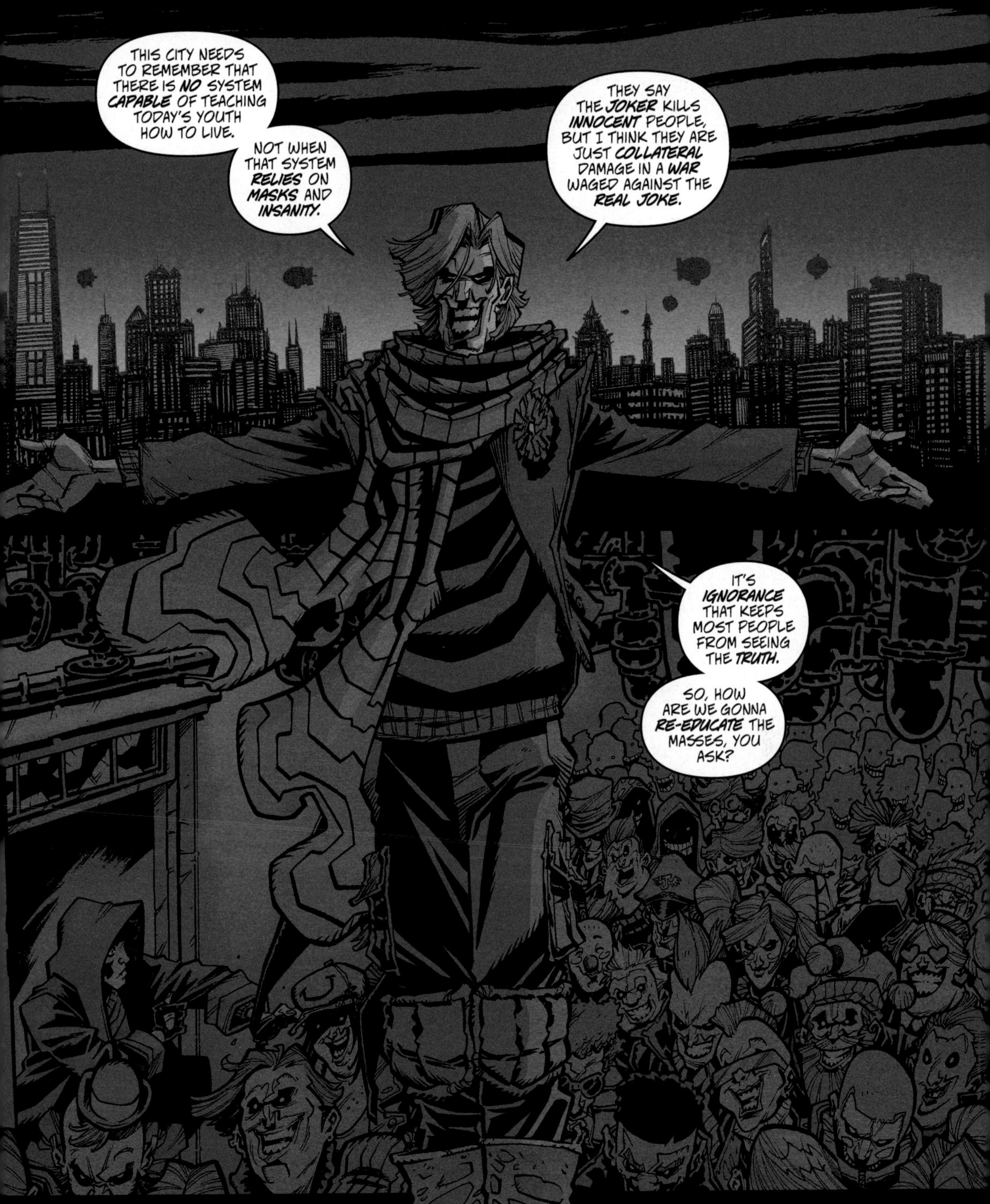
THIS CITY NEEDS TO REMEMBER THAT THERE IS NO SYSTEM CAPABLE OF TEACHING TODAY'S YOUTH HOW TO LIVE.
NOT WHEN THAT SYSTEM RELIES ON MASKS AND INSANITY.
THEY SAY THE JOKER KILLS INNOCENT PEOPLE, BUT I THINK THEY ARE JUST COLLATERAL DAMAGE IN A WAR WAGED AGAINST THE REAL JOKE.
IT'S IGNORANCE THAT KEEPS MOST PEOPLE FROM SEEING THE TRUTH.
SO, HOW ARE WE GONNA RE-EDUCATE THE MASSES, YOU ASK?

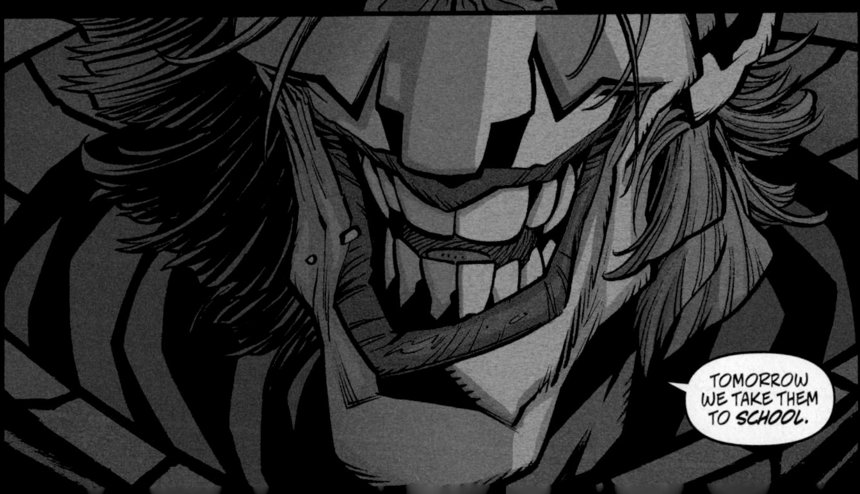
TOMORROW WE TAKE THEM TO SCHOOL.

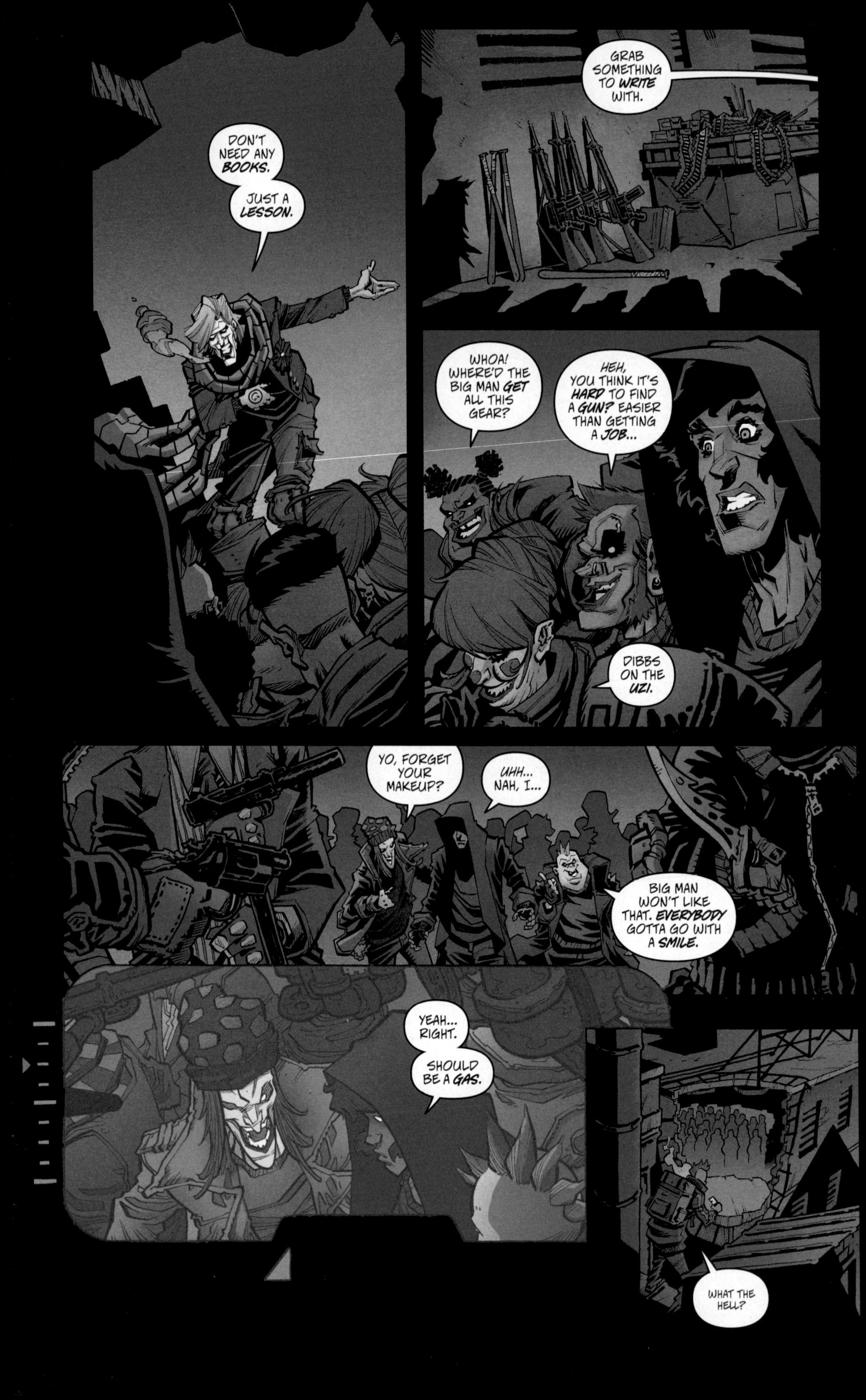
DON'T NEED ANY BOOKS.
JUST A LESSON.
GRAB SOMETHING TO WRITE WITH.
WHOA! WHERE'D THE BIG MAN GET ALL THIS GEAR?
HEH, YOU THINK IT'S HARD TO FIND A GUN? EASIER THAN GETTING A JOB...
DIBBS ON THE UZI.
YO, FORGET YOUR MAKEUP?
UHH... NAH, I...
BIG MAN WON'T LIKE THAT. EVERYBODY GOTTA GO WITH A SMILE.
YEAH... RIGHT.
SHOULD BE A GAS.
WHAT THE HELL?

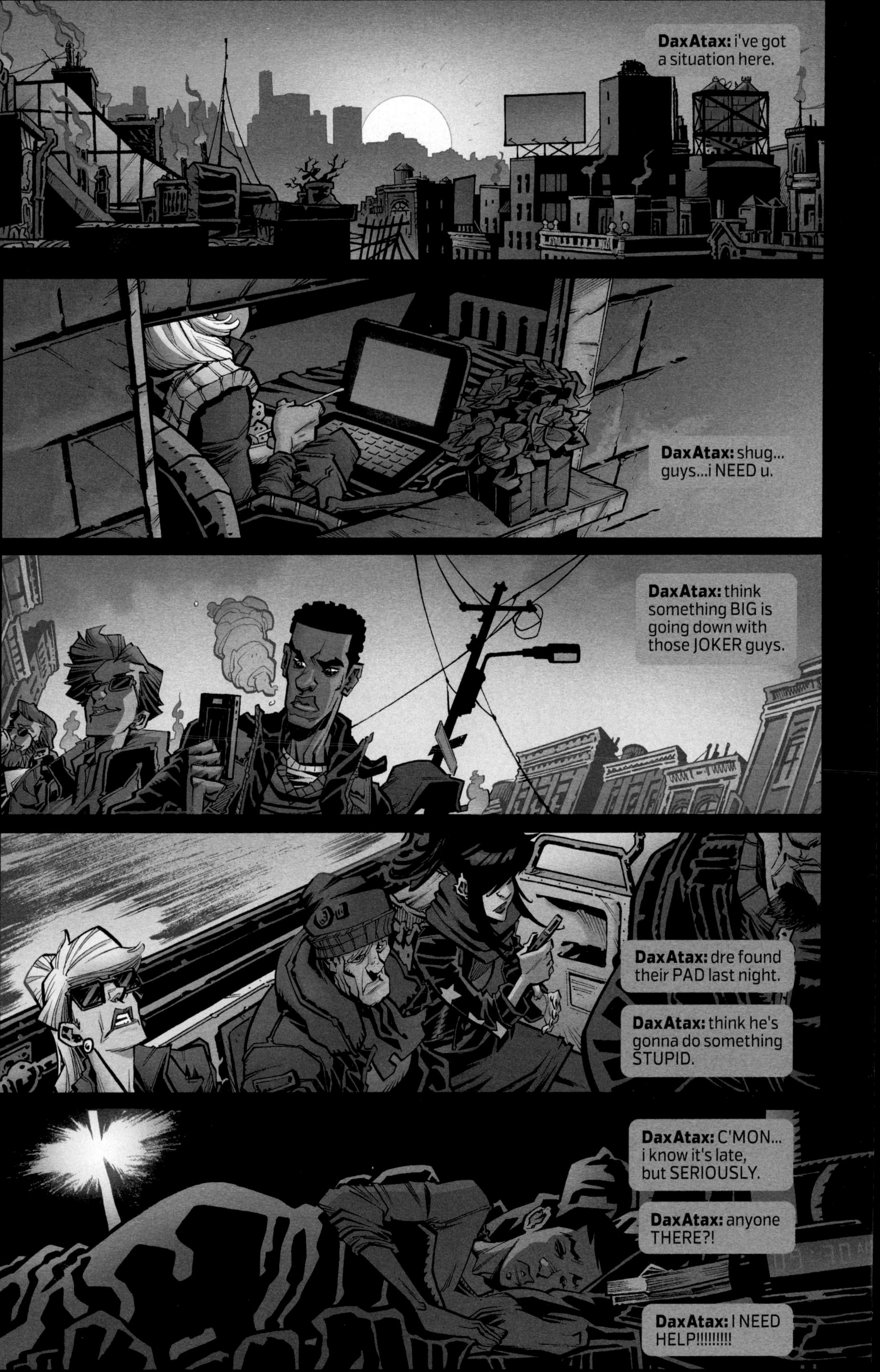

DaxAtax: i've got a situation here.
DaxAtax: shug... guys...i NEED u.
DaxAtax: think something BIG is going down with those JOKER guys.
DaxAtax: dre found their PAD last night.
DaxAtax: think he's gonna do something STUPID.
DaxAtax: C'MON... i know it's late, but SERIOUSLY.
DaxAtax: anyone THERE?!
DaxAtax: I NEED HELP!!!!!!!!!

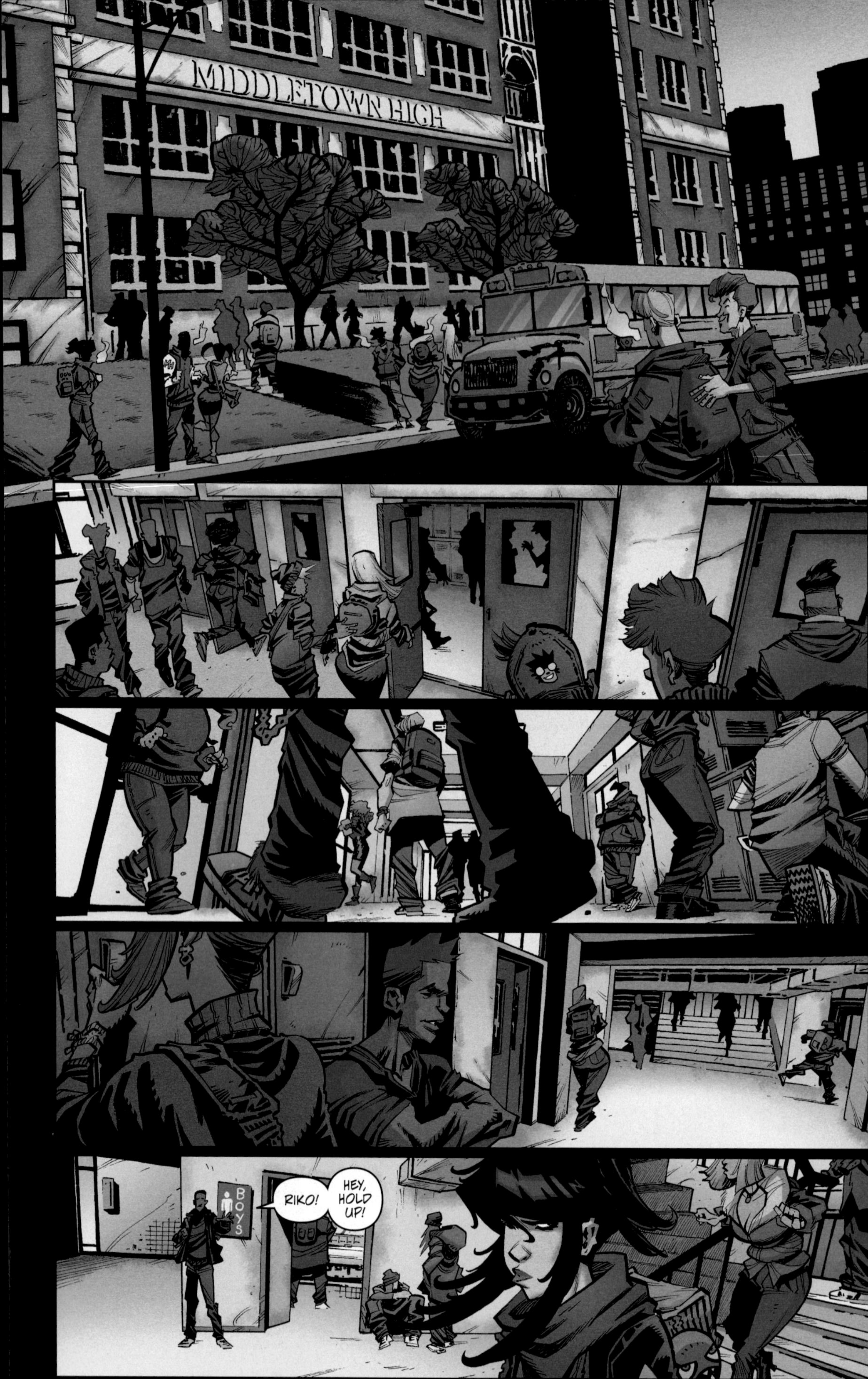
MIDDLETOWN HIGH
BOYS
RIKO!
HEY, HOLD UP!

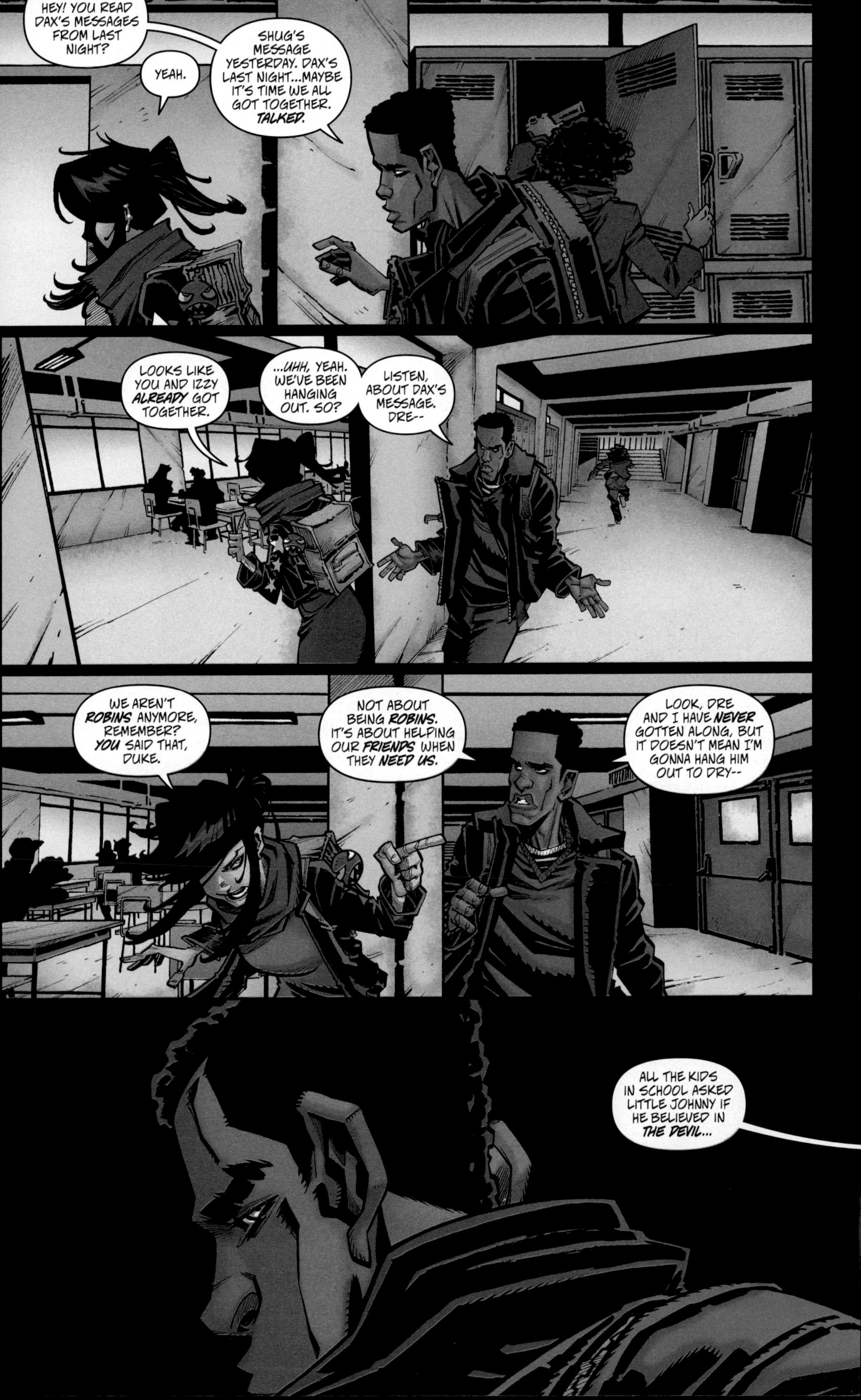
HEY! YOU READ DAX'S MESSAGES FROM LAST NIGHT?
YEAH.
SHUG'S MESSAGE YESTERDAY. DAX'S LAST NIGHT...MAYBE IT'S TIME WE ALL GOT TOGETHER. TALKED.
LOOKS LIKE YOU AND IZZY ALREADY GOT TOGETHER.
...UHH, YEAH. WE'VE BEEN HANGING OUT. SO?
LISTEN, ABOUT DAX'S MESSAGE. DRE--
WE AREN'T ROBINS ANYMORE, REMEMBER? YOU SAID THAT, DUKE.
NOT ABOUT BEING ROBINS. IT'S ABOUT HELPING OUR FRIENDS WHEN THEY NEED US.
LOOK, DRE AND I HAVE NEVER GOTTEN ALONG, BUT IT DOESN'T MEAN I'M GONNA HANG HIM OUT TO DRY--
ALL THE KIDS IN SCHOOL ASKED LITTLE JOHNNY IF HE BELIEVED IN THE DEVIL...

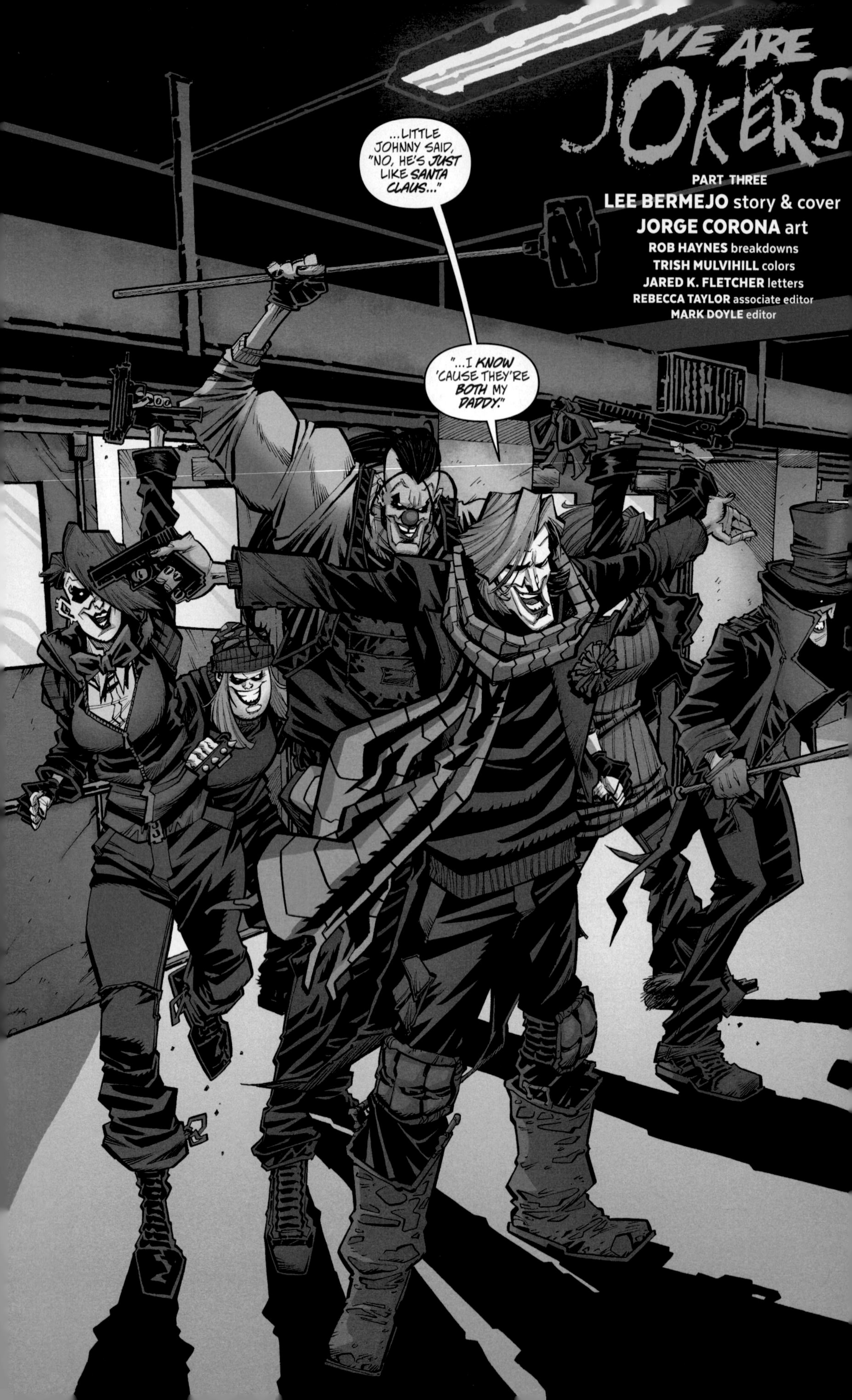
WE ARE JOKERS
PART THREE
LEE BERMEJO story & cover
JORGE CORONA art
ROB HAYNES breakdowns
TRISH MULVIHILL colors
JARED K. FLETCHER letters
REBECCA TAYLOR associate editor
MARK DOYLE editor
...LITTLE JOHNNY SAID, "NO, HE'S JUST LIKE SANTA CLAUS..."
"...I KNOW 'CAUSE THEY'RE BOTH MY DADDY."

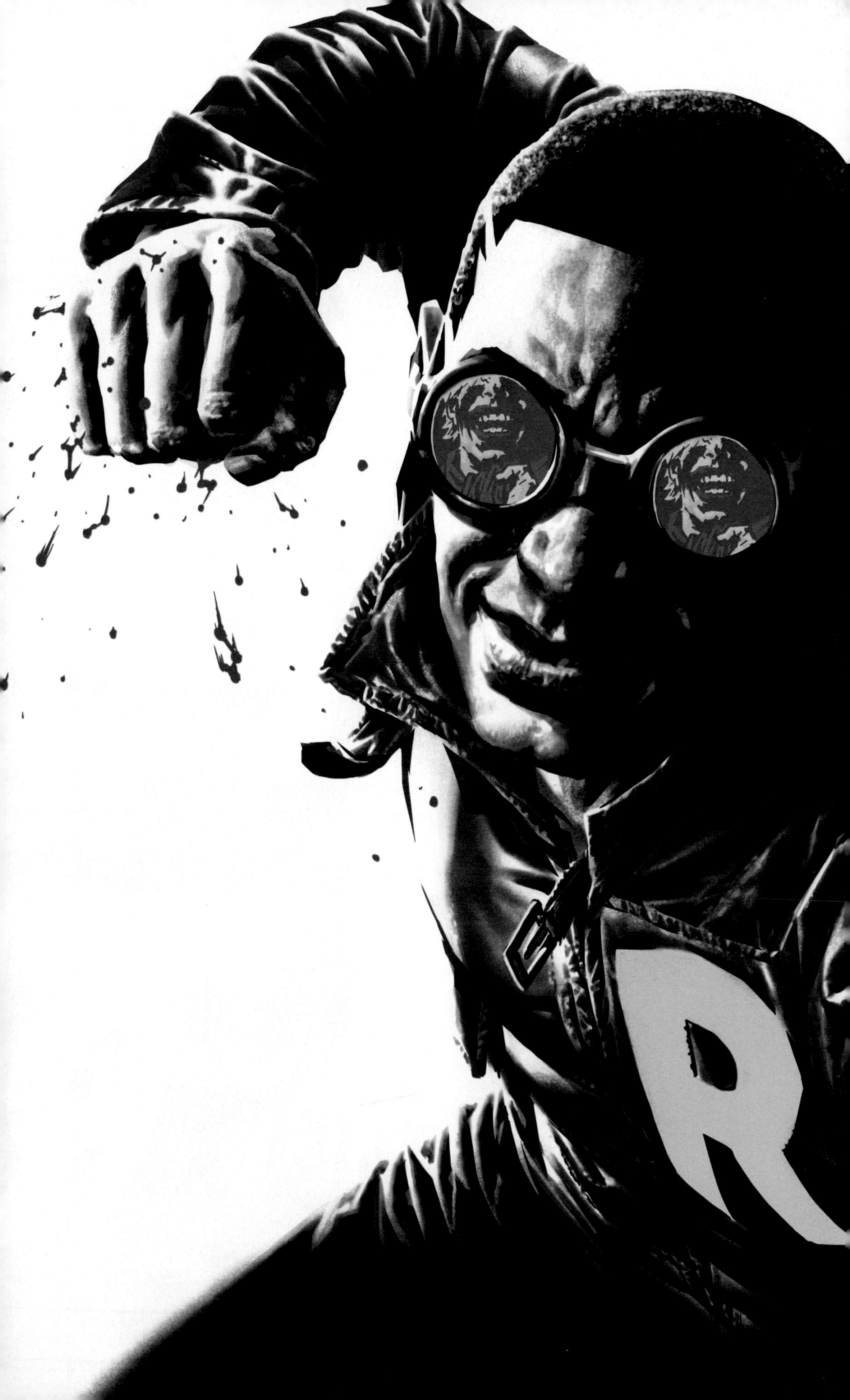

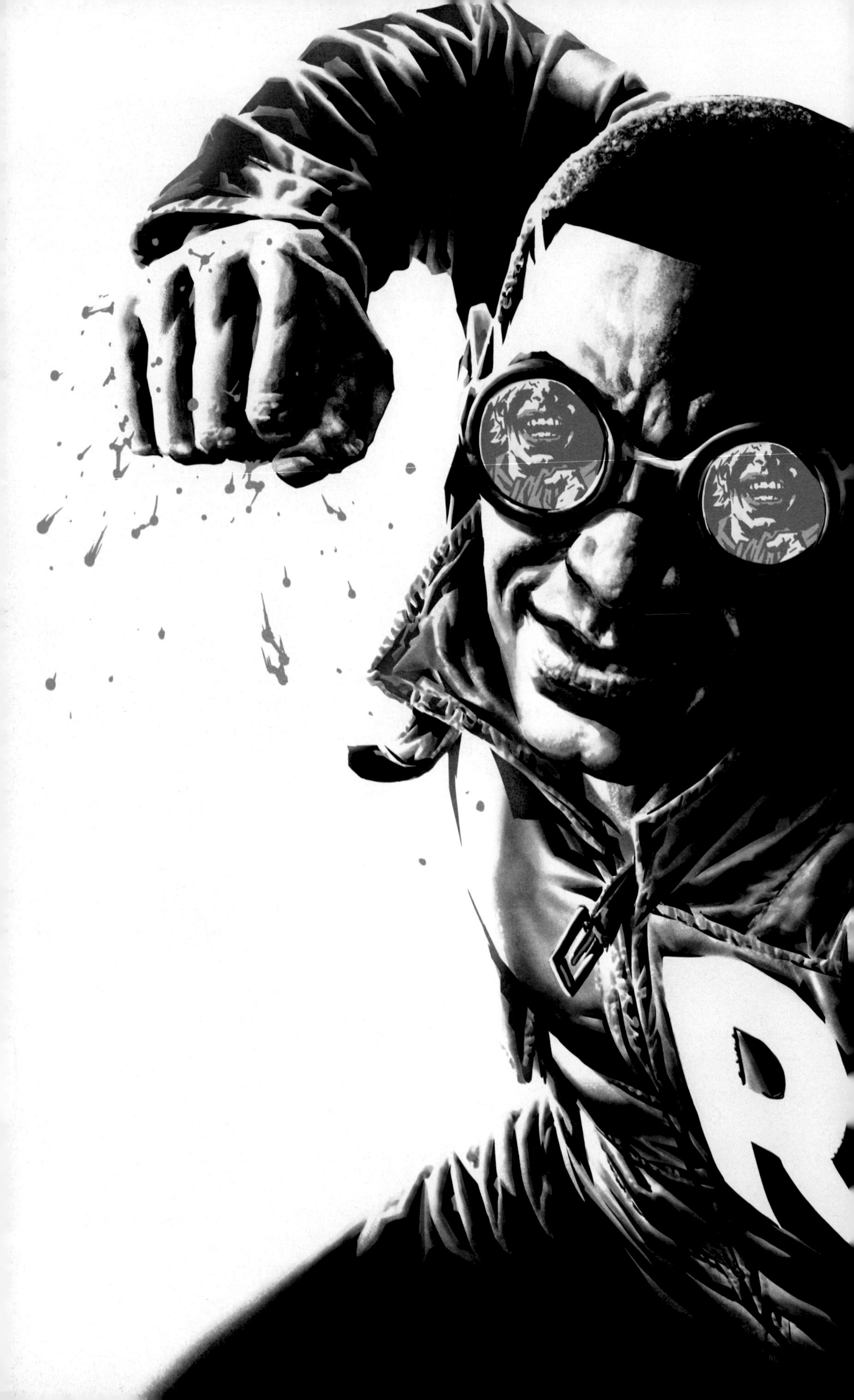

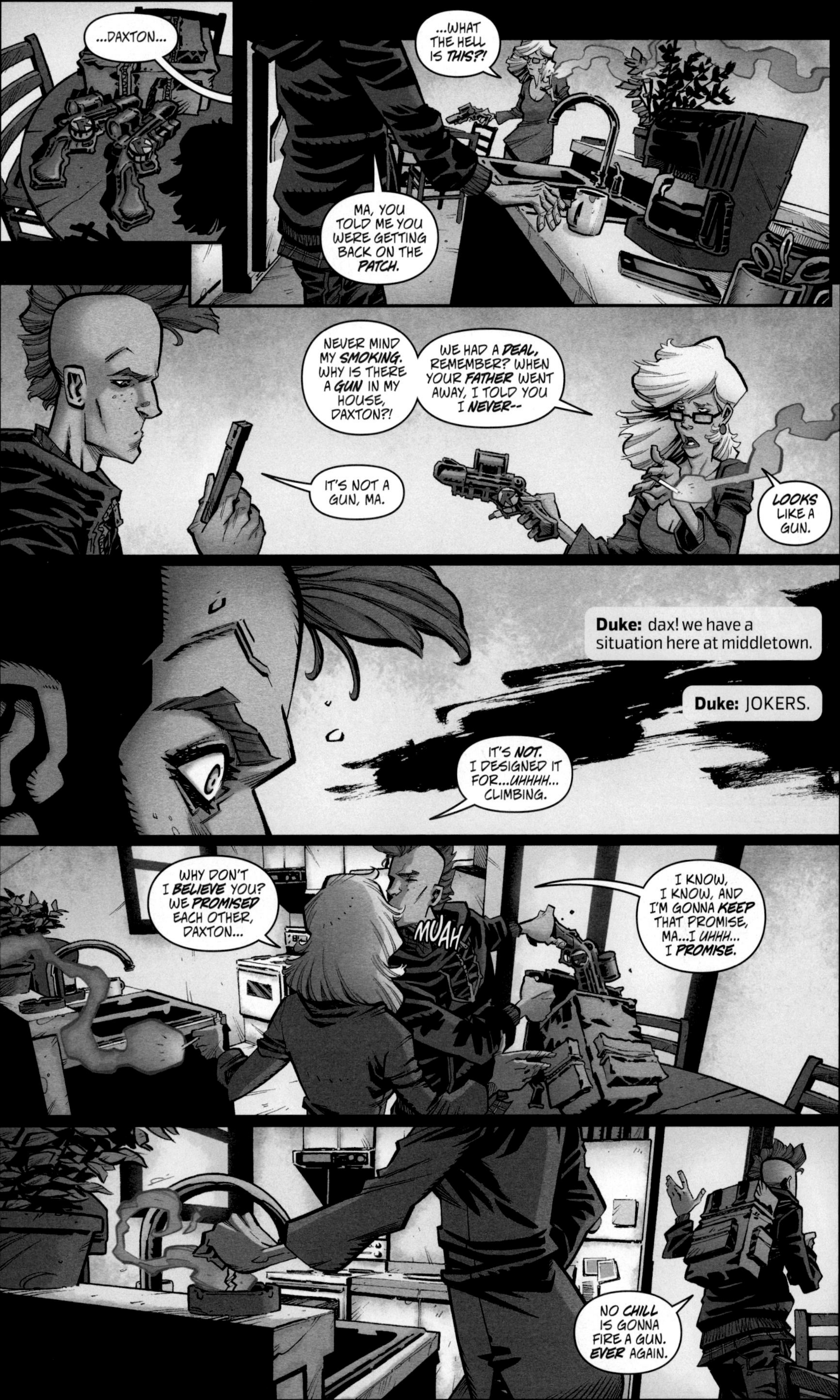
...DAXTON...
...WHAT THE HELL IS THIS?!
MA, YOU TOLD ME YOU WERE GETTING BACK ON THE PATCH.
NEVER MIND MY SMOKING. WHY IS THERE A GUN IN MY HOUSE, DAXTON?!
WE HAD A DEAL, REMEMBER? WHEN YOUR FATHER WENT AWAY, I TOLD YOU I NEVER--
IT'S NOT A GUN, MA.
LOOKS LIKE A GUN.
Duke: dax! we have a situation here at middletown.
Duke: JOKERS.
IT'S NOT. I DESIGNED IT FOR...UHHHH... CLIMBING.
WHY DON'T I BELIEVE YOU? WE PROMISED EACH OTHER, DAXTON...
MUAH
I KNOW, I KNOW, AND I'M GONNA KEEP THAT PROMISE, MA...I UHHH... I PROMISE.
NO CHILL IS GONNA FIRE A GUN. EVER AGAIN.

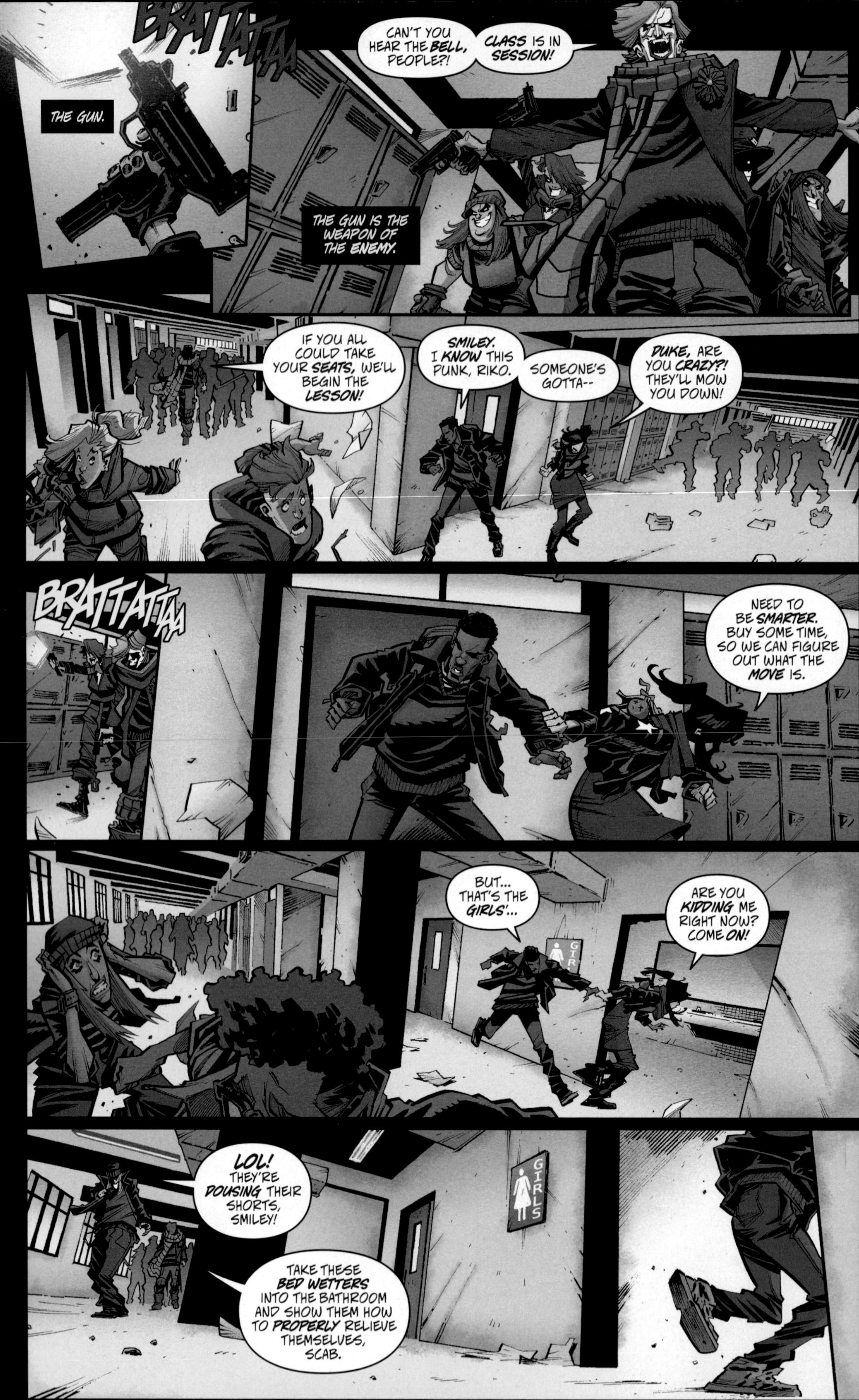
BRATTATTAA
THE GUN.
CAN'T YOU HEAR THE BELL, PEOPLE?!
CLASS IS IN SESSION!
THE GUN IS THE WEAPON OF THE ENEMY.
IF YOU ALL COULD TAKE YOUR SEATS, WE'LL BEGIN THE LESSON!
SMILEY. I KNOW THIS PUNK, RIKO.
SOMEONE'S GOTTA--
DUKE, ARE YOU CRAZY?! THEY'LL MOW YOU DOWN!
BRATTATTAA
NEED TO BE SMARTER. BUY SOME TIME, SO WE CAN FIGURE OUT WHAT THE MOVE IS.
BUT... THAT'S THE GIRLS'...
GIRLS
ARE YOU KIDDING ME RIGHT NOW? COME ON!
LOL! THEY'RE DOUSING THEIR SHORTS, SMILEY!
GIRLS
TAKE THESE BED WETTERS INTO THE BATHROOM AND SHOW THEM HOW TO PROPERLY RELIEVE THEMSELVES, SCAB.

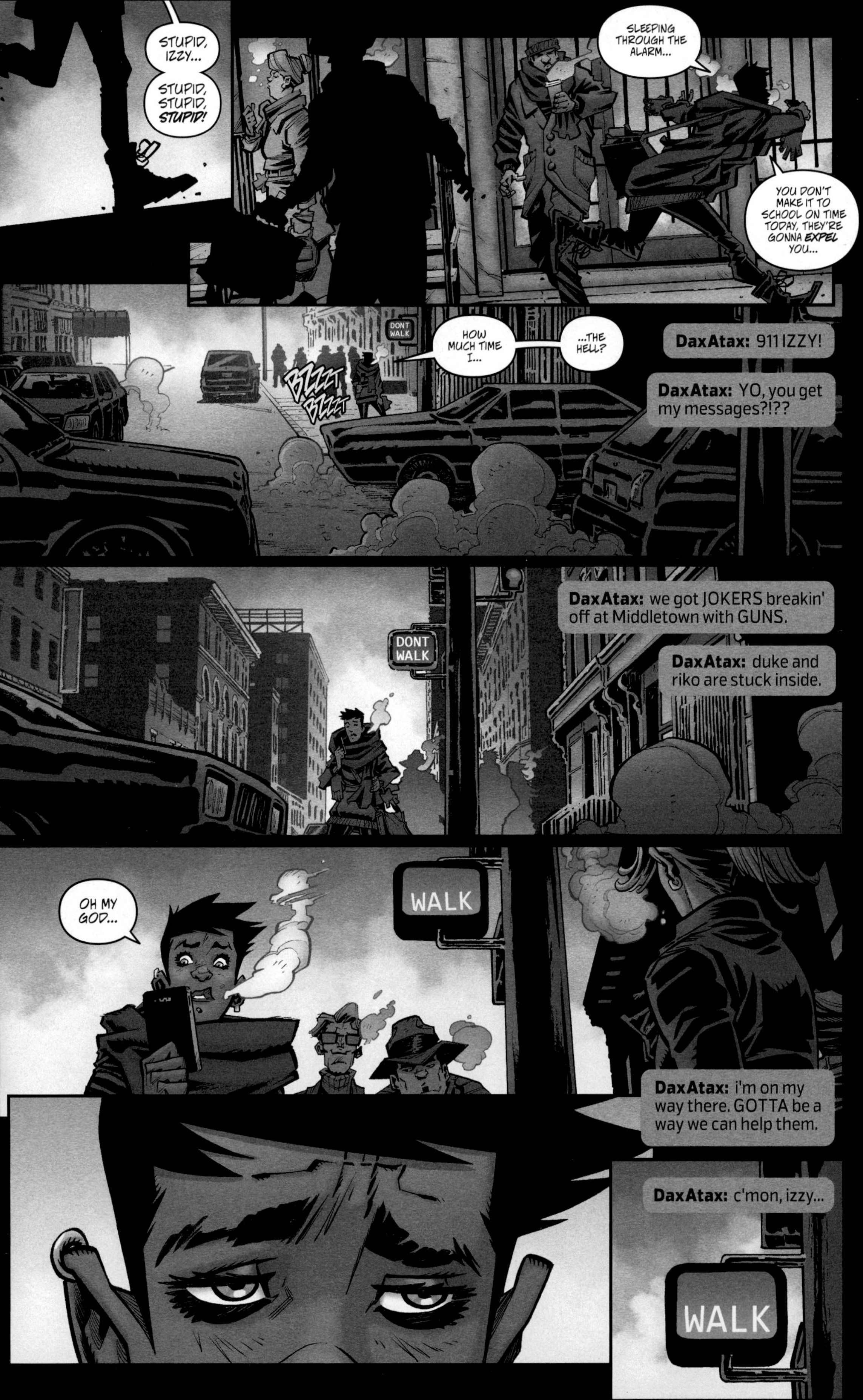
STUPID, IZZY...
STUPID, STUPID, STUPID!
SLEEPING THROUGH THE ALARM...
YOU DON'T MAKE IT TO SCHOOL ON TIME TODAY, THEY'RE GONNA EXPEL YOU...
DONT WALK
BZZZT BZZZT
HOW MUCH TIME I...
...THE HELL?
DaxAtax: 911 IZZY!
DaxAtax: YO, you get my messages?!??
DONT WALK
DaxAtax: we got JOKERS breakin' off at Middletown with GUNS.
DaxAtax: duke and riko are stuck inside.
OH MY GOD...
WALK
DaxAtax: i'm on my way there. GOTTA be a way we can help them.
DaxAtax: c'mon, izzy...
WALK

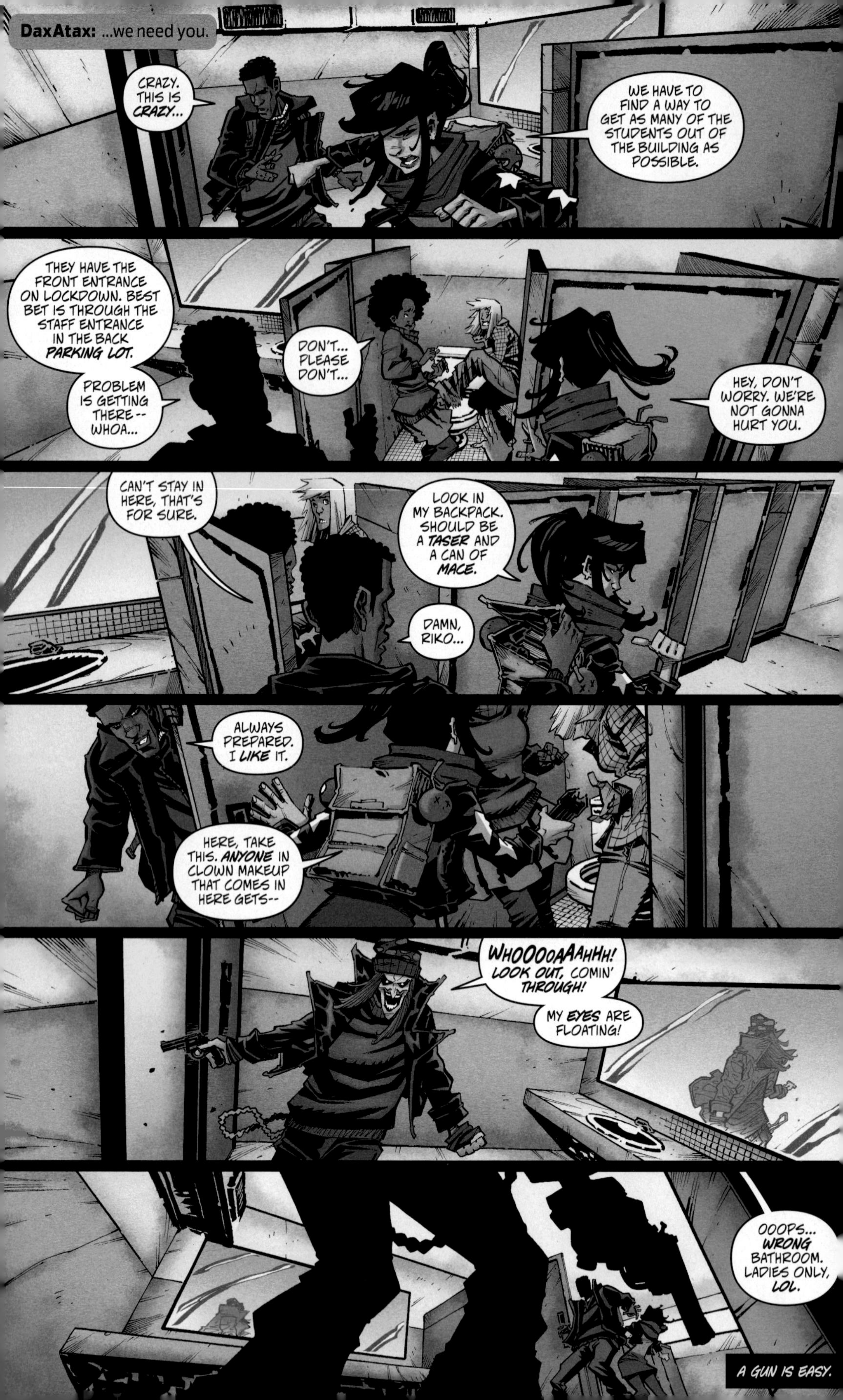
DaxAtax: ...we need you.
CRAZY. THIS IS CRAZY...
WE HAVE TO FIND A WAY TO GET AS MANY OF THE STUDENTS OUT OF THE BUILDING AS POSSIBLE.
THEY HAVE THE FRONT ENTRANCE ON LOCKDOWN. BEST BET IS THROUGH THE STAFF ENTRANCE IN THE BACK PARKING LOT.
PROBLEM IS GETTING THERE-- WHOA...
DON'T... PLEASE DON'T...
HEY, DON'T WORRY. WE'RE NOT GONNA HURT YOU.
CAN'T STAY IN HERE, THAT'S FOR SURE.
LOOK IN MY BACKPACK. SHOULD BE A TASER AND A CAN OF MACE.
DAMN, RIKO...
ALWAYS PREPARED. I LIKE IT.
HERE, TAKE THIS. ANYONE IN CLOWN MAKEUP THAT COMES IN HERE GETS--
WHOOOOAAAHHH! LOOK OUT, COMIN' THROUGH!
MY EYES ARE FLOATING!
OOOPS... WRONG BATHROOM. LADIES ONLY, LOL.
A GUN IS EASY.

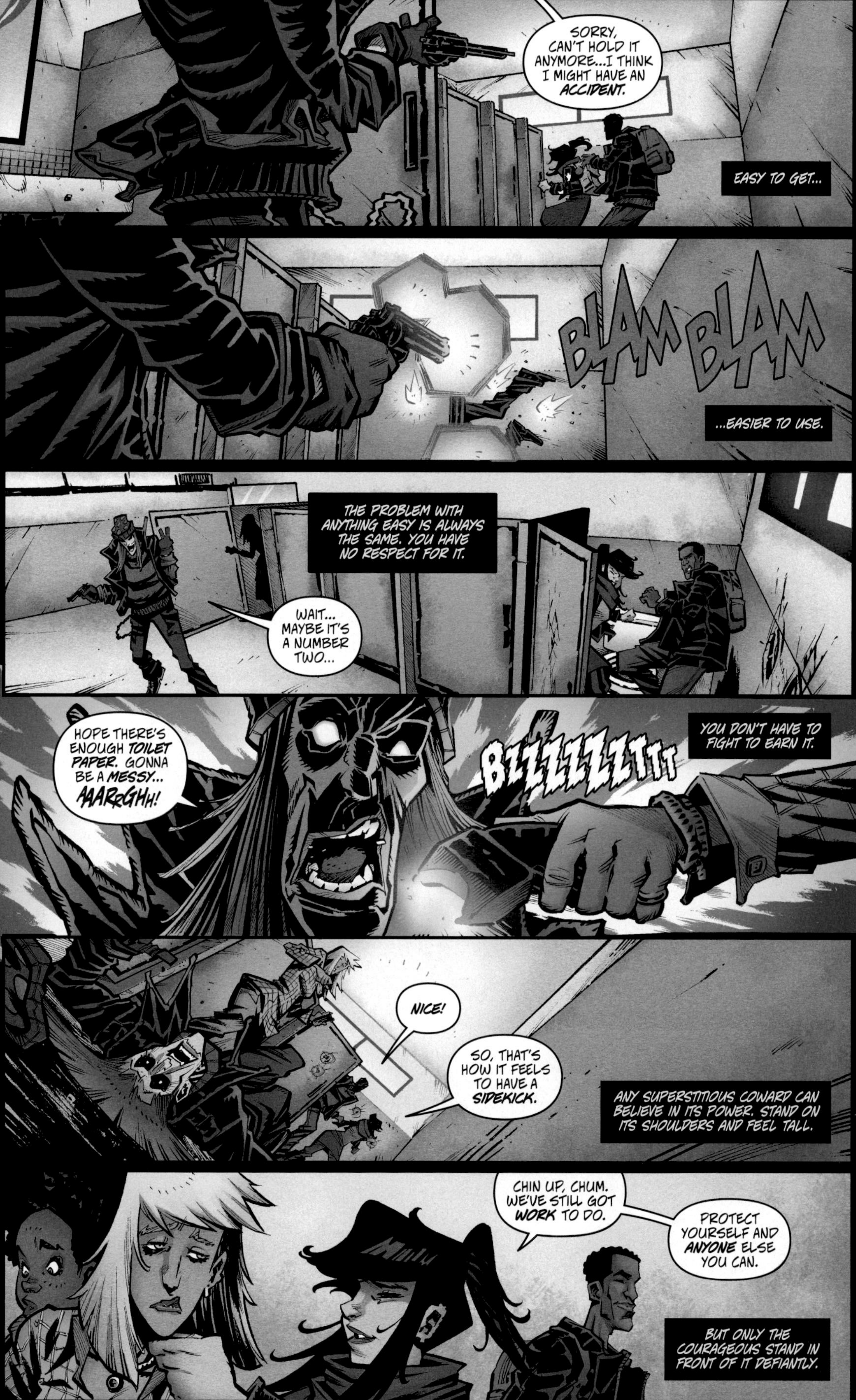
SORRY, CAN'T HOLD IT ANYMORE...I THINK I MIGHT HAVE AN *ACCIDENT.*
EASY TO GET...
BLAM BLAM
...EASIER TO USE.
THE PROBLEM WITH ANYTHING EASY IS ALWAYS THE SAME. YOU HAVE NO RESPECT FOR IT.
WAIT... MAYBE IT'S A NUMBER TWO...
HOPE THERE'S ENOUGH *TOILET PAPER.* GONNA BE A *MESSY*... *AAARRGHH!*
YOU DON'T HAVE TO FIGHT TO EARN IT.
BZZZZZZTTT
NICE!
SO, THAT'S HOW IT FEELS TO HAVE A *SIDEKICK.*
ANY SUPERSTITIOUS COWARD CAN BELIEVE IN ITS POWER. STAND ON ITS SHOULDERS AND FEEL TALL.
CHIN UP, CHUM. WE'VE STILL GOT *WORK* TO DO.
PROTECT YOURSELF AND *ANYONE* ELSE YOU CAN.
BUT ONLY THE COURAGEOUS STAND IN FRONT OF IT DEFIANTLY.

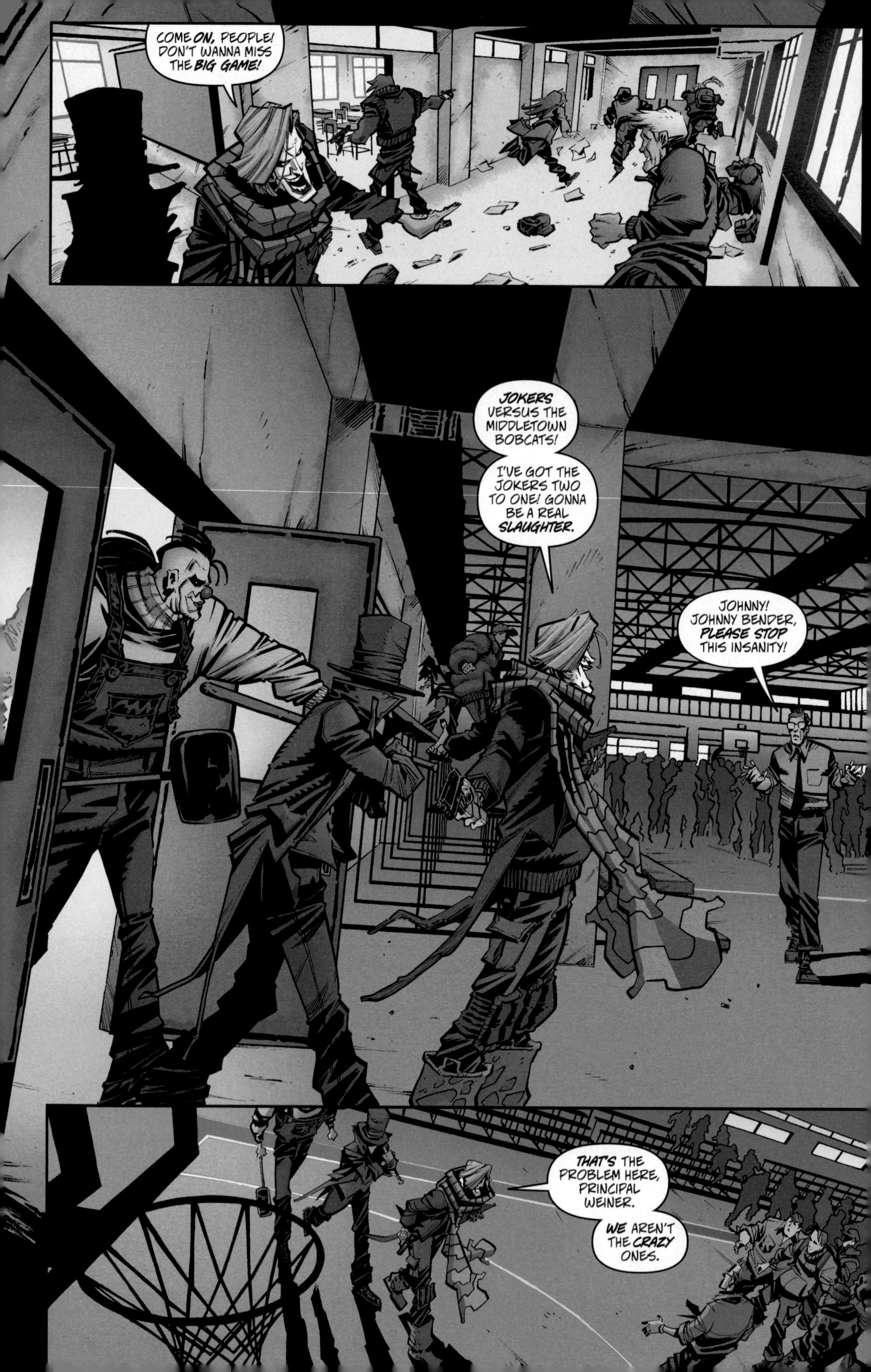

COME ON, PEOPLE! DON'T WANNA MISS THE BIG GAME!
JOKERS VERSUS THE MIDDLETOWN BOBCATS!
I'VE GOT THE JOKERS TWO TO ONE! GONNA BE A REAL SLAUGHTER.
JOHNNY! JOHNNY BENDER, PLEASE STOP THIS INSANITY!
THAT'S THE PROBLEM HERE, PRINCIPAL WEINER.
WE AREN'T THE CRAZY ONES.

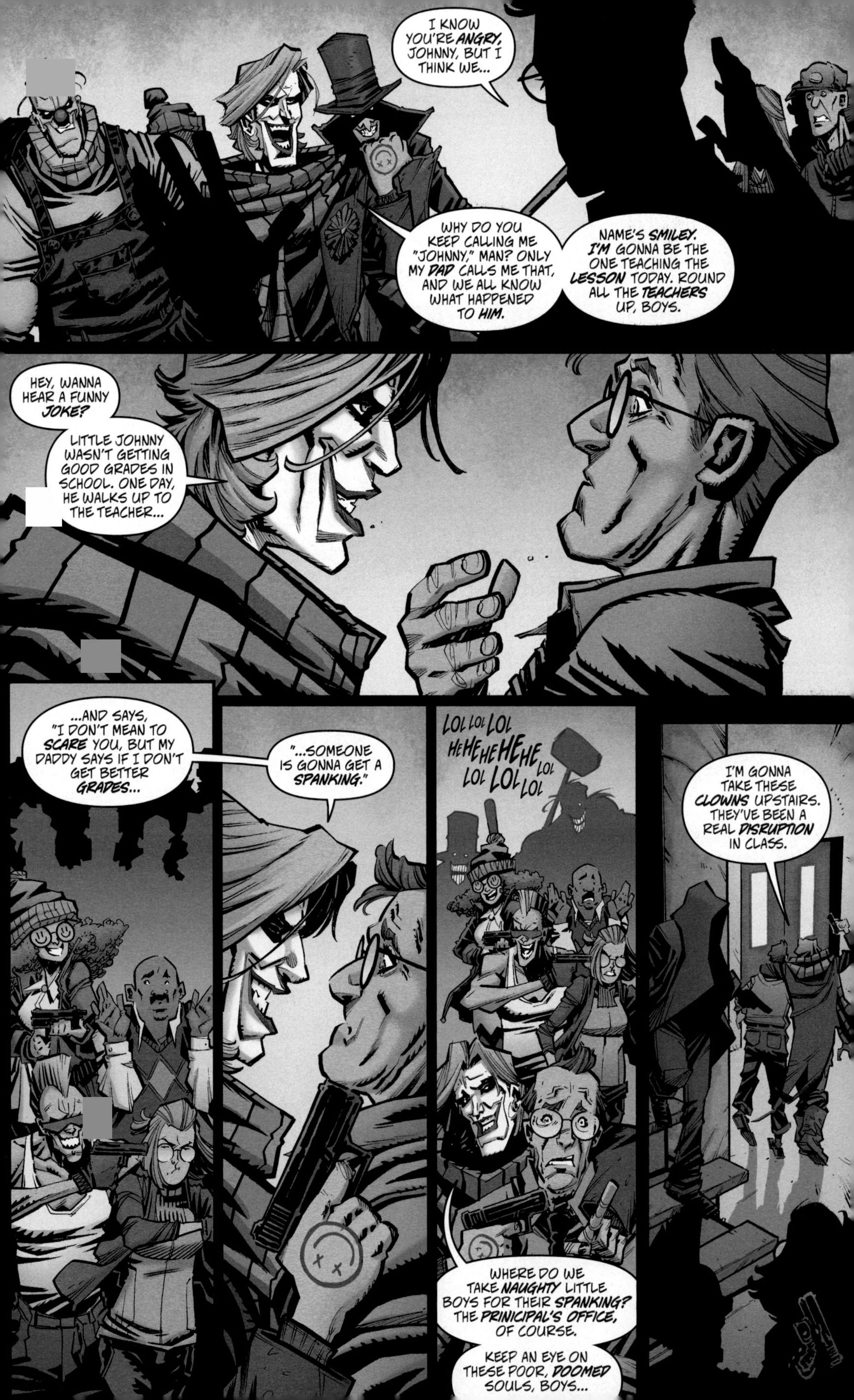
I KNOW YOU'RE ANGRY, JOHNNY, BUT I THINK WE...
WHY DO YOU KEEP CALLING ME "JOHNNY," MAN? ONLY MY DAD CALLS ME THAT, AND WE ALL KNOW WHAT HAPPENED TO HIM.
NAME'S SMILEY. I'M GONNA BE THE ONE TEACHING THE LESSON TODAY. ROUND ALL THE TEACHERS UP, BOYS.
HEY, WANNA HEAR A FUNNY JOKE?
LITTLE JOHNNY WASN'T GETTING GOOD GRADES IN SCHOOL. ONE DAY, HE WALKS UP TO THE TEACHER...
...AND SAYS, "I DON'T MEAN TO SCARE YOU, BUT MY DADDY SAYS IF I DON'T GET BETTER GRADES...
"...SOMEONE IS GONNA GET A SPANKING."
LOL LOL LOL HEHEHEHEHE LOL LOL LOL LOL
WHERE DO WE TAKE NAUGHTY LITTLE BOYS FOR THEIR SPANKING? THE PRINICIPAL'S OFFICE, OF COURSE.
KEEP AN EYE ON THESE POOR, DOOMED SOULS, BOYS...
I'M GONNA TAKE THESE CLOWNS UPSTAIRS. THEY'VE BEEN A REAL DISRUPTION IN CLASS.

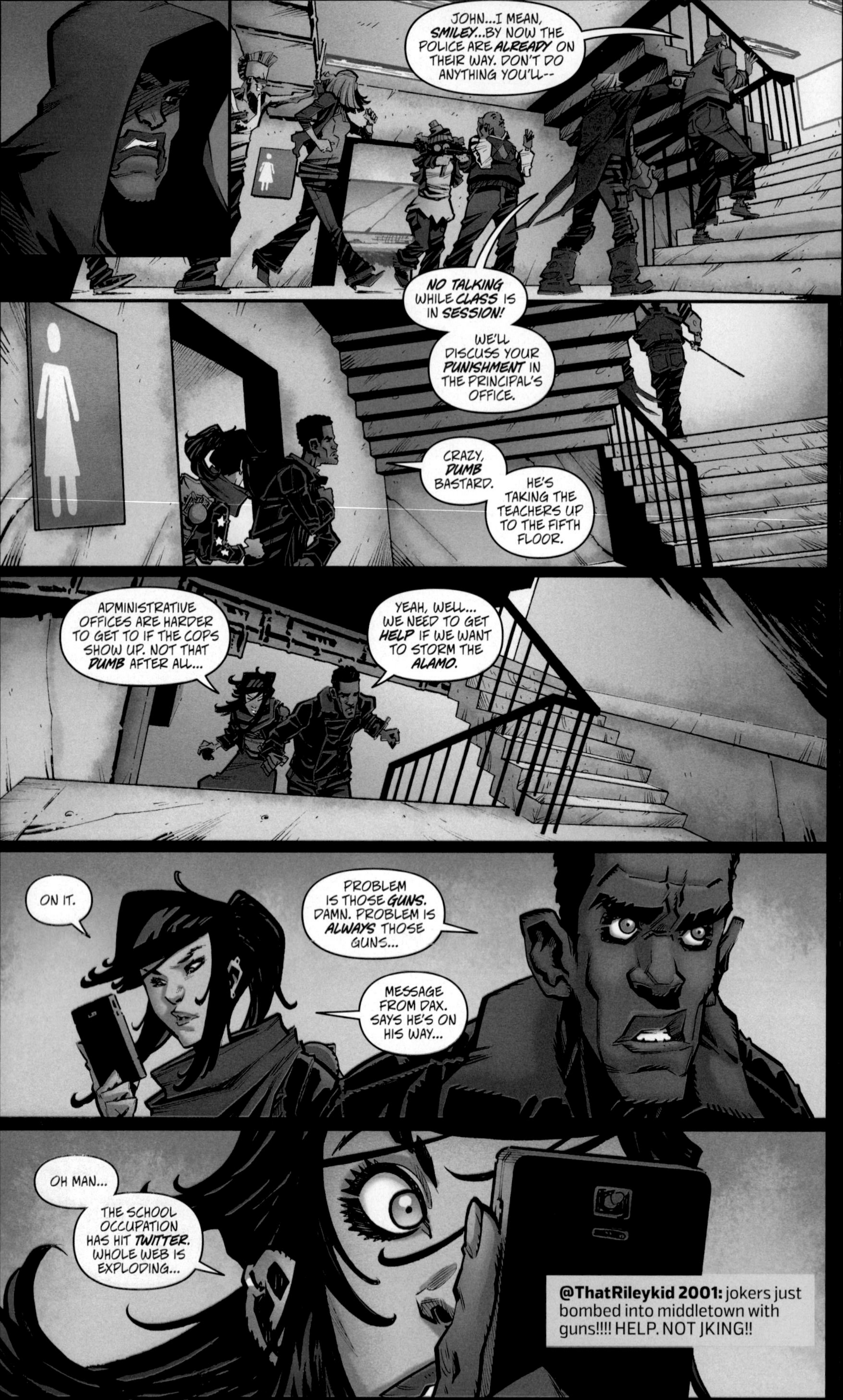

JOHN...I MEAN, SMILEY...BY NOW THE POLICE ARE ALREADY ON THEIR WAY. DON'T DO ANYTHING YOU'LL--
NO TALKING WHILE CLASS IS IN SESSION!
WE'LL DISCUSS YOUR PUNISHMENT IN THE PRINCIPAL'S OFFICE.
CRAZY, DUMB BASTARD.
HE'S TAKING THE TEACHERS UP TO THE FIFTH FLOOR.
ADMINISTRATIVE OFFICES ARE HARDER TO GET TO IF THE COPS SHOW UP. NOT THAT DUMB AFTER ALL...
YEAH, WELL... WE NEED TO GET HELP IF WE WANT TO STORM THE ALAMO.
ON IT.
PROBLEM IS THOSE GUNS. DAMN. PROBLEM IS ALWAYS THOSE GUNS...
MESSAGE FROM DAX. SAYS HE'S ON HIS WAY...
OH MAN...
THE SCHOOL OCCUPATION HAS HIT TWITTER. WHOLE WEB IS EXPLODING...
@ThatRileykid 2001: jokers just bombed into middletown with guns!!!! HELP. NOT JKING!!

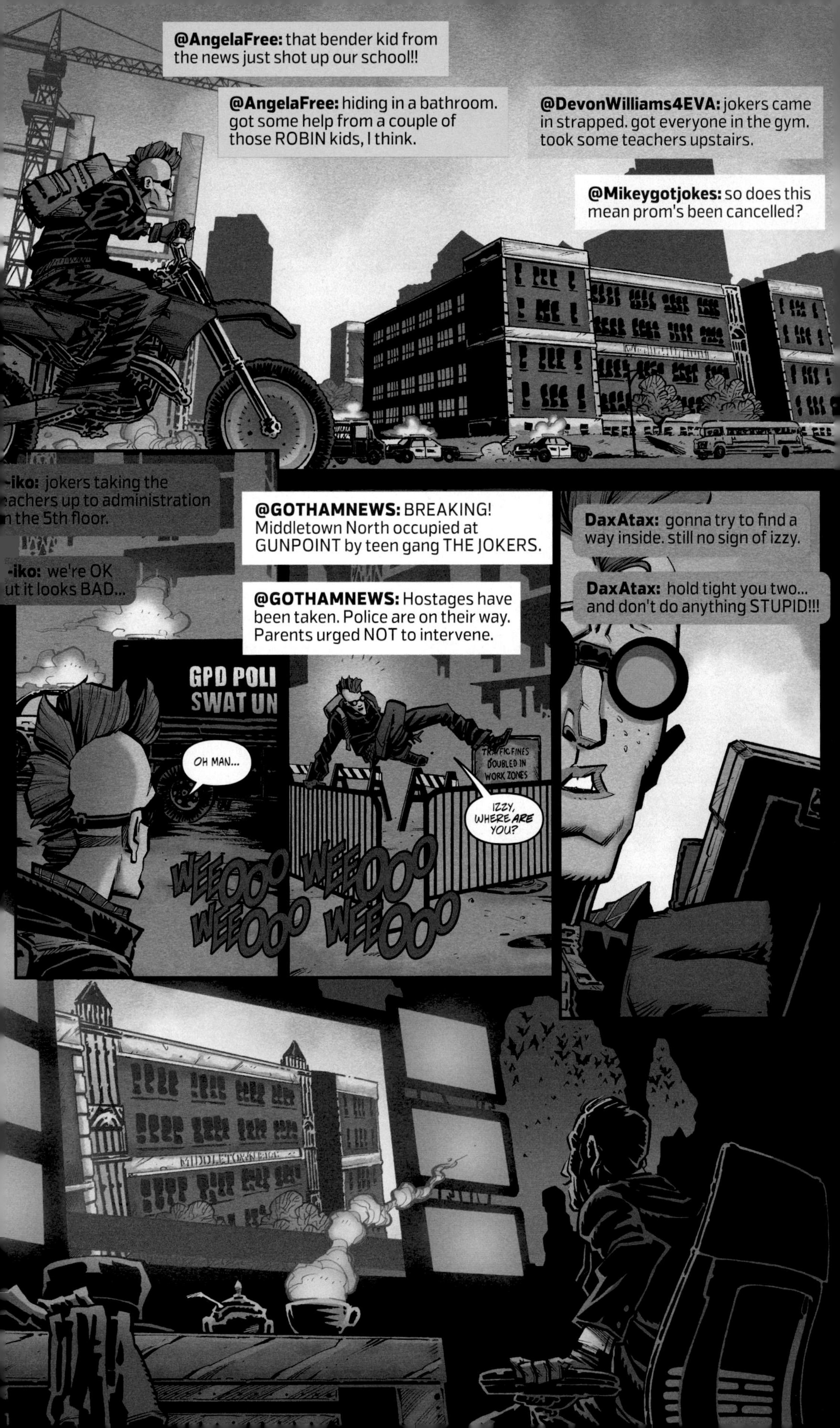

@AngelaFree: that bender kid from the news just shot up our school!!
@AngelaFree: hiding in a bathroom. got some help from a couple of those ROBIN kids, I think.
@DevonWilliams4EVA: jokers came in strapped. got everyone in the gym. took some teachers upstairs.
@Mikeygotjokes: so does this mean prom's been cancelled?
-iko: jokers taking the achers up to administration n the 5th floor.
-iko: we're OK ut it looks BAD...
GPD POLI
SWAT UN
OH MAN...
WEEOOO WEEOOO
WEEOOO WEEOOO
@GOTHAMNEWS: BREAKING! Middletown North occupied at GUNPOINT by teen gang THE JOKERS.
@GOTHAMNEWS: Hostages have been taken. Police are on their way. Parents urged NOT to intervene.
TRAFFIC FINES DOUBLED IN WORK ZONES
IZZY, WHERE ARE YOU?
DaxAtax: gonna try to find a way inside. still no sign of izzy.
DaxAtax: hold tight you two... and don't do anything STUPID!!!
MIDDLETOWN HIGH

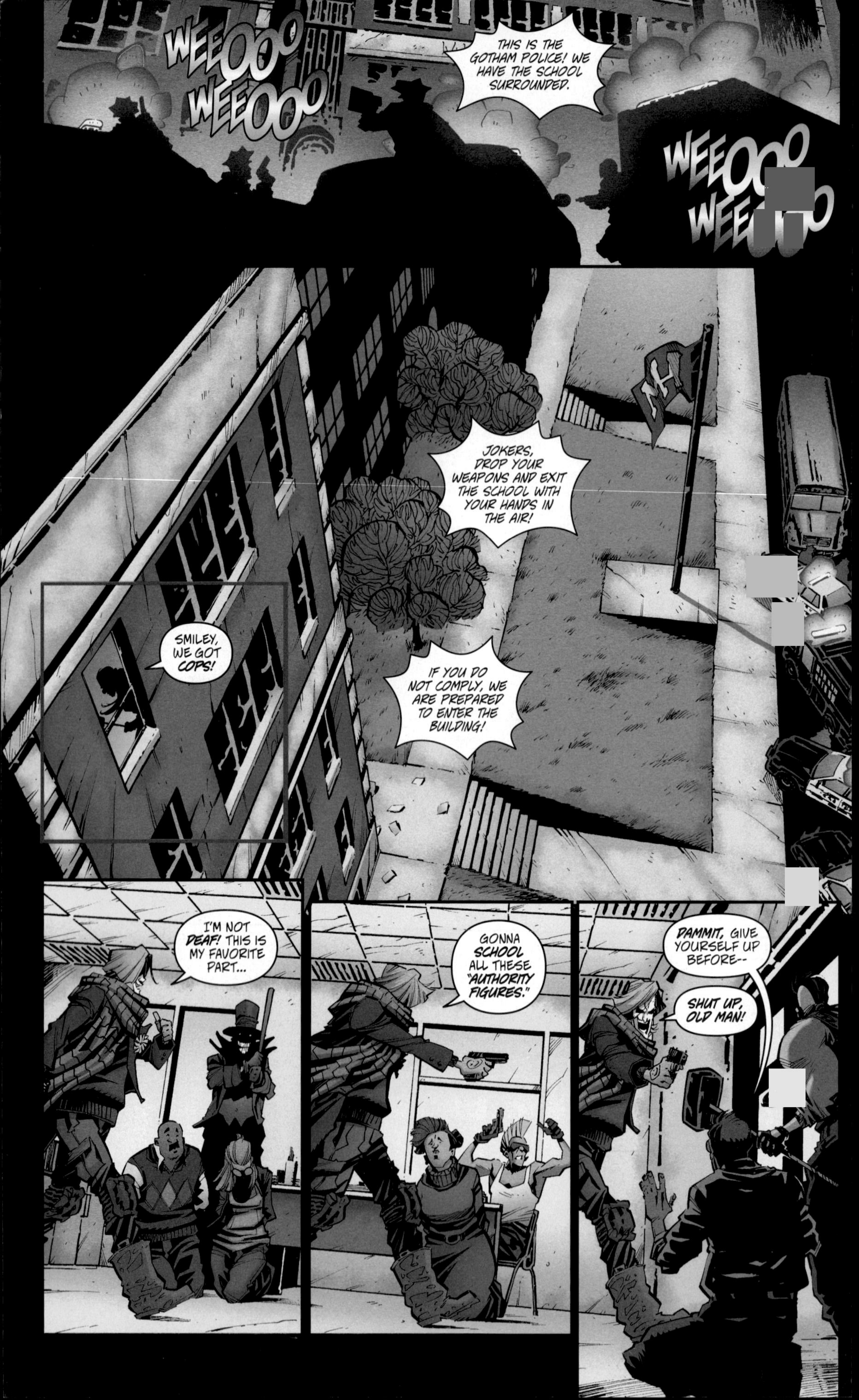

WEEOOO
WEEOOO
THIS IS THE GOTHAM POLICE! WE HAVE THE SCHOOL SURROUNDED.
JOKERS, DROP YOUR WEAPONS AND EXIT THE SCHOOL WITH YOUR HANDS IN THE AIR!
SMILEY, WE GOT COPS!
IF YOU DO NOT COMPLY, WE ARE PREPARED TO ENTER THE BUILDING!
I'M NOT DEAF! THIS IS MY FAVORITE PART...
GONNA SCHOOL ALL THESE "AUTHORITY FIGURES."
DAMMIT, GIVE YOURSELF UP BEFORE--
SHUT UP, OLD MAN!

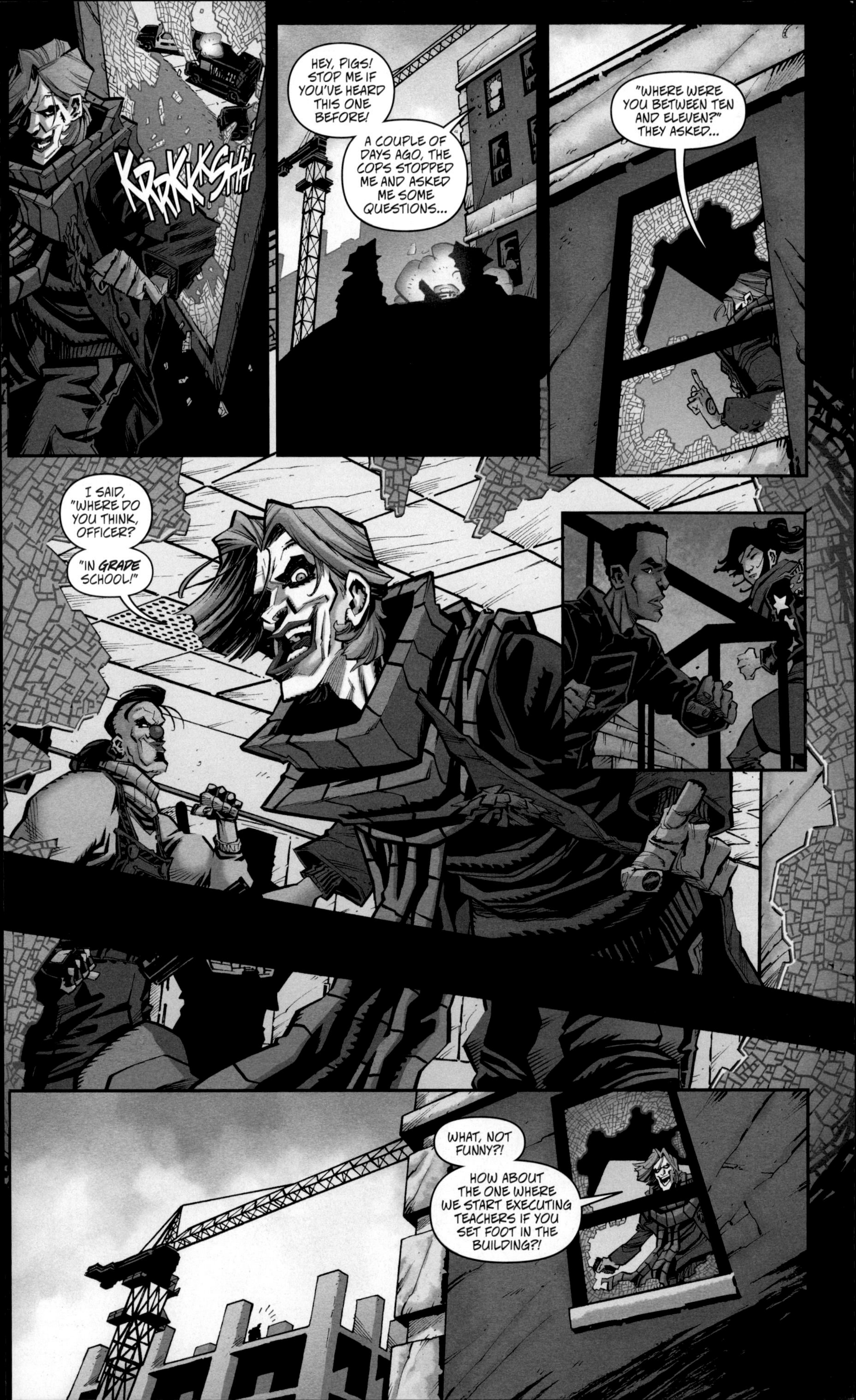
KRKKKSHH
HEY, PIGS! STOP ME IF YOU'VE HEARD THIS ONE BEFORE!
A COUPLE OF DAYS AGO, THE COPS STOPPED ME AND ASKED ME SOME QUESTIONS...
"WHERE WERE YOU BETWEEN TEN AND ELEVEN?" THEY ASKED...
I SAID, "WHERE DO YOU THINK, OFFICER?
"IN GRADE SCHOOL!"
WHAT, NOT FUNNY?!
HOW ABOUT THE ONE WHERE WE START EXECUTING TEACHERS IF YOU SET FOOT IN THE BUILDING?!

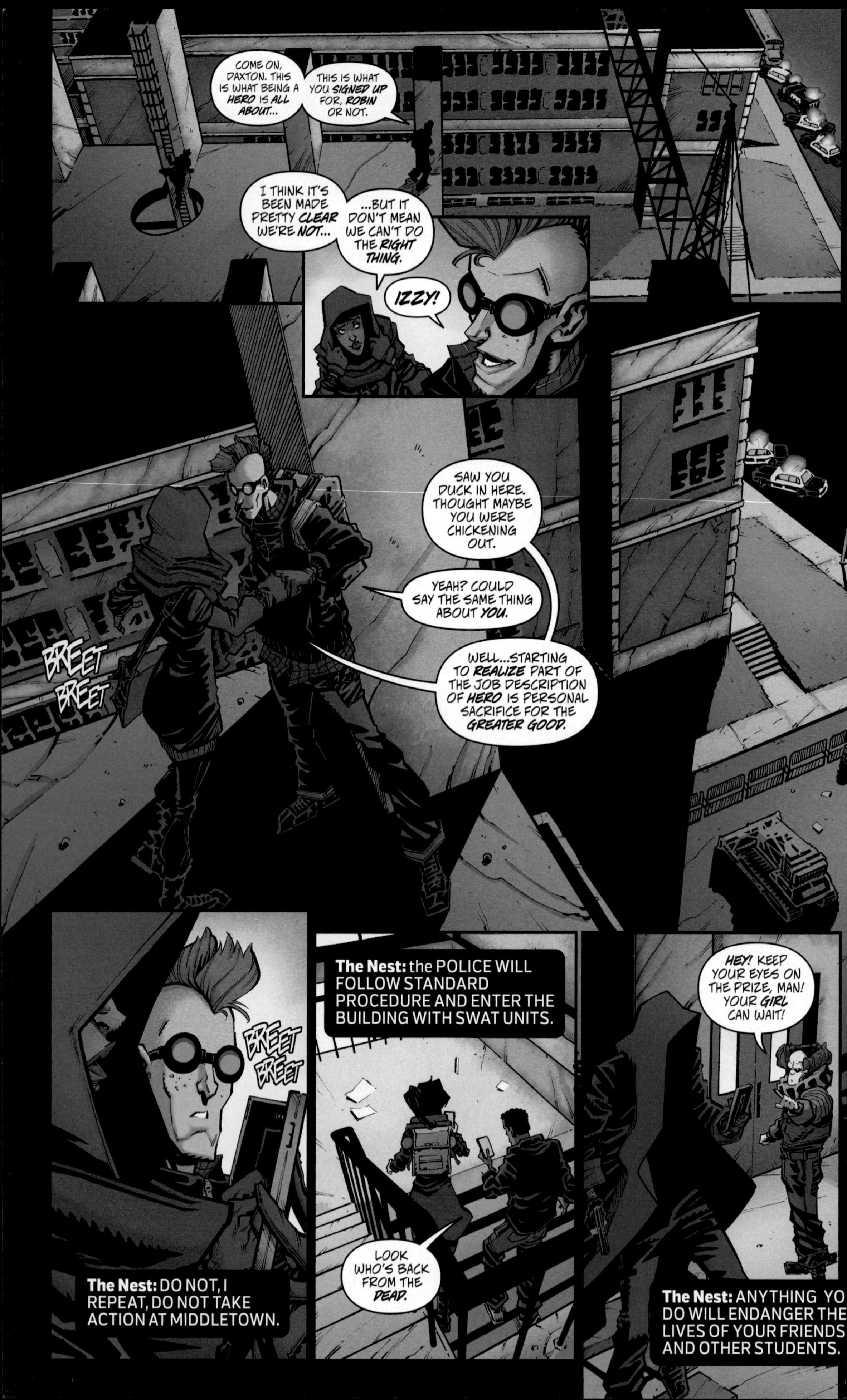
COME ON, DAXTON. THIS IS WHAT BEING A HERO IS ALL ABOUT...
THIS IS WHAT YOU SIGNED UP FOR, ROBIN OR NOT.
I THINK IT'S BEEN MADE PRETTY CLEAR WE'RE NOT...
...BUT IT DON'T MEAN WE CAN'T DO THE RIGHT THING.
IZZY!
SAW YOU DUCK IN HERE. THOUGHT MAYBE YOU WERE CHICKENING OUT.
YEAH? COULD SAY THE SAME THING ABOUT YOU.
WELL...STARTING TO REALIZE PART OF THE JOB DESCRIPTION OF HERO IS PERSONAL SACRIFICE FOR THE GREATER GOOD.
BREET BREET
BREET BREET
The Nest: DO NOT, I REPEAT, DO NOT TAKE ACTION AT MIDDLETOWN.
The Nest: the POLICE WILL FOLLOW STANDARD PROCEDURE AND ENTER THE BUILDING WITH SWAT UNITS.
LOOK WHO'S BACK FROM THE DEAD.
HEY! KEEP YOUR EYES ON THE PRIZE, MAN! YOUR GIRL CAN WAIT!
The Nest: ANYTHING YO DO WILL ENDANGER THE LIVES OF YOUR FRIENDS AND OTHER STUDENTS.

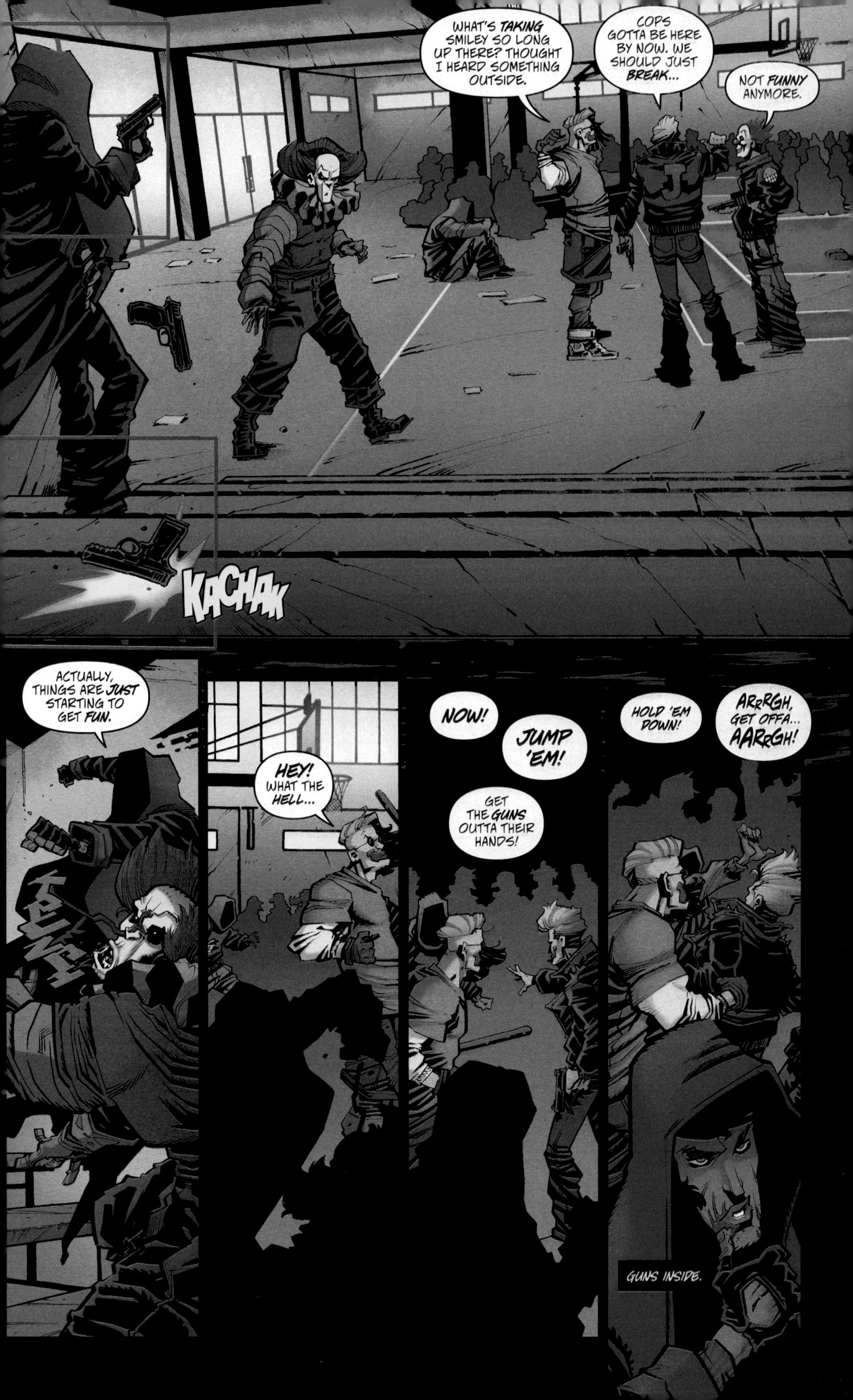
WHAT'S TAKING SMILEY SO LONG UP THERE? THOUGHT I HEARD SOMETHING OUTSIDE.
COPS GOTTA BE HERE BY NOW. WE SHOULD JUST BREAK...
NOT FUNNY ANYMORE.
KACHAK
ACTUALLY, THINGS ARE JUST STARTING TO GET FUN.
HEY! WHAT THE HELL...
NOW!
JUMP 'EM!
GET THE GUNS OUTTA THEIR HANDS!
HOLD 'EM DOWN!
ARRRGH, GET OFFA... AARRGH!
GUNS INSIDE.

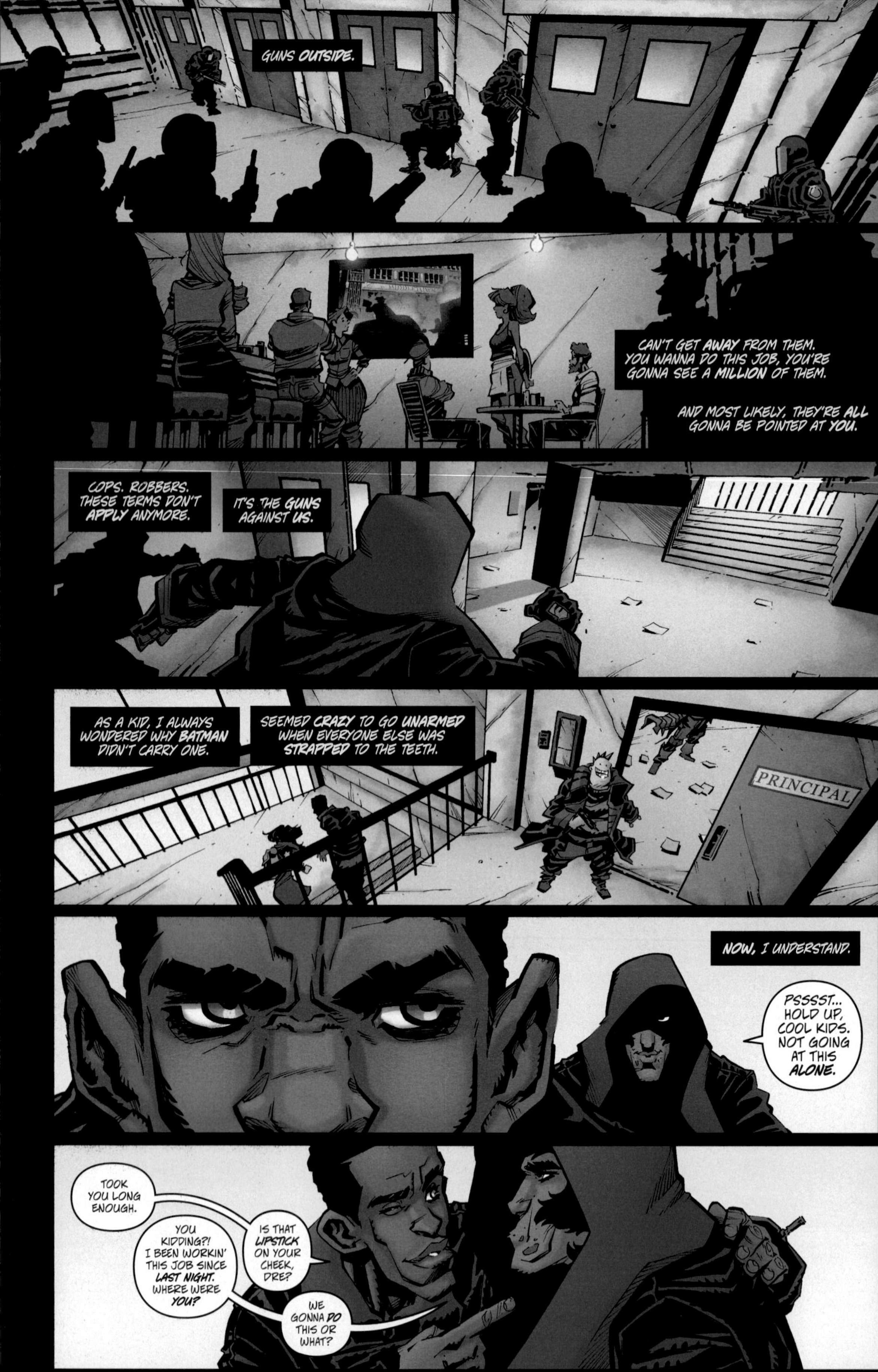
GUNS OUTSIDE.
CAN'T GET AWAY FROM THEM. YOU WANNA DO THIS JOB, YOU'RE GONNA SEE A MILLION OF THEM.
AND MOST LIKELY, THEY'RE ALL GONNA BE POINTED AT YOU.
COPS. ROBBERS. THESE TERMS DON'T APPLY ANYMORE.
IT'S THE GUNS AGAINST US.
AS A KID, I ALWAYS WONDERED WHY BATMAN DIDN'T CARRY ONE.
SEEMED CRAZY TO GO UNARMED WHEN EVERYONE ELSE WAS STRAPPED TO THE TEETH.
PRINCIPAL
NOW, I UNDERSTAND.
PSSSST... HOLD UP, COOL KIDS. NOT GOING AT THIS ALONE.
TOOK YOU LONG ENOUGH.
YOU KIDDING?! I BEEN WORKIN' THIS JOB SINCE LAST NIGHT. WHERE WERE YOU?
IS THAT LIPSTICK ON YOUR CHEEK, DRE?
WE GONNA DO THIS OR WHAT?

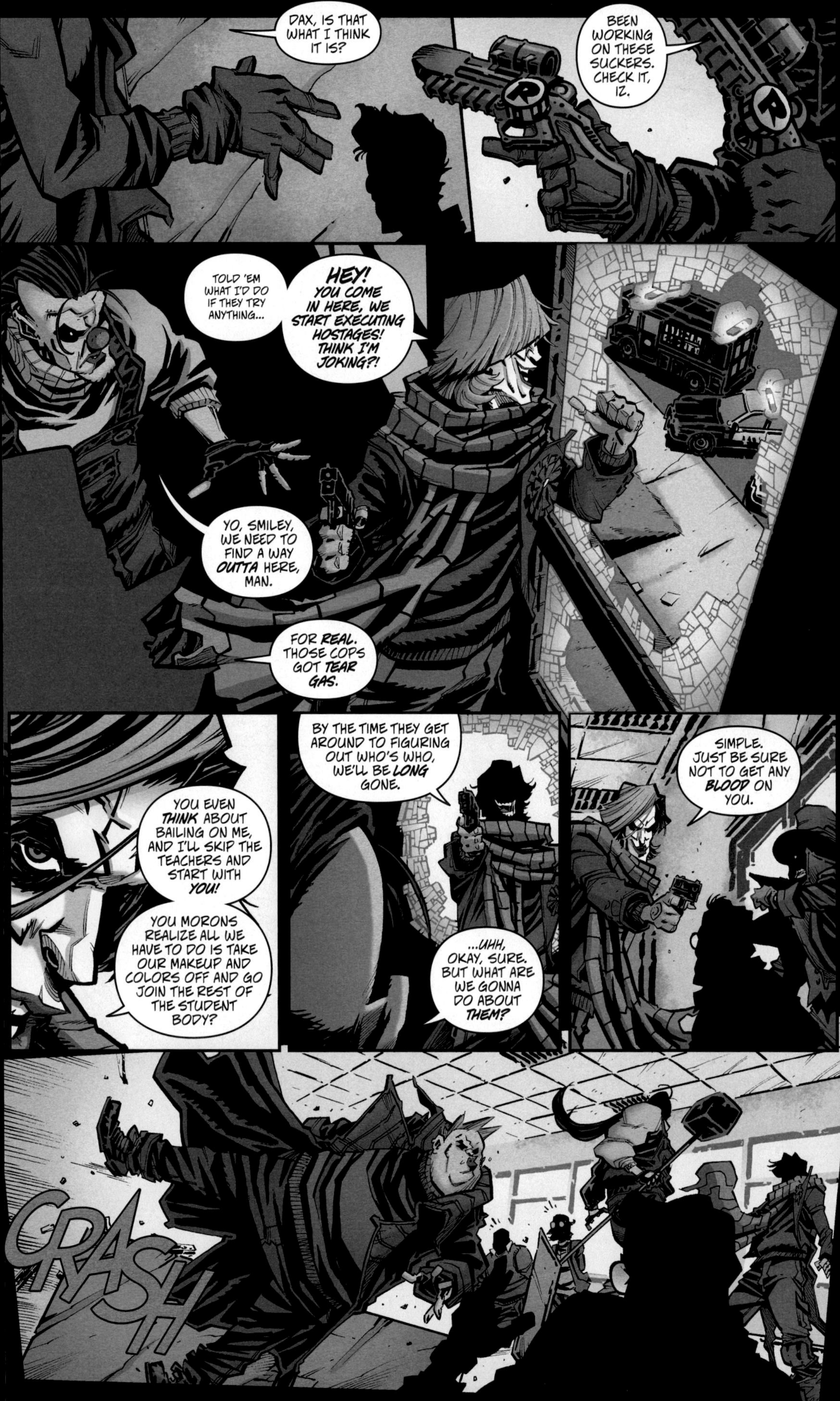
DAX, IS THAT WHAT I THINK IT IS?
BEEN WORKING ON THESE SUCKERS. CHECK IT, IZ.
TOLD 'EM WHAT I'D DO IF THEY TRY ANYTHING...
HEY! YOU COME IN HERE, WE START EXECUTING HOSTAGES! THINK I'M JOKING?!
YO, SMILEY, WE NEED TO FIND A WAY OUTTA HERE, MAN.
FOR REAL. THOSE COPS GOT TEAR GAS.
YOU EVEN THINK ABOUT BAILING ON ME, AND I'LL SKIP THE TEACHERS AND START WITH YOU!
YOU MORONS REALIZE ALL WE HAVE TO DO IS TAKE OUR MAKEUP AND COLORS OFF AND GO JOIN THE REST OF THE STUDENT BODY?
BY THE TIME THEY GET AROUND TO FIGURING OUT WHO'S WHO, WE'LL BE LONG GONE.
...UHH, OKAY, SURE. BUT WHAT ARE WE GONNA DO ABOUT THEM?
SIMPLE. JUST BE SURE NOT TO GET ANY BLOOD ON YOU.
CRASH

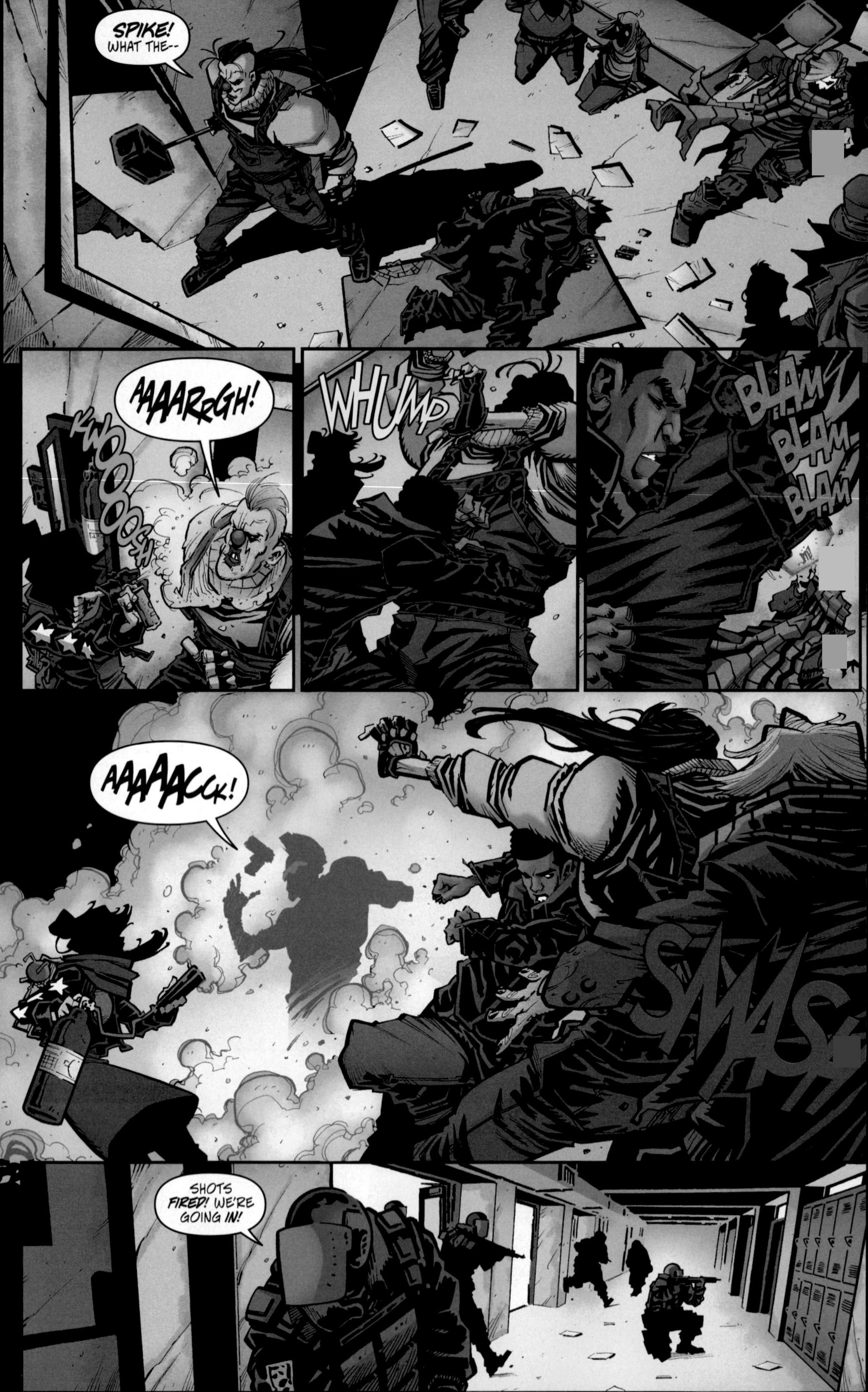
SPIKE! WHAT THE--
KWOOOOOSH
AAAARRGH!
WHUMP
BLAM BLAM BLAM
AAAAACCK!
SMAS
SHOTS FIRED! WE'RE GOING IN!

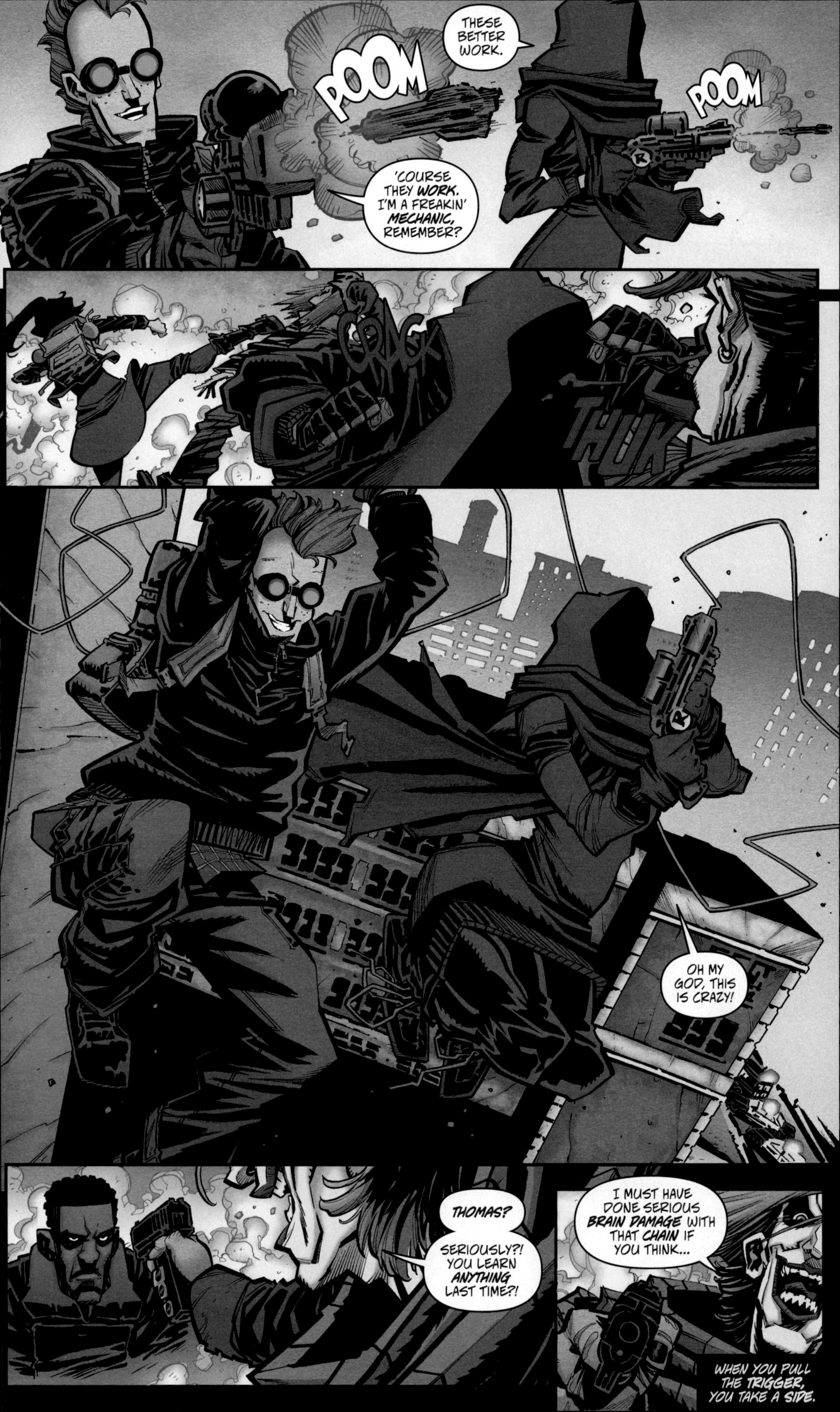
POOM
THESE BETTER WORK.
POOM
'COURSE THEY WORK. I'M A FREAKIN' MECHANIC, REMEMBER?
CRACK
THUK
OH MY GOD, THIS IS CRAZY!
THOMAS?
SERIOUSLY?! YOU LEARN ANYTHING LAST TIME?!
I MUST HAVE DONE SERIOUS BRAIN DAMAGE WITH THAT CHAIN IF YOU THINK...
WHEN YOU PULL THE TRIGGER, YOU TAKE A SIDE.

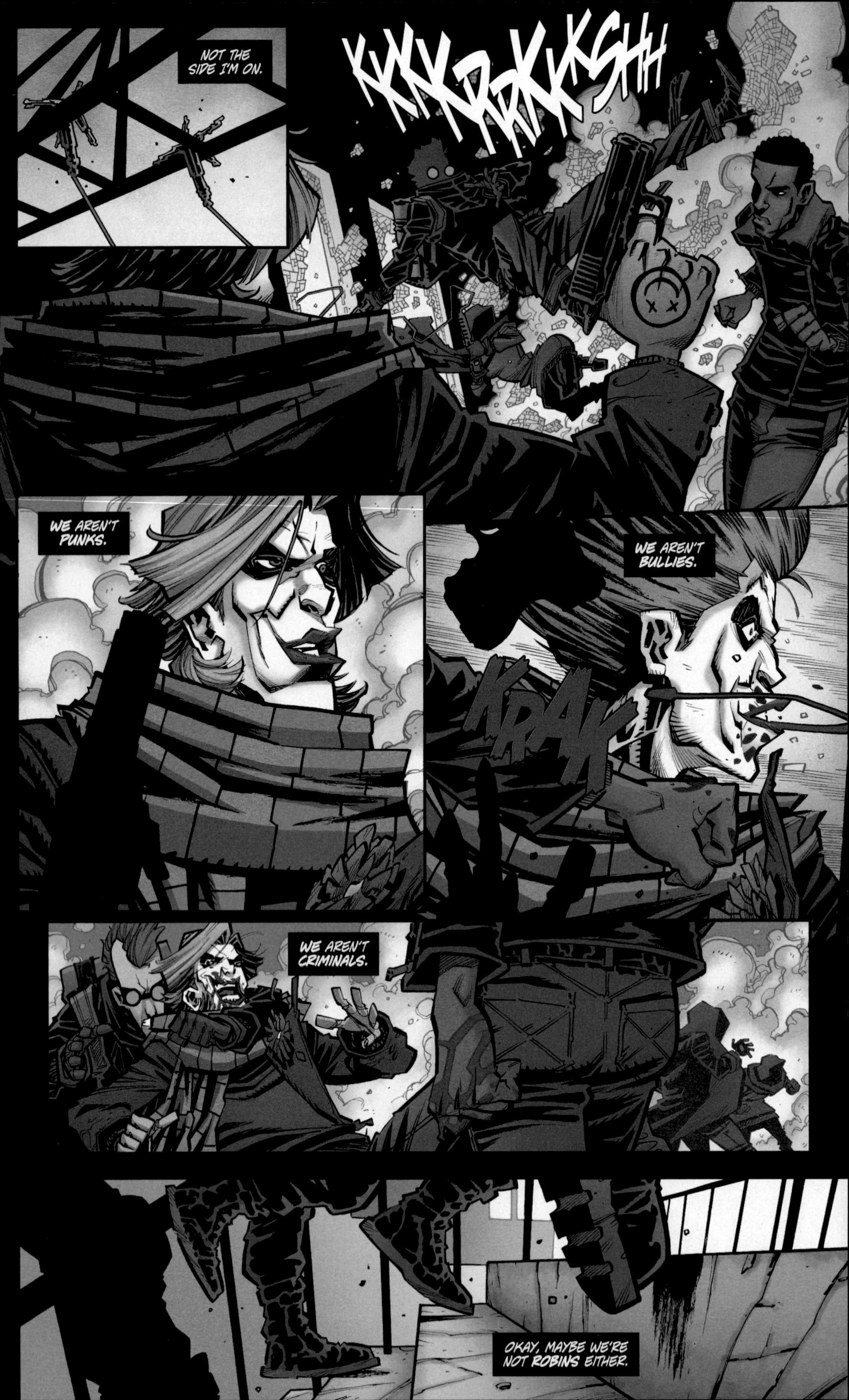
NOT THE SIDE I'M ON.
KKKKRRKKKSHH
WE AREN'T PUNKS.
WE AREN'T BULLIES.
KRAK
WE AREN'T CRIMINALS.
OKAY, MAYBE WE'RE NOT ROBINS EITHER.

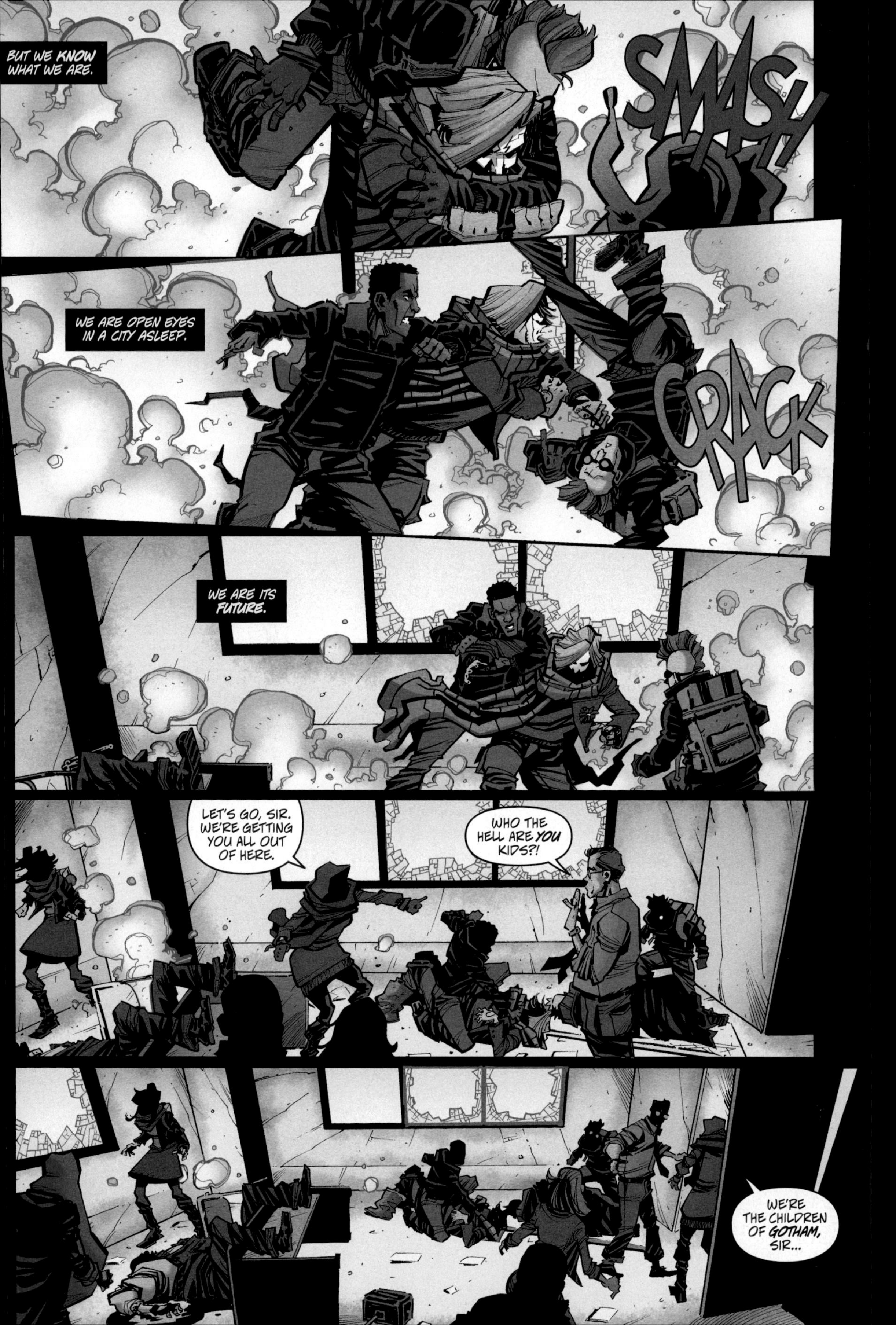
BUT WE KNOW WHAT WE ARE.
SMASH
WE ARE OPEN EYES IN A CITY ASLEEP.
CRACK
WE ARE ITS FUTURE.
LET'S GO, SIR. WE'RE GETTING YOU ALL OUT OF HERE.
WHO THE HELL ARE YOU KIDS?!
WE'RE THE CHILDREN OF GOTHAM, SIR...

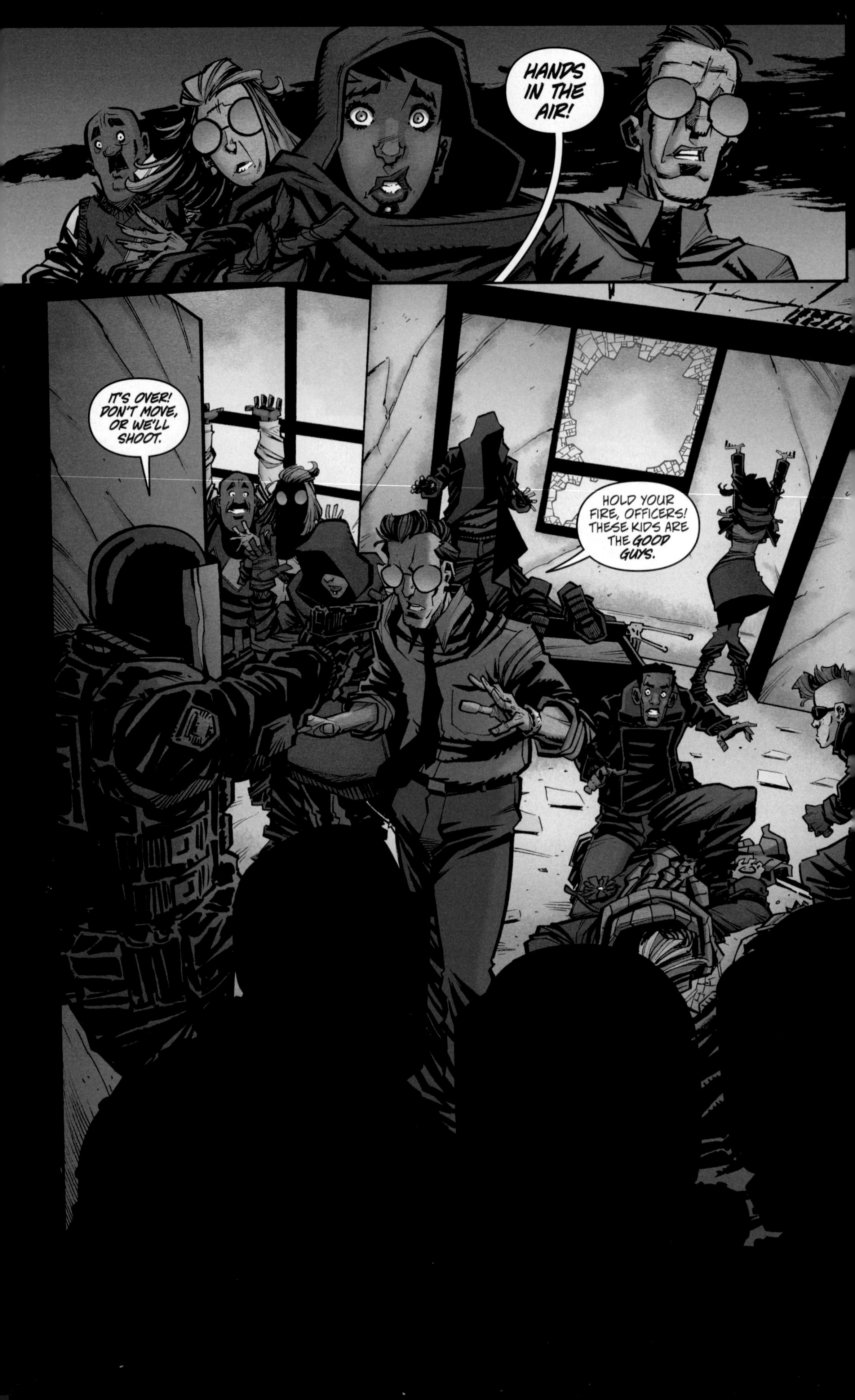
HANDS IN THE AIR!
IT'S OVER! DON'T MOVE, OR WE'LL SHOOT.
HOLD YOUR FIRE, OFFICERS! THESE KIDS ARE THE GOOD GUYS.

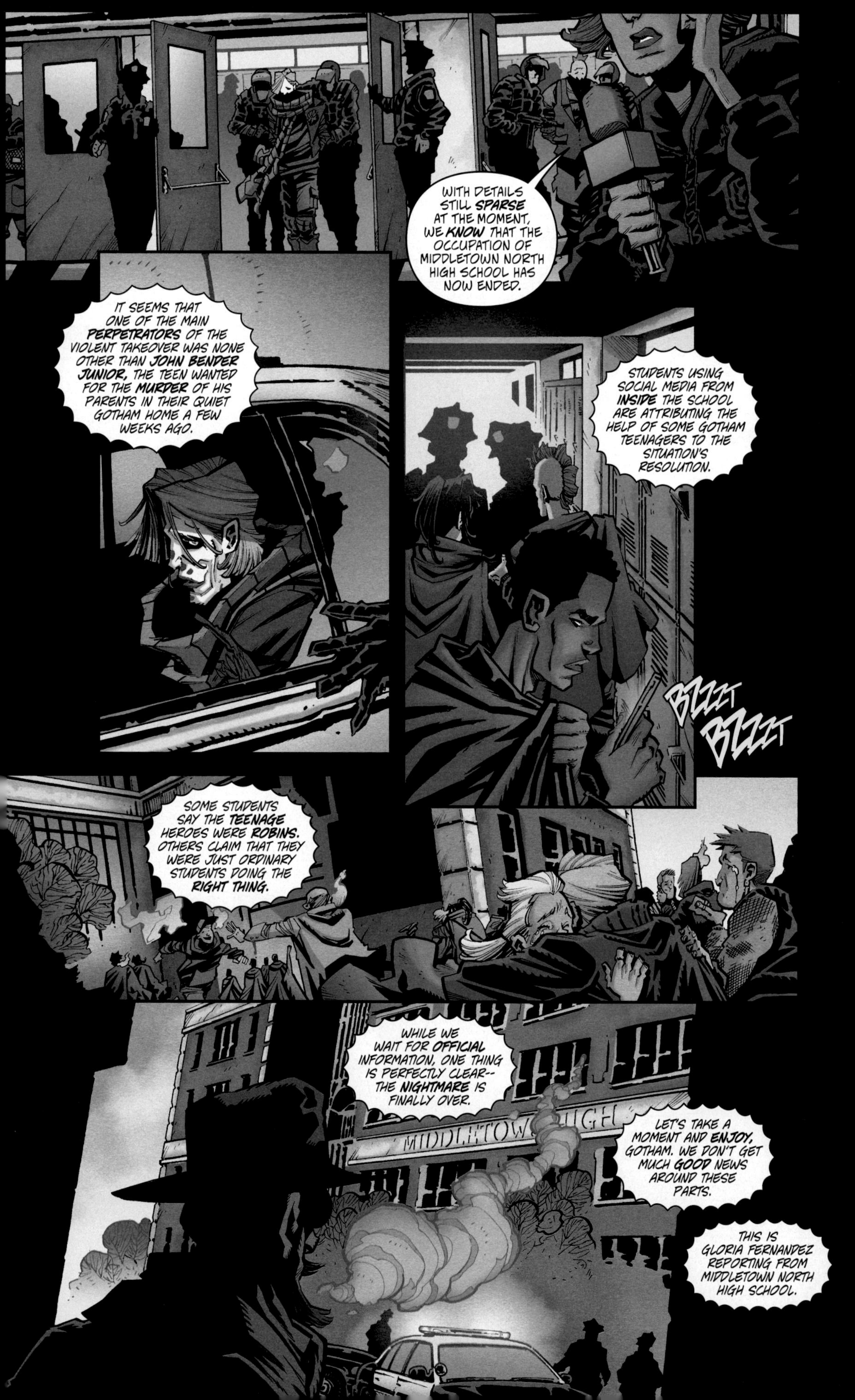
WITH DETAILS STILL SPARSE AT THE MOMENT, WE KNOW THAT THE OCCUPATION OF MIDDLETOWN NORTH HIGH SCHOOL HAS NOW ENDED.
IT SEEMS THAT ONE OF THE MAIN PERPETRATORS OF THE VIOLENT TAKEOVER WAS NONE OTHER THAN JOHN BENDER JUNIOR, THE TEEN WANTED FOR THE MURDER OF HIS PARENTS IN THEIR QUIET GOTHAM HOME A FEW WEEKS AGO.
STUDENTS USING SOCIAL MEDIA FROM INSIDE THE SCHOOL ARE ATTRIBUTING THE HELP OF SOME GOTHAM TEENAGERS TO THE SITUATION'S RESOLUTION.
BZZZT
BZZZT
SOME STUDENTS SAY THE TEENAGE HEROES WERE ROBINS. OTHERS CLAIM THAT THEY WERE JUST ORDINARY STUDENTS DOING THE RIGHT THING.
WHILE WE WAIT FOR OFFICIAL INFORMATION, ONE THING IS PERFECTLY CLEAR-- THE NIGHTMARE IS FINALLY OVER.
LET'S TAKE A MOMENT AND ENJOY, GOTHAM. WE DON'T GET MUCH GOOD NEWS AROUND THESE PARTS.
THIS IS GLORIA FERNANDEZ REPORTING FROM MIDDLETOWN NORTH HIGH SCHOOL.

SO YOU STILL *READ* THE MESSAGES I SEND.

FOR A MOMENT I THOUGHT THEY HAD FALLEN ON *DEAF EARS.*

WE'RE *LISTENING.* TO *OURSELVES* NOW.

LOOK, WE *APPRECIATE* YOUR HELP... *REALLY*...

...BUT WE CAN'T KEEP RELYING ON A *MYSTERY MAN* AND HIS BAG OF EXPENSIVE *TRICKS* TO SHOW US THE WAY.

I'VE BEEN DOING THIS JOB A *LONG* TIME, YOUNG MAN. TO DO SO ALONE IS *FOLLY.*

THAT'S JUST IT. WE AIN'T-- WE *AREN'T* ALONE.

AND WE'VE *GOT* THIS.

FROM NOW ON, WE DO THINGS *OUR WAY.*

AND DO YOU KNOW WHAT *YOUR* WAY *IS?*

THAT'S JUST IT...

WE AREN'T *DYING* TO FIND OUT.

WE ARE JOKERS **PART FIVE**

LEE BERMEJO story & cover **JORGE CORONA** art

ROB HAYNES breakdowns TRISH MULVIHILL colors JARED K. FLETCHER letters
JOHN ROMITA JR. Variant Cover inks by DANNY MIKI colors by BRAD ANDERSON
REBECCA TAYLOR associate editor MARK DOYLE editor

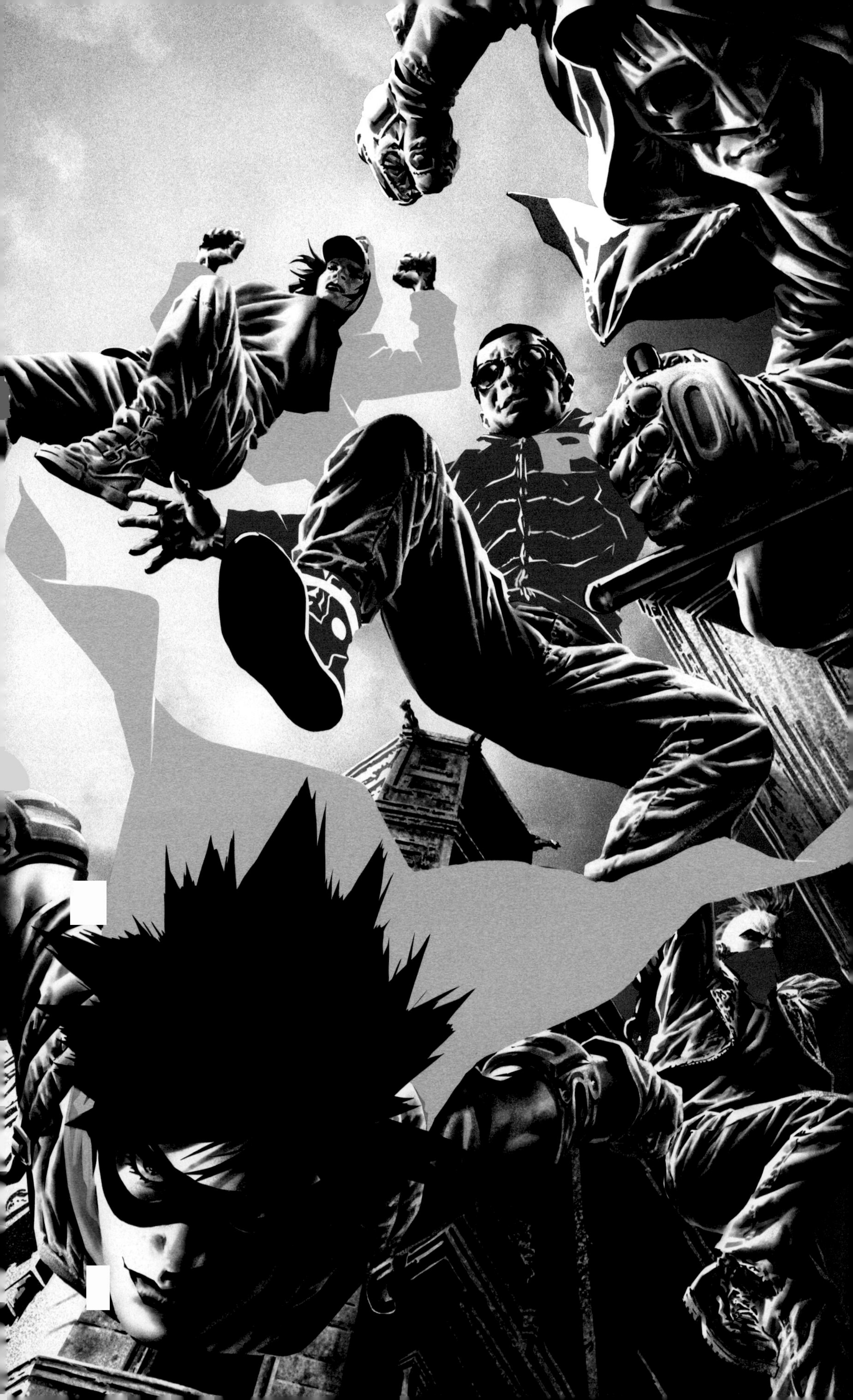

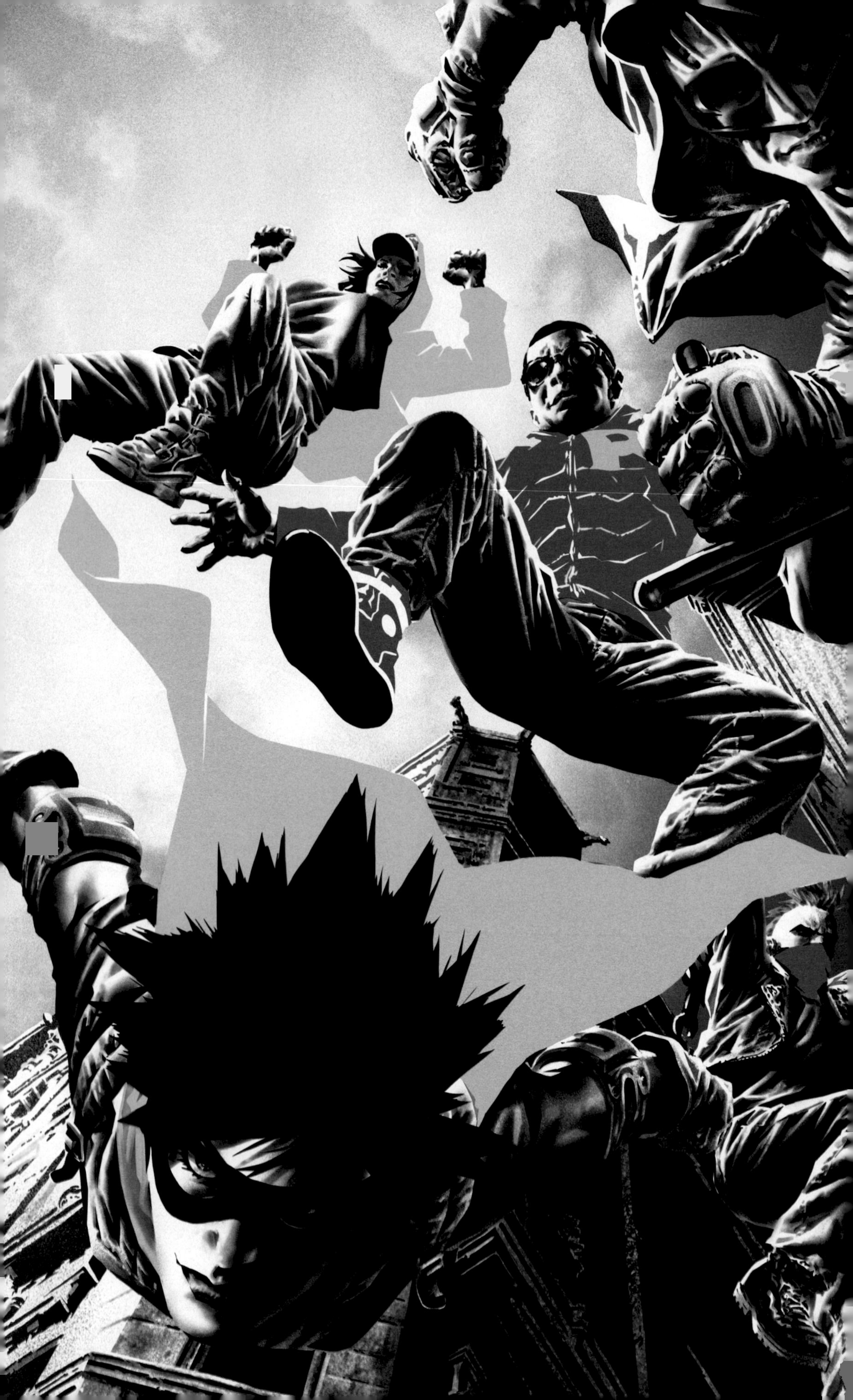

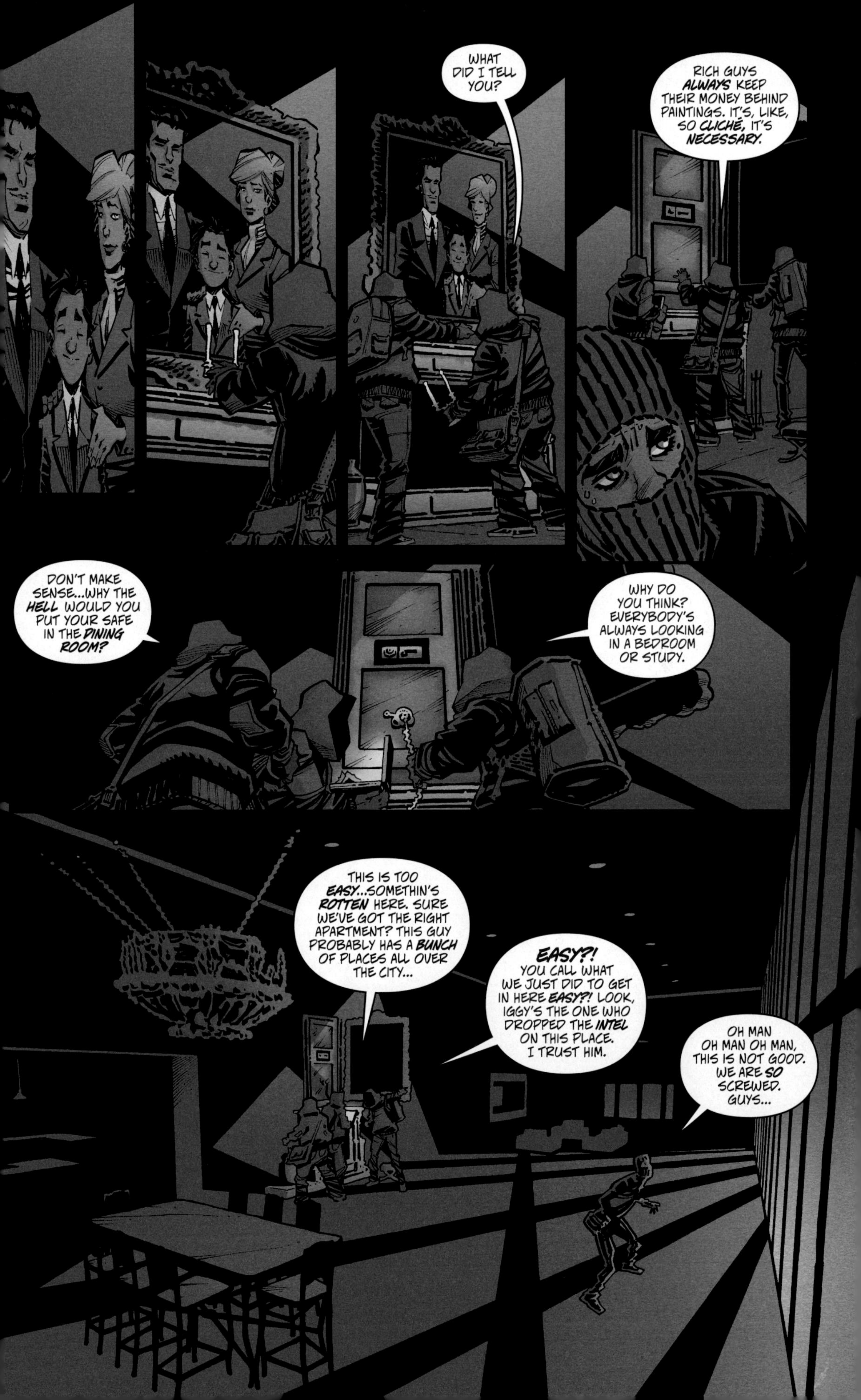
WHAT DID I TELL YOU?
RICH GUYS ALWAYS KEEP THEIR MONEY BEHIND PAINTINGS. IT'S, LIKE, SO CLICHÉ, IT'S NECESSARY.
DON'T MAKE SENSE...WHY THE HELL WOULD YOU PUT YOUR SAFE IN THE DINING ROOM?
WHY DO YOU THINK? EVERYBODY'S ALWAYS LOOKING IN A BEDROOM OR STUDY.
THIS IS TOO EASY...SOMETHIN'S ROTTEN HERE. SURE WE'VE GOT THE RIGHT APARTMENT? THIS GUY PROBABLY HAS A BUNCH OF PLACES ALL OVER THE CITY...
EASY?! YOU CALL WHAT WE JUST DID TO GET IN HERE EASY?! LOOK, IGGY'S THE ONE WHO DROPPED THE INTEL ON THIS PLACE. I TRUST HIM.
OH MAN OH MAN OH MAN, THIS IS NOT GOOD. WE ARE SO SCREWED. GUYS...

THE HERO BUSINESS

LEE BERMEJO story & cover **JORGE CORONA** art
ROB HAYNES breakdowns **TRISH MULVIHILL** colors **JARED K. FLETCHER** letters
REBECCA TAYLOR associate editor **MARK DOYLE** editor

...THIS IS GONNA GO BAD.

CISCO. A.K.A.: REDBIRD16. TWO WEEKS AGO.

YOU LOOK SOOOO BEAUTIFUL, LITTLE KAYLA DOLL. I WANT TO TAKE YOU WITH ME TO--

MARIEL, HOW MANY TIMES DO I HAVE TO TELL YOU NOT TO BRING TOYS TO THE TABLE? CISCO, PUT THE PAPER DOWN. IT'S DINNER TIME.

THAT'S IT! THAT'S THE LAST TIME I GET OUTED FOR A CONTRACT BY WAYNE ENTERPRISES!

YOUTH HEROES SAVE MIDDLETO

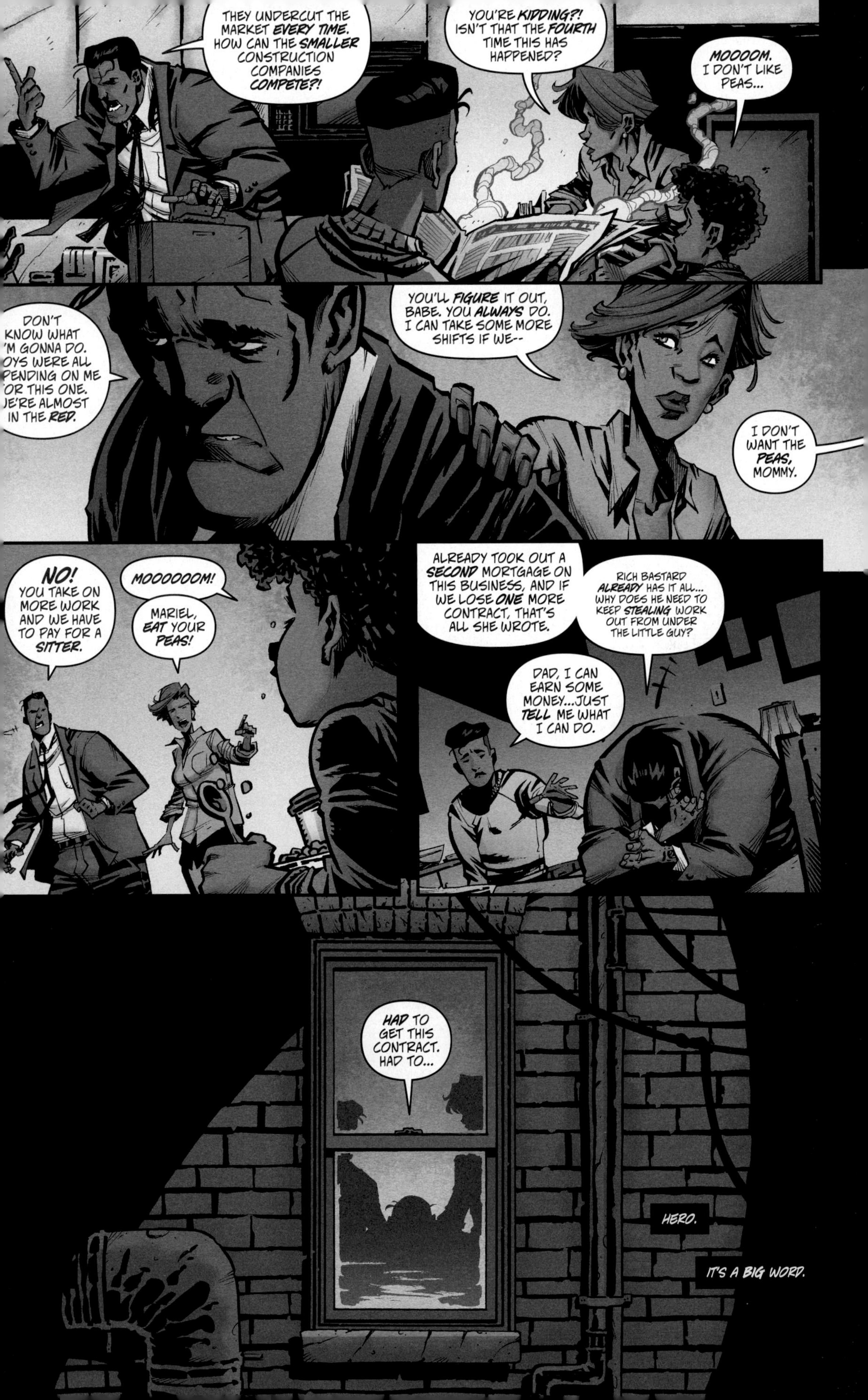
THEY UNDERCUT THE MARKET EVERY TIME. HOW CAN THE SMALLER CONSTRUCTION COMPANIES COMPETE?!
YOU'RE KIDDING?! ISN'T THAT THE FOURTH TIME THIS HAS HAPPENED?
MOOOOM. I DON'T LIKE PEAS...
DON'T KNOW WHAT I'M GONNA DO. BOYS WERE ALL DEPENDING ON ME FOR THIS ONE. WE'RE ALMOST IN THE RED.
YOU'LL FIGURE IT OUT, BABE. YOU ALWAYS DO. I CAN TAKE SOME MORE SHIFTS IF WE--
I DON'T WANT THE PEAS, MOMMY.
NO! YOU TAKE ON MORE WORK AND WE HAVE TO PAY FOR A SITTER.
MOOOOOOM!
MARIEL, EAT YOUR PEAS!
ALREADY TOOK OUT A SECOND MORTGAGE ON THIS BUSINESS, AND IF WE LOSE ONE MORE CONTRACT, THAT'S ALL SHE WROTE.
RICH BASTARD ALREADY HAS IT ALL... WHY DOES HE NEED TO KEEP STEALING WORK OUT FROM UNDER THE LITTLE GUY?
DAD, I CAN EARN SOME MONEY...JUST TELL ME WHAT I CAN DO.
HAD TO GET THIS CONTRACT. HAD TO...
HERO.
IT'S A BIG WORD.

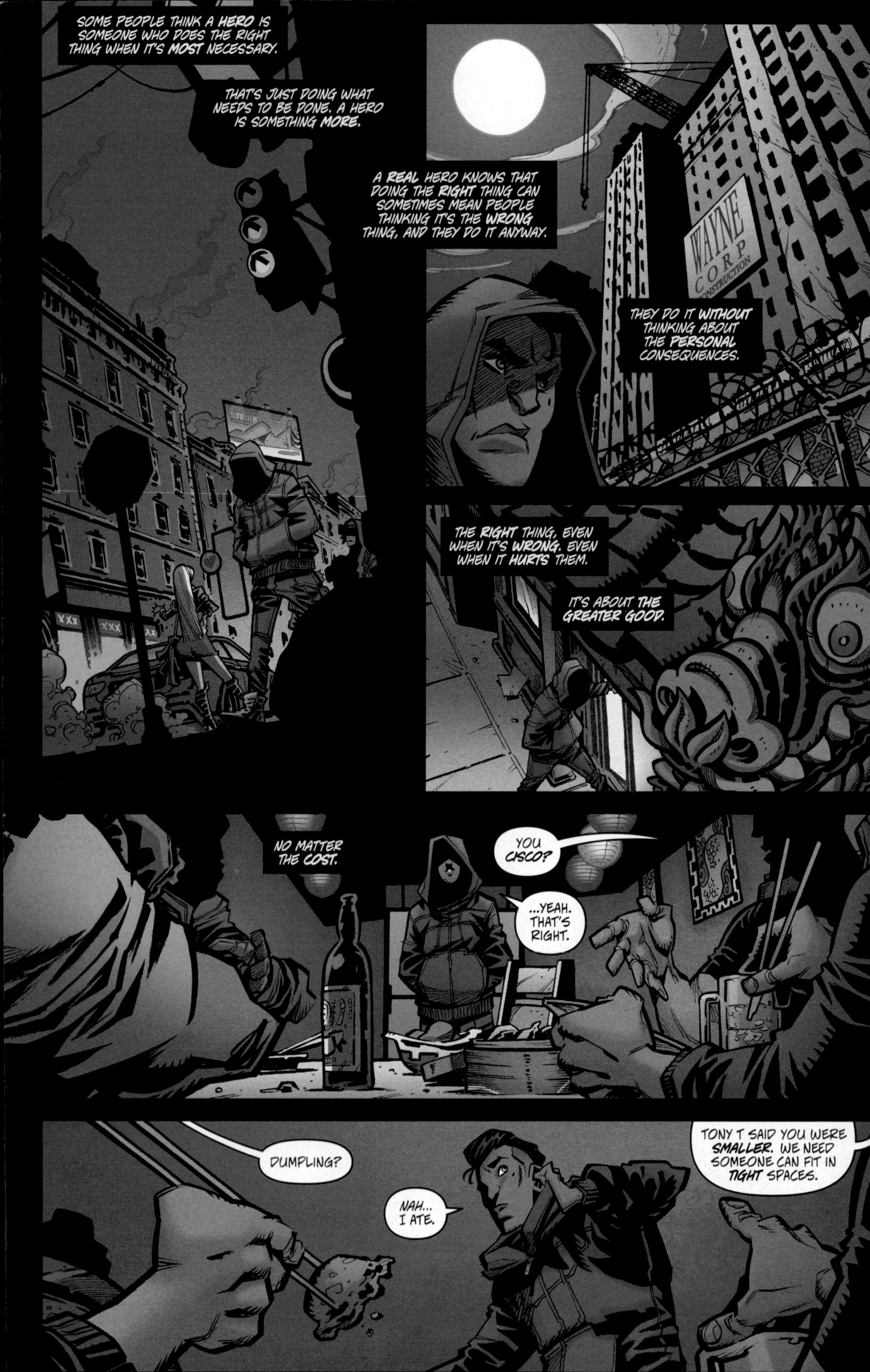
SOME PEOPLE THINK A HERO IS SOMEONE WHO DOES THE RIGHT THING WHEN IT'S MOST NECESSARY.
THAT'S JUST DOING WHAT NEEDS TO BE DONE. A HERO IS SOMETHING MORE.
A REAL HERO KNOWS THAT DOING THE RIGHT THING CAN SOMETIMES MEAN PEOPLE THINKING IT'S THE WRONG THING, AND THEY DO IT ANYWAY.
WAYNE CORP CONSTRUCTION
THEY DO IT WITHOUT THINKING ABOUT THE PERSONAL CONSEQUENCES.
THE RIGHT THING, EVEN WHEN IT'S WRONG. EVEN WHEN IT HURTS THEM.
IT'S ABOUT THE GREATER GOOD.
NO MATTER THE COST.
YOU CISCO?
...YEAH. THAT'S RIGHT.
DUMPLING?
NAH... I ATE.
TONY T SAID YOU WERE SMALLER. WE NEED SOMEONE CAN FIT IN TIGHT SPACES.

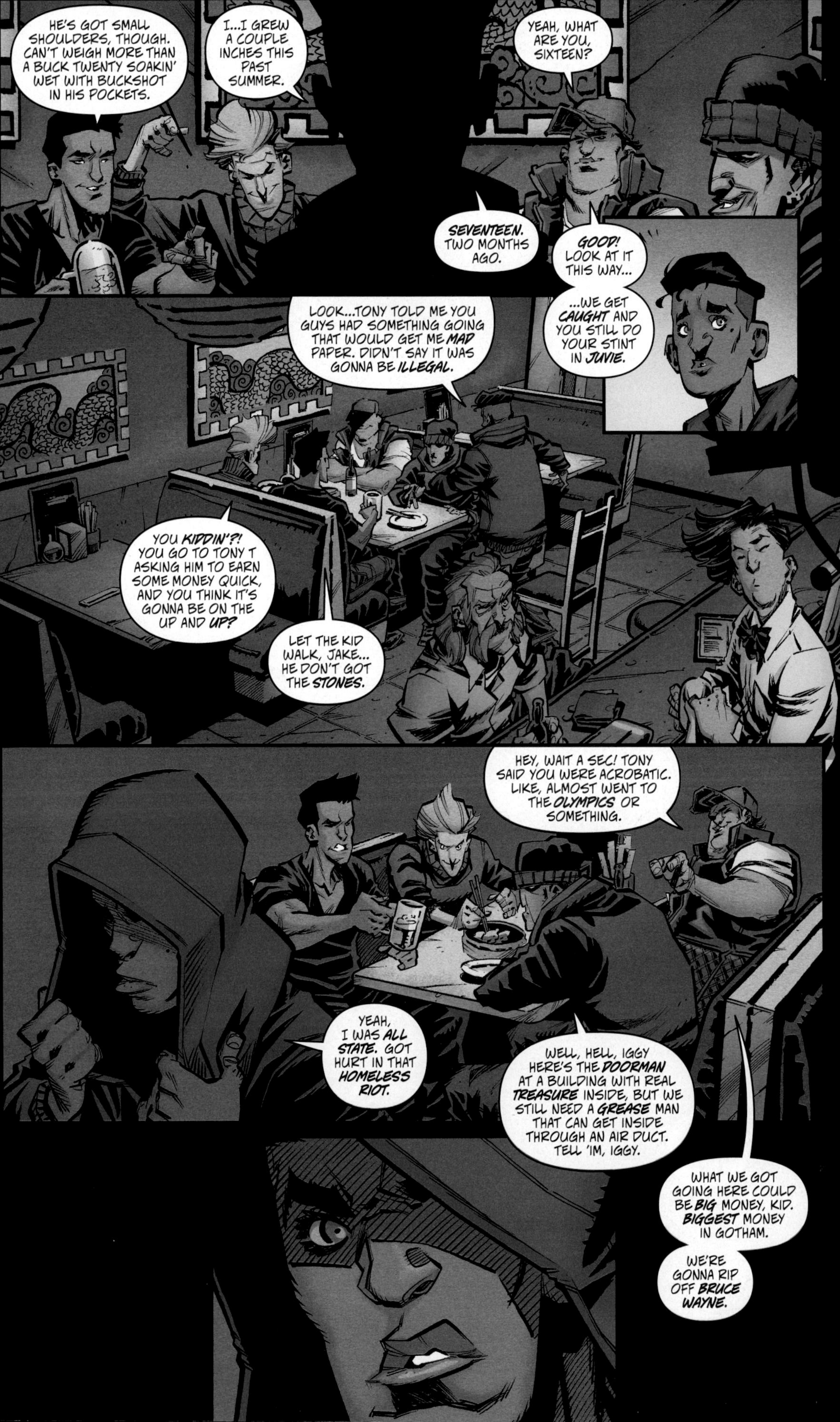
HE'S GOT SMALL SHOULDERS, THOUGH. CAN'T WEIGH MORE THAN A BUCK TWENTY SOAKIN' WET WITH BUCKSHOT IN HIS POCKETS.
I...I GREW A COUPLE INCHES THIS PAST SUMMER.
YEAH, WHAT ARE YOU, SIXTEEN?
SEVENTEEN. TWO MONTHS AGO.
GOOD! LOOK AT IT THIS WAY...
...WE GET CAUGHT AND YOU STILL DO YOUR STINT IN JUVIE.
LOOK...TONY TOLD ME YOU GUYS HAD SOMETHING GOING THAT WOULD GET ME MAD PAPER. DIDN'T SAY IT WAS GONNA BE ILLEGAL.
YOU KIDDIN'?! YOU GO TO TONY T ASKING HIM TO EARN SOME MONEY QUICK, AND YOU THINK IT'S GONNA BE ON THE UP AND UP?
LET THE KID WALK, JAKE... HE DON'T GOT THE STONES.
HEY, WAIT A SEC! TONY SAID YOU WERE ACROBATIC. LIKE, ALMOST WENT TO THE OLYMPICS OR SOMETHING.
YEAH, I WAS ALL STATE. GOT HURT IN THAT HOMELESS RIOT.
WELL, HELL, IGGY HERE'S THE DOORMAN AT A BUILDING WITH REAL TREASURE INSIDE, BUT WE STILL NEED A GREASE MAN THAT CAN GET INSIDE THROUGH AN AIR DUCT. TELL 'IM, IGGY.
WHAT WE GOT GOING HERE COULD BE BIG MONEY, KID. BIGGEST MONEY IN GOTHAM.
WE'RE GONNA RIP OFF BRUCE WAYNE.

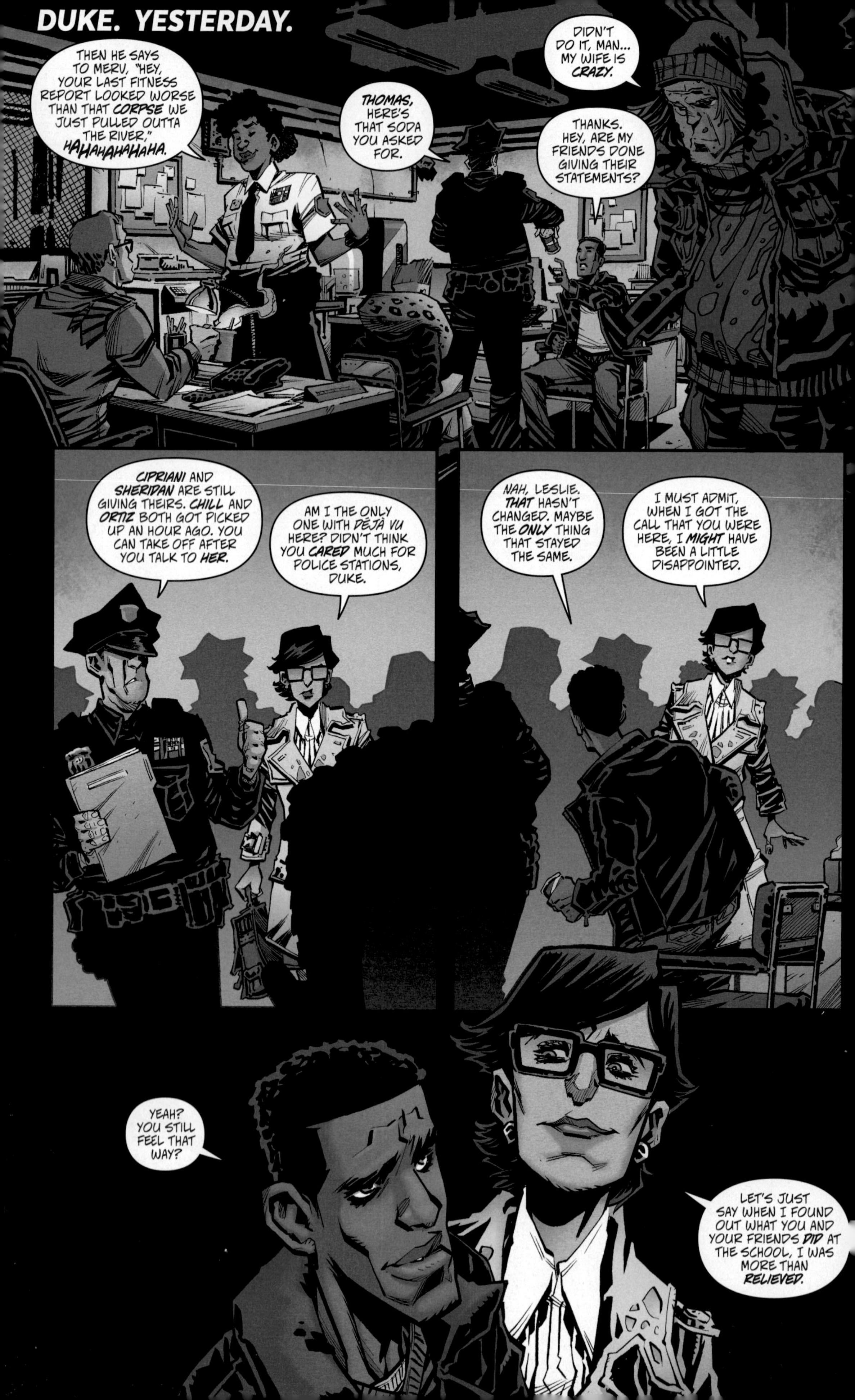
DUKE. YESTERDAY.
THEN HE SAYS TO MERU, "HEY, YOUR LAST FITNESS REPORT LOOKED WORSE THAN THAT CORPSE WE JUST PULLED OUTTA THE RIVER," HAHAHAHAHAHA.
THOMAS, HERE'S THAT SODA YOU ASKED FOR.
DIDN'T DO IT, MAN... MY WIFE IS CRAZY.
THANKS. HEY, ARE MY FRIENDS DONE GIVING THEIR STATEMENTS?
CIPRIANI AND SHERIDAN ARE STILL GIVING THEIRS. CHILL AND ORTIZ BOTH GOT PICKED UP AN HOUR AGO. YOU CAN TAKE OFF AFTER YOU TALK TO HER.
AM I THE ONLY ONE WITH DÉJÀ VU HERE? DIDN'T THINK YOU CARED MUCH FOR POLICE STATIONS, DUKE.
NAH, LESLIE. THAT HASN'T CHANGED. MAYBE THE ONLY THING THAT STAYED THE SAME.
I MUST ADMIT, WHEN I GOT THE CALL THAT YOU WERE HERE, I MIGHT HAVE BEEN A LITTLE DISAPPOINTED.
YEAH? YOU STILL FEEL THAT WAY?
LET'S JUST SAY WHEN I FOUND OUT WHAT YOU AND YOUR FRIENDS DID AT THE SCHOOL, I WAS MORE THAN RELIEVED.

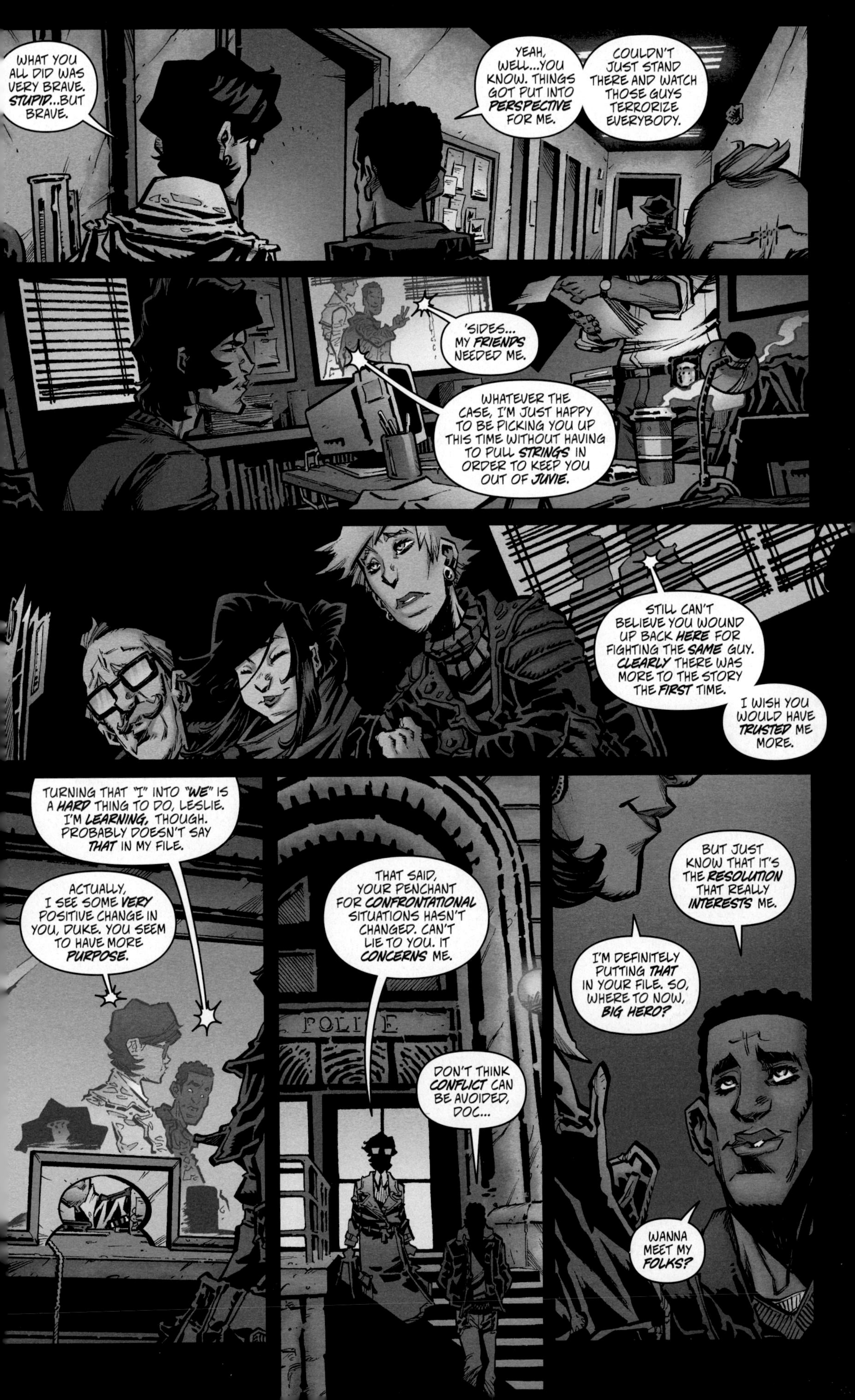
WHAT YOU ALL DID WAS VERY BRAVE. STUPID...BUT BRAVE.
YEAH, WELL...YOU KNOW. THINGS GOT PUT INTO PERSPECTIVE FOR ME.
COULDN'T JUST STAND THERE AND WATCH THOSE GUYS TERRORIZE EVERYBODY.
'SIDES... MY FRIENDS NEEDED ME.
WHATEVER THE CASE, I'M JUST HAPPY TO BE PICKING YOU UP THIS TIME WITHOUT HAVING TO PULL STRINGS IN ORDER TO KEEP YOU OUT OF JUVIE.
STILL CAN'T BELIEVE YOU WOUND UP BACK HERE FOR FIGHTING THE SAME GUY. CLEARLY THERE WAS MORE TO THE STORY THE FIRST TIME.
I WISH YOU WOULD HAVE TRUSTED ME MORE.
TURNING THAT "I" INTO "WE" IS A HARD THING TO DO, LESLIE. I'M LEARNING, THOUGH. PROBABLY DOESN'T SAY THAT IN MY FILE.
ACTUALLY, I SEE SOME VERY POSITIVE CHANGE IN YOU, DUKE. YOU SEEM TO HAVE MORE PURPOSE.
THAT SAID, YOUR PENCHANT FOR CONFRONTATIONAL SITUATIONS HASN'T CHANGED. CAN'T LIE TO YOU. IT CONCERNS ME.
POLICE
DON'T THINK CONFLICT CAN BE AVOIDED, DOC...
BUT JUST KNOW THAT IT'S THE RESOLUTION THAT REALLY INTERESTS ME.
I'M DEFINITELY PUTTING THAT IN YOUR FILE. SO, WHERE TO NOW, BIG HERO?
WANNA MEET MY FOLKS?

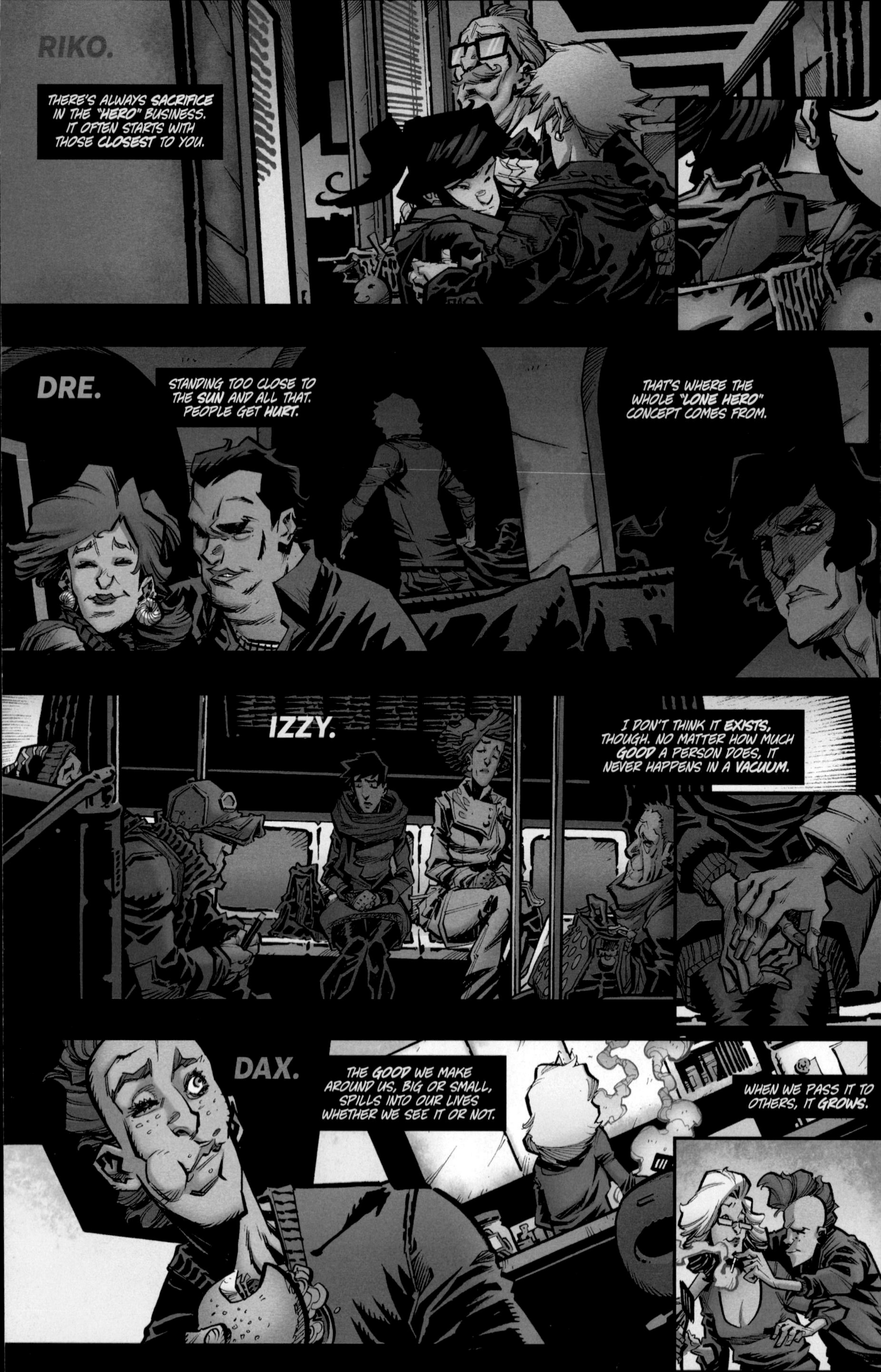
RIKO.
THERE'S ALWAYS SACRIFICE IN THE "HERO" BUSINESS. IT OFTEN STARTS WITH THOSE CLOSEST TO YOU.
DRE.
STANDING TOO CLOSE TO THE SUN AND ALL THAT. PEOPLE GET HURT.
THAT'S WHERE THE WHOLE "LONE HERO" CONCEPT COMES FROM.
IZZY.
I DON'T THINK IT EXISTS, THOUGH. NO MATTER HOW MUCH GOOD A PERSON DOES, IT NEVER HAPPENS IN A VACUUM.
DAX.
THE GOOD WE MAKE AROUND US, BIG OR SMALL, SPILLS INTO OUR LIVES WHETHER WE SEE IT OR NOT.
WHEN WE PASS IT TO OTHERS, IT GROWS.

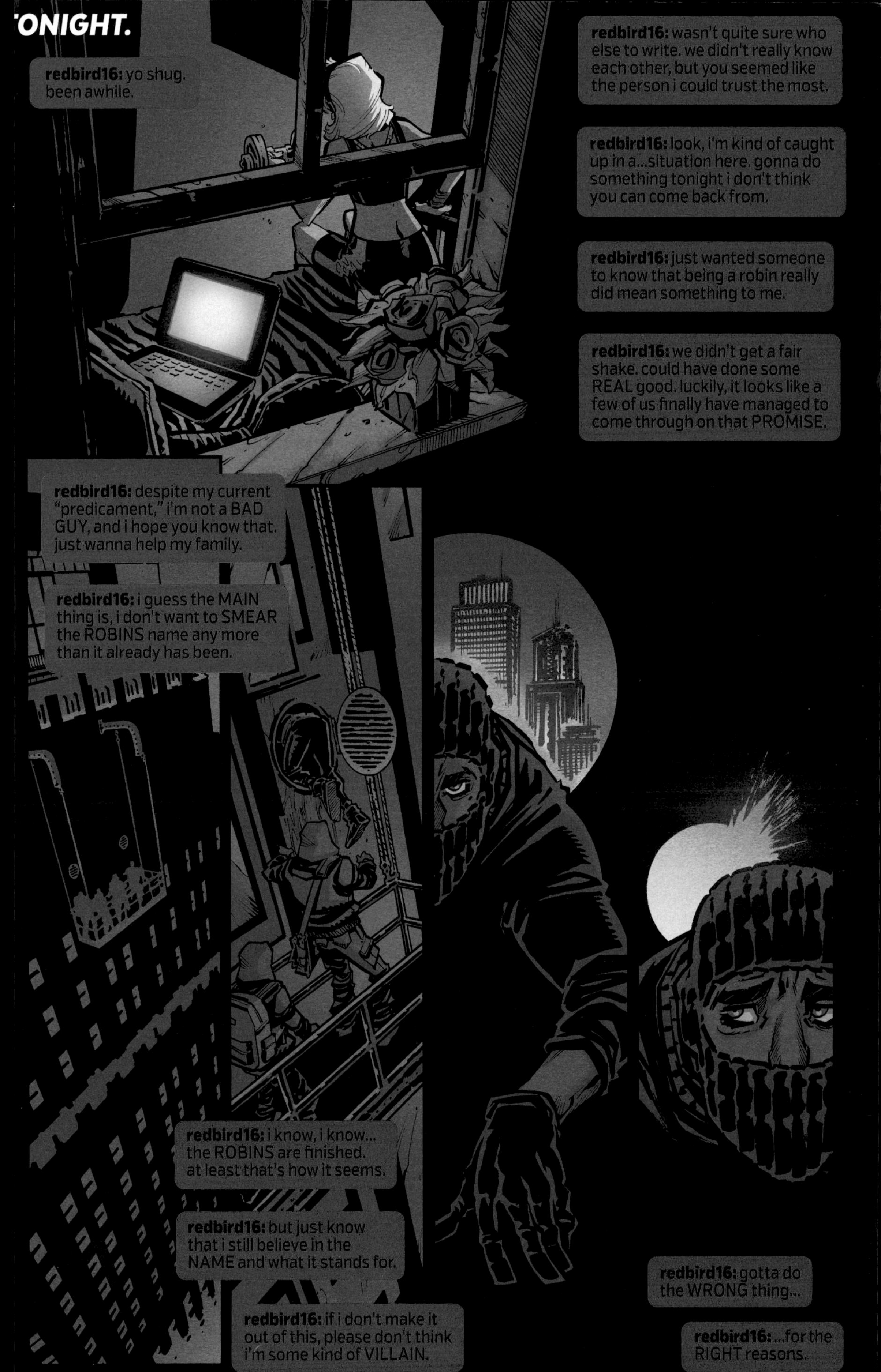
'ONIGHT.
redbird16: yo shug. been awhile.
redbird16: wasn't quite sure who else to write. we didn't really know each other, but you seemed like the person i could trust the most.
redbird16: look, i'm kind of caught up in a...situation here. gonna do something tonight i don't think you can come back from.
redbird16: just wanted someone to know that being a robin really did mean something to me.
redbird16: we didn't get a fair shake. could have done some REAL good. luckily, it looks like a few of us finally have managed to come through on that PROMISE.
redbird16: despite my current "predicament," i'm not a BAD GUY, and i hope you know that. just wanna help my family.
redbird16: i guess the MAIN thing is, i don't want to SMEAR the ROBINS name any more than it already has been.
redbird16: i know, i know... the ROBINS are finished. at least that's how it seems.
redbird16: but just know that i still believe in the NAME and what it stands for.
redbird16: if i don't make it out of this, please don't think i'm some kind of VILLAIN.
redbird16: gotta do the WRONG thing...
redbird16: ...for the RIGHT reasons.

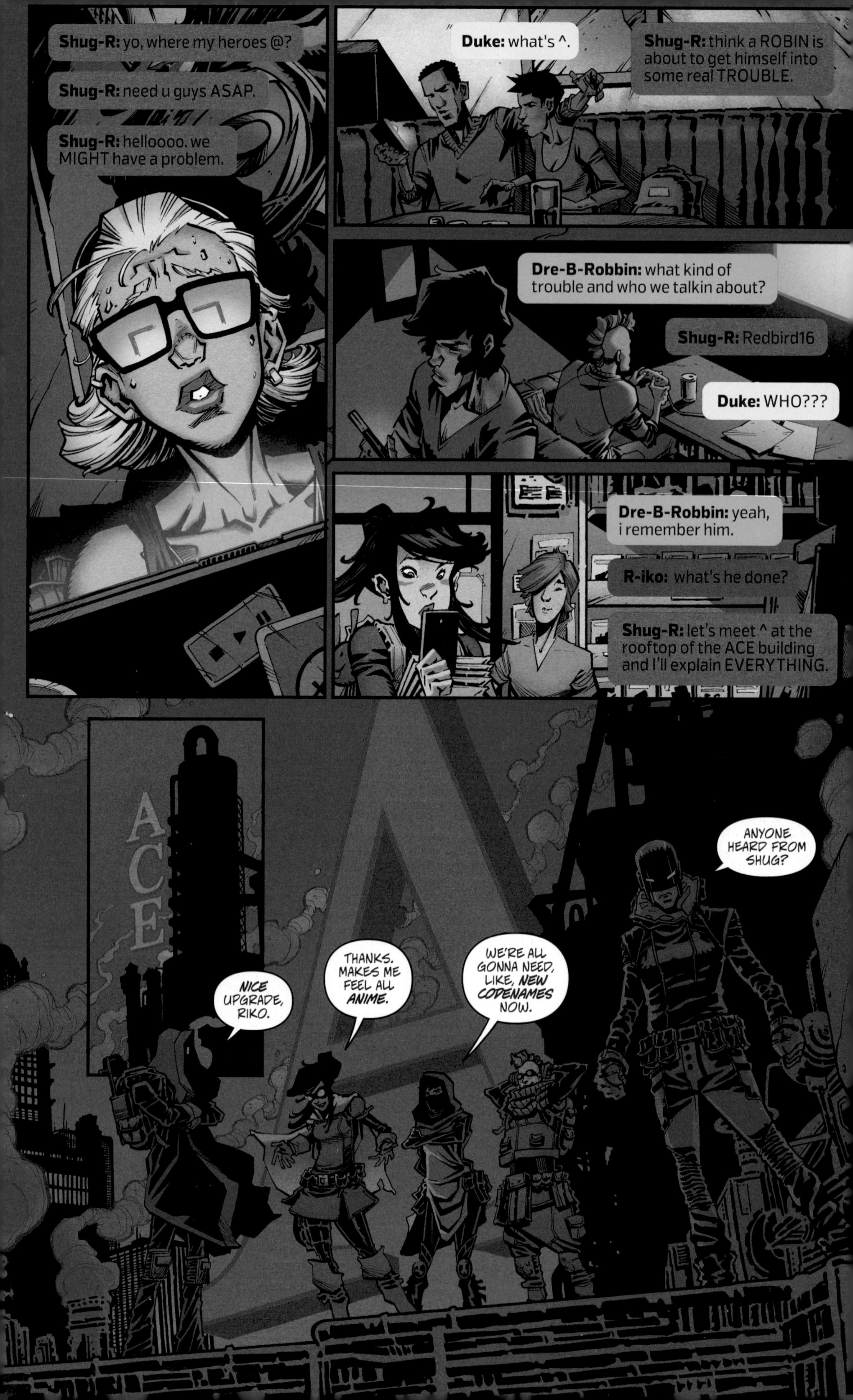

Shug-R: yo, where my heroes @?
Shug-R: need u guys ASAP.
Shug-R: helloooo. we MIGHT have a problem.
Duke: what's ^.
Shug-R: think a ROBIN is about to get himself into some real TROUBLE.
Dre-B-Robbin: what kind of trouble and who we talkin about?
Shug-R: Redbird16
Duke: WHO???
Dre-B-Robbin: yeah, i remember him.
R-iko: what's he done?
Shug-R: let's meet ^ at the rooftop of the ACE building and I'll explain EVERYTHING.
ACE
ANYONE HEARD FROM SHUG?
NICE UPGRADE, RIKO.
THANKS. MAKES ME FEEL ALL ANIME.
WE'RE ALL GONNA NEED, LIKE, NEW CODENAMES NOW.

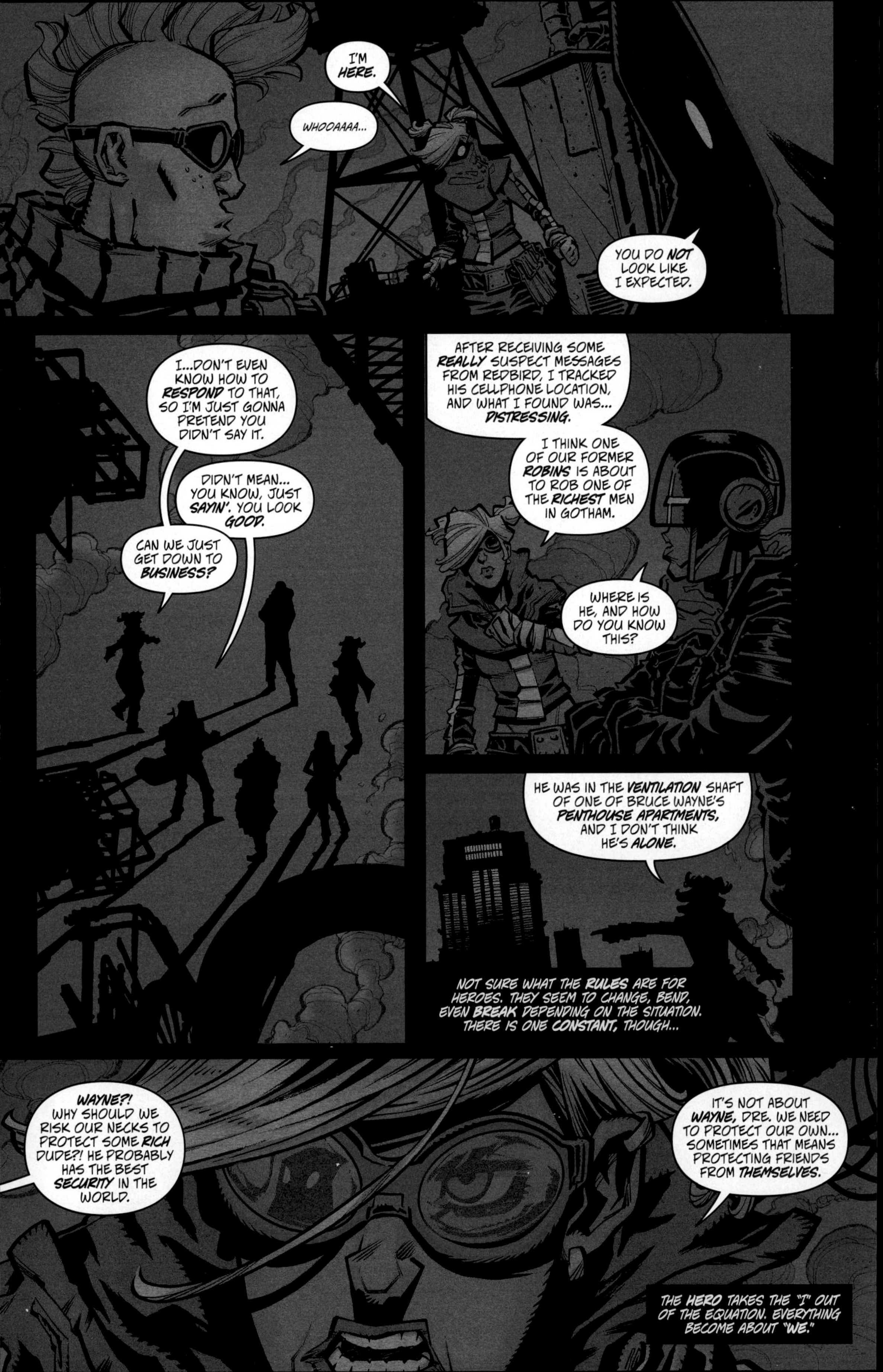
I'M HERE.
WHOOAAAA...
YOU DO NOT LOOK LIKE I EXPECTED.
I...DON'T EVEN KNOW HOW TO RESPOND TO THAT, SO I'M JUST GONNA PRETEND YOU DIDN'T SAY IT.
DIDN'T MEAN... YOU KNOW, JUST SAYIN'. YOU LOOK GOOD.
CAN WE JUST GET DOWN TO BUSINESS?
AFTER RECEIVING SOME REALLY SUSPECT MESSAGES FROM REDBIRD, I TRACKED HIS CELLPHONE LOCATION, AND WHAT I FOUND WAS... DISTRESSING.
I THINK ONE OF OUR FORMER ROBINS IS ABOUT TO ROB ONE OF THE RICHEST MEN IN GOTHAM.
WHERE IS HE, AND HOW DO YOU KNOW THIS?
HE WAS IN THE VENTILATION SHAFT OF ONE OF BRUCE WAYNE'S PENTHOUSE APARTMENTS, AND I DON'T THINK HE'S ALONE.
NOT SURE WHAT THE RULES ARE FOR HEROES. THEY SEEM TO CHANGE, BEND, EVEN BREAK DEPENDING ON THE SITUATION. THERE IS ONE CONSTANT, THOUGH...
WAYNE?! WHY SHOULD WE RISK OUR NECKS TO PROTECT SOME RICH DUDE?! HE PROBABLY HAS THE BEST SECURITY IN THE WORLD.
IT'S NOT ABOUT WAYNE, DRE. WE NEED TO PROTECT OUR OWN... SOMETIMES THAT MEANS PROTECTING FRIENDS FROM THEMSELVES.
THE HERO TAKES THE "I" OUT OF THE EQUATION. EVERYTHING BECOME ABOUT "WE."

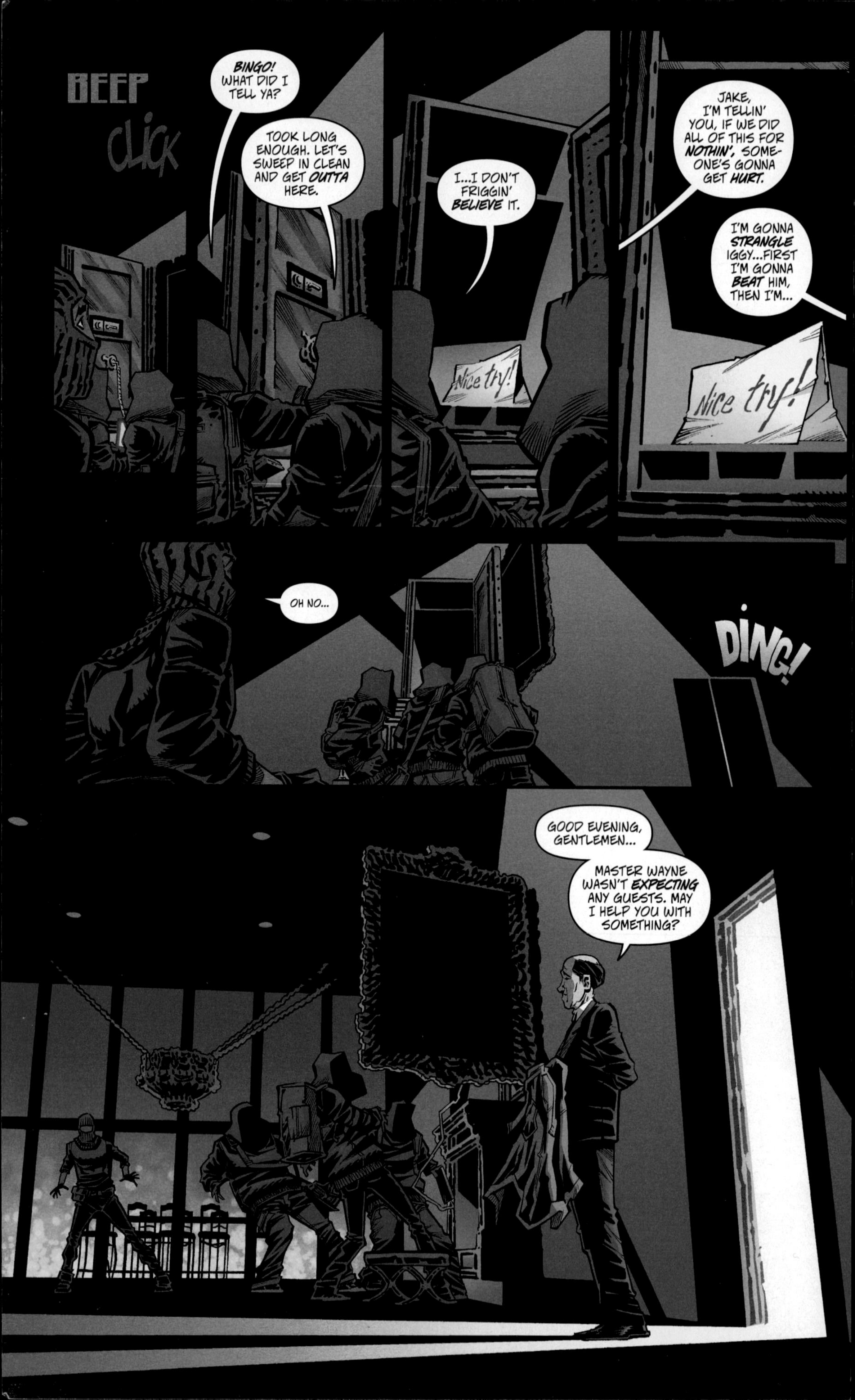
BEEP
CLICK
BINGO! WHAT DID I TELL YA?
TOOK LONG ENOUGH. LET'S SWEEP IN CLEAN AND GET OUTTA HERE.
I...I DON'T FRIGGIN' BELIEVE IT.
Nice try!
JAKE, I'M TELLIN' YOU, IF WE DID ALL OF THIS FOR NOTHIN', SOME-ONE'S GONNA GET HURT.
I'M GONNA STRANGLE IGGY...FIRST I'M GONNA BEAT HIM, THEN I'M...
Nice try!
OH NO...
DING!
GOOD EVENING, GENTLEMEN...
MASTER WAYNE WASN'T EXPECTING ANY GUESTS. MAY I HELP YOU WITH SOMETHING?

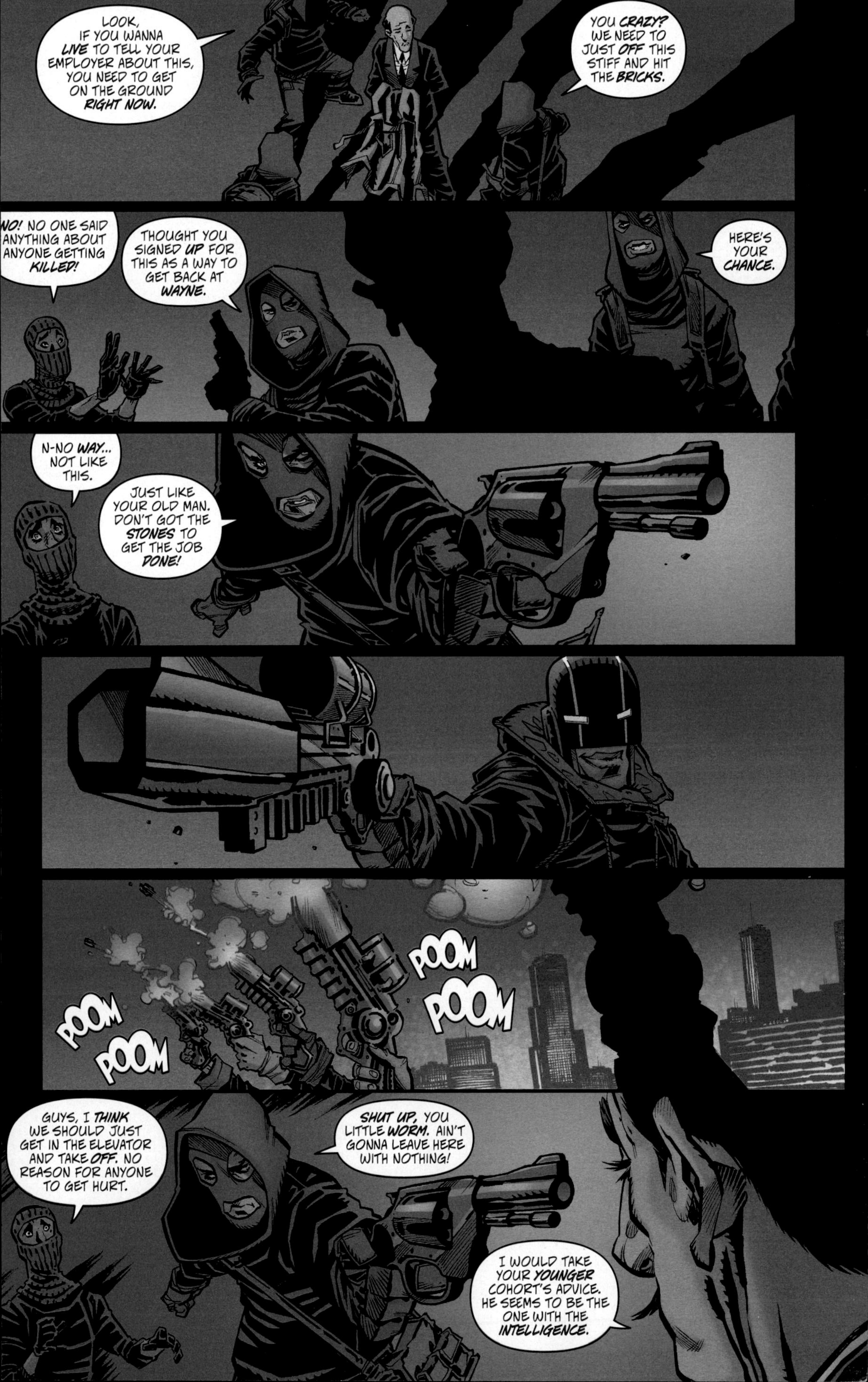
LOOK, IF YOU WANNA LIVE TO TELL YOUR EMPLOYER ABOUT THIS, YOU NEED TO GET ON THE GROUND RIGHT NOW.
YOU CRAZY? WE NEED TO JUST OFF THIS STIFF AND HIT THE BRICKS.
NO! NO ONE SAID ANYTHING ABOUT ANYONE GETTING KILLED!
THOUGHT YOU SIGNED UP FOR THIS AS A WAY TO GET BACK AT WAYNE.
HERE'S YOUR CHANCE.
N-NO WAY... NOT LIKE THIS.
JUST LIKE YOUR OLD MAN. DON'T GOT THE STONES TO GET THE JOB DONE!
POOM
POOM
POOM
POOM
GUYS, I THINK WE SHOULD JUST GET IN THE ELEVATOR AND TAKE OFF. NO REASON FOR ANYONE TO GET HURT.
SHUT UP, YOU LITTLE WORM. AIN'T GONNA LEAVE HERE WITH NOTHING!
I WOULD TAKE YOUR YOUNGER COHORT'S ADVICE. HE SEEMS TO BE THE ONE WITH THE INTELLIGENCE.

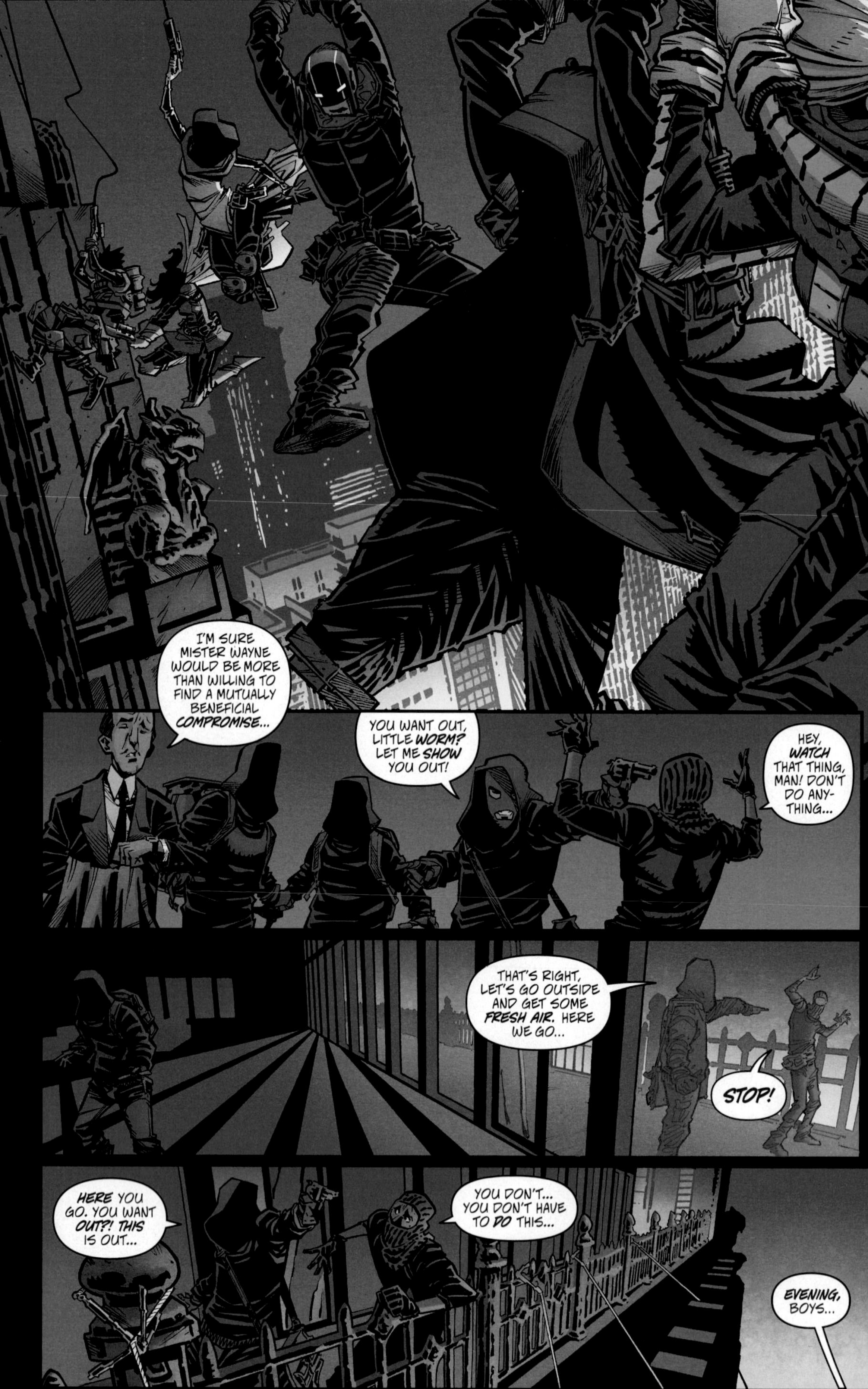
I'M SURE MISTER WAYNE WOULD BE MORE THAN WILLING TO FIND A MUTUALLY BENEFICIAL *COMPROMISE*...
YOU WANT OUT, LITTLE *WORM?* LET ME *SHOW* YOU OUT!
HEY, *WATCH* THAT THING, MAN! DON'T DO ANY-THING...
THAT'S RIGHT, LET'S GO OUTSIDE AND GET SOME *FRESH AIR.* HERE WE GO...
STOP!
HERE YOU GO. YOU WANT *OUT?! THIS* IS OUT...
YOU DON'T... YOU DON'T HAVE TO *DO* THIS...
EVENING, BOYS...

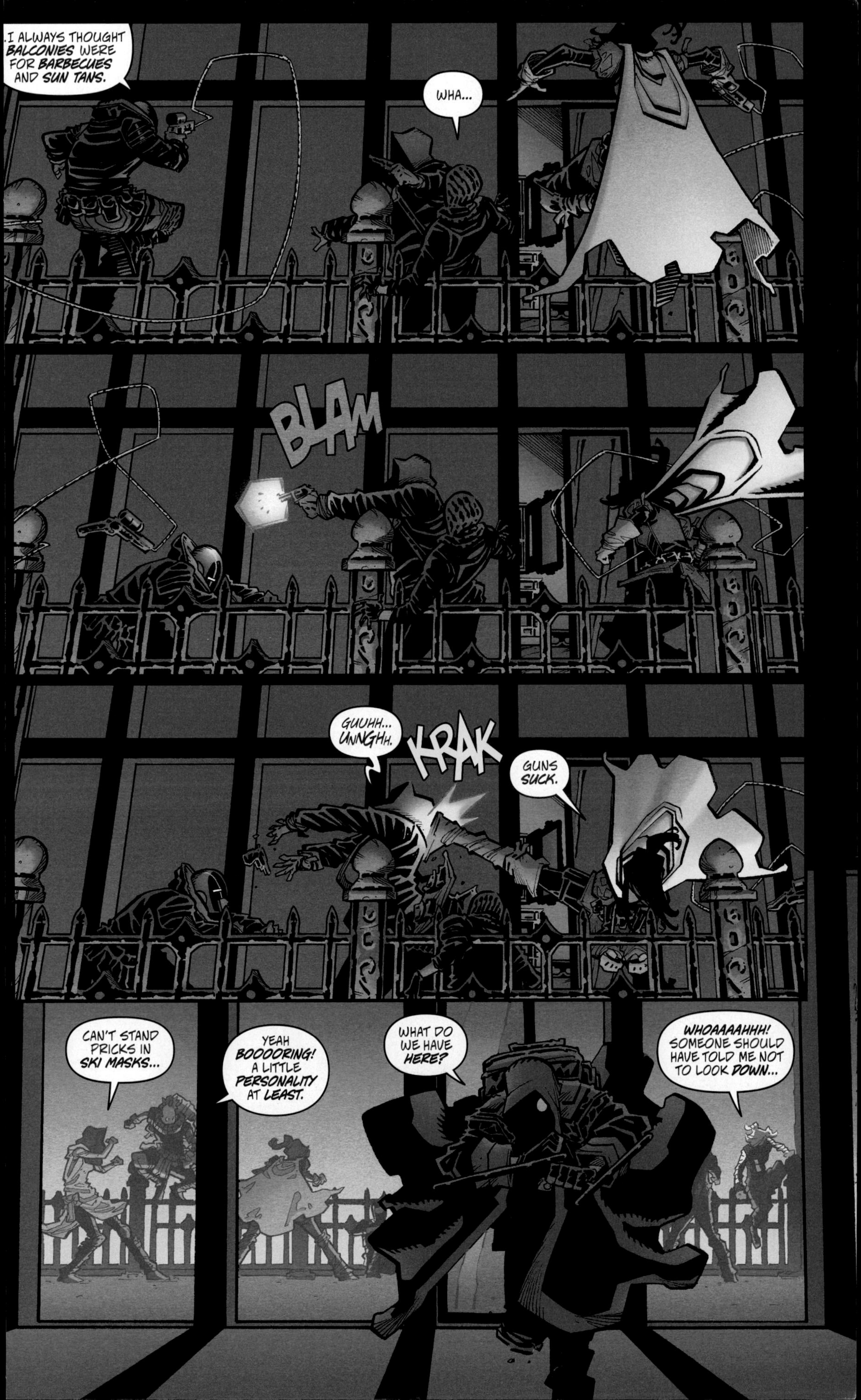

...I ALWAYS THOUGHT BALCONIES WERE FOR BARBECUES AND SUN TANS.
WHA...
BLAM
GUUHH... UNNGHH.
KRAK
GUNS SUCK.
CAN'T STAND PRICKS IN SKI MASKS...
YEAH BOOOORING! A LITTLE PERSONALITY AT LEAST.
WHAT DO WE HAVE HERE?
WHOAAAAHHH! SOMEONE SHOULD HAVE TOLD ME NOT TO LOOK DOWN...

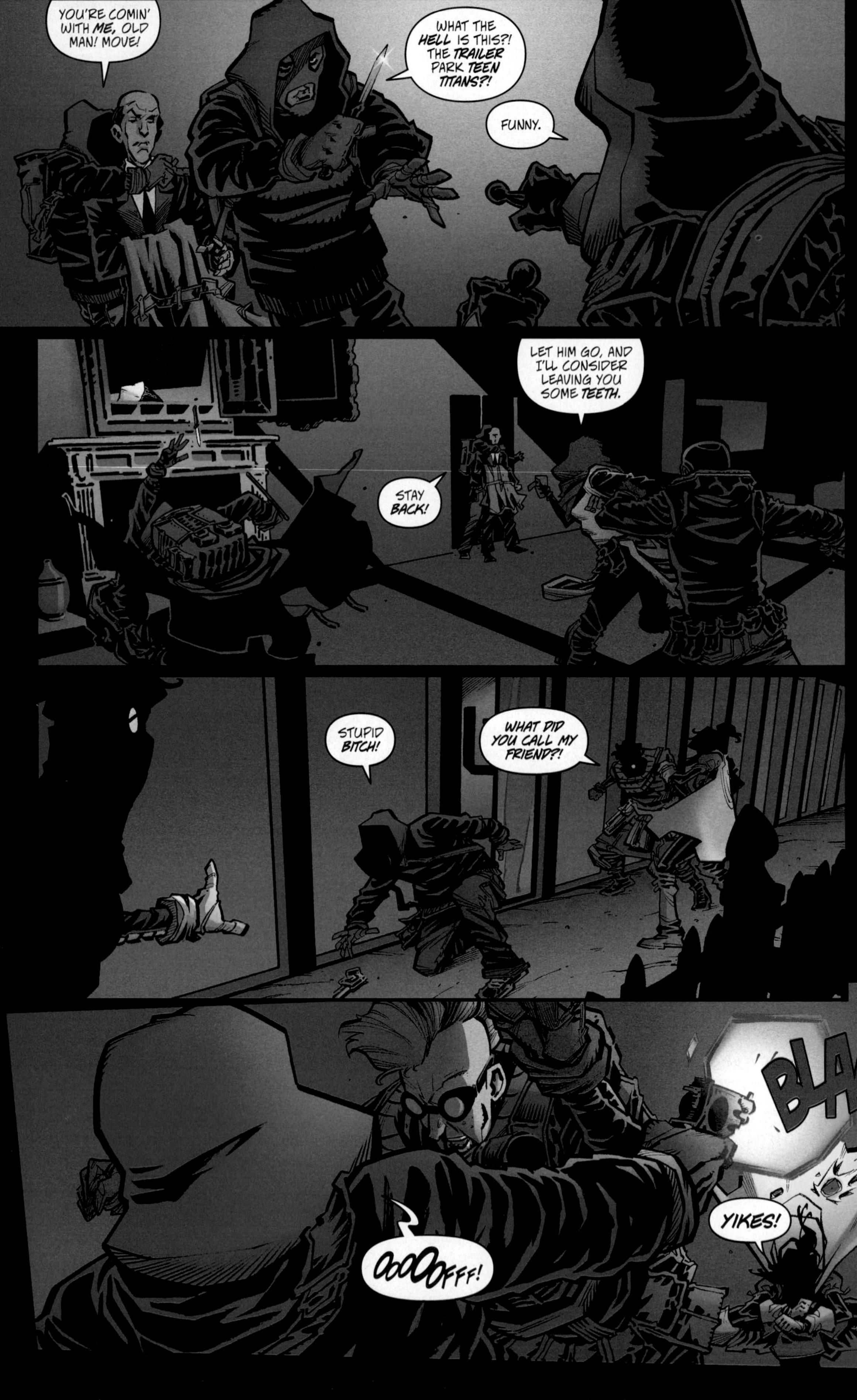
YOU'RE COMIN' WITH ME, OLD MAN! MOVE!
WHAT THE HELL IS THIS?! THE TRAILER PARK TEEN TITANS?!
FUNNY.
LET HIM GO, AND I'LL CONSIDER LEAVING YOU SOME TEETH.
STAY BACK!
STUPID BITCH!
WHAT DID YOU CALL MY FRIEND?!
YIKES!
OOOOOFFF!

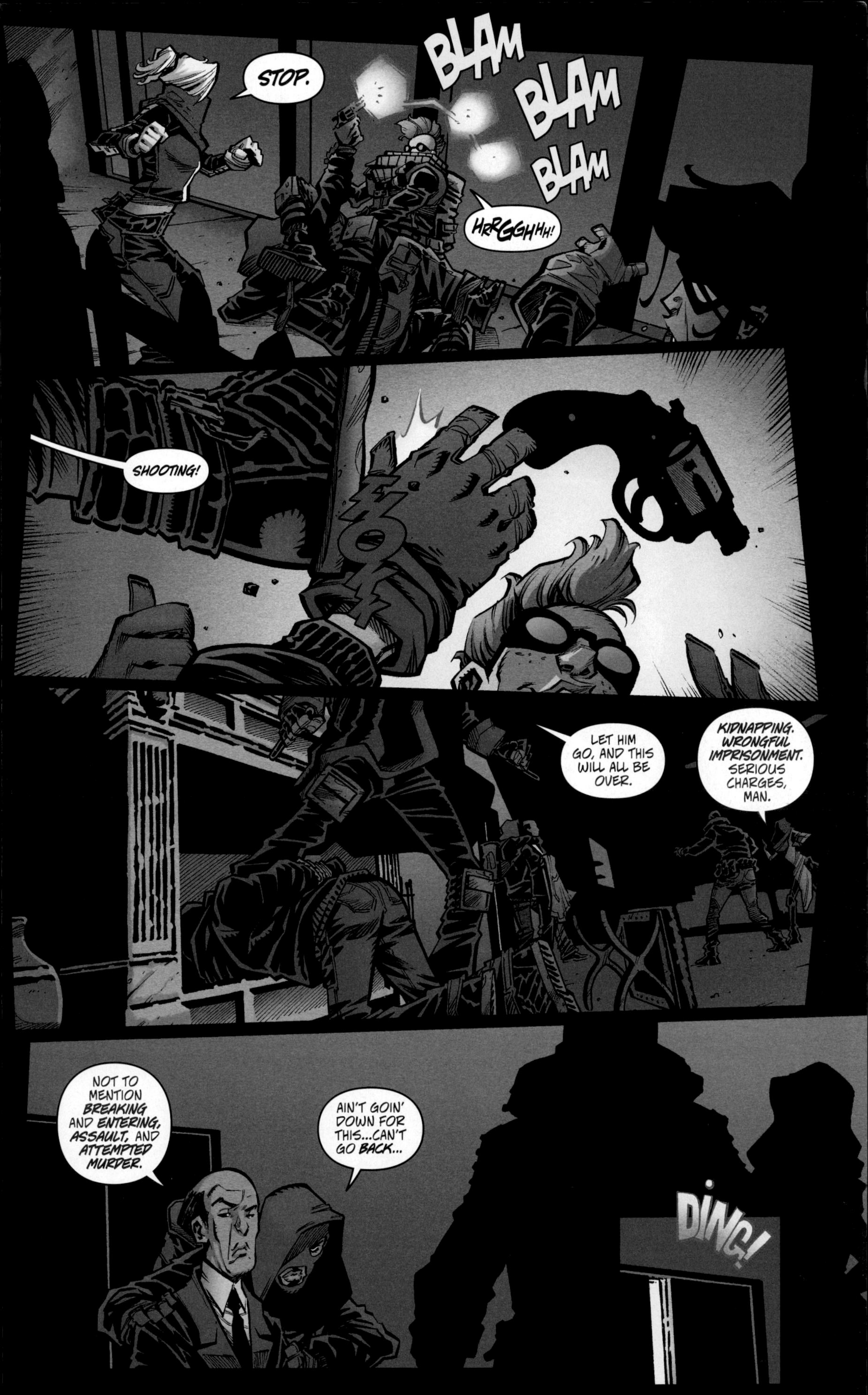
STOP.
BLAM
BLAM
BLAM
HRRGGHHH!
SHOOTING!
LET HIM GO, AND THIS WILL ALL BE OVER.
KIDNAPPING. WRONGFUL IMPRISONMENT. SERIOUS CHARGES, MAN.
NOT TO MENTION BREAKING AND ENTERING, ASSAULT, AND ATTEMPTED MURDER.
AIN'T GOIN' DOWN FOR THIS...CAN'T GO BACK...
DING!

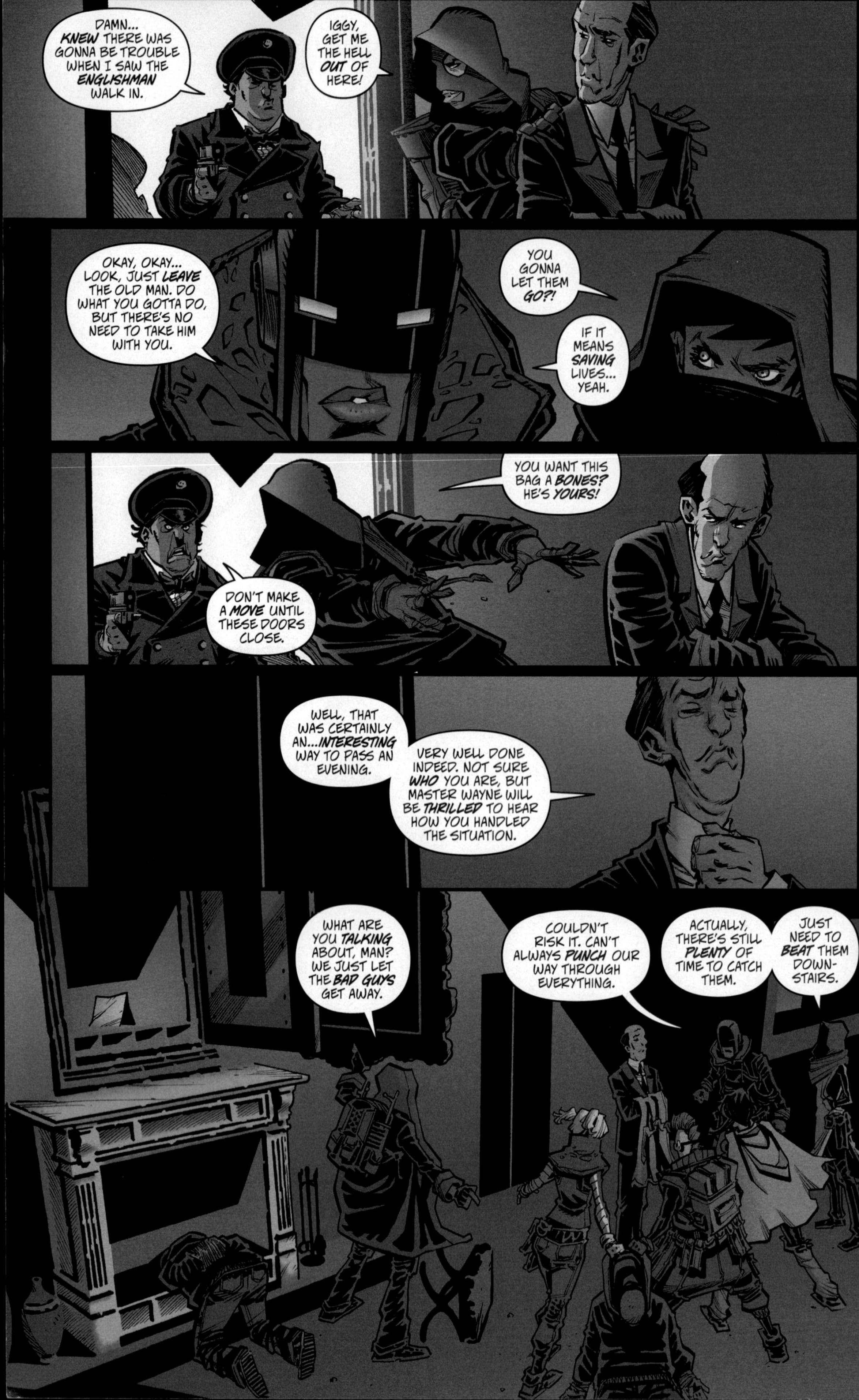
DAMN... KNEW THERE WAS GONNA BE TROUBLE WHEN I SAW THE ENGLISHMAN WALK IN.
IGGY, GET ME THE HELL OUT OF HERE!
OKAY, OKAY... LOOK, JUST LEAVE THE OLD MAN. DO WHAT YOU GOTTA DO, BUT THERE'S NO NEED TO TAKE HIM WITH YOU.
YOU GONNA LET THEM GO?!
IF IT MEANS SAVING LIVES... YEAH.
YOU WANT THIS BAG A BONES? HE'S YOURS!
DON'T MAKE A MOVE UNTIL THESE DOORS CLOSE.
WELL, THAT WAS CERTAINLY AN...INTERESTING WAY TO PASS AN EVENING.
VERY WELL DONE INDEED. NOT SURE WHO YOU ARE, BUT MASTER WAYNE WILL BE THRILLED TO HEAR HOW YOU HANDLED THE SITUATION.
WHAT ARE YOU TALKING ABOUT, MAN? WE JUST LET THE BAD GUYS GET AWAY.
COULDN'T RISK IT. CAN'T ALWAYS PUNCH OUR WAY THROUGH EVERYTHING.
ACTUALLY, THERE'S STILL PLENTY OF TIME TO CATCH THEM.
JUST NEED TO BEAT THEM DOWN-STAIRS.

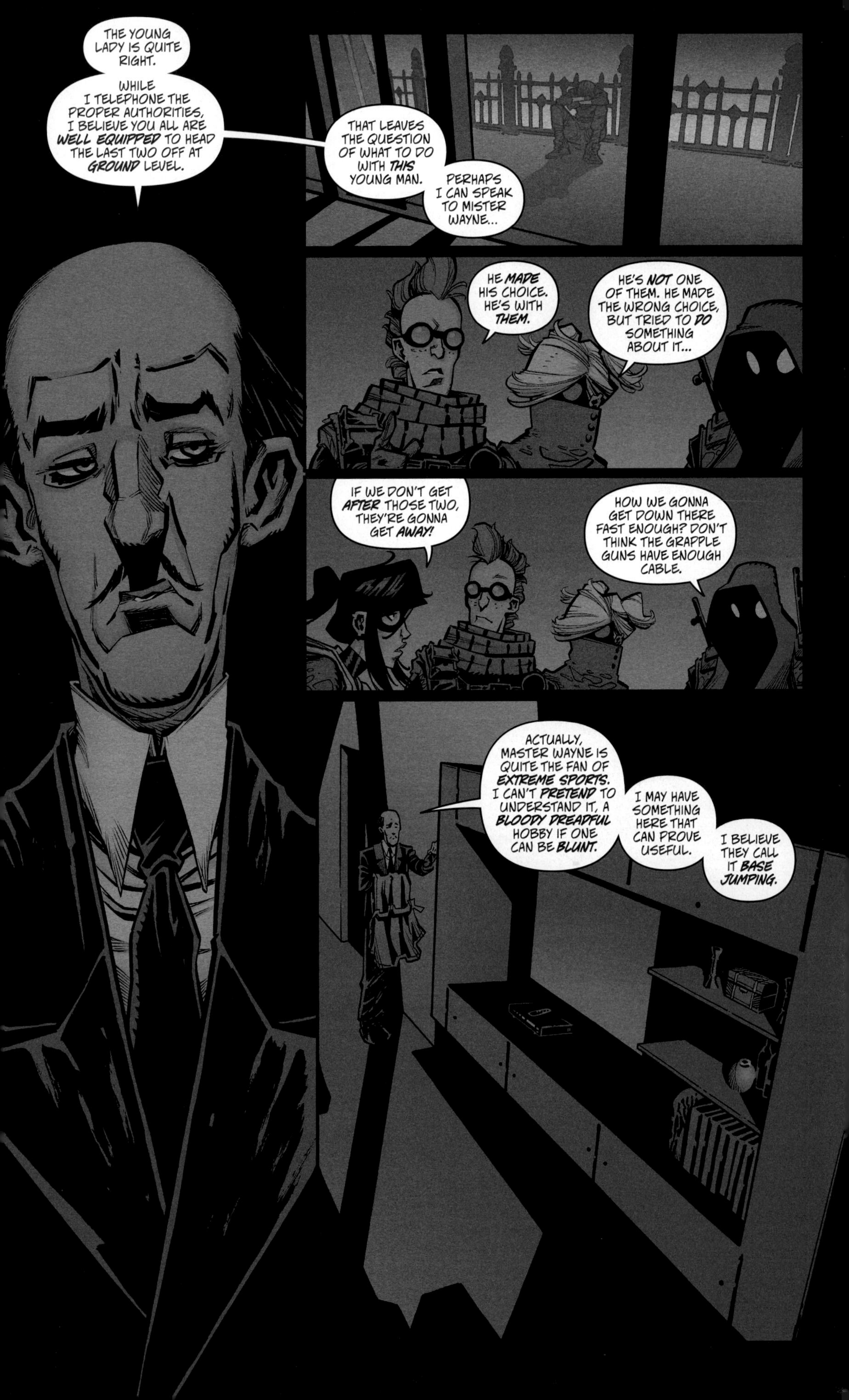
THE YOUNG LADY IS QUITE RIGHT.
WHILE I TELEPHONE THE PROPER AUTHORITIES, I BELIEVE YOU ALL ARE WELL EQUIPPED TO HEAD THE LAST TWO OFF AT GROUND LEVEL.
THAT LEAVES THE QUESTION OF WHAT TO DO WITH THIS YOUNG MAN.
PERHAPS I CAN SPEAK TO MISTER WAYNE...
HE MADE HIS CHOICE. HE'S WITH THEM.
HE'S NOT ONE OF THEM. HE MADE THE WRONG CHOICE, BUT TRIED TO DO SOMETHING ABOUT IT...
IF WE DON'T GET AFTER THOSE TWO, THEY'RE GONNA GET AWAY!
HOW WE GONNA GET DOWN THERE FAST ENOUGH? DON'T THINK THE GRAPPLE GUNS HAVE ENOUGH CABLE.
ACTUALLY, MASTER WAYNE IS QUITE THE FAN OF EXTREME SPORTS. I CAN'T PRETEND TO UNDERSTAND IT, A BLOODY DREADFUL HOBBY IF ONE CAN BE BLUNT.
I MAY HAVE SOMETHING HERE THAT CAN PROVE USEFUL.
I BELIEVE THEY CALL IT BASE JUMPING.

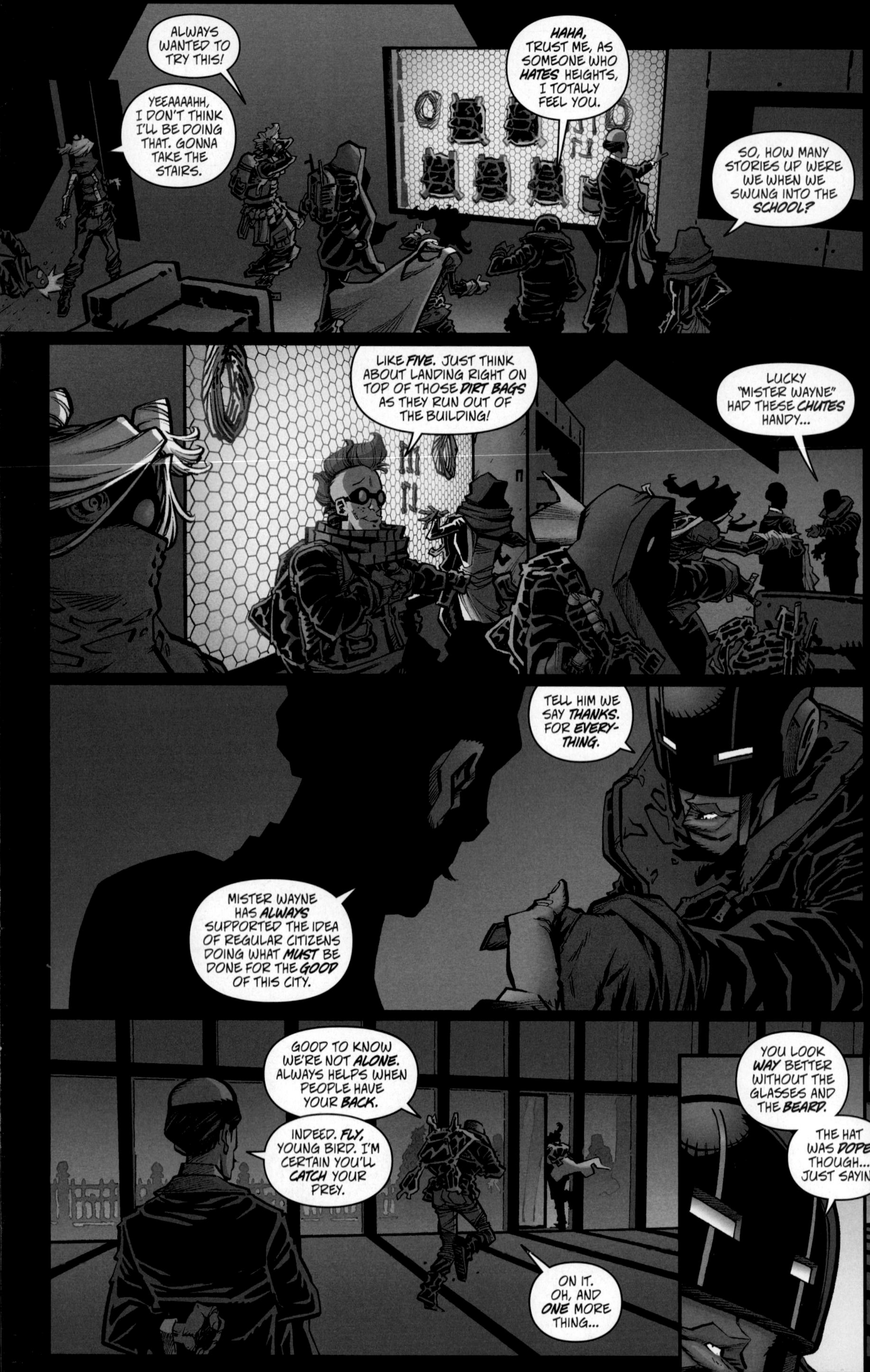
ALWAYS WANTED TO TRY THIS!
YEEAAAAHH, I DON'T THINK I'LL BE DOING THAT. GONNA TAKE THE STAIRS.
HAHA, TRUST ME, AS SOMEONE WHO HATES HEIGHTS, I TOTALLY FEEL YOU.
SO, HOW MANY STORIES UP WERE WE WHEN WE SWUNG INTO THE SCHOOL?
LIKE FIVE. JUST THINK ABOUT LANDING RIGHT ON TOP OF THOSE DIRT BAGS AS THEY RUN OUT OF THE BUILDING!
LUCKY "MISTER WAYNE" HAD THESE CHUTES HANDY...
TELL HIM WE SAY THANKS. FOR EVERY-THING.
MISTER WAYNE HAS ALWAYS SUPPORTED THE IDEA OF REGULAR CITIZENS DOING WHAT MUST BE DONE FOR THE GOOD OF THIS CITY.
GOOD TO KNOW WE'RE NOT ALONE. ALWAYS HELPS WHEN PEOPLE HAVE YOUR BACK.
INDEED. FLY, YOUNG BIRD. I'M CERTAIN YOU'LL CATCH YOUR PREY.
ON IT. OH, AND ONE MORE THING...
YOU LOOK WAY BETTER WITHOUT THE GLASSES AND THE BEARD.
THE HAT WAS DOPE THOUGH... JUST SAYIN'

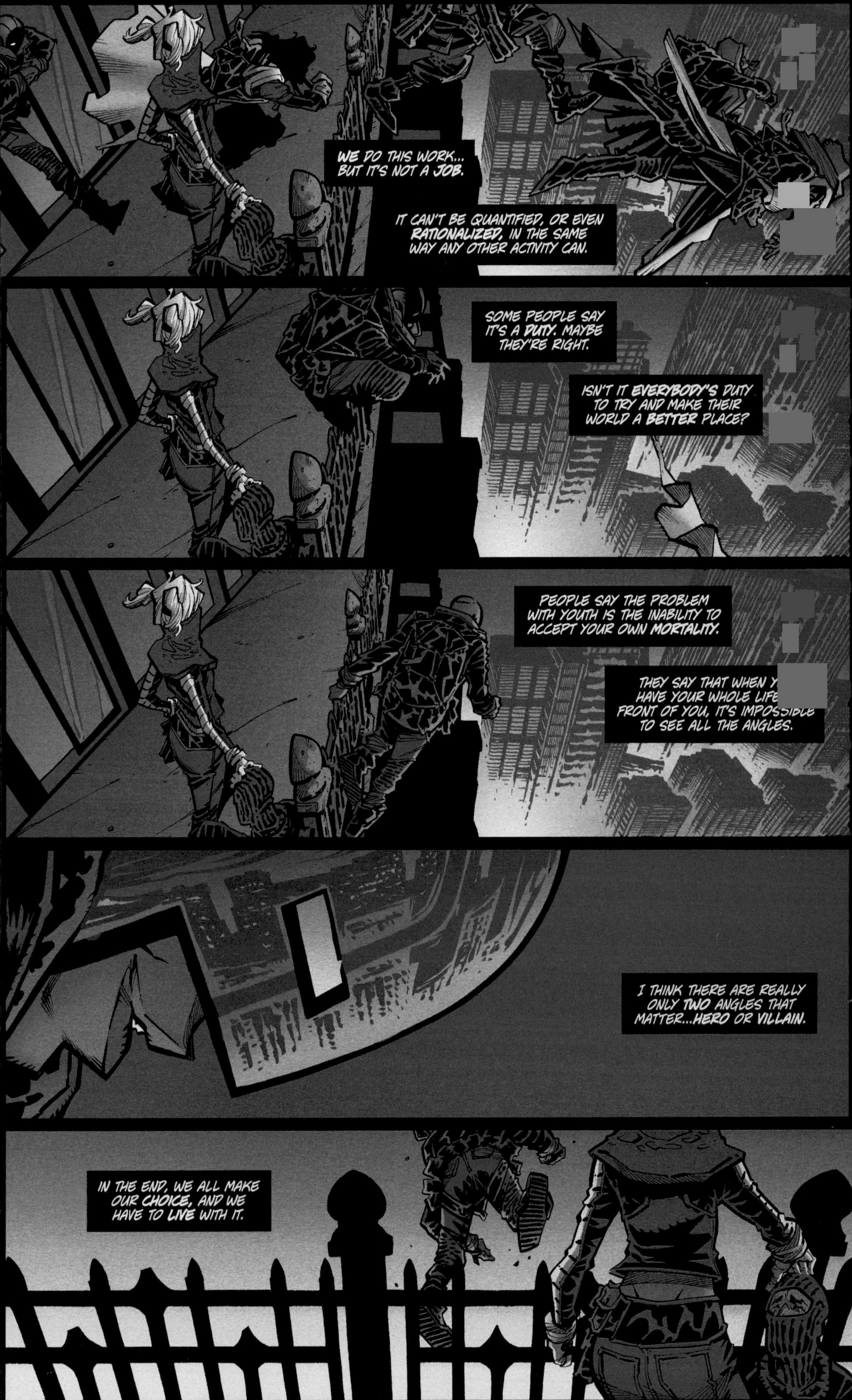
WE DO THIS WORK... BUT IT'S NOT A JOB.
IT CAN'T BE QUANTIFIED, OR EVEN RATIONALIZED, IN THE SAME WAY ANY OTHER ACTIVITY CAN.
SOME PEOPLE SAY IT'S A DUTY. MAYBE THEY'RE RIGHT.
ISN'T IT EVERYBODY'S DUTY TO TRY AND MAKE THEIR WORLD A BETTER PLACE?
PEOPLE SAY THE PROBLEM WITH YOUTH IS THE INABILITY TO ACCEPT YOUR OWN MORTALITY.
THEY SAY THAT WHEN Y HAVE YOUR WHOLE LIFE FRONT OF YOU, IT'S IMPOSSIBLE TO SEE ALL THE ANGLES.
I THINK THERE ARE REALLY ONLY TWO ANGLES THAT MATTER...HERO OR VILLAIN.
IN THE END, WE ALL MAKE OUR CHOICE, AND WE HAVE TO LIVE WITH IT.

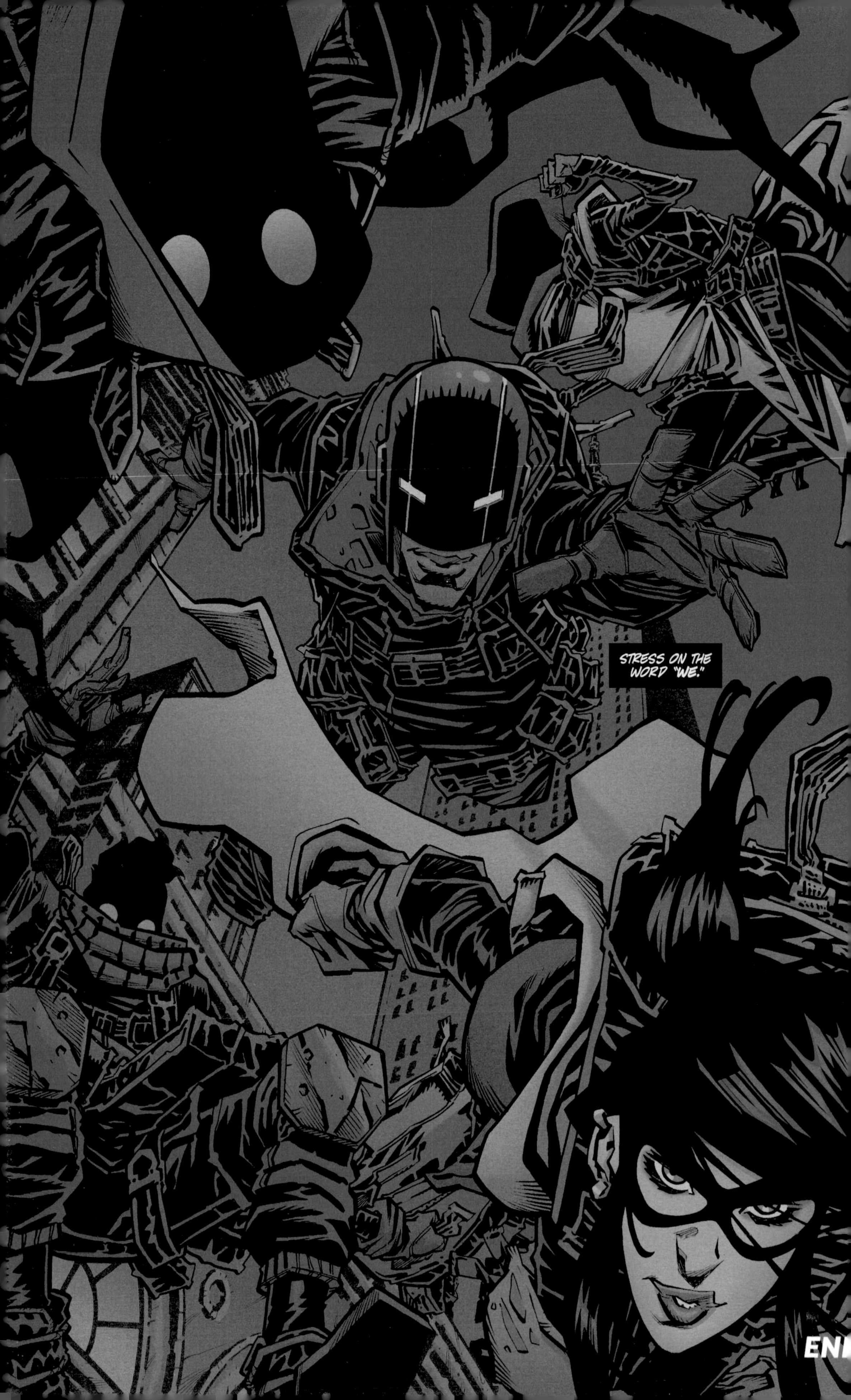
STRESS ON THE WORD "WE."
EN

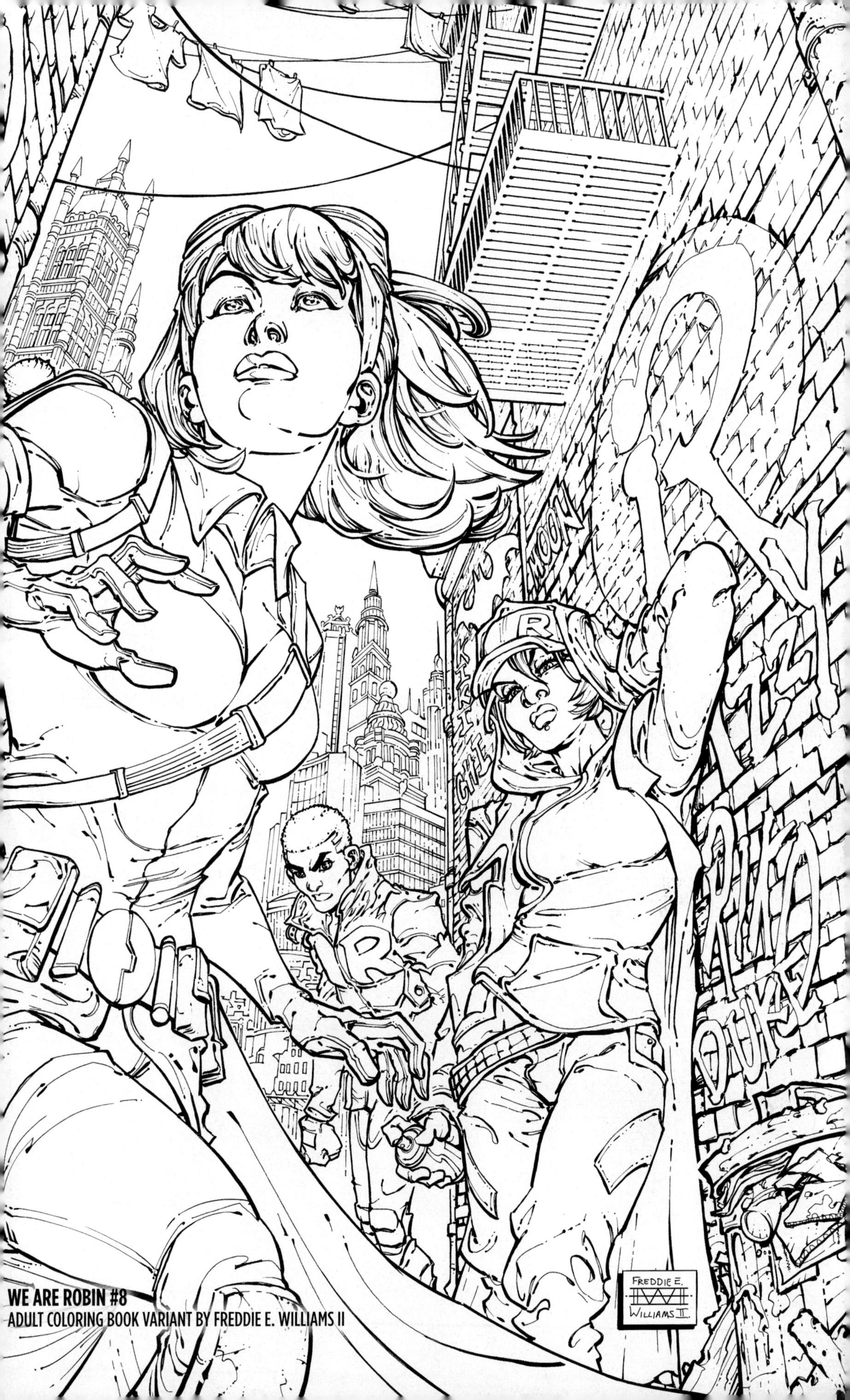
FREDDIE E.
WILLIAMS II

WE ARE ROBIN #8
ADULT COLORING BOOK VARIANT BY FREDDIE E. WILLIAMS II

WE ARE ROBIN #9
VARIANT BY NEAL ADAMS, SANDRA HOPE & TOMEU MOREY

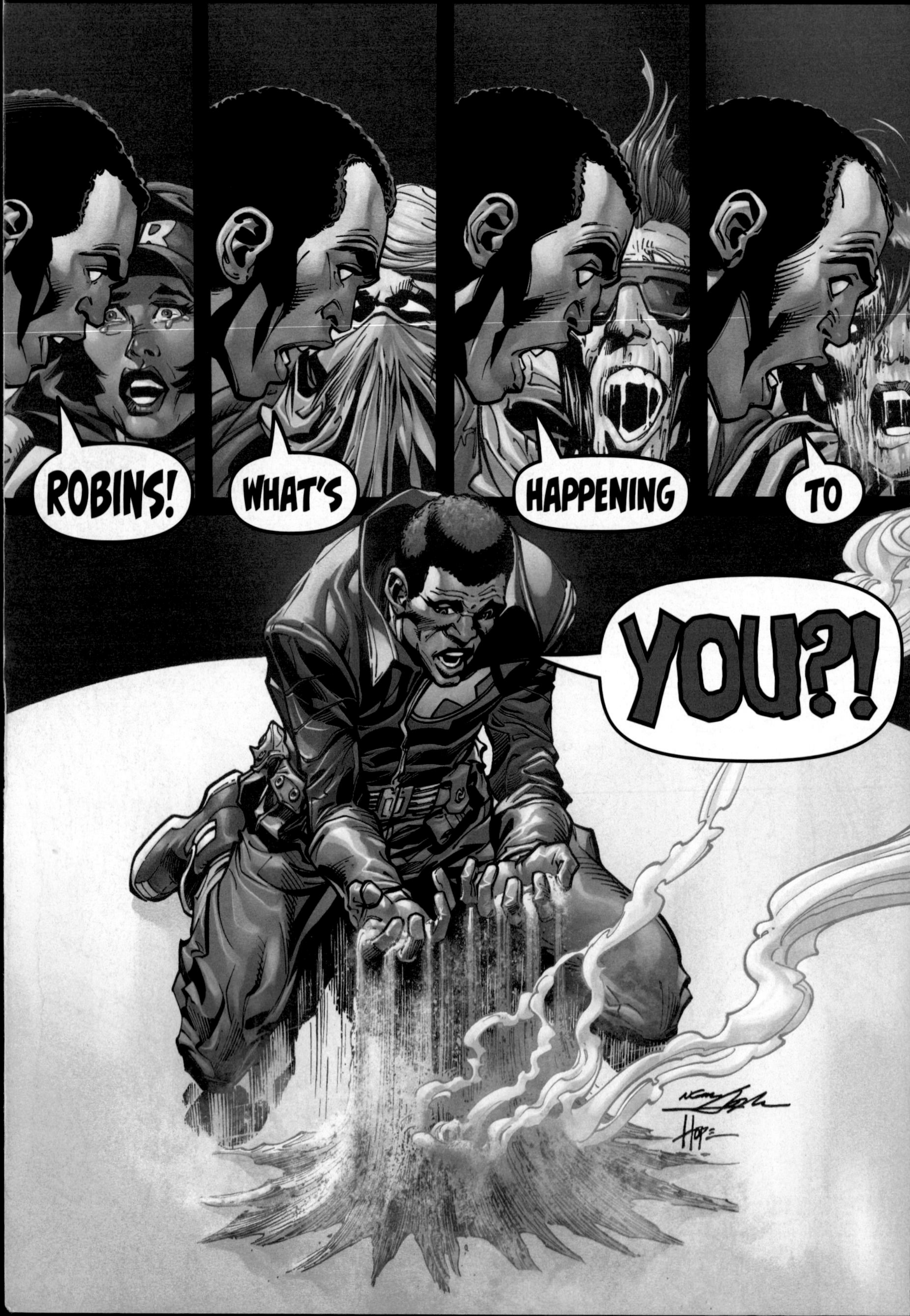
ROBINS!
WHAT'S
HAPPENING
TO
YOU?!

WE ARE ROBIN #11
VARIANT BY JOHN ROMITA JR., DANNY MIKI, & BRAD ANDERSON

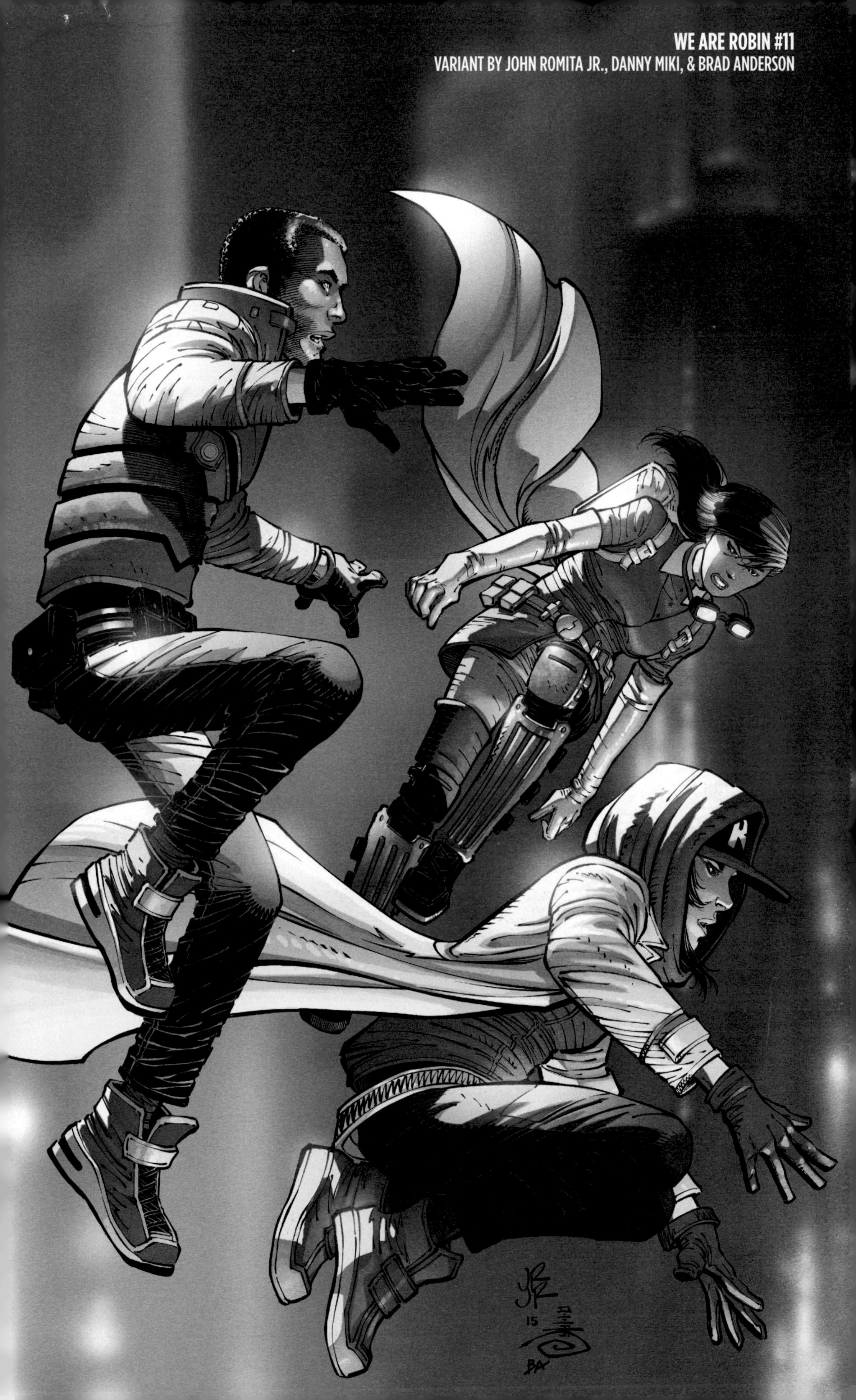

"[Writer Scott Snyder] pulls from the olde. aspects of the Batman myth, combines it with sinister-com elements from the series' best period, and gives the who thing terrific forward-spin."—ENTERTAINMENT WEEKL

START AT THE BEGINNING!

BATMAN VOLUME 1: THE COURT OF OWLS

BATMAN VOL. 2: THE CITY OF OWLS

with SCOTT SNYDER and GREG CAPULLO

BATMAN VOL. 3: DEATH OF THE FAMILY

with SCOTT SNYDER and GREG CAPULLO

BATMAN: NIGHT OF THE OWLS

with SCOTT SNYDER and GREG CAPULLO

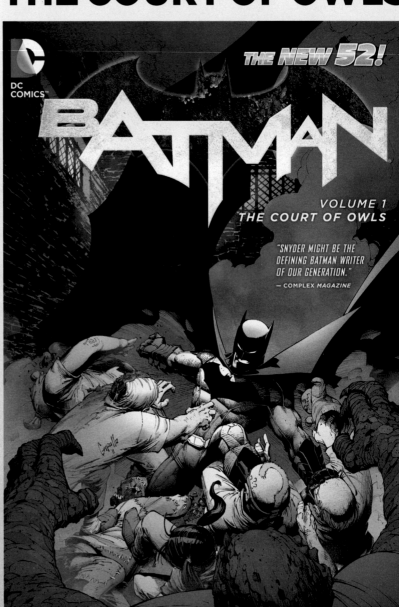

SCOTT **SNYDER** GREG **CAPULLO** Jonathan **GLAPION**